SOCIOLOGICAL INTERPRETATIONS OF EDUCATION

SOCIAL ANALYSIS
A Series in the Social Sciences
Edited by Richard Scase, University of Kent

Beyond Class Images:
Exploration in the Structure of
Social Consciousness
Howard H. Davis

Fundamental Concepts and the
Sociological Enterprise
C.C. Harris

Urban Planning in a Capitalist Society
Gwyneth Kirk

The State in Western Europe
Edited by Richard Scase

Autonomy and Control at the Workplace:
Contexts for Job Redesign
Edited by John E. Kelly and Chris W. Clegg

The Entrepreneurial Middle Class
Richard Scase and Robert Goffee

Capitalism, the State and Industrial Relations:
The Case of Britain
Dominic Strinati

Alcohol, Youth and the State
Nicholas Dorn

The Evolution of Industrial Systems
T.W. Leggatt

Sociological Interpretations of Education

DAVID BLACKLEDGE and BARRY HUNT

CROOM HELM
London ● Sydney ● Dover, New Hampshire

© 1985 David Blackledge and Barry Hunt
Croom Helm Ltd, Provident House, Burrell Row,
Beckenham, Kent BR3 1AT
Croom Helm Australia Pty Ltd, First Floor, 139 King Street,
Sydney, NSW 2001, Australia

British Library Cataloguing in Publication Data

Blackledge, D.C.
 Sociological interpretations of education. —
 (Social analysis)
 1. Educational sociology
 I. Title   II. Hunt, Barry J.   III. Series
 370.19′.01   LC191

 ISBN 0-7099-0647-1
 ISBN 0-7099-0676-5 Pbk

Croom Helm, 51 Washington Street, Dover, New Hampshire 03820, USA

Library of Congress Cataloging in Publication Data

Blackledge, D.C. (David C.)
 Sociological interpretations of education.
 (Social analysis)
 Includes bibliographical references and index.
 1. Educational sociology.   I. Hunt, Barry J.
(Barry James), 1945-   II. Title.   III. Series.
LC181.B58   1985   370.19   85-4145
ISBN 0-7099-0647-1
ISBN 0-7099-0676-5 (pbk.)

Filmset by Mayhew Typesetting, Bristol, England
Printed and bound in Great Britain
by Billing & Sons Limited, Worcester.

CONTENTS

List of Tables and Figures

Preface   ix

1. Introduction   1

Part I Durkheim and the Functionalist Tradition   5

2. Émile Durkheim   7

3. The Modern Durkheimians   27

4. The Functionalist Approach to Education   64

5. An Assessment of the Functionalist Approach   98

Part II The Marxist Perspective   111

6. The Marxist Perspective — An Introduction   113

7. The Marxist Analysis of Education: Theories of Direct Reproduction   134

8. The Marxist Analysis of Education: Resistance, Relative Autonomy and Voluntarism   179

9. An Evaluation of the Marxist Perspective   198

Part III The Interpretive Approach   231

10. The Micro Interpretive Approach — An Introduction   233

11. Micro Interpretive Approaches: Some Studies of Teachers and Pupils   249

12. The 'New' Sociology of Education   290

13. Conclusion: The Weberian Perspective   316

Bibliography   338

Index   344

LIST OF TABLES AND FIGURES

TABLES

4.1 Turner's Folk Norms   79
4.2 Hopper's Typology   82
4.3 Hopper's Dimensions for the Regulation of Ambition   84
11.1 Hammersley's Typology   256

FIGURES

2.1 A Model of the Overlapping of Social Class Values   25
7.1 Bowles and Gintis's Framework for a Path Analysis   145
11.1 A Model of Teacher–Pupil Interaction, Constraints
     and Expectations   250
11.2 Woods's Modes of Adaptation   267
11.3 Hargreaves's Coping Strategies   286

To Richard, Philip and Julian

PREFACE

We would like to thank Richard Scase for his helpful comments on an earlier draft of this book, and Hilary Walford for her expert editing of the typescript. We are also grateful to Denis Fleisch for supplying us with a considerable amount of information on the ethnomethodological view of education, and to Frances Blow for her advice on education in the nineteenth century.

Barry Hunt would also like to thank the Principal of Trinity and All Saints' College for granting him study leave in the autumn of 1983, which enabled him to complete part of his contribution to this book.

The writing of this book has involved a great deal of close co-operation between the authors. Some of the chapter have been jointly written, namely the Introduction and Chapters 3, 4, 5 and 7. Generally speaking, this has meant that each of us has been responsible for different sections of a chapter. For example, in Chapter 3 Barry Hunt wrote the section on the work of David Hargreaves, David Blackledge that on Basil Bernstein. Chapter 4 was mainly written by David Blacklege, except for much of the discussion of the work of Talcott Parsons.

With regard to the remainder of the book, a division of labour gradually developed. David Blackledge write Chapters 2, 10 and 11; Barry Hunt was responsible for Chapters 6, 8, 9, 12 and 13.

1 INTRODUCTION

Our aim in this book is to provide a clear account of the major sociological perspectives on education. For many years we have been teaching courses in the sociology of education and have often found that students are discouraged from reading extensively in the area by the complex language and style of a number of writers. In such writing any intrinsic difficulties of the subject matter are magnified by obscurities in presentation. However, these sociologists frequently have important and interesting things to say about the role of education in modern society. What we have set out to do, therefore, is to try to present such ideas in a readily intelligible manner, accompanied by an assessment of their validity. In this way we hope to give students the confidence to approach such writers directly and thus deepen their understanding of the ideas.

Three Approaches

We have organised the book into three parts corresponding to what we see as the three major sociological approaches to education, namely (1) Durkheim and the functionalist tradition, (2) the Marxist perspective and (3) the interpretive approach. Although we have sought to give a reasonably full account of each perspective, we have not attempted to provide an exhaustive review of all of the literature. Rather, whilst trying to convey something of the range of ideas within a particular tradition of thought, we have confined ourselves to a consideration of the most important or interesting writers, or those who are most representative of a particular perspective.

For example, in Part I we discuss the work of two of the major figures in the whole field of sociology, Émile Durkheim and Talcott Parsons. No serious outline of the sociology of education could omit Durkheim. Not only was he a 'founding father' of the discipline of sociology, but he also devoted his talents to a thorough study of education. His views on education have recently been taken up and developed by the 'modern Durkheimians'. David Hargreaves has drawn upon Durkheim's concepts of egoism, anomie and individualism in his analysis of contemporary education, whilst Basil Bernstein has employed some of Durkheim's other central ideas in his writings on educational change.

Similarly, it is important to examine the work of Talcott Parsons as he was *the* dominant figure in functionalist sociology in the 1950s and

1960s; indeed, his theories were required reading for a whole generation of sociologists. The writings of Ralph Turner and Earl Hopper exemplify the approach taken by other functionalists to education. Their work also illustrates the way in which attempts have been made to develop complex typologies of social and educational systems. Finally, the writings of Ioan Davies and Dennis Smith provide a good example of the type of debate that often goes on within the sociology of education — debates which ultimately lead to the development of more adequate perspectives on education.

In addition to giving an account of each of the major sociological interpretations of education, we have also provided an extensive commentary on each approach. This takes one of three forms: a 'Comments' section at the end of a chapter (as, for example, in Chapters 2 and 12); a 'Comments' section at the end of each major part of a chapter (as in Chapter 3); or a separate chapter which provides a commentary on a whole approach (as with Chapter 5 on functionalism and Chapter 9 on the Marxist perspective).

The Development of the Sociology of Education

In what follows we shall of course explain the nature of each perspective in detail. Here we want to provide some introduction to the ideas by briefly describing the development of the sociology of education.

Although some of the classical sociologists of the nineteenth and early twentieth centuries had made important contributions to the study of education — Émile Durkheim (1858–1917), as we have seen, wrote extensively on the subject — it was not until the 1950s and early 1960s that the sociology of education emerged as a distinct area of inquiry. During these early years the work in the discipline tended to be of two types. First, there was the tradition of 'political arithmetic'. This was chiefly concerned with the problem of social class and educational attainment, and studies of family and class background were combined with investigations into 11+ selection and streaming. Second, functionalist theory was used to relate education to the economy, social mobility and the political order, as well as being applied to the study of school organisation and, through role theory, to teacher–pupil interaction.

Functionalism, however, had major empirical and logical difficulties, and was felt to be politically conservative. This situation led to the development of alternative approaches in mainstream sociology, namely social action theory and phenomenology. As far as the sociology of education was concerned, it was the work of Berger and Luckmann, Dawe and Cicourel which had a major impact.[1] The result was the development of two forms of the interpretive approach. On the one hand, interpretive sociologists devoted themselves to the study of 'micro' social processes in the classroom and school. Drawing upon the insights of interactionism and ethnomethodology, in addition to phenomenology, they set about analysing in detail classroom interaction, teachers' and pupils' 'definitions of the situation' and the role of language. On the other hand, we witnessed the emergence of the 'new' sociology of education with the publication in 1971 of the volume *Knowledge and Control,*[2] which focused attention on knowledge as a social construct.

More recently, the recognition of the limitations of ethnography, combined with the re-emergence of Marxism, has produced a renewed concern with 'macro' social processes. Attention has again been focused on the relationship of education to the economy and the political order — but now with a very different interpretation of the relationship from that found in functionalist theory.

Marxists have approached the matter in one of two ways. Either they see education as assisting in the process of the 'reproduction' or maintenance of capitalist 'relations of production'; or they view education as a 'site of resistance' to the demands of the capitalist system. Pluralists and Weberians have taken issue with their analysis, arguing that Marxists have overemphasised the importance of the economy to the detriment of other factors. Furthermore, Weberian sociology has attempted to link the macro and micro approaches to education by arguing that what goes on in schools and classrooms must be related to wider social processes. The interaction of teachers and pupils certainly contributes to the development of the educational system. However, the existing social and economic structure also influences and conditions the action people take.

The Structure of the Book

Finally, we need to draw attention to certain additional features of the book's organisation. First, there is the ordering of the sections of the book. Although, as we have seen, certain forms of interpretive approach developed, chronologically, before the Marxist perspective, we shall be treating the Marxist analysis of education in advance of the interpretive. Our reason for doing this is that both the functionalist and Marxist approaches are macro in focus (as we have just noted). Despite many other differences, they both deal with the relationship of education to the wider society. They pay little attention to micro social processes of classroom interaction and they neglect the importance of the actors' definitions of the situation. There seems a certain logic, therefore, in examining such macro theories in advance of a consideration of micro interpretive approaches.

Secondly, and obviously related to this, the treatment of authors in the book is not chronological. Marxist writers are considered before the micro interpretive sociologists; and the modern Durkheimians, although writing at the same time as these two groups (the 1970s and early 1980s), are discussed in the first section of the book following our account of the work of their mentor, Émile Durkheim.

Thirdly, we need to stress that, because of our approach to the subject, a small number of authors are discussed in more than one place in the book, and the order of treatment of their work is not necessarily chronological. The most obvious example of this is David Hargreaves who, over the years, has changed his perspective on education. Hargreaves's early work was very much in the interpretive mould. Hence the prominence we give to his *Interpersonal Relations and Education*[3] in Chapter 10. We also discuss his early empirical study of 'interaction processes and day-to-day behaviour' in a northern secondary school[4] in Chapter 9, as it provides material which is relevant to our assessment of the Marxist tradition. In his more recent writing, however, Hargreaves has adopted a Durkheimian stance. As a result, a detailed discussion of *The Challenge for the Comprehensive School*[5] appears in Chapter 3.

NOTES

1. P. Berger and T. Luckmann, *The Social Construction of Reality* (Allen Lane, London, 1967); A. Dawe, 'The Two Sociologies', *British Journal of Sociology*, vol. 21, no. 2 (1970); A. Cicourel, *Method and Measurement in Sociology* (Free Press, New York, 1964); A. Cicourel and J. Kitsuse, *The Educational Decision Makers* (Bobbs-Merrill, Indianapolis, 1963).

2. M.F.D. Young (ed.), *Knowledge and Control* (Collier-Macmillan, London, 1971).

3. D. Hargreaves, *Interpersonal Relations and Education*, Student edition (Routledge and Kegan Paul, London, 1975).

4. D. Hargreaves, *Social Relations in a Secondary School* (Routledge and Kegan Paul, London, 1967), p. vii.

5. D. Hargreaves, *The Challenge for the Comprehensive School: Culture, Curriculum and Community* (Routledge and Kegan Paul, London, 1982).

PART I

DURKHEIM AND THE FUNCTIONALIST TRADITION

2 ÉMILE DURKHEIM

Discipline is necessary in schools; corporal punishment should be abolished; there should be a core curriculum based on science; education must teach people self-discipline; education is essential if society is to remain orderly. These are some of the conclusions Émile Durkheim reached in his study of education; and they are not just unsupported assertions but conclusions firmly based on his theory of man and society. In saying this we do not claim that Durkheim's reasoning is always accurate, or that all his ideas are well founded, but we do suggest that a study of Durkheim helps us to adopt a more rational view of what education does, and ought to do, in modern society.

Durkheim's thinking about education was based on three major aims: (1) to establish sociology as a discipline of academic standing; (2) to apply the methods of natural science, as he understood them, to the study of society; (3) to discover how an orderly society was maintained, particularly in the complex modern world. By briefly examining what Durkheim had to say about these matters, we can gain a better understanding of his educational sociology.

SOCIOLOGY

To establish sociology as an academic discipline, Durkheim tries to show that its subject matter is distinct from that of other areas, particularly that of psychology. To do this he argues that 'society' is the subject matter of sociology and that the 'social' dimension of things is distinct from the 'individual' dimension. He argues that there is a qualitative difference between society and the individual, and that no study of the individual can give us an understanding of society. Copper and tin can combine to make a new substance, bronze, which is quite unlike either of its component parts. Inorganic chemicals combine to make living organisms which are quite distinct and different from them. In the same way, Durkheim argues in *The Rules of Sociological Method*,[1] society, although it is made up of individuals, is different and distinct from its component parts.

There are a number of ways to understand what Durkheim is trying to say. If we think of the English or French language; or of all the different forms of marriage that have existed and do exist; or of the various legal and moral codes to be found throughout the world; then it becomes clear that from studying the individual person we could never anticipate such differences or such variety. Therefore, concludes Durkheim, we must look at language, marriage, legal and moral *systems* rather than at individuals. This means, in Durkheim's terms, that we must recognise the distinctiveness of social phenomena and of the social dimension of things.

By the term 'social' Durkheim means a number of things. In the first place, anything social is 'general' and 'collective'. Certain ideas, values and beliefs can be found throughout a society and often persist for long periods of time. Frequently, they are more enduring than individual members of society: they were there before the individual was born and they will be there after he is dead. Christianity's beliefs and values, for example, have a history beyond any individual Christian and these beliefs and values have been, and are, shared by many people. Christianity as a belief system, therefore, is general and collective. Durkheim realises, of course, that things, like ideas, beliefs and values, only exist because individuals hold them and put them into practice. The point he is making that such things can and must be studied separately from the individuals who hold them.

So far, there is probably little in what we have said that many would find unacceptable. However, Durkheim's notion of the social involves more than this. Individuals, he believes, are 'constrained' by social pressures. This is often experienced, Durkheim argues, in moral matters where we are constrained to conform to a set of values which we have not made, or been part of making. Such constraint often takes the form of 'external' pressure: to act 'morally' brings praise, to act 'immorally' brings criticism or punishment. But people conform to moral values, not just from a desire for reward or for fear of punishment, but because they feel they *ought* to do so. Morality, therefore, can constrain people from 'within' as well as externally. Society's morality becomes part of the individual's personality: it penetrates his self and consciousness. The process whereby social phenomena, such as society's morality, becomes part of the individual's personality is called 'socialisation'.

The most contentious aspect of Durkheim's idea of the 'social' and of society remains, however, to be considered. For Durkheim, not only is society distinct from individuals, not only does it mould them, but society is a reality in its own right (or *sui generis* as Durkheim usually says). Society has an existence independent of, and external to, individuals; it has its own 'laws' of evolution; it changes people, but is not changed by them. In a way, society is analogous to 'nature'. There are laws of nature, like gravity, which constrain men whether they like it or not. In the same way, Durkheim seems to think, there are laws of society (not just the laws passed by Parliament or Congress) which constrain men, again whether they like it or not. The scientist can learn to understand nature and use the laws of nature to man's benefit. In the same way, the social scientist can learn to understand the laws of society and use them to promote human well-being.

It is also useful in trying to understand this aspect of Durkheim's thought to compare his conception of society with certain forms of religious belief. The Christian or Jew believes that God made man. God is seen as greater than man, having an existence of his own and indicating to man how he should act. Only conformity to God's will can lead to satisfaction in life; and God's will is made known by prophets, theologians and by the use of man's reason. For Durkheim, society replaces God and stands in a similar relation to man.[2] Society is greater than man, it has an existence of its own, it indicates to man, through socialisation, how man should act. Failure to conform to society leads to dissatisfaction in life. Furthermore, the social scientist takes the part of the prophet or theologian in indicating what society requires.

There is something rather appealing, not least to certain sorts of social scientists, in this view. For example, it could be argued that the vast majority of people do not wish to risk their lives in war. Self-preservation is an important and powerful instinct. Yet, in times of war people feel compelled to risk their lives and they even enter situations in which death is almost certain. In such circumstances, the vast majority are subjected to a force which leads them to act against a powerful natural instinct. Since all men share this instinct, it could well be argued that the power that overrides it cannot come from any one man or all men. The power must come from some force greater than man, and independent of man's desires or instincts. That force must be society.

Clearly then, Durkheim's way of looking at society as a reality in its own right does have advantages. It opens up new ways of thinking about the condition of man. Yet Durkheim's approach is also unacceptable in many respects. His attempt to establish sociology as a unique discipline leads him to overstate his case. The chief problem with Durkheim's notion of society is that it tends to reduce human freedom and creativity to nothing. Durkheim also seems to confuse 'the one and the many'. He seems to suggest that, since society is independent of and external to any one individual, it is independent of and external to all individuals. But clearly this is false. Finally, at Steven Lukes points out in his excellent study of Durkheim's life and work,[3] Durkheim's use of the term 'constraint' is unacceptably broad. The term is normally used to refer only to those 'external' pressures where, for example, an individual conforms to certain rules or demands because of the threat of punishment for not so doing. But it is misleading to extend the use of the term to refer to 'internal' pressures. When people 'internalise' certain moral rules they make them their own. Consequently, they have a feeling of being 'committed' to them, not 'constrained' by them. Such 'commitment' is a positive thing, whereas 'constraint' is a negative phenomenon. As Lukes says, Durkheim wanted to draw attention to the various ways in which individuals are affected by social forces, but to speak only of 'constraint' is wrong-headed. It fails to do justice to the wide-ranging nature of society's influence over the individual.

METHODS OF SOCIOLOGY

Closely related to his views on society are Durkheim's proposals for the methods to be employed in the study of social phenomena or of 'social facts' (as Durkheim liked to call them). Since society, like nature, is something real it can be understood by the methods of natural science. Therefore, social facts — such as moral systems and values, social institutions, customs and popular opinions — must be treated like things in nature.

To Durkheim, this means that, when we attempt to understand any particular part of society, such as education, we must first provide a definition of the phenomenon to be studied. Having done this we should then seek an explanation of the social fact that is both 'causal' and 'functional' in nature. By a causal explanation of a social fact Durkheim means one that shows 'how it originated or why it is what it is'.[4] But such a causal explanation, he insists, must not be couched in terms of the purposes, intentions and actions of individuals or of identifiable groups of individuals; but rather in terms of 'impersonal' social forces.[5] Thus, in seeking to understand the development of the educational system in Britain, the explanation should be at the level of education's relation to the economy, the political system, the class system and currents of opinion in society, rather than making reference to the policies and actions of individuals such as Shuttleworth, Morant, Butler or the aims and activities of groups of individuals in, say, the 'education world' such as the local authority and teacher associations. Similarly a functional explanation of a social fact must examine its usefulness to society rather than individuals. It must determine the way in which it serves 'the general needs of the social organism'[6] rather than the ends or needs of individuals. Essentially this means that sociologists must consider the part that any social phenomenon plays in the maintenance of social order and social stability.

Durkheim's analysis of education naturally incorporates both a causal and a functional explanation of this particular social fact.

Causal Explanation

Durkheim's study of the development of education in France is a good example of his ideas about causal explanation.[7] 'Educational transformations', he writes, 'are always the result and the symptom of the social transformations in terms of which they are to be explained.'[8] In other words, education changes as society changes.

It is important to be clear as to what Durkheim means by 'changes in society'. In keeping with what we have said above, Durkheim does not consider ideas and theories — whether about education or anything else — to have an independent causal role. Certainly fresh thinking about, say, educational matters does have an influence on the development of new systems of education. But such educational theory is itself, in Durkheim's words, a 'manifestation' or 'expression' of more basic changes in the social structure. (And it is worth noting that, in this respect, Durkheim's views are similar to those of certain brands of Marxism which see ideas, beliefs and theories — 'ideology' — as, in themselves, ineffective in bringing about changes in the social system; rather they reflect and accompany changes in the economic and social structure.)

To illustrate his point Durkheim considers the educational changes associated with the Renaissance. These were basically twofold.

Firstly, the study of classical literature replaced the rigorous logical training that was central to the scholasticism of the Middle Ages. The emphasis now was on attractiveness of presentation, elegance of form and a refined and polished style, rather than the development of the power of reason.

The cause of this change, according to Durkheim, was not that nothing was previously known of classical literature and that it was now 'rediscovered'. Rather, in the Middle Ages 'its virtues were not appreciated because they did not meet any contemporary need'.[9] In the sixteenth century, however, the situation was different. In Durkheim's view, there had been certain important social changes deriving from developments in the economic sphere. The most important of these was 'the discovery of America and the trade route via the Indies [which] had galvanized economic activity by opening new worlds in which it could operate'.[10] Such changes produced general economic prosperity; and as the bourgeoisie, in particular, became richer and more powerful, it began to imitate the life-style of the aristocracy. As a consequence, it demanded a form of education suited to that end. Education's aim became that of producing 'an elegant and fluent nobleman able to hold his own in a salon and possessing all the social graces'.[11]

Secondly, education started to give more attention to the individual and his needs. This, says Durkheim, can be seen in the educational activity of the Jesuits. The Jesuits, a new religious order in the Catholic Church, turned to education to fight Protestantism. They disliked the pagan humanism of the Classics, but realised that classical literature was in keeping with the spirit of the age. They therefore used classical texts to exemplify Christian virtues.

The Jesuits also developed new methods of education. They believed, as Durkheim says, that 'there can be no good education without contact at once continuous and personal between the pupil and the educator'.[12] This system made the child subject to continuous pressure, but that pressure was adjusted to suit the personality of each pupil. Education thus became, in Durkheim's terms, more 'individualised'.

Once again we find Durkheim arguing that the cause of the transformation that the Jesuits initiated is to be found in more general social changes. By the sixteenth century, he says, the unity of Europe had dissolved. The fundamental beliefs and doctrines of the Christian faith were no longer held in common. Each nation now possessed its 'own special mode of thought and feeling'[13] and had established its own identity. This process Durkheim describes as a 'movement towards individualisation and differentiation'[14] (a central theme in Durkheim's writing, as we shall see), and as the 'root cause' of the Reformation, which is an important element of the Renaissance. During the Renaissance, therefore, men began to develop more as individuals, and education had to change accordingly. In the Middle Ages, by contrast, 'the notion of the individual personality was relatively undeveloped' and so teaching was 'impersonal', being directed at the 'indistinct crowd' of pupils.[15]

> With the Renaissance . . . the individual began to acquire self-consciousness; he was no longer . . . merely an undifferentiated fraction of the whole . . . he was a person . . . who experienced at least the need to fashion for himself his own way of thinking and feeling.[16]

The principles underlying the Jesuit system were, therefore, well grounded in the condition of society in the sixteenth century. With the development of individualism in society as a whole, education had to become more personalised in nature.

Thus we have here one more example of Durkheim's 'social determinism'. New ideas about education, and the attempts by individuals and groups to put them into practice, are not in themselves the effective cause of changes in the educational system. Rather, they are a reflection of more general social changes.

Functional Explanation

In the book *Education and Sociology*[17] we find Durkheim's functional explanation of education. Education is there defined as 'the influence exercised by adult generations on those not yet ready for social life'.[18] Since the content of education varies from society to society, and from time to time, Durkheim concludes that it is impossible, by the use of reason alone, to specify what the content of education ought to be. What we must do is look at society and see how education fits into it. When we do this we will see that education is social in nature; and that it is a means to an end. But the end, insists Durkheim, is defined by society, not by the individuals being educated nor by the teachers and educational administrators. The prime function of education is not to develop the individual's abilities and potentialities for their own sake. Rather it is to develop those abilities and capacities that society needs. Thus it was not important in earlier educational systems to promote scientific or rational thinking; but, as such thinking is essential in modern society, it is now developed in pupils in schools.

All societies, Durkheim suggests, need a certain amount of specialisation. One of the functions of education is to prepare people for the particular milieu for which they are destined. Even so, all forms of education contain a common core which all children receive. Each society, Durkheim says, sets up 'an ideal of man, of what he should be, as much from the intellectual point of view as from the physical and moral'.[19] The general function of education must be to

> arouse in the child: (1) a certain number of physical and mental states that the society to which he belongs considers should not be lacking in any of its members; (2) certain physical and mental states which the particular group (caste, class, family, profession) considers, equally, ought to be found among all those who make it up.[20]

Each society needs some basic similarity of thought, values and norms among its members if it is to continue; it also requires some specialisation, for the division of labour is necessary to maintain society. Education fulfils society's needs in these respects: its satisfies society's requirements. But in creating the new generation for society, education is also laying down the conditions for society to perpetuate itself. In this sense, education has the function of preserving and developing society.

Education's function of fitting people into society is accomplished in the process of socialisation. During the socialisation process the child is formed according to society's requirements: 'The man whom education should realise in us is not the man such as nature has made him, but as society wishes him to be; and it wishes him such as its internal economy calls for.'[21] Durkheim insists, however, that although such socialisation is required by society it is also necessary and desirable when looked at from the individual's point of view. The alternative to socialised man is man in a state of 'anomie'.

The idea of 'anomie' is particularly developed in Durkheim's study of suicide.[22] In his book *Suicide*, Durkheim points out that there was an increase in suicides in times of sudden trade depression, and also in times of economic boom. The former is easy to understand; but it is more difficult to understand why, when things are going well, businessmen should kill themselves. Durkheim's explanation is that the stability of the individual personality is dependent upon the stability of society. In times of sudden economic growth, the constraints coming from society are unexpectedly lifted, aspirations expand to a level which can never be satisfied and life starts to become unsatisfactory and pointless:

> No living being can be happy or even exist unless his needs are sufficiently proportioned to his means . . . But how [can anyone] determine the quantity of well-being, comfort or luxury legitimately to be craved by a human being? Nothing appears in man's organic or in his psychological constitution which sets a limit to such tendencies . . . It is not human nature which can assign the variable limits necessary to our needs. They are thus unlimited so far as they depend on the individual alone.[23]

Thus Durkheim assumes that human appetites are unlimited and, as a consequence, incapable of satisfaction. The individual will not limit his desires, but will try to satisfy them all. The end result of living in this state of anomie is perpetual unhappiness. Men suffer, says Durkheim, from 'the malady of infinite aspirations'.[24] To live a satisfying life, to find a purpose in life, man must have his wants confined to what is achievable. Since no man is capable of voluntarily restricting his desires, the necessary constraints must come from a source which is both powerful and independent of men's will. This is society. So education, in socialising man according to society's requirements, does the individual a service: it provides him with values and norms, and thus gives the individual a framework by means of which he can live a satisfying life. As Durkheim says:

> Whereas we showed society fashioning individuals according to its needs, it could seem, from this fact, that the individuals were submitting to an insupportable tyranny. But in reality they are themselves interested in this submission; for the new being that collective influence, through education, builds up in each of us, represents what is best in us. Man is man, in fact, only because he lives in society.[25]

This view of the nature of man is one of the basic ideas on which Durkheim's theory of education is built. If man is as he describes him, then the implications are clear. Education must provide the norms and values the child needs. It must also, thinks Durkheim, provide a cognitive framework in terms of which the child can come to understand the world and acquire knowledge. This involves creating a stable and structured environment in which these things are clearly defined and where conformity to them is demanded by those in authority. Since all are subjected to the school regime, education will build up the necessary consensus for society to continue. Durkheim, then, clearly disagrees with the educationalists who think that there are natural moral values and ways of thinking in children. He would oppose the view that education must develop the child's potentialities, except in so far as these are needed by society.

For Durkheim, then, the functions of education are: to preserve society; to socialise and humanise man by providing the normative and cognitive frameworks he lacks. However, the precise methods used in education and the actual content of education cannot be specified in advance; it is necessary to understand the way society is developing in order to grasp the particular part education will play. Durkheim believed that he had discovered the way society was developing in his work *The Division of Labour in Society*[26] and it is necessary to look at his thinking on this point to gain further insight into his views on education.

MODERN SOCIETY

The Nature of Modern Society

Durkheim distinguishes two general types of society, roughly corresponding to pre-industrial and modern society. The earlier type of society tended to be based on the clan system, while modern society has a complex division of labour. The earlier form of society was bound together by what Durkheim calls 'mechanical solidarity'.[27] What united the members was that they shared a strong 'collective conscience'. That is, all members tended to hold the same values, abide by the same norms and think in much the same way. There was little scope for individuality; the collective conscience defined how to behave in fairly precise ways. Should anyone fail to abide by the common rules and regulations, then he would be subject to violent punishment. This was not so much revenge, but a sign of the outrage society felt about its rules being broken. Furthermore, there was no great difference between the collective conscience and the individual's conscience; people were very similar in their attitudes, outlooks and personalities. The collective conscience had a religious character and great moral authority. Durkheim thinks that this sort of society was in the process of evolution to a new form. The development of large cities, better means of communication and, possibly, larger populations had increased 'moral density'. More people were in more frequent relationships and the way society was integrated had to change. The new, developing form of order Durkheim calls 'organic solidarity'.

A society integrated by organic solidarity is characterised by the high level of the division of labour; it is a society in which work is divided into specialist and expert groups. Society is analogous to an organism (hence the term organic). Just as the body of an animal has different parts (organs), each of which has a specialist function, so, too, society is composed of specialised parts, each of which has a function to perform. In the animal the parts need each other: the lungs need the heart, the heart needs the lungs. Similarly with organic solidarity, society is integrated by the interdependence of the parts, each needing the others. In this form of society, the law serves to preserve the balance between the different social elements. For the individual, it is no longer enough to belong to a clan and follow the traditional ways; society is too complex. The individual can find himself in many, different situations. It is necessary that he has room for personal initiative and reflection. The old collective conscience, which gave fairly detailed rules and regulations concerning individual conduct, becomes inappropriate in the complicated new society. What happens is that the collective conscience becomes more general; it provides abstract values which the individual must apply for himself in his everyday situations. But, for this to operate, society must develop individuality among its members, so that they can intelligently apply the abstract values to their lives. The dignity of the individual becomes emphasised, as too does the right of equality of opportunity among individuals and the need to be committed to one's function in society.

Durkheim, then, sees the developing society as one in which respect for the individual is a moral obligation laid upon its members; it is held together by the dependence of the parts on each other. It has a complex division of labour and members must feel the duty to fulfil their roles within their specialist groups. To function effectively, society must ensure that there is equality of opportunity. Should it fail to do so, social conflict will follow. Class conflict is a symptom of the resistance to the evolution of society which will disappear once true equality and social justice are attained.

Towards the end of *The Division of Labour in Society*, Durkheim suggests that the evolution from mechanical to organic solidarity has been rapid.

> Our faith has been troubled; tradition has lost its sway; individual judgement has been freed from collective judgement. But, on the other hand, the functions which have been disrupted in the course of the upheaval have not had time to adjust themselves to one another; the new life which has emerged so suddenly has not been able to be completely organized, and above all, it has not been organized in a way to satisfy the need for justice which has grown more ardent in our hearts.[28]

What was the solution? Partly it was the further development of social justice and increasing equality of opportunity. But, given the nature of man, as Durkheim understood it, it was also necessary to provide constraints. One possibility was the development of codes of ethics within occupational groups, similar to those of the medical profession. If these codes were developed by all groups, the division of labour would be strengthened and the individual would be helped to avoid the dangers of being anomic.

Moral Education

There is a significant part for education to play in the new, developing society. As we have noted above, education's function is to maintain stability in society and socialise man; the sort of person produced by education, Durkheim argued, is the one required by society. But, what sort of person would that be, and how would education go about producing him? In the book *Moral Education*, which is a posthumous collection of Durkheim's lectures, we get some suggestions.

Characteristics of Morality. In *Moral Education* Durkheim appears to be trying to solve the problem of how man can be saved from the possibility of anomie, in a society in which the traditional constraints and religious morality are dying; a society, moreover, which demands that the individual act on his own to apply the general moral principles to everyday life.

Durkheim says he will adopt the method of examining 'morality as a fact',[29] but hardly abides by this. He thinks that there are three characteristics which all moral systems share: (1) the 'spirit of discipline'; (2) 'attachment to social groups' by the individual; and (3) the 'self-determination or autonomy' demanded by modern morality.

With regard to the first characteristic, the 'spirit of discipline', in a long and complex argument, Durkheim suggests that moral conduct involves abiding by norms which we are not free to change. Morality thus makes our conduct consistent and regular and demands that we submit to the authority of moral rules. In order to be able to do this we must have the spirit of self-discipline, we must be able to restrain our desires and appetites. But it is not in the nature of man to be able to do this for himself; consequently self-restraint can only be developed by experiencing external restraint. But, Durkheim insists, the spirit of discipline is not the same as blind submission to society. We should teach children the benefits of self-restraint and show them that the only way to be happy 'is to set proximate and realizable goals, corresponding to the nature of each person'.[30] This first aspect of morality, then, is closely related to Durkheim's notion of anomie and his idea that man is in need of constraint.

The second characteristic of morality is 'attachment to social groups'. Durkheim wishes to show that moral action involves acting in the interests of society.

> To act morally is to act in terms of the collective interest . . . Now, it is evident that a moral act must serve some living and sentient being and even more specifically a being endowed with consciousness . . . Above and beyond me as a conscious being, above and beyond those sentient beings who are other individual human beings, there is nothing else save that sentient being that is society.[31]

This is one of Durkheim's most extreme statements on the nature of society, in which he endows it with both life and consciouness. Society, he is saying, can have interests of its own which may differ from those of any one member or, indeed, of all members. His reasoning is as follows. Any action that is dedicated to the furthering of an individual's own interest is not a moral action. If this is the case, then to do something which benefits another individual is equally a non-moral action; and to do something which results in all individuals benefiting, or getting what they, as individuals, want, is non-moral also. Consequently, moral actions are those which benefit the reality we call society. There is no other possibility.

Durkheim's argument here is obviously unsound. Actions which benefits others *are* regarded as moral actions. Equally, there are some actions which benefit a society or a group which are clearly immoral, for example, those which promoted the interests of Nazi Germany.

The third element of morality is autonomy. In modern society, says Durkheim, 'one of the fundamental axioms of our morality — even perhaps *the* fundamental axiom — is that the human being is the sacred thing par excellence'.[32] Because of this we are unable to accept the imposition of morality upon us. We demand to know the reason why we should follow rules and regulations. In other words, we demand autonomy. Durkheim tries to relate autonomy to the 'spirit of discipline' and 'attachment to groups' by using the example of science. Science has allowed man to understand the laws of nature and to adapt to these laws. However, man is still subjected to the laws of nature. What scientific understanding does is to allow man to become more autonomous in that he can know why he must do something. He can conform to the laws of nature with knowledge and understanding. If a science of morality were developed, then man could understand the causes and functions of morality and conform rationally. Rational conformity is not constraint. Autonomy, then, for Durkheim, means the rational acceptance of society's morality: it does not imply that a person can choose his own, personal moral code. This form of rational acceptance of moral precepts is unique, thinks Durkheim, to modern society; previous religious moral systems have rested on the belief in God as the giver of morality. Only secular morality can give rise to a rational understanding of why a person should accept a moral code.

Morality Applied to Education. Having laid down the basic elements of morality, Durkheim tries to apply his ideas to schools. While children exhibit frequent changes of mood, they are also very susceptible to ideas and commands. The school must build on this susceptibility to develop the spirit of discipline. Rules are very important in this process. When a child enters the school, he is faced with rules that bind him and others equally. These rules are more general than the ones he has experienced at home. By being subjected to school discipline the child learns that there are general rules that he must accept. However, school discipline should not be too detailed or all-embracing; this would only serve to make the child a rebel or to make him so dependent on external rules that he could not develop the self-discipline required in modern society.

Punishment is important; it shows the child that the rules are binding on all and worthy of respect. Physical punishment would be counter-productive since it offends against the basic principle of modern morality — respect for the dignity of man. There must be a sliding scale of punishment going from individual reproach, to showing disapproval before the class, to communicating with parents and, finally, suspension from the school. At each stage the teacher should explain why the punishment is being applied. This is the process, Durkheim suggests, by which self-discipline should be developed in the child.

The child's natural attachment to places and people is the key to the development of the second element of morality, attachment to groups. The school must be organised so that the child can lead a communal life. The school must give the child an image of the group to which he belongs. Each class has a personality of its own; the teacher, as director of the class, must develop its unity and solidarity. Collective punishments and rewards can be used for this purpose, from time to time. The headteacher must organise the school in such a way that the child recognises that his own class is part of the larger whole. By this process of identification with groups, the child is led to attach himself to the wider society.

There is little said, in *Moral Education*, about the third element of morality. It is clear that Durkheim felt that children needed to know the reason for acting morally; they must, therefore, have an understanding of their own society and its needs. The best way to develop this understanding is through science. As Durkheim says: 'The clearer our notion of reality, the more apt we are to behave as we should. It is science that teaches us what is. Therefore, from science, and from it alone, must we demand the ideas that guide action, moral action as well as any other.'[33] Science employs observation and reason to demonstrate the complexity of the world; once this is understood men can use their rational capacities to act sensibly. By studying science, and especially by studying society in a scientific way, children can be led freely and willingly to accept the morality of their society. Once they recognise their dependence on society, their need for external constraint will diminish and children will begin to understand why they must behave in a moral way.

Clearly, in this part of his argument, Durkheim, rather like Plato before him, assumes that, if people know what is desirable, they will act to achieve the desirable end. This is rather like saying that, if people know that smoking is unhealthy, they will give up smoking; similarly, if people know that wearing seat belts is safer than not wearing them in a car, they will wear them. Unfortunately, everyday experience does not confirm this view. There is, clearly, some connection between what we know and the way we act, but knowledge of itself does not determine action. However, when linked into the other elements of morality, it is possible to argue that Durkheim's ideas would create a stable society, if his ideas about the nature of man and society were substantially correct.

Durkheim's ideas in *Moral Education* are in some senses conservative. He clearly demands a structured class and school in which moral values are clear and conformity to them is expected. Children need to be disciplined, for their own sake as well as that of society. Punishment is therefore necessary. Children must be brought to see that their own individual desires are less important than the desires of the class or school or society. But, on the other hand, Durkheim would put scientific understanding above all other forms of study in education. Science will allow rational action to dominate other forms of action. It will permit the child to see why he should act morally. Here Durkheim gives a moral value to the teaching of science; science should be taught not only because it aids the economy, but because it helps man to understand his society and to conform, willingly, to its demands.

As well as a course on moral education, Durkheim presented lectures on intellectual education. Here he argued that the basic ideas we use to organise our thinking — concepts like cause, effect, law, space, number, life, consciousness, society — are given to us by society. Just as it is necessary that all members share common values for society to continue, so it is equally necessary for them to share a common set of blueprints which will guide their thinking. Put rather simply, people must think in the same way, if not think the same thoughts, for society to remain orderly. Science will provide the pattern for thinking in the modern world. This aspect of Durkheim's thought has received little attention, although, as we shall see in Chapters 3 and 7, it has been developed by Bernstein and by Bourdieu.

COMMENTS

Society as a Reality

Durkheim's view of society is, in many respects, an easy target for criticism. We have noted that society is presented as a reality in its own right, having the characteristics of a God, being independent of man, having its own laws of development and shaping man according to its own requirements. Man appears to be powerless to shape his own life except where society gives him the freedom to do so. Whatever man thinks, whatever he values, whatever his personality, appear to be determined by society. The individual plays little part in his own development.

As we said earlier, Durkheim confuses 'the one and the many'. It may well be true that one man is powerless against the forces of society, and even that particular groups of individuals are similarly powerless, but this does not mean that all men, especially when acting together, are unable to resist or change society.

Peter Berger and Thomas Luckmann[34] give us, we think, a more balanced view of the relationship between the individual and society. They suggest that, when men interact, they produce values, norms, language, ideas, social institutions and the like. People acting together thus create society — which is the name we give for the complex product of human interaction. But, they note, when people produce values, ideas and social institutions, these products do constrain individuals. If a group creates a language, for example, then each individual member has to use the rules of the language if he wishes to communicate. So Durkheim is, to some extent, correct in seeing the way that the 'social dimension' influences the individual who is part of a group or society. Berger and Luckmann also suggest that a child, born into an existing group, is faced with ideas, values and a language. His society appears to be a given fact, the language of the group is the only language in his life. The rules of language allow many ways of communication, just as the rules of chess allow many different games to be played, but the rules are given to the child. In this context it is interesting to note what a Marxist author, R. Sharp, has recently said.

> Yet it is important to query what is meant by the notion of the individual — merely the biological organism, with a definite physical make up and potential, or does the concept include some reference to the individual's ideas, aspirations, abilities, freedom, moral dispositions and other cultural attributes? If the latter, then our concept is of an individual already social, the product of society and history, not *qua* animal, a pre-social, merely biological being. We should therefore eschew any arbitrary opposition between the individual on the one hand and society and history on the other.[35]

So, while we need to recognise that society is the term which we give to the product of human interaction, we must also realise that the individual is, indeed, shaped by his social environment. Durkheim, by emphasising this aspect of human life, allows us to understand education in a new way.

The Nature of Man

With regard to Durkheim's view of the nature of man, certain modifications are necessary. It is quite possible that, if some people are cut off from the rules and regulations of society, they become anomic and lead a meaningless life. Social stability and personal stability, too, may be related together in the way that Durkheim suggests. However, we would argue that man is not asocial, but has a natural inclination to live a social life with others. Indeed, given the physical dependence of the infant on adults, it is difficult to think of man as not being social. Because he needs to relate to others, man has to accept the rules of the group or, with others, invent rules for social life. Man makes rules, as well as being bound by pre-existing rules. Any observation of children's play shows us this. When children invent games or form a gang, they make rules. The rules, once made, are regarded as binding on all. Of course there are arguments and threats, individuals try to change the rules to suit themselves. Individuals may withdraw. While Durkheim gives no recognition of the rule-making process, he does stress the importance of rules for social order. He also makes the important point that the individual makes the rules of society a part of his personality in the socialisation process. But, since he gives little recognition to the rule-making capacities of man, he fails to see that the individual could remake the rules of society and develop his own personality. The individual does not create himself from nothing, but has the capacity to adapt himself, and to adapt the rules with which he is faced in society.

Education

In looking at Durkheim's views on education, we feel there are a number of difficulties that need to be mentioned. He suggests that education transmits society's ideals of man — physical, moral and intellectual. When we apply this to British education, it is not clear what these ideals are, or, indeed, if any ideals are transmitted to all pupils. There are many arguments about the 'aims' of education, but little information on what education actually does. Perhaps one way to discover the ideal that education attempts to transmit is to look at the sort of person who is rewarded by the educational system. If we adopt this line of approach, we will have to distinguish the type of person rewarded by the system of education and the type of person rewarded by individual teachers. In some cases these two may be the same, but not necessarily so. The teacher may reward hard work, or a co-operative pupil. The system may reward, with certificates, a 'clever' but lazy person, or one who thinks only of his own success. It is not easy to say, then, what the ideals are that the educational system transmits, or attempts to transmit. Academic ability, that is the ability to deal with abstractions rather than concrete issues, seems to be highly regarded. A good memory, linguistic fluency, ability to spell well and the ability to work individually also seem to be important. Bourdieu develops this line of argument more fully; we could, possibly, suggest that the ideal of education is embodied in the Oxbridge graduate, since that is the type of personality that is most highly rewarded by the educational system.

Durkheim assumes that the educational system is successful in the process of inculcating the values or ideals it attempts to transmit. In Britain, this is by no means self-evident. Paul Willis suggests that certain pupils actually reject the sort of personality that they see as demanded for educational success.[36] How common this is, is difficult to say, but every secondary school seems to contain some pupils for whom the present educational system must be said to have failed. Durkheim failed to note the possibility of the clash of home and school and assumed that the school socialisation process must be succcessful.

Lastly, we must ask to what extent the ideals of education (assuming there are such ideals) are those of society. Durkheim seems to argue that there must be some basic values or principles that all members of the society share, otherwise there would be conflict and chaos in society. The function of the school is to pass on these basic values. But if we ask, of modern Britain, what are the basic, shared values, it is not easy to come up with very much. Possibly respect for life, desire for material well-being, a happy family life could be represented as society's ideals. Over and above such rather vague generalities, it is difficult to find any ideals of society.

However, there is an alternative view which seems to be consistent with the present workings of the British educational system. British society may be seen as a series of social groups (or classes), each having its own system of values (see Figure 2.1). If we imagine that these classes are in a hierarchy, integration could be brought about by having an overlap of values. That is to say, the people in group 1 have some values, but not all, in common with those in group 2; the people in group 2 have some values in common with those in group 3; and so on. The point is that there are no common values which all groups share.

If British society is something similar to this, then we can suggest that the educational system attempts to transmit the ideals of some, but not all, groups in society. The children of the groups whose ideals are transmitted are more likely to accept the system and be successful in it. The children of the other groups will tend to be less successful and

Figure 2.1: A Model of the Overlapping of Social Class Values

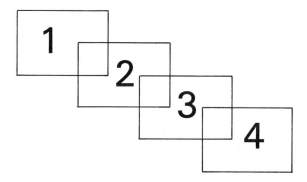

possibly reject the socialisation process involved in education. There will be different responses to the educational experience and the system will begin to separate people with different values. This can actually contribute to order in society, by ensuring that the groups do not come into contact with one another, and that the groups have little in common with each other. This system of overlap and separation would account for order in society as successfully as a consensus in values, and may explain the operation of the educational system in a more satisfactory way than the explanation offered by Durkheim.

NOTES

1. É. Durkheim, *The Rules of Sociological Method* (Free Press, New York, 1964).

2. And, we might note, replaces any other force which, it has been thought, controls and moralises man. For example, the state as the embodiment of reason and man's higher self; 'positive science'; philosopher–kings; the Communist Party as the vanguard of the proletariat; and even reason itself. (Society, Durkheim says, is 'the authority which demands to be respected even by reason itself. We feel that it dominates . . . the whole of our nature, even our rational nature.' Quoted in Z. Bauman, *Towards a Critical Sociology* (Routledge and Kegan Paul, London, 1976), p. 15.)

3. S. Lukes, *Émile Durkheim: His Life and Work* (Allen Lane, London, 1973).

4. Durkheim, *The Rules*, p. 90.

5. For a good discussion of this issue, see I. Berlin, 'Historical Inevitability' in *Four Essays on Liberty* (Oxford University Press, London, 1969).

6. Durkheim, *The Rules*, p. 95.

7. É. Durkheim, *Evolution of Educational Thought*. An extract is reprinted in J. Karabel and A.H. Halsey (eds.), *Power and Ideology in Education* (Oxford University Press, New York, 1977), and the references below are to this source.

8. Ibid., p. 92.

9. Ibid., p. 96.

10. Ibid., p. 93.

11. Ibid., p. 94.
12. Ibid., p. 101.
13. Ibid., p. 94.
14. Ibid., p. 94.
15. Ibid., p. 104.
16. Ibid., p. 104.
17. É. Durkheim, *Education and Sociology* (Free Press, New York, 1956).
18. Ibid., p. 71.
19. Ibid., p. 70.
20. Ibid., p. 70.
21. Ibid., p. 122.
22. É. Durkheim, *Suicide: A Study in Sociology* (Routledge and Kegan Paul, London, 1952).
23. Ibid., pp. 246–7
24. É. Durkheim, *Moral Education* (Free Press, New York, 1961), p. 40.
25. Durkheim, *Education and Sociology*, pp. 75–6.
26. É. Durkheim, *The Division of Labour in Society* (Free Press, New York, 1964).
27. Durkheim, *The Division of Labour, passim.*
28. Ibid., p. 809.
29. Durkheim, *Moral Education*, p. 23.
30. Ibid., p. 49.
31. Ibid., p. 59.
32. Ibid., p. 107.
33. Durkheim, *Moral Education*, p. 274.
34. P. Berger and T. Luckmann, *The Social Construction of Reality* (Allen Lane, London, 1967).
35. R. Sharp, *Knowledge, Ideology and the Politics of Schooling* (Routledge and Kegan Paul, London, 1980), p. 105.
36. P. Willis, *Learning to Labour* (Saxon House, Farnborough, 1977).

3 THE MODERN DURKHEIMIANS

In this chapter we wish to investigate the ways in which two eminent contemporary sociologists have tried to apply the insights of Émile Durkheim. For many years Durkheim was classified as a type of functionalist who thought that education had the job of socialising children into society's values. Only Bernstein and more recently Hargreaves have recognised his deeper insights.

Over the years Hargreaves has consistently employed a subjectivist or interpretive approach very different from that of Durkheim, as we shall discuss in Chapter 10. However, he has now adopted his ideas about the threats to social solidarity in modern society. Like Durkheim he believes that the school's function is to promote dignity. The secondary school is, however, more likely to develop a form of individualism which is either egoistic or anomic rather than moral. While we do not necessarily accept Hargreaves's arguments, we feel that he has redirected our attention in an interesting and fruitful way. He brings out the tension between the 'needs' of the individual and of the collectivity and suggests ways in which the school could be reorganised to counter the malaise he detects. Thus, after many years of lying dormant, Durkheim's original ideas have provoked a lively response in an author whom we would have expected to reject them.

Bernstein has always acknowledged his debt to Durkheim. He takes over many of his concepts, notably the distinction between organic and mechanical solidarity. He uses these ideas to develop his speculations on the way that education is changing and to try to relate these assumed changes to the principles of solidarity in society. Unfortunately as we shall see, Bernstein's style is very opaque and for this reason his ideas are difficult to understand. Nonetheless his intention of relating education to the basis of order in society echoes one of Durkheim's preoccupations, although Bernstein's execution falls short of that of his mentor.

Although Bernstein was writing in the Durkheimian tradition before Hargreaves, we intend, in what follows, to look at the work of Hargreaves first as we feel that his work relates more directly and immediately to Durkheim's ideas on education.

David Hargreaves

INDIVIDUALISM AND PERSONAL DIGNITY

Hargreaves's starting-point in his book *The Challenge for the Comprehensive School* is his view that education has become a threat to the dignity of many pupils, especially those from the 'working class'. In order to resist this assault on their dignity, many working-class pupils — by which he means those who come from 'the complex communities that live in inner-city terraced cottages, in high-rise flats and in council estates'[1] — have developed a school 'counter-culture'. This counter-culture is not, as is often thought, a consequence of the clash between the values of the school and the values of working-class children. Rather, it has developed because of the decline of the working-class 'community'.

In the traditional working-class community, says Hargreaves:

> the working-class pupil's identity was strongly rooted in home life, in the extended family, in his clear occupational future in father's footsteps or in her anticipated marriage in a home not far from mother. To be born working class was for most people to inherit a clear past, a stable present and a predictable future, even though that future might appear bleak and financially insecure. Nurtured in such a culture and social structure, the school could be treated as an alien institution staffed by distant and alien teachers.[2]

Such a world has now largely disappeared, claims Hargreaves. As a consequence, the working-class child seeks a sense of community and of his own dignity in youth sub-cultures.

Hargreaves regards the promotion of dignity as 'the principal aim for secondary education'.[3] But, he says, the promotion of dignity has a strong social or corporate element: 'we must rescue the concept of dignity from its individualistic connotations.'[4] For Hargreaves believes that 'to acquire dignity a person must achieve a sense of competence, of making a contribution to, and of being valued by, the groups to which he or she belongs'.[5] And here we come to a central theme of Hargreaves's recent thinking, namely that 'our education generally is excessively individualistic'.[6] He believes there has developed a 'culture of individualism' in which 'the social functions of education have become trivialized'.[7]

'Individualism' in education begins, says Hargreaves, with Rousseau and runs through the 'progressivism' of Dewey to the 'child-centred' philosophy of the present day. It concentrates exclusively on the development of the individual and his or her capacities and potentialities, and has spread throughout the educational system. 'The working vocabulary of teaching', Hargreaves argues, 'reflects the cult of individualism. When teachers talk about their aims, the rhetoric is replete with concepts such as "individual development", "personal growth" and a whole host of concepts — independence, autonomy, self-reliance, initiative — which can all be prefaced with the word "individual".'[8] 'On this view,' concludes Hargreaves, 'education is not primarily concerned with creating a certain kind of society; rather its primary duty is the promotion of the educated individual.'[9]

It must not be thought, however, that Hargreaves is totally opposed to such a conception of education. On the contrary, he regards such a concern for individual pupils as of 'inestimable benefit'.

> The fault with the culture of individualism [he writes] does not lie with the humanistic sentiments and ideals which it enshrines; in themselves they are far from being reprehensible. The error lies in the repudiation of the nineteenth-century concerns with the social functions of education and the attempt to substitute individual functions in their place.[10]

This does not mean that Hargreaves wants to return wholesale to a nineteenth-century conception of education. He argues that the concern with 'social needs' in the nineteenth century jeopardised the education of the individual. Hargreaves believes, however, that today we have gone to the opposite extreme. The exclusive attention in education on the individual prevents us from attending to the needs of society.

THE SOCIAL FUNCTIONS OF EDUCATION

What then does a concern with the 'social functions' of education involve? According to Hargreaves it means that we must ask two questions. 'First, what sort of society do we want to create or maintain? Second, what is the role of education in creating or maintaining such a society?'[11]

Society

Hargreaves's basic answer to the first of these questions is that he wants a society in which there is a greater concern for, and feeling of, 'community' and 'social solidarity'. He claims that his understanding of these concepts is very much in the Durkheimian tradition. Indeed his whole argument about the 'culture of individualism' and the neglect of education's social functions is, he stresses, 'merely an elaboration of the thesis put forward by Émile Durkheim'.[12]

We saw in Chapter 2 that one of Durkheim's major aims was to discover the basis of social order. Hargreaves points out that Durkheim was particularly concerned with the 'threats to solidarity in advanced industrial society', and sums up the old master's diagnosis in the following way:

> In essence Durkheim believed that the lack of solidarity and integration in modern society sprang from an excessive individualism — from what he termed 'egoism' and 'anomie' which arise when private interests and greed burst forth beyond social regulation and group controls.[13]

Hargreaves believes this judgement is still sound. As he puts it: 'If Durkheim had lived to the present day he would, I believe, now judge our society to be more deeply affected by egoism and anomie than it was in his own day.'[14]

Hargreaves also feels that Durkheim's solution to this problem is still correct. There is a need for the 'collective' and 'corporate' experiences which will provide the necessary control of individual conduct. If men are to act morally and have a sense of dignity, they must be subject to the experience of group solidarity. Hargreaves approvingly quotes Durkheim to the effect that: 'Everything which is a source of solidarity is moral . . . morality consists in being solidary with a group.'[15]

Education

Education has a vital role to play in this process, and here Hargreaves tackles the second question. As he puts it:

> Morality and solidarity, then, are founded on our group experiences and in fact we all belong to several groups — family groups, occupational groups, political parties, religious bodies, leisure groups, ethnic and national groups. But it is the institution of the school which offers all its members a particularly early and intensive opportunity for participation in group life and a thorough socialization in collective experiences.[16]

And he continues by arguing that it is:

> the teacher's duty to provide pupils with the most vivid experience of group life and its demands, with respect both to the groups to which the pupil now belongs and to which he will belong after school . . . the teacher's burden is to transmit to pupils the authoritative

demands that group life makes on all, both teachers and pupils. The teacher is the instrument, not the author, of the moral power and authority that emanates from group life . . .[17]

In more concrete terms, this means that the teachers ought to be developing a sense of 'loyalty to the school', a concern for 'the honour of the school', as well as resurrecting such notions of 'esprit de corps' and 'team spirit'. To those who say that these are antiquated and redundant ideas, Hargreaves replies by arguing that young people 'need' such corporate experiences, and today seek them in their own 'counter-cultures'. 'Loyalty and honour are not dead; they are celebrated on the terraces of professional football matches each Saturday afternoon and among the supporters of so-called pop music groups.'[18]

Hargreaves warns, however, that this stress on the social functions of education must not be taken too far.

Too great an emphasis on the corporate [he says] is oppressive and dangerous; the stultifying effects of collective and conformity on creativity, imagination, freedom and autonomy are so obvious and so generally accepted that they need not be rehearsed here. In repudiating the cult of individualism in education I am not, of course, pleading for it to be replaced by a new cult of corporatism.[19]

Hargreaves is seeking, therefore, a form of corporate experience which is productive of social solidarity, but which also respects the 'fundamental *rights* and dignity of all individuals'.[20] At this stage of his argument he quotes from Durkheim's article 'Individualism and the Intellectuals', pointing out that Durkheim made a distinction between two types of individualism, namely 'egoistic' individualism and a form which is concerned with

the glorification not of the self, but the individual in general. Its motive force is not egoism but sympathy for all that is human, a wider pity for all sufferings, for all human miseries, a more ardent desire to combat and alleviate them, a greater thirst for justice. Is this not the way to achieve a community of all men of goodwill?[21]

It is this second form of individualism — let us, for want of a better expression, call it 'non-egoistic' individualism — that Hargreaves seeks to promote. But it is a form of individualism in which 'collective experiences' are central; and schools have a vital role to play. As Hargreaves says:

'collective experiences in school are embryonic experiences of social solidarity; and because such experiences will sometimes threaten the rights of individuals, they are experiences in learning to recognise and respect the rights of individuals.'[22]

INDIVIDUALISM

First, the distinction between the two forms of individualism is crucial in the assessment of Hargreaves's view, and we feel that Hargreaves fails to appreciate the significance of it for his general thesis. For, having recognised that there exists an 'egoistic' and 'non-egoistic' form, Hargreaves nevertheless identifies the individualism of the 'culture of individualism' with the egoistic type. Without any supporting evidence, he attributes to his opponents a belief in 'egoistic' individualism and, indeed, uses the words 'individualism' and 'egoism' and 'anomie' interchangeably throughout the discussion (see, for example, the quotation on p. 30 above). It never seems to occur to him that many of those concerned with the 'development of the individual' are advancing an individualism of the non-egoistic type and would repudiate an individualism of the egoistic form just as readily as he or Durkheim. What child-centred progressive teacher, for example, would embrace the sort of individualism condemned by Durkheim in 'Individualism and the Intellectuals'? For in that work Durkheim's target is what he terms 'the narrow utilitarianism and utilitarian egoism of Spencer and the economists'.[23] It involves the 'apotheosis of comfort and private interest, that egoistic cult of self for which utilitarian individualism has justly been reproached'.[24] In other words, it is an individualism that is concerned with the pursuit of pleasure and self-satisfaction — where the aim, in Durkheim's words, is to 'indulge our instincts'.

This form of individualism surely has nothing in common with the theory or practice of contemporary educators. On the contrary, we would contend that, generally speaking, teachers today share a concern for a non-egoistic form of individualism. If one examines Durkheim's description of this type of individualism, it is difficult to see how, in essentials, it differs from the individualism of today.[25]

Furthermore, Hargreaves says that our 'excessively individualistic concept of education' has lead to a neglect of education's 'social functions' and diverted attention away from asking questions about the sort of society we want to create or maintain. We see no reason to suppose, however, that, as Hargreaves describes them, the individualists of the present day neglect social aims and purposes. Take, for example, his description of 'developmental' and 'moral' individualism. Developmental individualism, we are told, is 'centrally concerned with the development of the individual person'; and teachers imbued with this doctrine 'see their pre-eminent goals to be the development of the intellectual abilities and moral character of individual pupils'. In so far as such individualism is concerned with moral character, it is obviously closely linked with the concept of 'moral' individualism.

Yet to be 'moral' *means* that a person is not concerned solely about himself and the pursuit of his own selfish ends. For example, William Frankena says that a person is taking 'the moral point of view' '. . . if one is not being egoistic, one is doing things on principle, one is willing to universalise one's principles, and in so doing one considers the good of everyone alike.'[26] A central feature of moral conduct, therefore, is that people take into account and strive to promote the well-being of others. In so doing people are surely seeking a 'social' aim or purpose, and trying to create a certain type of society. Hargreaves berates the individualist for not being concerned with inequalities and injustices, etc. But to act morally means to be concerned that all people receive equal consideration and respect, and that their claims are justly treated. By definition, then, injustice and inequality offend a person with a developed moral sense. The creation of a society without inequalities and injustice must be the aim, therefore, of a moral and developmental individualism.

Such considerations also lead us to reject Hargreaves's claim that it is a fallacy to think a 'good' society can be created out of 'good' individuals. The 'fallacy of individualism', says Hargreaves, involves the belief that 'if only schools can successfully educate every pupil in self-confidence, independence and autonomy, then society can with confidence be left to take care of itself. The good society will be automatically produced by the creation of good individuals.'[27] But if by 'good' Hargreaves means 'morally' good, then a society composed of morally good individuals must be a good society. In so far as individuals possess the qualities just described, the result must be a society without injustice, exploitation, etc. Such a society will possess the features that Hargreaves himself admires.

Self-development

With regard to the notion of 'self-development' — the growth and development of our capacities and potentialities — it might seem that Hargreaves is on firmer ground. For as Lukes points out in his book *Individualism*

— to which Hargreaves makes reference — the ideal of self-development has indeed been conceived as an *anti*-social process 'with the individual set apart from and hostile to society (as among some of the early Romantics)'; or as an *extra*-social process 'when the individual pursues his own path free of social pressures (as with Mill)'. However, Lukes makes it clear that it has also been conceived as a 'highly social' process, 'where the individual's self-development is achieved through community with others (as with Marx or Kropotkin)'; and he quotes Marx's statement from *The German Ideology* that: 'Only in community with others has each individual the means of cultivating his gifts in all directions.'[28] In Marx's essay 'On James Mill' we find the same view being expressed. The essential idea is that alone we are impoverished, together we grow and develop. Individual capacities can only be cultivated in conditions of harmonious collaborations with others.

The notion of self-development, then, is certainly not tied to some sort of egoism, nor is it hostile to the pursuit of social aims and purposes. Even where, as in Mill, the individual requires to be left alone to develop his capacities and potentialities, the *consequences* of this process are regarded as socially beneficial. Mill says that, by cultivating our individuality,

> human beings become a noble and beautiful object of contemplation; and as the works partake the character of those who do them, by the same process human life also becomes rich, diversified and animating, furnishing more abundant aliment to high thoughts and elevating feelings, and strengthening the tie which binds every individual to the race, by making the race infinitely better worth belonging to. In proportion to the development of his individuality, each person becomes more valuable to himself and is therefore capable of becoming more valuable to others.[29]

Self-development, on this view then, helps to create a better type of society (and there is a lengthy discussion in Mill's essay on the social effects of the development of individuality). David Reisman, a contemporary writer, echoes Mill's opinion when he says that 'we depend for our advance, in morals no less than in physical science, on individuals who have developed their individuality to a notable degree'.[30]

There is little support, therefore, for Hargreaves's view that a concern for the development of the individual detracts from the pursuit of social aims and purposes. On the contrary, for many individualists the one is thought to follow naturally from the other; or the two aims are considered to be closely interrelated.

Individual and Social Aims

There is also another sense in which the pursuit of 'individual' and 'social' aims is linked. As we have seen, Hargreaves criticises individualists for being primarily concerned with the development of the educated individual neglecting the question of 'What sort of society do we want?' Yet in the opinion of many social and political thinkers, the only way to answer this question is to ask in turn 'What sort of life do we as *individuals* want?' 'For how do we know', says Greaves, 'what we want of [society] unless we know what we want for ourselves out of life as members of the community.'[31]

Furthermore, if we are considering the merits of one form of society as opposed to another, then, as Field suggests, we must 'go back to ultimate ends' and address the question of what the final test is by which any set of social institutions is to be judged. Field says that, according to the Greeks, the final test involves looking at *the kind of people and the pattern of behaviour* that is likely to be produced by one type of social system as compared to another. We need to consider, in other words, what effect any social structure 'is likely to have on the general character, lives and behaviour of the people concerned'.[32] For permanent institutions necessarily have an impact on our pattern of life.

If we consider, for example, a society in which absolute power is in the hands of a small group or class of individuals — such as in a police state, a society ruled by a land-owning aristocracy, or a Communist Party dictatorship — then certain personal characteristics or qualities of mind will necessarily result. As Field puts it:

> Obviously the first characteristic required from the mass of the people will be the habit of absolute and implicit obedience [to] authority. They must have no will of their own and it would be dangerous even for them to have opinions which might conflict with those of their rulers . . . Of course, it would be a good thing for them to think about doing their own jobs well. But any attempt to think for themselves or develop critical views about public questions or the general interests of the community would necessarily have to be discouraged . . . It looks as if the great virtue of an ordinary citizen in such a state would lie in minding his own business and not having any ideas outside of it.[33]

Furthermore, many such societies will also foster credulousness and suggestibility as a consequence of the likelihood that there will be periodic demands for blind loyalty to the rulers' policies.

Now one of the main reasons why most of us would not be in favour of such a form of social and political organisation is because we do not wish to encourage the development of such qualities in people. On the contrary, we think that independence of mind, an interest in public affairs and a willingness to think about and discuss them, a sense of responsibility for the community, and a respect for and tolerance of others are the attitudes of mind which are desirable. But individuals with characteristics such as these — whom most of us would consider to have well-developed capacities and potentialities — can only be produced in a society of a very different type. Such a society needs to be 'open' and free, and one in which the people are able ultimately to control those in positions of power and authority. In other words, such a society needs to be democratic — be it a 'capitalist' or 'socialist' democracy. The point we wish to stress, however, is that we want such a society precisely because of the sorts of people that can 'develop' or flourish there. This is not to say, of course, that people will necessarily become well-developed individuals with the sort of qualities listed above. Only that without such a form of society there is no possibility at all of these characteristics being developed on a large scale.

Our conclusion, then, is that the creation of a certain type of society goes hand in hand with the development of individuals with qualities such as independence, autonomy and respect for others. Any 'individualist' must, because of his individualism, have a desire for that form of society which permits the development of individuality. An individualist cannot ignore social and political questions, for, as we have seen, individual development requires a certain form of social organisation. It may be that some proponents of the doctrine do not always fully appreciate this; but it is not an intrinsic part of their individualism, rather of their failure to see its implications. Similarly, someone like Hargreaves who is concerned with social aims and purposes will, by virtue of that fact, be brought back to a consideration of the sorts of individuals he thinks desirable.

MODERN SOCIAL ILLS

Next we wish to consider Hargreaves's contention that present-day societies are deeply affected by egoism and anomie and that the solution to the problem lies in the moralising effect of group life. For in his view the extension of collective experiences of social solidarity will bring about that control of individual conduct which is necessary if individuals are to act morally rather than selfishly. According to Hargreaves, there is a need for the restoration of a greater sense of 'community' with all the regulation of individuals that that involves.

It must be stressed that this diagnosis of society's ills, and the proposed remedy or cure, are based upon a particular view of man or of human nature. In his article comparing Durkheim's notion of 'anomie' with Marx's concept of 'alienation',[34] Lukes convincingly argues that we can only make sense of these concepts (embodying as they do hypotheses concerning the relation of the individual to society) if we take into account what Durkheim and Marx see as the 'healthy', 'natural' or 'normal' condition of the individual in society. The meaning of these concepts only becomes clear, in other words, if one knows what it is not to be alienated or anomic.[35] And such conceptions of the 'healthy' condition of the individual in society involve a theory of human nature.

Lukes goes on to point out that: 'The doctrines of Marx and Durkheim about human nature are representative of a long and distinguished tradition of such doctrines in the history of political and social theory.'[36] Durkheim belongs to the tradition of Hobbes, Freud and (we would add) conservative social theorists, who see man as 'a bundle of desires, which need to be regulated, tamed, repressed, manipulated and given direction for the sake of social order and individual happiness.'[37] On this view coercion, external authority and restraint are necessary for the sake of the well-being of society as a whole and of its individual members.

The second tradition includes Rousseau, Marx, the 'Utopian' socialists and (we would say) liberals such as J.S. Mill. For these thinkers 'man is still an angel, rational and good, who requires a rational and good society in which to develop his essential nature'.[38] In their opinion, it is social organisation which is at fault not human nature. The individual's and society's problems derive not from the nature of man, but from the unjustifiable constraints and restrictions placed upon man's nature. What we need to do, therefore, is to reform or abolish those institutions which repress or obscure man's essential goodness. Some control of the individual is necessary, but this involves only as much restriction of a person's freedom as is compatible with the freedom of the rest.

Lukes summarises the essential differences between the views of Durkheim and Marx, and thus of the two traditions, by saying that: 'Social constraint is for Marx a denial and for Durkheim a condition of human freedom and self-realization.'[39]

Community

Hargreaves says that 'at the centre' of his thinking is the belief that we must strive to resolve the conflict which exists between the various groups that make up society. 'The resolution of conflict', he argues, 'requires solidary communities throughout society, communities of men and women with dignity and a commitment to the basic rights of man.'[40] The school has an important role to play in this process. It must introduce a 'community-centred curriculum' which is 'organized around community studies and the expressive arts'.[41] The aim of such a curriculum, Hargreaves asserts, is 'to endow our children with the knowledge and skills to be active and useful members of their communities'.[42]

The first question to ask with regard to all of this is: What essentially does Hargreaves mean by 'community'? Hargreaves himself points out that the concept of 'community' 'is a flabby and sometimes vacuous one'.[43] He notes that for many 'the instant connotation of community is a local residential community', although some people use it to refer to a unit as small as a street or as large as a nation or a continent.[44] However, the central meaning of 'community' in Hargreaves's work is based, we feel, on his understanding of the nature of traditional working-class communities. Such communities, he believes, provided the individual with a defence against the problems of egoism and anomie. They created a sense of belonging, rootedness and fixed identity among their members. There was a feeling of 'solidariness' with the group and out of this developed standards of moral conduct. Hargreaves bemoans the passing of such communities, and, in seeking to establish 'solidary communities' throughout society, he seems to take them as a model. By this we do not mean that he wants to turn the clock back; rather, he wishes to restore their essential features or recreate them in a new form.

Hargreaves recognises, however, that traditional working-class communities had their drawbacks:

> There is, of course, a real danger of romanticizing the working class communities of the past . . . It is easy to forget the horrors and conflicts that existed in working-class communities, their conservatism, their xenophobia, their sexism in which so many women were imprisoned.[45]

Even so Hargreaves understates the disadvantages both of the traditional working-class community and of the communitarian ideal as such. For example, he recognises that the extended family brought with it 'tensions and restrictions', yet he feels these are counter-balanced by the

> continuity, the transmission of values and practices, and considerable mutual help and support. Mum could teach her daughter the skills of being a housewife and mother, and looked after the children as well as keeping a close eye on the progress of the marriage. Secrets were

hard to keep and privacy difficult to guard, but the compensation was often a protection against loneliness, isolation and deprivation.[46]

There are a number of things that need to be said about such a view. First, the idea that important skills and values were transmitted in traditional working-class communities between, say, mother and daughter, is surely suspect. What is often striking about such communities is the extent of the ignorance among working-class women concerning such matters as diet and childbirth. They often lacked basic knowledge in these areas and were just as likely to be transmitting 'old wives' tales' as reliable information. Furthermore, with the extension of secondary education and the spread of courses in 'home economics' and 'health education', daughters are just as likely to have been teaching their mothers as learning from them.

Second, and more important, Hargreaves also exaggerates the extent to which working-class communities provided a warm and protective environment for their members. Traditional working-class communities could often be narrow, restrictive and small-minded worlds devoid of any understanding and sympathy for an individual's needs. There was often a stifling atmosphere in which independence of mind and attempts at self-direction were squashed out of a concern for 'what people will say'. The freedom and autonomy of the individual were sacrificed, therefore, to the maintenance of the community's customs and traditions.

It is not surprising, perhaps, that Hargreaves should neglect such features of working-class community life. For, as we have seen, he belongs to that tradition of thought in which the control and regulation of the individual is regarded as necessary for the sake of social order and individual happiness — and life in a 'solidary community' certainly provides such control. Hargreaves himself admits — in the passage just quoted — that privacy in traditional working-class communities was difficult to guard. But 'privacy' is another word for 'negative freedom' or that absence of constraints which allows the individual to act as he or she chooses; and such 'choice' or self-determination is regarded by many — socialists and liberals alike — as an ultimate value or end-in-itself. R.H. Tawney, for example, once said that 'a man is most himself when he thinks, wills and acts'; J.S. Mill that it is 'the privilege and proper condition' of a human being to decide how he or she shall live; and I. Berlin, commenting on this outlook, that 'those who have ever valued liberty for its own sake believed that to be free to choose, and not to be chosen for, is an inalienable ingredient in what makes human beings human'.

For all these writers human 'dignity' depends upon such self-direction.

But self-direction may not be compatible with the pursuit of the communitarian ideal. Indeed, many see an increase in individual freedom to be the chief benefit of the decline of the traditional community. Ralf Dahrendorf, for example, points out that the consistent liberal 'gets impatient with the illusion of a community that robs the individual of this opportunity for decision and reduces him from a free person to a bee tied to the hive'.[47] He argues that 'the loss of community' is no loss at all, in fact it has been a liberating and emancipating development.[48] Furthermore, the German communitarian tradition, and the work of Tönnies in particular, is, Dahrendorf believes, profoundly reactionary and illiberal. It is, he says, 'a barrier on the road to modernity'.[49]

In certain forms, then, the ideal of community conflicts with other values which are central to the ethos of modern society. Of course, modern society itself is not without its critics — it has often been described by communitarians as 'anonymous' and 'impersonal'. Yet, as R. Plant points out in his discussion of the work of one critic of the community ideal, Harvey Cox:

> What the communitarian calls, with prejudice, 'anonymity', Cox would call, with equal prejudice, 'autonomy'; what the communitarian would call 'anomie' or 'normlessness', Cox would call 'freedom'; what the communitarian would condemn as the atomistic nature of contemporary society, Harvey Cox would praise as its independence.[50]

In Cox's view, then, the anonymous nature of secular urban life is a prerequisite for freedom, independence and autonomy. David Reisman writes in a similar vein about the benefits to be derived from the 'impersonal' nature of modern life. He says that:

> One of the interesting semantic expressions of our own disenchantment is that of bewailing our society as 'impersonal'. What would the member of the village group or small town not give at times for an impersonal setting where he was not constantly part of a web of gossip and surveillance.[51]

Reisman also comments on the relationship between 'society' and 'community' — which he defines as 'the larger territorial organization' and the 'environing group' respectively. He points out that:

> As so defined, society, the larger territorial organization, often provides the mechanism by which individuals can be protected against

the group, both by formal legal procedures such as a bill of rights, and by the fact that large-scale organization may permit the social mobility by which individuals can escape from any particular group.[52]

Of course, Hargreaves — as we have seen — emphasises that the individual must be protected against the group or community, and he seeks a balance between the interests of the community and those of the individual. However, in belonging to that tradition of thought which sees the control of the individual through social integration as crucial to social and psychological well-being, Hargreaves is prevented from recognising that psychological and social 'health' depend upon the freedom and self-direction of the individual. Such 'individual' values have, for him, a truly secondary place.

The question of whether these individual values can, nevertheless, be reconciled with some alternative conception of community is, we believe, of vital importance. It has recently been explored, for example, in the books by Kamenka and Plant.[53] Plant, for instance, asks: 'is there a sense and a definition of community which is relevant to modern autonomous individualistic urban life?'[54] If there is, Hargreaves certainly does not provide it.

Community-centred Curriculum

This brings us to a discussion of Hargreaves's views on the 'community-centred curriculum' and especially to his contention that the comprehensive school ought to reduce the importance of what he calls the 'cognitive-intellectual' component of the curriculum. For Hargreaves believes that schools still accord a central place to cognitive–intellectual abilities and skills. It is by no means uncommon, he says, to hear teachers and headteachers extolling the virtues of other types of abilities and skills — the 'aesthetic–artistic', the 'affective–emotional', the 'physical–manual' and the 'personal–social'. But, in practice, they give them a secondary place. For the actual curriculum of schools transmits the message that what really counts are cognitive–intellectual abilities.

Hargreaves, however, takes the view that 'the cultivation of intellectual ability should not be the cardinal aim of education in the secondary school'.[55] For 'an education based on the cognitive–intellectual grammar school curriculum has been found wanting as the most appropriate education'.[56] He believes that such an academic curriculum must be replaced by one that is 'more comprehensive and balanced'.[57] It should concentrate on 'community studies' and the 'expressive arts' and concern itself with the other four types of ability listed above. Cognitive–intellectual skills will not be discarded, 'since they play an important part in so many communities'.[58] But schools must come to recognise that such knowledge and skills are not always the most important.

The problem with this view is that it underestimates the extent to which the cognitive–intellectual permeates all other types of activity and is fundamental to other forms of ability and skill. Take, for example, the personal–social and affective–emotional. In so far as a person is concerned with determining what ought to be done in personal and social affairs, he must recognise that such judgements can only be made on the basis of a great deal of *knowledge* — of the physical world, of society, of the interests and feelings of other people, of the principles on which objective moral judgements must rest. As Hirst and Peters say: 'Only in so far as one *understands* other people can one come to care about them and actively seek their good.'[59] Similarly, if, like Hargreaves, you have as an objective the resolution of the conflict between the various groups that make up society, then your first task must be to *understand* such conflict, that is, *explain* its character and causes. But such 'knowledge', 'understanding' and 'explanations' are surely the result of cognitive–intellectual activity.

Furthermore, although Hargreaves wants to downgrade the importance of the cognitive–intellectual, he himself cannot help but recognise its importance. For example, he says that the education system needs to prepare young people for an active role in society 'where they *understand* the nation's problems and are willing to help to solve them'.[60] He also wants the reformed curriculum to make people capable of 'reasoned criticism' of such things as social, political and economic matters, radio, television, newspapers, novels, plays and scientific experiments and theories.[61] But what else does cognitive–intellectual activity consist of if not such reasoned criticism? Also, we must recognise that the ability to be critical does not arise spontaneously or develop in a vacuum. A person needs to be provided with forms of knowledge and experience with which to be critical: 'People have to be trained to think critically . . . It is largely a product of the company which people keep, from which they pick up the mode of experience which enables them to manage on their own.'[62] In other words, initially we learn the reasoned criticism of, say, social, political and economic matters through the reasoned criticism of others; and such criticism is most likely to be found in the work of sociologists, political philosophers and scientists, and economists. But what are the disciplines of sociology, political philosophy and science, and economics if not examples of cognitive–intellectual activity?

Hargreaves's attack, therefore, is misdirected. As we have seen, he says that 'the cognitive–intellectual grammar school curriculum has been found wanting'. However, it is one thing to have as your target the grammar school curriculum; it is quite another to call into question cognitive–intellectual activity itself. Hargreaves may well be right to suggest that the secondary school curriculum is too narrow and that there is little justification for thinking only in terms of traditional 'subjects', rather than, say, community studies. For, if a person is concerned to develop an appreciation of the different forms of knowledge and understanding, we should recognise that we can probably achieve these ends by means of various types of curriculum. But whatever form the curriculum takes, we would maintain that cognitive–intellectual activity will still be central.

In addition, Hargreaves, like many other writers, draws too sharp a distinction between the cognitive–intellectual on the one hand, and the affective–emotional on the other. They speak as though our mind and our emotions/feelings were unconnected. Gilbert Ryle has characterised this view as follows:

> In our abstract theorizing about human nature we are still in the archaic habit of treating ourselves and all other human beings as animated department stores, in which the intellect is one department, the will is another department and the feelings a third department.[63]

But such a view, says Ryle, is a 'sheer fairy story', for the intellect and the feelings are not separable in this way. Let us consider, for example, 'feelings' of amusement at a joke or of indignation at the injustice of an allegation. With regard to the former Ryle asks:

> Is it true . . . that you can separate off in it, first, an intellectual operation of considering the point of the joke and secondly, an induced throb, spasm or pang of feeling tickled by it? Can you imagine having the tickle without having seen the point; and can you imagine seeing the point of the joke and feeling, just for once, not amusement, but vertigo, nausea, awe, anxiety or compunction instead?[64]

The answer, says Ryle, is 'no' and that is because the 'cognitive' process of appreciating a joke's wit and the 'feeling' of being tickled by it are not separable operations 'but are all features of the same thing, namely appreciating the joke'.[65]

Furthermore our 'feelings' are not, as it were, given once and for all, remaining untouched by the degree of development of our intellect or our level of understanding. 'The sense of humour', says Ryle, 'is an educable thing; certain sorts of jokes are above the heads of people of certain ages.'[66] The same is true of our 'feelings' of indignation at the perpetration of an injustice. Such feelings are not akin to purely physical sensations such as seasickness. Rather, as our understanding of the world increases, we come to learn to feel indignation at certain types of acts. Ryle stresses that only thinking beings can have such feelings, because in order to feel indignant at the injustice of an allegation we have to be able to recognise or understand that an injustice has occurred.

In the light of these considerations Hargreaves's suggestion that the cognitive–intellectual should play a smaller part in the curriculum in favour of other types of abilities and skills must be considered suspect. For, if our affective–emotional and personal–social skills are to be developed, the cognitive–intellectual component of them must be recognised and this component must be central to the school curriculum.

We have devoted a great deal of space to an assessment of Hargreaves's views, because we consider that his work merits careful attention. Hargreaves provides us with a coherent and well-written analysis of contemporary education. He brings together a large amount of material and shapes it into a well-structured whole. In concentrating on what we regard as its weak points we would not like to leave the reader with the impression that it does not also have considerable strengths. Hargreaves makes many acute observations about contemporary educational theory and practice.

Basil Bernstein

INTRODUCTION

In this section we will look at the way that Bernstein has taken up and developed some of Durkheim's ideas. However, at the outset, we feel we must point to a crucial difference between Durkheim and Bernstein, namely the latter's failure to relate education explicitly to the wider society. For example, when Bernstein talks of 'social order' it is never clear whether he is talking about the social order of the school, or of society, or of both. Bernstein deals in an interesting way with the changes that are occurring within education, and many of the changes that he predicted seem to be happening today. However, he is very vague as to why these changes are occurring, and he does not adequately trace the significance of the changes within education for our understanding of the way that the wider society is organised. Perhaps the difference between Durkheim and Bernstein can be shown by quoting Bernstein who says: 'I have always found it difficult to move towards a more general macro-analysis until I have some grip upon the local relationships at the micro-aspect.'[67] In other words, Bernstein feels the need to understand what is happening in a part of society before venturing to look at society as a whole. Durkheim, we suggest, tended to have a view of the nature of society as a whole and then move to the analysis of a particular part in order to check his general view. This crucial difference in approach leads Bernstein into a rather vague and undeveloped statement of the part education plays in helping to establish order in society.

We will not devote much time to Bernstein's socio-linguistic thesis. Suffice it to say that he is very much aware of the class nature of society and the impact of class on education, something that Durkheim neglected. Bernstein suggests that class values affect the pattern of socialisation of children. Members of one group adopt a 'personal' approach to the raising of their children in which they are sensitive to the changes and development of the child and modify their demands and expectations as the child develops. Other people adopt a 'positional' approach to their children, in which the demands they make on the child are related to the age, sex and status of the child — infant or baby or youth. In this latter form of socialisation, the child learns that what is expected of it depends on factors not under its control. It also learns that parts of life are divorced from each other: the life of the baby, child and youth are separated and unrelated. In the 'personal' approach, the child learns that the different parts of his life are related together and flow into each other, because of the way it has been treated by parents. To use terms that Bernstein develops later, the 'positional' family socialisation is characterised by 'strong classification' and the 'personal' family socialisation is characterised by 'weak classification'.

Bernstein suggests that the language code that is used in the different patterns of socialisation is very important. Positional socialisation patterns are usually accompanied by the 'restricted' code of language, while the 'personal' regime tends to put over an 'elaborated' code of language. (Bernstein uses other terms for these codes in his various articles.) Roughly speaking, the 'elaborated' code allows its user to see relationships between aspects of experience that are hidden to users of the 'restricted' code and it enables people to make explicit their meanings; whereas the restricted code works on the assumption that the listener has the same experience as the speaker and has an implicit understanding of the speaker's meanings. The elaborated code is the code of education and thus middle-class pupils who arrive in school with the elaborated code are better placed for educational success than working-class children.

There has been a great deal of debate and argument about this aspect of Bernstein's work which we cannot develop here in detail. We merely summarise his ideas to indicate that he is aware of the importance of social class in education and that he does see a relationship between the way that education is changing and the social class system in Britain.

CHANGES IN EDUCATION

In a brief article 'Open Schools — Open Society?'[68] Bernstein uses the terms organic and mechanical solidarity to try to analyse changes in the school. His thesis is that the school is moving from mechanical to organic solidarity. 'Mechanical solidarity' is defined as having the following characteristics: individuals share a common set of beliefs and conduct is regulated in a very detailed way; roles are ascribed; punishment is repressive; there is little tension between an individual's private beliefs and his role obligations. 'Organic solidarity' is defined by the following characteristics: individuals relate to each other through a complex interdependence of specialised functions; roles are achieved; there is more variation in people's values. Bernstein points out that he is dealing with what he sees as a trend, which will be found to a greater extent in some schools than in others, and which 'at the moment may exist at the ideological rather than the substantive level'.[69]

Bernstein then looks at different aspects of the school to show how the changes are occurring. He believes that there is a move away from the transmission of common values in schools, with control based on the teachers' position or status, to a situation in which control is based on the recognition of differences between individuals. There are more subjects taught and more people involved in the authority hierarchy. The teachers' role is more complex with many more sub-roles. For pupils, their position within the school is based more and more on their individual qualities and less on such things as age, sex and IQ. The class is a less popular form of organisation, with sets and all-ability groups taking the place of the class. There is now greater variation in the size of teaching groups and pupils will find themselves in many different teaching groups. There is a change in the aims of teaching too, with a move towards the discovery of principles and topic work. The teacher is becoming more of a problem poser rather than the problem-solver and is more likely to work with other teachers rather than being insulated and autonomous within the classroom. The distinction between subjects is being replaced with the notion of integrated themes, and this will affect the relationship among staff. More and more the individual teacher will have to 'achieve' his role relative to other members of staff. For the pupil, too, there is more choice and the role of the pupil is less well defined by the organisation of the school. The clear-cut distinction between the school and the outside world is being eroded.

Bernstein summarises these changes by suggesting that we are moving from a situation of education in depth to one of education in breadth. This move weakens the authority structure in the school which was based on the teacher's position in the subject hierarchy, but it requires a fundamental consensus among staff on the integrating themes. Another way of understanding the changes is to suggest that we are seeing a change from the 'purity of categories' to 'the mixing of categories'. That is, we are seeing a shift from the school having a clear-cut set of values which it transmitted to the pupils, to one where values are more ambiguous and more 'open to the influence of diverse values from outside'.[70] The move from purity to mixing of categories is also seen in the tendency to combine subjects instead of keeping them separate and to mixing teaching groups instead of having pupils in the same class all the time.

These changes may cause difficulties for staff and pupils, who can become confused about where one subject ends and another begins, about where one role ends and another begins, and about what the structure of the school actually is. It is possible that as a reaction to these ambiguities pupils will form 'closed' peer groups which may develop their own clear-cut distinctions.

To summarise, Bernstein suggests that there is a change evident in some parts of the educational system which can be seen as a move from education in depth to education in breadth. This movement affects the role of the teacher and pupil, the organisation of knowledge and the authority structure within the school. Bernstein says little about why such a shift is happening. At one point he states: 'One origin of the purity and mixing of categories may be in the general social principles regulating the mixing of diverse groups in society.'[71] This apart, we are left to infer why the changes are taking place and what the consequences are for the wider society of such changes. It is possible that Bernstein thinks, following Durkheim, that education is moving from mechanical to organic solidarity because society is developing in this direction; but this is not made explicit. It may be that Bernstein thinks that the changes in education will bring about changes in the wider society as the title 'Open Schools — Open Society?' seems to imply. But again, this is not made clear.

COMMENT

Some comments are appropriate before we move on to examine the ways that Bernstein has developed his ideas. We should note that Bernstein was writing in 1967 and that many of the trends that he mentions have indeed become more obvious with the development of education. Streaming is now less popular than previously and there is a move towards setting and mixed-ability teaching. In secondary education there are many more options available than ten years ago and more emphasis given to pastoral care in schools. The teachers' role does seem to have become more complex and it is possible that to a greater extent teachers have to win control over pupils rather than having it given automatically because they are teachers. In terms of the curriculum we are seeing, to some extent, a movement away from subject specialism. The DES report of 1980 suggested that we should think of organising the curriculum along the lines of the different sorts of experience that we can offer to pupils, and then fit subjects into this framework.[72] We have recently seen the notion of skill training become central to a lot of thinking in education, particularly that of the Further Education Unit.[73] Primary schools, after the abolition of the 11+ examination, have tended to move, in curriculum terms, in the direction indicated by Bernstein. These trends have not been uniform throughout the educational system; we suspect that the developments Bernstein mentions are to be found in the primary areas and among the less academic groups in the secondary sphere. The 'mixing of categories' may be found in the early stages of higher education, but is quickly replaced by the traditional pure subject specialisms. The same may be true of secondary education where the examination system still maintains a relatively 'pure' system of curriculum organisation. So we would comment that Bernstein has certainly detected a trend and that this trend is growing; however, the traditional system still has a strong hold. Had Bernstein noted that the trend was more popular among selected groups of younger or less able pupils, this could have influenced his ideas about the changing nature of control in schools. We would also say that the changes may be more apparent than real, that is, a school may appear to use an integrated approach but a closer investigation may reveal that it is still structured on subject lines.

We are not altogether happy with Bernstein's use of the terms organic and mechanical solidarity. As we have previously pointed out, these terms are used by Durkheim to refer to the way societies are organised. In organic solidarity, while it is true that roles are achieved, that individuals are placed in many roles and that the values of society become more general, it is also true that the society is composed of specialist groups. Each group has its own specific function and order is brought about by the interdependence of these groups. The trends that Bernstein plots seem to suggest the erosion of specialist groups with the mixture of categories. If this is the case, then the trend would seem to be against the development of organic solidarity.

Finally, we would suggest that there is a way of using a Durkheimian line of reasoning to add depth to Bernstein's analysis. It might be argued that what we are seeing today is the development of a common way of thinking. In a pluralistic society order is not brought about by shared values, since there are many value systems. One way in which a basis of social order could be developed would be to have everyone sharing a common approach to solving problems, a common frame of thinking. The development of an integrated, rather than a subject specialist curriculum, and of a project method, could be seen as a way of getting all members of the society to accept the same rules for problem-solving. In this way education could be one method of producing the basis for order in society. This idea is not incompatible with Bernstein's analysis and it may lie at the back of his thinking. If so, it needs to be made explicit.

EDUCATIONAL KNOWLEDGE

Bernstein has developed his ideas further in a number of articles. We will look at what is perhaps his most influential article, entitled 'On the Classification and Framing of Educational Knowledge'.[74]

The distribution of power and the 'principles of control' are reflected, so Bernstein thinks, in the way that a society 'selects, classifies, distributes, transmits and evaluates the educational knowledge it considers to be public'.[75] Both Durkheim and Marx have, apparently, shown this to be the case. We have to admit that we do not understand what Bernstein means by 'principles of control'. The term 'social control', when used in sociology, refers to the forms of external pressure (economic, political, military and from family) which constrain us to act in certain ways. The term also refers to the internalisation of values, norms and ideas which we use when we act 'naturally'. It may be that Bernstein is distinguishing these two meanings. External constraint may be understood as the 'distribution of power', internalised constraint as 'control'. The principles of control would then be the basic rules or values internalised in socialisation. This seems the best elaboration of what Bernstein means, but he does not make the distinction clear. If we are right, it appears that by looking at education we can get some idea about external and internal constraint in society.

Bernstein begins by seeing education as composed of curriculum (what is defined as valid knowledge); pedagogy (what is defined as valid transmission) and evaluation (what is defined as valid realisation of the knowledge transmitted). Furthermore — and here we come to the really important ideas — all schools and colleges divide the day up into units of time. These may be long or short units. What happens in a unit of time is called a content. It is best at this stage to think of contents as the subject matter of a lesson. The contents, or subject matter, of a lesson may be well insulated from the subject matter of another lesson, or the contents may be related together. In addition, in lessons the teacher or the pupil, or both, may have little control over what is done, when it is done and how it is done. Alternatively, they may have a lot of control over these things.

Classification and Framing

Bernstein now introduces two concepts to describe these features. The concept of 'classification' is used to refer to the relationship of contents. When classification is strong, then the contents are well insulated from each other and the boundaries between contents are strong and clear. Think of the traditional school or university where what is done in one period has little to do with what was done in the period before. Weak classification means that the boundaries between contents are weak and blurred. The concept of 'framing' is used to refer to the control of what is transmitted or received. 'Thus frame refers to the degree of control teacher and pupil possess over the selection, organization, pacing and timing of the knowledge transmitted and received in pedagogical relationship.'[76] Strong frame means the teacher and pupil have little control; weak frame means they have more control.

It is appropriate here to note that Bernstein does not distinguish between teacher control and pupil control. However, it may be that frame is weak for the teacher and strong for the pupil in the same lesson, or vice versa. Similarly, Bernstein confounds what is transmitted and what is received; again these should be distinguished. It is interesting to note that, in a later formulation of the term frame, Bernstein says: 'Where framing is strong, then the acquirer has little control over the selection, organization and pacing of the transmission.'[77] In this formulation, framing refers only to the pupil, the 'acquirer', and not to the teacher.

When we have knowledge organised along the lines of strong classification, then this gives rise 'to what we here call a collection code'.[78] If there is an attempt to reduce the strength of the classification, then we have an 'integrated' code. The term code is left undefined here, but we are fairly sure what Bernstein means. Code refers to the basic principles, or rules, of organisation. Thus, in organising the way we measure, we can have a decimal code of centimetres, metres, etc. or we can have a feet and inches code. In counting money we can have a decimal or a 'pounds, shillings and pence' code. In the same way, when putting knowledge together the basic principle could be of keeping parts well separated (a collection code), or putting them together (an integrated code).

Having defined his terms, Bernstein suggests that England has a collection code with very strong classification and relatively weak framing. In Europe we find strong classification and very strong framing and in the USA relatively weak classification and framing. In England we find that students specialise early and that a subject identity and loyalty are developed. As pupils progress they become more specialised, learning more and more about less and less, and their subject loyalty is increased. When they become teachers and lecturers, they in turn transmit subject loyalty and identity, and so the system perpetuates itself. Because the subject has become so much a part of the teachers' and pupils' identity, they will resist any attempt to change the form of curriculum organisation.

There are certain characteristics of the collection code which Bernstein pulls out for attention. With a collection code, knowledge becomes rather like private property to which only a few have access. It is only the few who are admitted to the 'ultimate mystery' of the subject, that is, nothing is certain and given but everything is capable of being understood in different ways. Most pupils never realise this. Educational knowledge is divorced from everyday, common-sense knowledge and so pupils are socialised into the view that everyday reality is unrelated to knowledge. Learning, in the collection code, goes from surface knowledge towards the deeper structure of concepts and theories. Finally, the collection code generates a particular power system within the school and education generally.

In contrast, the integrated code has its own characteristics. Because the parts of knowledge have to be put together, integration demands that the deep structure, the basic principles, be revealed early. The parts of knowledge have to be integrated about a theme and this means that teachers must work together. The consequence of this is that a common method of teaching and common modes of evaluation will develop among teachers. So, while pupils may have more choice and more control, teachers will, individually, have less control over the method of teaching. From the individual teacher's point of view, framing will be strong. The power structure will be different from that found with the collection code.

In the collection code power is usually vested in the heads of departments. It is they who make decisions and try to win favourable allocations. Teachers work with others in the same department and usually do not talk about the presentation of knowledge with non-departmental staff. As Bernstein puts it: 'social order arises out of the hierarchical nature of the authority relationships, out of the systematic ordering of differentiated knowledge in time and space, out of an explicit, usually predictable, examination procedure.'[79] Integration codes encourage co-operation among teachers who must make decisions about teaching. Thus horizontal relationships are formed and power is shifted from the top to the lower orders who do the teaching. At the same time there has to be a shift in identities, for the teachers can no longer see themselves as subject experts.

While a clear-cut hierarchy of power is present in the collection code, the advent of integrated codes can create problems of order. To avoid this four conditions must be satisfied:

1. There must be explicit consensus among teachers about the integrating theme and thus 'a *high* level of ideological consensus among staff'.[80]
2. The linkage between the integrating idea and the knowledge presented must be explicitly worked out by the staff involved. Teachers will have to learn to negotiate a course.
3. There will have to be a committee system of staff, and possibly students, to give feedback and monitor the course.
4. There will have to be multiple criteria of assessment which cover such 'inner' attributes as motivation, co-operation, etc. More of the personality of the pupil will become subject to observation.

Bernstein finishes by noting an apparent paradox. The collection code with its explicit hierarchies of power seems to be an expression of mechanical solidarity. But it produces specialised personnel, which is typical of organic solidarity. The integrated code with its weak classification and with staff having to achieve their roles with others seems to be an expression of organic solidarity. However, since staff will have to develop a shared ideology and shared ways of teaching and evaluating, then the outcome is likely to be pupils with less specialisation and with a fair degree of consensus obtained implicitly through exposure to their education. This non-specialised consensus seems to be characteristic of mechanical solidarity.

TYPES OF PEDAGOGY

Bernstein develops some of his ideas further in the article 'Class and Pedagogies — Visible and Invisible'.[81] Here he looks at the new forms of education which he thinks are developing in infant schools. To do this he develops the notions of visible and invisible pedagogy.

A visible pedagogy has strong classification and frame. Here the roles of the teacher and pupil are well defined, the sequencing of learning is clearly set out and the criteria used to assess whether a pupil has learned are explicitly stated. An invisible pedagogy is characterised by weak classification. The roles of teacher and pupil are not so clearly distinguished, the definition of who is a teacher and who is a pupil is implicit rather than explicit. The teacher observes the pupil, particularly at play, to discern signs that the pupil is ready to progress. Since the signs of readiness are based on individual development and on theories of development that the teacher holds, there can be no explicitly defined sequencing of learning. The sequence depends on the child's development as understood by the teacher. Much more of the pupil is open to inspection with the invisible pedagogy; aspects of emotional stability, motivation and peer relationships are taken into account. The pupil, being unaware of the theories of development, cannot know the rules that are used to define the sequencing of learning. Here the rules are implicit, rather than explicitly stated. An interesting example of this form of invisible pedagogy was reported to us recently, where a child who had completed the first year of an ITA reading programme was told to begin it all again because 'she had lost confidence'. In the invisible pedagogy, the criteria of successful learning are not defined and are implicitly stated.

As Karabel and Halsey note, Bernstein argues that the invisible pedagogy of the open classroom in the infant school, 'thought by its proponents to be universally progressive, actually reflects the life situation of a particular social group — the new middle class'.[82] A new method of socialisation has been developed by a new social group and is finding its way into the education system. The new middle class has adopted a 'person' rather than an 'individual' form of socialisation. To develop this notion Bernstein says:

> It is clear that in advanced industrial societies, especially in the West, there has been a considerable increase in the division of labour of social control based upon specialized modes of communication (symbolic control). This has created a vast range of occupations dedicated to the symbolic shaping and reshaping of the population. With this increase in the division of labour of symbolic control, I suggest there

has also developed a change in emphasis in the *form* of socialization; from the creation of strongly bounded but specialized *individuals* to more weakly bounded but specialized *persons*. Durkheim foresaw this as a development of organic solidarity, and he was concerned with its consequences for inner discipline. I do not think that he quite saw that this development carried its own *structure* of integration, nor did he see its social function: to shift the relationships between visible and invisible forms of control.[83]

To highlight the distinction between individual and person Bernstein suggests that Durkheim argued that the division of labour in the economy had led to the development of individualism in modern society. The individual was now regarded as sacred and worthy of respect. As Lukes says: 'Durkheim maintained that a new set of values had become institutionalised in modern societies, rendering the individual sacred, attaching moral value to individual autonomy, and justifying individual freedom and rights — and it was this which he chose to call "individualism".'[84]

With the development of the communication and education industry, Bernstein thinks, there has been a development of a new middle class. This new class is not a property-owning group; it owes its position in society to its ability to control the various forms of communications. Put in the terms used by Pierre Bourdieu, this class has cultural not economic capital. When Durkheim dealt with 'individualism' in modern society he was thinking about the old middle class. The new middle class has developed the notion of 'person' as the product of socialisation; the old middle class saw the 'individual' as the product of socialisation. The distinction between person and individual is made by Bernstein in the following passage. 'Whereas the concept of the *individual* leads to specific, unambiguous role identities and relatively inflexible role performances, the *concept* of the person leads to ambiguous personal identity and flexible role performances.'[85] What Bernstein appears to be driving at here (and again we point out the difficulty of understanding what he says) is that the new middle class is developing a new form of socialisation which produces an individual capable of fitting into a large range of roles and of performing a role in a number of different ways. The development of the 'person' is brought about by weak classification and by observing many aspects of personality. Control is not developed by putting the child in clearly defined situations in which the rules and values are explicitly stated; rather control is brought about by developing as much variety as possible within the child. Rigid structures can limit the development of variety and are rejected; concentration on one aspect of personality can also limit variety, so many facets of the child must be observed and developed. Socialisation into an explicit value system would reduce variety, so the values must be implicitly stated and intuited by the developing person. Bernstein thus argues that the form of socialisation of the new middle class is that of invisible pedagogy. The form of socialisation in the infant school is also invisible pedagogy. But the new middle class is facing a problem in that the form of secondary education is visible pedagogy.

Bernstein goes on to elaborate his ideas further by noting that in the new middle class it is the mother who is the crucial agent of socialisation rather than the nanny of the old middle class. The invisible pedagogy assumes that time is a flexible quality not to be divided into distinct periods. The concept of space is also flexible; space can be used for a variety of purposes and more space is needed. Invisible pedagogy also brings in a new form of social control.

> Because the hierarchy is implicit (*which does not mean it is not there, only that the form of its realization is different*), there is a relative absence of *strongly marked* regulation of the child's acts, communication objects, spaces, times and progression. In what lies the control? We will suggest that control inheres in *elaborated interpersonal communication* in a context where maximum surveillance is possible. *In other words, control is vested in the process of interpersonal communication.* A particular function of language is of special significance, and its realization is of an elaborated form in contrast to the more restricted form of communication where the pedagogy is visible.[86]

Thus it appears that the new middle class uses the elaborated mode of speech, which the old middle class apparently did not do. Further, the invisible pedagogy of the infant school uses an elaborated mode, but presumably the visible pedagogy of secondary education uses a more restricted code. This contradicts the earlier socio-linguistic thesis of middle class and the schools using elaborated codes.

COMMENTS

Before making some general comments on Bernstein's developments of Durkheim, we wish to note that, in the article dealt with above, Bernstein seems to be confused as to what Durkheim means by individualism. We feel that there is little evidence in Durkheim to suggest that individualism in organic solidarity leads to specific and unambiguous identities and inflexible role-performances. Indeed, as we have already noted, Lukes sees the notion as referring to such things as respect for individual autonomy, freedom and rights. Of course, it might be argued that, as Durkheim thought, one of the ways to avoid anomie was to produce groups with their own ethical systems which would give a morality to their members, and that these 'professional ethics' would lead to inflexible role-performance. However, since Durkheim placed so much emphasis on individualism as the central value of modern society, it could just as well be argued that the principle of individualism would be incorporated into the various ethics that groups develop. The notion of 'person' as defined by Bernstein seems to us to be more akin to Durkheim's idea of anomie. Bernstein insists that the socialisation is into implicitly rather than explicitly stated rules and values; but this seems to run counter to Durkheim's views in *Moral Education* where he consistently demands that the structure of the school and its discipline should be explicitly and clearly related to the children's socialisation.

It may be obvious that we have had some difficulty in trying to describe Bernstein's ideas. This may be due to our own inadequacies; but we suggest that it is also because of the opacity of Bernstein's language. Too often he fails to define important concepts clearly, and this failure means that the subsequent elaboration is confused.

Bernstein is certainly aware of the changes that are occurring in education. He draws our attention to changes in curriculum, in the roles of the teacher and the pupil, and in authority relations in school. Bernstein seems to think that all these developments are linked together by some underlying, unifying principle. He talks of a shift from mechanical to organic solidarity in schools and of a move from a collection to an integrated code in the curriculum. He also seems to believe that these educational changes are related to changes in the wider society — though exactly how is not clear. The terms 'classification' and 'frame' are introduced to help clarify the nature of the changes in education and to relate them to changes in society generally. In a later work[87] these concepts are also used to deal with the specific link between education and the economy.

Classification

However, when we look carefully at the term 'classification', we immediately find confusion. Part of the definition of strong classification is that the content of a unit of time is well insulated from the content of another unit of time. Weak classification exists when the contents of units of time are not well insulated. For example, a possible organisational feature of school life is the double period, with no break between the lessons. Here the contents of one period are not insulated from the next, so we presume that Bernstein would say that we have weak classification. At the end of the second period the pupils may well have a lesson in a different subject; so now we have strong classification. Or again, in a junior school we can often find a teacher beginning the morning by looking at the weather and recording it on wall charts with the pupils. This may then be immediately followed by maths. Here we have strong classification within a unit of time. Our examples suggest that defining classification by the contents of a unit of time is confusing unless the term 'unit of time' is defined. Do we think of a unit of time as being defined by the school bell, or is it the content that defines the unit of time? We are not told.

Bernstein also says that classification depends on the strength of the insulation between the contents; but who defines the strength? In a lesson on war poetry, for example, a teacher may discuss life in the trenches. To the teacher this is part of teaching English, but the pupils may see it as History. From the teacher's point of view classification is weak, from the pupil's strong. It may be argued, of course, that Bernstein, in formulating the concept of classification, is thinking in terms of the general organisation of knowledge as presented by the timetable, so that exceptions do not matter. To this we would reply that Bernstein has to show that what the timetable says and what in fact happens in practice is similar. He cannot assume that integration occurs because the timetable says it does.

These confusions are made worse when we come to look at the concepts of collection and integrated code. Strong classification defines a collection code, while weakened classification defines an integrated code. How weak does the classification have to be before we have an integrated code? From whose point of view do we measure the strength of the classification, headmaster's, teacher's or pupil's? Since there appears to be a sliding scale from collection to integration (with some undefined cut-off point), why call them two distinct codes? Bernstein defines code in the following way: 'a code is a regulative principle, tacitly acquired, which integrates relevant meanings, the form of their realization and their evoking contexts.'[88] If we have two codes we have two regulative principles, two different rules for organising curricula. But Bernstein defines one code by strong classification, the other by weaker classification. Here we have one principle, classification, but apparently two codes. Confusion reigns again.

However, there is a second, possibly more fruitful, element to the definition of the term 'classification'. Here Bernstein refers to the boundaries between contents being clearly defined. This seems to be a development of the idea of the purity of categories that he talked about in the article 'Open Schools — Open Society?'[89] A category may be understood to be a sort of conceptual box or label into which particular pieces of experience are placed. In the traditional academic education in Britain knowledge has been placed into certain categories or boxes. There are the sciences, the humanities, the arts. These general categories are also subdivided into physics and chemistry, history and geography, and so on. But the term 'category' can also be used of the boxes we have for understanding the social world. Society can be divided up into the economy, the educational system, religion, the political system, social classes, the family. The term may be applied to social roles too: to the role of teacher, of pupil, of social worker, of priest, of police officer, and so on. It should be stressed that the method that is used to understand society or the curriculum — the set of boxes and what goes into each box — is a product of the development of society. Purity of categories exists when there is little or no confusion about which bit of experience goes into which box. In Britain we tend to think that there is no relationship between astronomy and psychology, but in other parts of the world these two aspects of experience are linked. Purity of categories will exist when there is a clear-cut distinction between what we call subjects in the curriculum. It will exist when there is little or no obvious relationship between education, the family and work, and when there are clear distinctions between acting as a teacher, a learner, a social worker and a policeman. The mixing of categories occurs when it is clear that the traditional curriculum boxes are not being used, when the school and the wider society are brought more and more together with work experience programmes and parents coming into school to teach the pupils. Similarly, when the role of the teacher begins to take on aspects of the social worker and policeman, the mixing of categories has occurred. Put briefly, the mixing of categories involves the breakdown of the traditional classificatory system, assuming such a system ever existed. If we take classification to mean the purity or mixing of categories, then Bernstein's work can suggest some interesting lines of investigation. We can ask about the extent to which the mixing of curriculum categories goes along with the mixing of role categories or the mixing of the school, family and economy categories. Unfortunately Bernstein does not go into these possibilities. Rather he seems to assume that the mixing of curriculum categories involves the mixing of other categories too, and he spends most of his time showing how, logically, this must happen. However, Ronald

King used data he had collected for other purposes to see to what extent changes in one category implied changes in others. His conclusions are interesting. He writes:

> the results presented here do not strongly support the concomitant idea that particular organizational forms and practices, conceptually similar when using various categories [weak or strong classification] would tend to be associated with one another . . . If the various kinds of closed/open, mixed/pure activities are not closely related, then the proposition that changes in these activities have an underlying, unifying factor is not strongly supported. Put simply, it is suggested that the introduction of one 'open' innovation into a school is not necessarily associated with moves to 'open up' other aspects of school, and may sometimes be associated with the closure of others. In addition, this analysis implies that the logical power of the concepts of openness, purity, and possibly educational codes, is greater than their explanatory power.[90]

In other words, Bernstein mistakenly assumes that a move from pure to mixed categories in one aspect of school life (for example, in the curriculum) necessarily involves a similar change in other aspects of school life (for example, in the teacher's role).

This is not surprising really, for the difficulties we mentioned earlier still remain, even if we take classification to refer to pure and mixed categories. We still have to ask: 'From whose point of view are the categories pure or mixed, the observer's, the headmaster's, the teacher's or the pupil's?' Bernstein seems to assume some sort of consensus. He assumes that if the timetable indicates a collection code then this is what happens or if the rhetoric of the school indicates an integrated code this too occurs. That this is not the case is demonstrated both by Sharp and Green, and by Andy Hargreaves, who show that there can be vast differences between what is said to be going on and what actually happens in the classroom.[91]

Framing

We now turn to look at the concept of 'framing', which also is confused. Strong framing exists when teacher and pupil have little or no control over the selection, organisation and pacing of knowledge. We have already mentioned, earlier in this chapter, the difficulties of failing to separate teacher and pupil control, and we would like to add further comments now. There appears, at first sight, to be an overlap between the ideas of classification and frame. Part of the definition of frame is the control over the organisation of knowledge by teacher and pupil. But the whole notion of classification is to do with how knowledge is organised, be it on the basis of pure or mixed categories. We can only suggest that Bernstein, in his unclear way, is trying to distinguish the context imposed on the teacher and pupil and the ability of the teacher and pupil to mould this context to what they want. Classification would then refer to the imposed context and frame to the adaptations of the teacher and pupils. There is some justification for this view, because Bernstein sees classification as related to power and framing as having something to do with what he calls the 'principles of control'. Again, we have to infer this, for Bernstein neglects to define the terms 'power' and 'control'. If we have guessed correctly, then what Bernstein is talking about is power. Classification refers to the ability of some individuals or groups to impose their ideas about the general organisation of education upon others; frame refers to the way that pupils and teachers reorganise the imposed context. The analysis would then relate to the wider level of groups imposing either strong or weak classification and to the micro-level of teachers and pupils trying to cope with the imposed situation. In some instances there is no option but to go along with what is imposed (strong frame), in others there is a lot of freedom (weak frame). Unfortunately Bernstein does not deal with the questions of who controls education or the limits of control in education.

We feel that, apart from the confusion that arises from his lack of adequate definitions, Bernstein has adopted the worst aspects of Durkheim and neglected the best. Bernstein fails to give any real explanation of the changes he sees happening in education; he does not say why they are occurring. We presume that this is because he assumes that, if changes are being brought about in education, this is because they are happening in the wider society. As society changes, so does education. Changes in education mean that there are changes in the wider society. If Bernstein can discover what new forms of social solidarity are developing in education, then he can assume that new forms of solidarity are developing in society. Following Durkheim, he can neglect the problem of power, for modern society is thought to be integrated through the division of labour and the interdependence of the parts of society. Similarly, since education is a method of socialisation, changes in education will inevitably bring new forms of personality out in the pupils, although Bernstein is aware of the mediation of class factors.

While we have been critical of Bernstein, we do feel that he has opened up important areas for investigation. Despite all the complexities and definitional difficulties, there is much to be gained from looking at the changes in curriculum, roles and the relationship of education to other parts of the society. We believe that the notion of purity and mixing of categories could be released from Bernstein's assumption of a unifying underlying trend and be used to ask some interesting questions about British education. The most important question we believe is what are the categories of knowledge held by people with power in education and how do these categories influence the form of education that pupils receive? Further, and here Bernstein has much to offer, what are the relationships between categories of knowledge and the class system and how effective is the educational system in transmitting categories of knowledge? These questions are significant because the categories of knowledge that we give to our children are the fundamental frameworks for making sense of experience, as Durkheim recognised in his last great work 'Elementary Forms of Religious Life'. However, it is only by rigorous critical examination that some of the fundamentally important ideas of Bernstein can be clarified and made useful.

NOTES

1. D. Hargreaves, *The Challenge for the Comprehensive School: Culture, Curriculum and Community* (Routledge and Kegan Paul, London, 1982), p. 13.

2. Ibid., p. 40.

3. Ibid., p. 83.

4. Ibid., p. 100.

5. Ibid., p. 100.

6. D. Hargreaves, 'A Sociological Critique of Individualism in Education', *British Journal of Educational Studies*, vol. 28, no. 3 (1980), p. 189.

7. Ibid., p. 187.

8. Ibid., p. 193.

9. Ibid., p. 188.

10. Hargreaves, *The Challenge*, p. 93.

11. Ibid., p. 85.

12. Hargreaves, 'A Sociological Critique', p. 189.

13. Ibid., p. 190.

14. Ibid., pp. 190–1.

15. Ibid., p. 192.

16. Ibid., p. 192.

17. Ibid., p. 193.

18. Ibid., p. 194.

19. Ibid., p. 196.

20. Ibid., p. 196.

21. Ibid., p. 196; see S. Lukes, 'Durkheim's "Individualism and the Intellectuals" ', *Political Studies*, vol. 17, no. 1 (1969).

22. Hargreaves, 'A Sociological Critique', p. 197.

23. Lukes, 'Durkheim's "Individualism and the Intellectuals" ', p. 20.

24. Ibid., p. 21.

25. We would also like to point out that what Durkheim has to say about these matters in 'Individualism and the Intellectuals' is inconsistent with the views expressed in most of the remainder of his work. This means that, whilst Hargreaves's arguments are in keeping with Durkheim's general position on individualism in modern society, the essay 'Individualism and the Intellectuals' provides no support for Hargreaves's stance. Indeed, in this article, Durkheim defends many of the ideas which are attacked by Hargreaves.

26. W. Frankena, *Ethics* (Prentice-Hall, Englewood Cliffs, 1973), p. 113.

27. Hargreaves, *The Challenge*, p. 93.

28. S. Lukes, *Individualism* (Blackwell, Oxford, 1973), pp. 71–2.

29. J.S. Mill, *On Liberty* (Dent, London, 1910), pp. 120–1.

30. D. Reisman, *Individualism Reconsidered* (Free Press, New York, 1954), p. 37.

31. H.R.G. Greaves, *The Foundations of Political Theory* (Bell, London, 1966), p. 4.

32. G.C. Field, *Political Theory* (Methuen, London, 1963), p. 121.

33. Ibid., p. 122.

34. S. Lukes, 'Alienation and Anomie' in P. Laslett and W.G. Runciman (eds.), *Philosophy, Politics and Society*, Third series (Blackwell, Oxford, 1969) (reprinted in S. Lukes, *Essays in Social Theory* (Macmillan, London, 1977). The page references in the following notes are to the Blackwell edition.

35. Ibid., p. 142.

36. Ibid., p. 144.

37. Ibid., p. 145.

38. Ibid., p. 145.

39. Ibid., p. 142.

40. Hargreaves, *The Challenge*, p. 183.

41. Ibid., p. 128.

42. Ibid., p. 134.

43. Ibid., p. 114.

44. Ibid., p. 135.

45. Ibid., p. 33.

46. Ibid., p. 30.

47. Quoted in R. Plant, *Community and Ideology* (Routledge and Kegan Paul, London, 1974), p. 34.

48. Ibid., p. 30.

49. Ibid., p. 33.

50. Ibid., p. 33.

51. Reisman, *Individualism Reconsidered*, pp. 34–5.

52. Ibid., p. 26.

53. E. Kamenka (ed.), *Community as a Social Ideal* (E. Arnold, London, 1982); Plant, *Community and Ideology*.

54. Plant, *Community and Ideology*, p. 36.

55. Hargreaves, *The Challenge*, p. 174.

56. Ibid., p. 147.

57. Ibid., p. 161.

58. Ibid., p. 135.

59. P.H. Hirst and R.S. Peters, *The Logic of Education* (Routledge and Kegan Paul, London, 1970), p. 62 (emphasis added).

60. Hargreaves, *The Challenge*, p. 161 (emphasis added).

61. Ibid., p. 139.

62. Hirst and Peters, *The Logic*, p. 31.

63. G. Ryle, 'Can Virtue Be Taught?', in R.F. Dearden, P.H. Hirst and R.S. Peters (eds.), *Education and Reason* (Routledge and Kegan Paul, London, 1975), p. 52.

64. Ibid., pp. 52–3.

65. Ibid., p. 53.

66. Ibid., p. 53.

67. B. Bernstein, *Class, Codes and Control*, 2nd edn (Routledge and Kegan Paul, London, 1977), vol. 3, p. 2.

68. Bernstein, 'Open Schools — Open Society?' in *Class, Codes and Control*.

69. Ibid., p. 69.

70. Ibid., p. 73.

71. Ibid., p. 74.

72. Department of Education and Science, *A Framework for the School Curriculum* (HMSO, London, 1980).

73. Further Education Curriculum Review and Development Unit (FEU), *Beyond Coping: Some Approaches to Social Education* (FEU, London, 1980).

74. Bernstein, 'On the Classification and Framing of Educational Knowledge' in *Class, Codes and Control*.

75. Ibid., p. 85.

76. Ibid., p. 89.

77. Bernstein, 'Aspects of the Relations Between Education and Production' in *Class, Codes and Control*, p. 179.

78. Bernstein, 'Classification and Framing', p. 90.

79. Ibid., p. 106.

80. Ibid., p. 107.

81. Bernstein, 'Class and Pedagogies — Visible and Invisible' in *Class, Codes and Control*.

82. J. Karabel and A.H. Halsey (eds.), *Power and Ideology in Education* (Oxford University Press, New York, 1977), p. 69.

83. Bernstein, *Class, Codes and Control*, p. 18.

84. S. Lukes, *Émile Durkheim: His Life and Work* (Allen Lane, London, 1973), p. 199.

85. Bernstein, *Class, Codes and Control*, p. 125.

86. Ibid., p. 135.

87. Bernstein, 'Aspects of the Relations Between Education and Production' in *Class, Codes and Control*.

88. Ibid., p. 180.

89. Bernstein, 'Open Schools'.

90. R. King, 'Bernstein's Sociology of the School', *British Journal of Sociology*, vol. 27, no. 4 (1976), p. 440.

91. R. Sharp and A. Green, *Education and Social Control: A Study of Progressive Primary Education* (Routledge and Kegan Paul, London, 1975); A. Hargreaves, 'The Ideology of the Middle School' in A. Hargreaves and L. Tickle (eds.), *Middle Schools: Origins, Ideology and Practice* (Harper and Row, London, 1980).

4 THE FUNCTIONALIST APPROACH TO EDUCATION

In Chapter 2 we showed that the issue of how order is achieved and maintained in society is central to Durkheim's work. This concern with the 'problem of order' is also fundamental to the functionalist perspective. Indeed, the whole theory revolves around providing an answer to it.

THE FOUNDATIONS OF SOCIAL ORDER

The functionalists suggest that we should begin with a logical analysis of the concept of 'society' and ask ourselves what has to happen if any society — large or small, simple or complex — is to survive and develop. Obviously, they say, the society must recruit new members as the older generation dies out. It must feed and clothe its members. There must be a common language and some agreement on basic values among members to prevent outright conflict. There also has to be some mechanism for ensuring that the young acquire the language and the common values. In addition, there has to be some way of ensuring co-ordination among the various parts of society and of responding to new developments and external threats. Clearly one could add to the list, but the central point they wish to make is that, if a society is to survive and develop, certain problems must be solved. There may, of course, be different ways of solving these basic problems, but the problems are common to all societies.

In so far as a society continues in a more or less orderly fashion, it follows that it must have found ways of solving the basic problems. Furthermore, as the problems do not go away but have to be dealt with continuously, the mechanisms for solving the problems must be fairly permanent features of the society. In functionalist theory these problem-solving mechanisms are called 'institutions'. Examples of these institutions are: the family, which helps in solving the problem of providing new members; economic institutions, which help feed and clothe the population; political institutions, which co-ordinate the activities of the different sectors of society; religious institutions, which assist in the maintenance of basic values; and education, which helps solve the problem of training the young. (Of course, institutions do provide services other than the ones mentioned and several institutions may contribute to the solution of one particular problem.) Another way of stating the point is to say that social institutions perform certain crucial 'functions' in society and in doing so they help to satisfy society's needs.

Like Durkheim, some functionalists also make use of an organic analogy. Society, they say, is like the human body. In the body, particular organs have specific functions. The lungs take in oxygen, the heart pumps blood, and so on. In addition, the organs of the body are interdependent: the heart needs oxygen which the lungs supply, while the lungs need blood to work effectively. Furthermore, the body's organs are themselves complex structures, and each part of the structure has its own function to perform. Finally, the basic unit of the body is the cell which also has a particular job to do. Likewise in society each part, or institution, has a specific function (or functions) and the different parts of society are dependent upon one another for various services. Education, for example, is connected in various ways to the economy, the family, the political and religious systems. Social institutions, too, are complex structures. Education is made up of different layers or sub-systems — primary, secondary, further and higher education — each of which has its own function(s) to perform within the organised whole. Furthermore, these different layers of the educational system are composed of smaller units, such as departments or classes, which in turn are made up of more basic units which we call roles. These roles are analogous to the cells of the human body and, like cells, make an important contribution to the effective functioning of the whole system of which they are a part.

In looking at society in this way, functionalists also believe that, once we know the general function of an institution — the problem it helps to solve — we can go on to trace the particular functions of its sub-systems. Within each of these sub-systems we can also discover the functions of the role and how these roles relate to and complement one another. For example, when we establish the function of education, we can understand how primary and secondary education contributes to the performance of this function. We can also see how the roles of headteacher, teacher and pupil are organised within any school so as to enable the school to function effectively.

Functionalists recognise, however, that the organic analogy can only be taken so far. For when they come to consider the reason why the basic units of the organism/society perform their functions in a satisfactory manner, they point to a major difference between the cells of the body and social roles. Within the body the cells are programmed by nature to perform their functions. Within society roles are filled by people who are not biologically programmed. If any institution is to function effectively and society to survive, people have to be forced, or induced, to act out their roles. It is at this point that functionalists introduce the concepts of culture and socialisation, and leave the organic analogy behind.

According to the functionalists, every society has a culture which includes values and norms. Indeed, there is a consensus on certain values and norms in every society. Values are standards that define some actions as desirable, others as undesirable. Norms are the rules and regulations of everyday life and are particular applications of values. For example, we may find within a culture the value of courtesy. The associated norms would include the rules of queuing, of opening doors for people, of children standing up for adults to sit down on a bus, and the like. Within particular parts of a culture, such as the educational system, other values and norms will be found. In teaching, for instance, professional conduct is valued with the associated norms of adequate preparation, prompt marking, punctuality, not criticising colleagues in public, etc.

The functionalists recognise that some individuals conform to the values and norms of their society only because they fear the consequences if they do not do what is expected of them. Especially important in this respect is the individual's concern not to incur the disapproval of others. The majority of individuals, however, come to accept the values and norms as valid. This, the functionalists believe, is because they have 'internalised' such values and norms during the socialisation process. They therefore fulfil the 'expectations' associated with their roles and, as a consequence, social institutions function effectively. Socialisation into culture thereby ensures order in society.

When functionalists apply their ideas to education they ask: what needs does education satisfy or what contribution does it make to society's stability? Traditionally two functions have been suggested — socialisation and selection — although there is disagreement about which one is the most important. Parsons, for example, stresses the former; Turner and Hopper the latter. It is possible, however, that different societies may develop different ways of solving the same problem, as is suggested by Turner and Hopper. In addition, new problems may be generated by adopting one solution rather than another, as Hopper tries to show.

We shall now look at the works of Parsons, Hopper and Turner and try to locate their ideas within the ongoing debate about both the functions of education and the adequacy of functionalism itself.

EDUCATION AS SOCIALISATION

Talcott Parsons

Talcott Parsons was one of the most influential functionalist authors. He produced a theory of society in which culture, social structure and personality are linked together in a logical and coherent way. The model of society that he developed gave two essential functions to education — socialisation and selection. However, the major function for Parsons, as will become clear shortly, was socialisation. Indeed it is Parsons's view that, without an efficient mechanism of socialisation, social order and harmony are impossible.

Parsons's account of education is mainly to be found in two places: in a chapter of the slim volume *The System of Modern Societies*[1] and in the essay 'The School Class as a Social System'.[2] In both cases, we are fortunately spared the worst excesses of Parsons's normal style — for it has to be said that most of the time Parsons seems to have got something against the English language. However, the writings on education are relatively free from his normal bombastic and near unintelligible prose.[3]

VALUE CONSENSUS

In *The System of Modern Societies* Parsons argues that recently there has been an 'educational revolution' as important as the democratic and industrial revolutions of the nineteenth and twentieth centuries, a revolution which has begun 'to transform the whole structure of modern society'.[4] In particular, claims Parsons, it reduces the importance of the market and of bureaucratic organisation. For example, the self-made man gaining economic success without any educational qualifications is increasingly becoming a myth.

A major characteristic of the educational revolution is its 'immense extension of equality of opportunity'.[5] Equality of opportunity, however, inevitably brings differences in attainment arising from differences in: (1) ability; (2) 'family orientations', that is, different aspirations and attitudes in the family in respect of education; (3) 'individual motivations' or variations in the level of interest in education and in the willingness of pupils to apply themselves and work hard. Differences in educational attainment also introduce new forms of inequality. For educational qualifications now largely determine the job one gets and, thereby, one's income, status and position in the system of social stratification.

In the essay 'The School Class as a Social System', Parsons's main theme is that education, having engendered new forms of inequality and thus potential division and conflict in society, helps to counteract the 'strain' involved by legitimating such inequalities. This is its major *function*. It does this through the process of 'socialisation'. Education inculcates the view that inequalities of income and status, which are a consequence of differences of educational attainment, are acceptable: that it is proper for those who do well in education to be highly rewarded. Education thus helps to spread the ideology of 'equal opportunity' and 'achievement'; and this ideology is one of the key elements of the 'common culture' which exists in modern society. Every society, in Parsons's view, has such a 'common culture'. All members of a society, he believes, share certain values or moral principles. Indeed, Parsons thinks that it is a condition of social order and social stability. What essentially holds a society together is the existence of a 'moral consensus' or a set of 'common values'. And in today's society the values of 'achievement' and 'equality of opportunity' are fundamental to such a consensus.

Parsons summarises his position very clearly in the following passage:

> Probably the most fundamental condition underlying this process [of education] is the sharing of common values by the two adult agencies involved — the family and the school, in this case the core of the shared valuation of *achievement*. It includes, above all, recognition that it is fair to give differential rewards for different levels of achievement, so long as there has been fair access to opportunity, and fair that these rewards lead on to higher-order opportunities, for the successful. There is thus a basic sense in which the elementary school class is an embodiment of the fundamental American value of equality of opportunity, in that it places value *both* on initial equality and on differential achievement.[6]

This stress by Parsons on 'the sharing of common values' is, as we have indicated above, one of the key ideas in his sociology — and has been recognised as such by most of his interpreters and critics. The notion that there must be some sort of consensus for society to be stable and orderly has, of course, a long history. For example, the early nineteenth-century sociologist Auguste Comte took the view that

> Ideas govern the world or throw it into chaos . . . The great political and moral crisis that societies are now undergoing is shown by a rigid analysis to arise out of intellectual anarchy . . . whenever the necessary

agreement on first principles can be obtained . . . the causes of disorder will have been arrested.[7]

A good account of the history of the idea of consensus can be found in P.H. Partridge, *Consent and Consensus*.[8] Essentially, however, it comes down to saying that serious conflict and division in society, leading ultimately to chaos and anarchy, can only be avoided by some overriding attachment to a particular set of ideas, values or principles. If the 'state of war' of 'everyman against everyman' (in Thomas Hobbes's famous words) is to be prevented, then all members of society must accept and be committed to certain general principles which transcend their particular ends, interests and beliefs.

Many writers have considered religion to provide such a basis for social solidarity. Comte, whom we mentioned above, quite self-consciously sought a substitute for religion; and in the mid-eighteenth century even someone like Rousseau felt that a 'civil religion' was a necessary feature of an ideal community. Parsons himself believes that 'the values of society are rooted in religion',[9] and recognises that secularisation and the decline of religious uniformity can lead to 'the destruction of the moral or value consensus'. However, such destruction has not happened in the United States, Parsons asserts, as 'strong moral commitments' have survived as a consequence of what he calls 'value generalization'. As he says: 'The underlying moral consensus has persisted, but it is now defined at a higher level of generality than in European societies that have institutionalized internal religious uniformity.'[10] Thus there have developed 'highly general values' which keep conflict over other values, ends, principles and interests in check.

The question naturally arises as to whether 'achievement' and 'equality of opportunity' are examples of such higher level values. Parsons does not define them as such in *The System of Modern Societies*, nor, for that matter, does he give any other examples of these higher level values. Indeed, as it stands in the book, the concept of higher level values is a vague, ill-defined notion, which is rather surprising in the light of the central position it occupies in Parsons's theory of society. We are, of course, told in 'The School Class as a Social System' that 'achievement' and 'equality of opportunity' prevent conflict and discontent arising among the 'losers in the competition' for high income and status, and thus perform a crucial integrative function. In the light of that fact, 'achievement' might be thought to constitute a higher level value. Yet the conflict which 'achievement' contains is conflict arising from the pursuit of the *same* end by the individuals concerned, namely high income and status, *rather than* the pursuit of different ends or values which was said to be the hallmark of a higher level value. We are thus still in the dark about the status of 'achievement' and without a concrete example of the all-important 'highly general values'.

SOCIETY AND EDUCATION

We shall have more to say about the idea of a 'value consensus' in Chapter 5. Now we must turn to a more detailed treatment of Parsons's view of the way education contributes to such a 'consensus' and to the maintenance of social order.

The Three Systems of Society

In 'The School Class as a Social System' Parsons argues that the school has two functions, that of 'the socialization of individuals and . . . their allocation to roles within society'.[11] For the moment we shall concentrate on the first of these — the key notion of socialisation.

The school is an 'agency of socialization', says Parsons, that is 'it is an agency through which individual personalities are trained to be motivationally and technically adequate to the performance of adult roles'.[12] He explains his meaning in the following crucial passage:

> The socialization functions may be summed up as the development in individuals of the commitments and capacities which are essential prerequisites of their future role-performance. Commitments may be broken down in turn into two components: commitment to the implementation of the broad *values* of society, and commitment to the performance of a specific type of role within the *structure* of society. Thus a person in a relatively humble occupation may be a 'solid citizen' in the sense of commitment to honest work in that occupation, without an intensive and sophisticated concern with the implementation of society's higher-level values . . . Capacities can also be broken down into two components, the first being competence or the skill to perform the tasks involved in the individual's roles, and the second being 'role-responsibility' or the capacity to live up to other people's expectations of the interpersonal behaviour appropriate to these roles. Thus a mechanic as well as a doctor needs to have not only the basic 'skills of his trade', but also the ability to behave responsibly toward those people with whom he is brought into contact in his work.

What is important about this passage is that, besides being a statement of the way in which education contributes to the maintenance of a 'value consensus', it also contains many of the basic concepts and ideas in Parsons's general sociological theory. In explaining the one we are, therefore, necessarily engaged in giving an account of the other.

The concepts of 'broad values', 'roles' and 'role-structure', and 'individual personalities' represent, according to Parsons, the basic elements or components of society. Parsons divides society into three parts or 'systems'[13] which he calls the 'cultural', 'social' and 'personality' systems. This is equivalent to saying that society is composed of 'culture', the 'social structure' and 'individuals'. We can therefore represent Parsons's view as follows:

Cultural system   = culture
Social system   ·   = social structure
Personality system = individuals

Next we need to describe the nature of these systems. The 'broad values' shared by all the members of society are the most important part of the *cultural* system (the other elements being norms and organised knowledge and beliefs).[14] As for the *social* system, this is made up of social roles: 'the most significant unit of social structures is not the person', says Parsons, 'but the role.'[15] 'The primary ingredient of the role', he continues, 'is the role-expectation.'[16] Role-expectations he then defines as follows: 'What an actor is expected to do in a given situation both by himself and others constitutes the expectations of that role.'[17] In other words, roles such as those of husband and wife, or headteacher, teacher and pupils, involve certain quite specific rights and duties which are recognised and accepted by all concerned. Finally, the *personality* system or individual personality is essentially composed of motives or needs — in Parsons's words 'need-dispositions'. He argues that some human needs or motives are innate or biologically given, but the most important are social in nature, that is, acquired during the socialisation process.

We can thus develop the above diagram in the following way:

Cultural system/   = shared values (+ norms, knowledge
culture   and beliefs)
Social system/   = a structure of social roles. Roles =
social structure   role expectations = shared expectations
                                   of behaviour
Personality system/   = needs acquired during socialisation
individuals

Having made clear what Parsons means by the terms cultural, social and personality systems, we must naturally go on to consider how he conceives the relationship between them. He argues that there is a 'hierarchy of control' between these systems,[18] that is, the cultural system controls the social which in turn controls the personality system. In other words, culture determines the nature of the social structure, and individual personalities are shaped in accordance with the demands of their culture and of their social roles. More specifically, the broad values of society define the nature of the roles the individual has to play. The problems and choices faced by an individual ('actor') during his life are solved by reference to the moral standards of the cultural system.[19] What individuals are expected to do in their positions in society — their 'role-expectations' — is defined by society's moral standards. To put it differently, culture manifests itself in social organisation. Furthermore, society is able to get individuals to do what is expected of them in their roles because their personalities are moulded accordingly. As Parsons says: 'the individual personality must be shaped around the definition of role-expectations.'[20] This is accomplished in the process of socialisation. Parsons defines socialisation as the process by which the values of society are internalised in the individual's personality.[21] Society's values become the individual's values. Parsons also speaks of socialisation involving the internalisation of need-dispositions. People become committed to the moral values of their society and to the performance of specific roles because they 'need' to do so. Role-expectations are fulfilled because the individual needs to fulfil them. As C. Wright Mills says, summarising Parsons's point: 'what is socially expected becomes individually needed.'[22] If individuals fail to do what is expected of them, they will meet with the disapproval of others. But as, in Parsons's view, people want a favourable response from others more than anything else, conformity to moral values and role-expectations is assured. As Parsons says on this point: 'What people want most is to be responded to, loved, approved and esteemed.'[23] In his view, man is an approval-seeking creature who can only obtain satisfaction by observing society's moral standards and by doing what is expected of him.

In this way, then, the values of society are perpetuated, roles properly played and social order and stability assured. It amounts to a theory of cultural and social determinism with individuals very much on the receiving end of things. This can be represented diagrammatically.

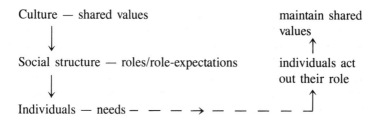

Education's part in this process is a major one, as a glance back at the passage from 'The School Class as a Social System' on p. 70 will reveal.

Education

Education is a major socialising agency developing in individuals the 'commitments and capacities' necessary for role-performance. It must develop commitment to society's broad values (especially achievement and equality of opportunity) and to the performance of a specific type of role within society. In addition, it must ensure that people are able to do what they are committed to. They must acquire, through education, a range of technical and social skills. In this way, education sustains the common culture of a society and provides the appropriate 'human material' for the social structure. It helps to maintain society as a well co-ordinated whole.

Parsons also tries to show how the socialisation and allocation functions are linked together in the school class. He argues that all pupils begin school as more or less equal. However, he does admit that sex role differences are established prior to school and that some pupils have a higher level of 'independence' on entry to school than others. By 'independence' is meant the pupil's 'level of self-sufficiency relative to guidance by adults, his capacity to take responsibility and to make his own decisions in coping with new and varying situations'.[24] Furthermore, it appears that pupils with a higher level of independence are likely to be successful in education, particularly on the academic side.

Parsons suggests that all pupils on entry to the school are treated equally: they are all given the same work, and are evaluated in the same way according to the same criteria. Gradually, however, they are differentiated on the axis of achievement: some do better than others and are given more rewards by the teacher. There are two types of achievement that can be obtained in education. 'One of these', says Parsons, 'is the more purely "cognitive" learning of information, skills, and frames of reference associated with empirical knowledge and technological mastery.' The other can be called 'moral' and involves 'responsible citizenship in the school community'. As Parsons says: 'Such things as respect for the teacher, consideration and co-operativeness in relation to fellow-pupils and good "work-habits" are the fundamentals, leading on to capacity for "leadership" and "initiative".'[25]

In the elementary school these two components are not clearly distinguished. Pupils are differentiated on the axis of achievement according to how well they live up to the expectations of the teacher who is the agent of the community. In the secondary school there is a clearer differentiation along the two dimensions, cognitive and moral. Parsons then suggests that: 'Those relatively high in "cognitive" achievement will fit better in specific-function, more or less technical roles; those high in "moral" achievement will tend toward diffuser, more "socially" or "humanly" oriented roles.'[26]

In effect, Parsons thinks that pupils are slowly differentiated into high achievers and low achievers, and that within each category they are further distinguished according to academic and social success. This process of differentiation, however, is also a process of socialisation. The value of achievement — which Parsons sees as being shared by family, school and community — is reinforced in pupils by the system of differentiation on the axis of achievement.

COMMENTS

Although the next chapter is devoted to a detailed examination of the functionalist theory, there are a number of specific criticisms of Parsons's view of education that it is appropriate to make now.

Parsons's thesis in 'The School Class as a Social System' rests on the assertion that all pupils begin from a basis of equality: this is essential if they are to accept later differentiation as fair and just. But a lot of evidence suggests that there is, in fact, a great deal of difference between social classes in the preparation of children for education.[27] Parsons might reply to this objection by arguing that, whilst this may be the case, the *school* is organised on the basis of equality — all pupils begin as equals from the school's point of view. Once again, however, there is evidence to suggest that pupils are not always treated equally by teachers, whose assumptions and preconceptions may influence their assessment of pupils' abilities. For example, R. Rist, in his three-year study of a school in St Louis, USA, found that:

after only eight days of kindergarten, the teacher made permanent seating arrangements based on what she assumed were variations in academic capability. But no formal evaluation of the children had taken place. Instead, the assignments to the three tables were based on a number of socio-economic criteria as well as on early interaction patterns in the classroom.[28]

In so far as this is the case, an important part of Parsons's thesis is destroyed.

Furthermore, Parsons, as we have already noted, states that both home and school value 'achievement'. When children come to school, they learn that others, besides their parents, value achievement and they gradually internalise the value, using it as a basis for locating themselves and others.

But, again, if Parsons's thesis is to hold, he would have to show that parents and school *mean* the same thing by 'achievement'. We would argue that it is true by definition that all people value 'achievement', but that it is not self-evident that they mean the same thing by it, nor that all people want to achieve the same things. For example, one person may want a quiet life, another power, yet another status. Some people are not ambitious. It is quite possible, also, that some parents regard school achievement as worthless, and schools may regard what parents would think of as achievement as equally worthless. If this is so, then it is difficult to see how Parsons can claim that both home and school value achievement, except in the most general and trivial sense of the word.

Finally, we would also dispute the validity of Parsons's view that educational qualifications, and not market position, determine success in the modern world. A person's socio-economic status has been repeatedly shown to be important for success in the educational system.[29] There is also some doubt that educational qualifications are a major determinant of occupational position.[30]

These criticisms must make us wary of a too ready acceptance of Parsons's ideas. Yet we must acknowledge that, from within the functionalist framework, he does provide us with an analysis which demonstrates that the major functions of education are socialisation and selection. Of these it is socialisation which is the dominant function, selection being of secondary significance.

EDUCATION AS SELECTION

Other authors who also adopt the functionalist perspective argue that selection is the major function. Perhaps the most well known of these authors are Turner and Hopper. Ralf Turner analyses the way that two societies try to solve the problem of maintaining order in a highly stratified situation. He looks at the way that elites are selected in England and the United States and argues that the two countries adopt rather different solutions to the same problem. Earl Hopper has tried to develop Turner's ideas further so that they can be used for international comparison. Educational systems are essentially selective systems. They differ in how they select, when they select, whom they select and why they select. Each society develops its own selective system, but in adopting one solution to the problem of selection a society runs into other problems, particularly those concerning the regulation of ambition. Hopper uses functionalist theory to see how different societies deal with the problem of selection and to suggest how the subsequent problems of motivating and de-motivating may be solved.

The ideas of Turner and Hopper have themselves been criticised by Davies and Smith. The criticisms are of two forms: firstly, they concern the lack of balance or precision; secondly, and more importantly, they concern the acceptability of the theoretical position taken by the authors.

We intend to look at this debate in some detail because it gives us a flavour of the type of argument that goes on and because it demonstrates the way that new perspectives are introduced into the analysis of education.

Ralf Turner

Under the title of 'Sponsored and Contest Mobility and the School System',[31] published in 1958, Ralf Turner attempted to use the functionalist framework to highlight the differences between the English and American educational systems. Both systems try to solve the same societal problem, but, he believes, do so in different ways.

Turner warns us that his descriptions are ideal types; they are meant to give us a guideline for understanding, but do not imply that every school will conform to the picture presented. (However, we would suggest that these ideal type descriptions should, to a great extent, conform to what happens in the educational system.) Turner also makes the point that he is dealing with only one aspect of education, the facilitation of social mobility, and that this aspect is not necessarily the most important feature of these educational systems.

SOCIAL MOBILITY

The issue of social mobility was very important in the 1950s and 1960s and is still a concern among sociologists today. We live in a stratified society and at each level there are differences in the amount of income, prestige and power. The elites at the top have considerably more than the average amount of income. For example, Westergaard and Resler[32] in 1975 estimated that the richest 1 per cent of the British population received 10 per cent of the total income, while the richest 10 per cent took home 30 per cent of the income of the country. Of course, income tax and benefits caused some redistribution, but not very much. The statistical journal *Social Trends* for 1978 estimated that the top 1 per cent of the population had 23 per cent of the marketable wealth of the country, while the bottom 50 per cent of the population owned 5 per cent. In terms of earnings in 1978 the average gross wage was about £99 per week. The top 10 per cent averaged about £158 while the bottom 10 per cent grossed £64 per week.[33] Differences in income probably reflect, and contribute to, differences in prestige and power, although it is much more difficult to quantify these. People do seem to rank occupations into broad status or prestige groups, although there is a lot of variation. There are also clear differences in the ability that some groups have to get their own way, but the issue of who has power and how much of it is very complex. The main point, however, is that our society can be pictured as class divided or stratified.

If we see society as stratified, then we could imagine a situation where every child remained in the same stratum as his parents. If this were the case, then there would be no mobility. On the other hand, we could imagine a society where the position in society of a child's family had no influence over the stratum he entered. In this second case mobility would be at a maximum. Societies tend to lie between these extremes. In our society there is some mobility, both upwards and downwards, but movements tend to be small. Comparatively few people are involved in 'long' movements.[34]

It has been suggested that there are good economic, political and moral reasons for promoting mobility. It would make economic sense for an able child of lower-class parents to rise in the class system. Politically it could be suggested that it would be dangerous to create a group of people with little income and no way of bettering themselves. Ethically it could be said that it is unjust to an individual to place him in a situation where his talents could not be used, or conversely, to place a person in a position of responsibility with which he could not cope.

People who wish to promote mobility have often thought that education could be used to engineer a more just and efficient society. In fact it appears that education is not very successful in changing the pattern of mobility in Britain. Halsey, Heath and Ridge, commenting on their findings on social class chances of educational success, say:

> This picture of unequal access to the superior secondary schools has remained depressingly constant over time. For the selective secondary schools as a group, chances of access rose at all levels of the class structure in the middle of our period, leading to some slight narrowing of class differentials, but they then fell back again to levels very like those of a generation earlier. Thus the likelihood of a working-class boy receiving a selective education in the mid 'fifties and 'sixties was very little different from that of his parents' generation thirty years earlier.[35]

Be that as it may, Turner feels that the mobility function of education is important enough to be worth studying.

CONTEST AND SPONSORED NORMS

Turner says: 'Every society must cope with the problem of maintaining loyalty to its social system and does so in part through norms and values, only some of which vary by class position.'[36] He adds, 'The most conspicuous control problem is that of ensuring loyalty in the disadvantaged classes.'[37]

Immediately we can see the functionalist assumptions at work. 'Society' is faced with a problem, the problem of maintaining order. There is a consensus on certain norms and values which help in the solution to the problem. Turner calls these norms 'organizing folk norms' which, he thinks, help to shape the way the educational systems of the United States and England are organised. The two countries have different folk norms and thus solve the problems in different ways. Turner then goes on to describe these differing folk norms, which are represented in Table 4.1.

The main thrust of Turner's analysis is clear. The twin problem of elite recruitment and the maintenance of the loyalty of the non-elites is solved in the United States by encouraging everyone to strive for elite status, and by trying to ensure that all are treated equally. The race analogy implies that the late sprinter could win and therefore there should be no early elimination. By the time it becomes obvious to people that they are not going to achieve elite status, loyalty to the system has been developed. Elites are controlled by the fear of being replaced by other

Table 4.1: Turner's Folk Norms

Contest Norm	Sponsored Norm
The method of acquiring elite status is like a race in which all start equal.	Future elites should be assigned their positions by the present elite or their agents.
The rules of the race are well known to all.	Only the elite can recognise the hidden talents of intelligence or vision.
Elite status is shown by the possession of wealth.	
There should be no early elimination. No special help should be given to the talented.	There should be early selection and specialist training for elite status. Future elites should be given the best training.
Most commonly found in a society with many elite groups in competition.	Most commonly found in a society with an established elite group.
Hope of elite status is kept alive until loyalty to the society is well established.	'Masses' are trained to see themselves as incompetent and to view the elite with a sense of mystery.
Elites are controlled by the recognition that they can be displaced by other elite groups.	Elites are socialised into benevolent paternalism and sensitivity to the opinion of fellow elites.

contenders. In England the system operates in a different way. Future elites are chosen by some secret criteria when quite young. They are then educated into a feeling that they should care for the rest of society and not abuse their position. The non-elites are educated into a feeling of relative incompetence to rule and thus to accept their station in life.

What Turner is describing in a generalised way is the basic organising folk norm that, he thinks, is commonly accepted in England or the United States. It is manifested in the official selection process, but, importantly, it is also held by the teachers and the population as a whole.

In the 1950s and 1960s it was fairly easy to show that the official selection routes were very different in England and the United States. England had the 11+ examination which sent the 'future elites' to the grammar school where they studied rather different subjects from the pupils in the secondary modern schools. Furthermore grammar schools had much better resources than the other schools. The United States, on the other hand, had a comprehensive system with no early, formal, separation of pupils. There was, so Turner suggests, no official differentiation of the curriculum, and it was generally assumed that 'the less successful require help to be sure that they stay in the contest'.[38] The different norms are also manifested today in Higher Education. In Britain we can see the 'sponsored norm' in the relatively small number of students who fail. Grants allow the students to be free from the necessity of working while they are at university or college, thus giving them more time to absorb the elite culture. Under the 'contest norm' in the United States many students drop out in the final stages of the race and, with some exceptions, students are expected to work their way through college. Indeed, Turner comments, 'in some instances schools include paid employment as a requirement for graduation'.[39]

Earl Hopper

TYPES OF SELECTION

Like Turner, Hopper, in his various papers on education, adopts a functionalist approach but, from time to time, drifts away from this point of view. Initially Hopper produces a 'theoretical statement' — which we take to mean that he is not too concerned to give evidence for his ideas at this stage. He assumes that the major function of education is selection. He says that the 'structure of educational systems especially those within industrial societies, can be understood primarily in terms of the structure of their selective processes'.[40] What Hopper tries to do in his essay 'A Typology for the Classification of Educational Systems' is to devise a system of characteristics which would allow us to compare and contrast educational systems in advanced industrial societies. In order to develop this 'typology' he thinks that it is necessary to ask four basic questions. (These questions refer to the total selection process, which itself can be seen as being made up of three stages: (1) selection into types and levels of ability; (2) appropriate instruction; and (3) allocation to jobs or further training.)

The four basic questions are:

1. How does selection occur?
2. When does it occur?
3. Who (i.e. what type of person) is selected?
4. Why are they selected (i.e. what justifications are given)?

The next stage of Hopper's argument is to suggest a number of logical possibilities connected with each question asked. Two extreme possibilities are suggested for 'how' selection occurs. On the one hand, selection could be standardised and centrally administered. This would require a national programme of education, with an identical examination and a department of civil servants to administer the system. The other possibility is to have a decentralised and unstandardised selection system in which there are no common elements throughout the society and no central organising agency. In both systems, continues Hopper, we would find an 'ideology of implementation', that is, a justification for the way the system is operated. In the former case, the ideology would be similar to Turner's sponsored norm, in the latter case to Turner's contest norm. Hopper stresses, however, that educational selection in the real world will fall somewhere between these two extremes.

In answer to the second question, of 'when' selection occurs, Hopper says that it may be early or late. 'The crucial distinction is how long before the completion of education have children been formally segregated into specialised routes.'[41] (Again, note the concentration on formal selection. Like Turner, it appears that Hopper is moving from the formal system to make assumptions about how participants define the situation. But, of course, informal selection may be just as important as formal selection.) Hopper suggests that, when selection occurs early, then the likely ideology of implementation will be 'elitist'. This ideology holds that abilities are innate and fixed, and that the amount of education a child receives should be related to future economic contributions. When selection occurs relatively late, then an 'egalitarian' ideology of implementation is likely to be found. This ideology emphasises the importance of environment, stresses the right of all to a maximum education and wants elites and non-elites to be educated side by side.

The final two questions of 'who' should be selected and 'why' they should be selected are taken together by Hopper. Here Hopper introduces us to a new notion, 'ideologies of legitimation'. He notes that elites have to justify their position and assimilate future leaders to avoid challenges. What is interesting here is the way that Hopper shifts perspective. The explanation is couched in terms of elite self-interest. However, he quickly returns to his functionalist view. He says that: 'One way in which most stratified societies have attempted to cope with such dilemmas is to develop fairly explicit ideologies which define the type of people whom the society values most highly.'[42] Given his previous statement, it would be more accurate to suggest that it is the powerful elite, rather than the 'society' which develops the ideology. The substitution of 'society' for 'elite'

Table 4.2: Hopper's Typology

Question	Answer	Ideology
How	Standardised	Sponsored ideology of implementation
	Unstandardised	Contest ideology of implementation
When	Early	Elitist ideology of implementation
	Late	Egalitarian ideology of implementation
Who	Diffuse skills	Particularistic ideology of legitimation
	Technical skills	Universalistic ideology of legitimation
Why	Diffuse skills and society's need	Paternalistic ideology of legitimation
	Diffuse skills and individual's right	Aristocratic ideology of legitimation
	Technical skills and society's needs	Communistic ideology of legitimation
	Technical skills and individual's right	Meritocratic ideology of legitimation

changes the argument considerably.

Hopper goes on to suggest that there are two types of person who may be valued. Society may value people who have what Hopper calls 'diffuse skills'. These cultural abilities are difficult to learn and are found in societies which have a 'particularistic ideology'. Alternatively, society may value people with 'technical skills'. If this is so, then a 'universalistic ideology' is to be found.

If the society justifies the choice of elites by saying that society needs people with diffuse skills then a 'paternalistic ideology' is operating. If the choice of people with diffuse skills is justified by suggesting it is the right of the individual who possesses these skills to have elite status, then an 'aristocratic ideology' exists. If the elite possess technical skills and their status is justified by reference to society's needs, then we find a 'communistic ideology', but, if the justification is in terms of the individual's right to elite status, then a 'meritocratic ideology' operates. We should note that the names of the ideologies are Hopper's and we are somewhat at a loss to know why he calls them what he does. The ideas are represented in Table 4.2.

THE REGULATION OF AMBITION

Hopper develops his typology further in the essay entitled 'Educational Systems and Selected Consequences of Patterns of Mobility and Non-Mobility in Industrial Societies: A Theoretical Discussion'.[43] Essentially he deals with the problem of motivation. He says that 'all industrial societies must strive to inculcate each of their successive cohorts with the desire to fill the most demanding and rewarding occupations'. With a characteristic shift of perspective, he adds that the people in power 'will strive to reduce and maintain at a low level the ambition of those personnel who fill essentially subordinate positions'.[44] The 'regulation of ambition', as Hopper calls it, has been noted before by others. Musgrave, in 1965, writing from a functionalist perspective, said: 'It is possible that the increase in educational opportunity may be so great that aspirations for upward mobility are generated in excess of the number of high positions that are available to the population of the country.' Should this happen, as Musgrave thinks it has in California, then: 'The function of selection is replaced by that of "cooling out" those with excess mobility aspirations.'[45]

Hopper takes up this problem. On the one hand, it is necessary to 'warm up' children so that they will try to attain high positions; on the other hand, it may be necessary to 'cool out' pupils who are not going to get elite status. While no society solves this problem fully, Hopper seems to feel that, unless adequate solutions are found, there is a likelihood of major problems of stability. The factors that influence the warming up/cooling down dilemma are the structure of the society itself and the structure of the educational system.

If a society exhibits 'high status rigidity', then we will find a number of clearly defined status groupings. These groups will have their own distinct life-styles and will restrict entry into the group. In a society like this it will be difficult, Hopper thinks, to warm up the lower classes, but easy to warm up the upper classes. In a society with low status rigidity, where entry into the rather ill-defined upper groups is comparatively easy, it will be easy to warm up the lower groups, relatively speaking, but difficult to cool them out at a later stage. It will also be more difficult to warm up the upper groups.

Having looked at the structure of society, Hopper goes through the typology we have outlined and tries to show how the structure of the educational system and its ideologies can affect the dilemma. He argues that, where selection is early, it is easy to warm up the upper classes but more difficult to cool them out; also it is difficult to warm up the lower classes. If selection is late, then it is easier to cool out the upper classes, but more difficult to cool out the lower classes; there is no great difference in warming up either class. Hopper also mentions here the advantages of an upper-class background when selection is early. When it occurs late, then the classes have had time to mix and the upper-class advantage is less obvious. He also notes that failure for the upper-class child leads to downward mobility whereas for the lower-class child it results in non-

Table 4.3: Hopper's Dimensions for the Regulation of
Ambition

Educational System or Ideology	Warm Up		Cool Out	
	Upper	Lower	Upper	Lower
Early selection	Easy	Hard	Hard	Easy
Late selection	Equal	Equal	Easy	Hard
Standardised selection	Equal	Equal	Hard	Easy
Unstandardised selection	Easy	Hard	Equal	Equal
Sponsored/elitist ideology	Easy	Hard	Hard	Easy
Contest/egalitarian ideology[a]	Equal	Equal	Equal	Equal
Paternalistic ideology	Easy	Hard	Hard	Easy
Aristocratic ideology	Easy	Hard	Hard	Easy
Communistic ideology	Hard	Easy	Hard	Easy
Meritocratic ideology	Hard	Easy	Hard	Easy

Note: a. Hopper also suggests that, in comparison with the sponsored/elitist
ideology, the contest/egalitarian ideology may warm up the lower classes more
easily and cool out the upper classes easily. Hopper's original text and chart seem
to be at odds.

mobility. With early selection the major problem lies with those who
are initially selected but who do not make it to the top. There is quite
a lot of provision for those initially rejected when it comes to finding
jobs, likewise those who reach the apex of the educational system are
well served. But there is very little done for the middle range who are
encouraged to identify with the elite but who are later rejected. Mostly
they have been educated for the next stage of the educational system not
for the jobs available to them. This segment is unprepared for the labour
market and their occupation will be at odds with what they had expected
to achieve.

Hopper continues in this way, examining the other questions he defines
as crucial to understanding education. Standardised systems cool out the
lower classes more easily than the upper classes, since the former can
blame the system or the 'establishment' for their failure. An unstandardised system warms up the upper classes due to their background
advantages.

Ideologies can work independently of the structure and affect the problem of warming up and cooling out. Sponsored and elitist ideologies
are more likely to warm up the upper classes while contest and egalitarian
ideologies are more likely to warm up the lower social classes. Hopper
goes on to analyse the various ideologies in terms of the problems of
warming and cooling. Table 4.3 represents Hopper's ideas in a simplified
form.

Hopper concludes his discussion by saying that, in a rigidly stratified society the best form of selection, in his opinion, would be one that is standardised, with late selection, a contest ideology and a meritocratic form of legitimation. On the other hand, in a society with a more flexible class structure, the most efficient form of selection, in his view, would be one that is still standardised, but with early selection, a sponsored ideology and paternalistic legitimation.

THE DEBATE ON SELECTION

Ioan Davies

Hopper's ideas have been criticised by Ioan Davies. Hopper's method, says Davies, ignores the complexity involved in studying education as a part of society, and is rather simplistic in the way it deals with the selection function. For example, Hopper fails to relate selection to the changing demands of the labour market. He does show how the economy influences the process of educational selection, but he assumes that all industrial societies are similar, whereas, in fact, differences in technology and the type of industry within a country will influence selection. Davies also suggests that Hopper assumes that there is a neat fit between selection in schools and the needs of the economy, when this is clearly not the case. Hopper's treatment of ideology is also weak, thinks Davies. He fails to appreciate that education 'is as much about the *creation* of ideologies as it is about anything else'.[46]

Davies's main criticism, however, is of Hopper's preoccupation with selection. This leads him, says Davies, to confuse the goals ascribed to education by bodies outside the educational system, with the goals of the people within the system itself. In other words, Hopper assumes that there exists a consensus on the goals of education. Further, even if we agree that selection is the most important function of education, we must still examine the conflict within society's ruling groups who have 'quite distinct value-systems which are in continual competition for the control of the educational system'.[47] What is important is to identify these competing groups and assess their relative importance. Davies says that, if we are to understand selection in education, we must look at a society's power structure in two major areas. Firstly, we should look at how national policy is made, recognising that the policy itself is a way of trying to resolve competing interests. Secondly, we should look at the way this policy is interpreted and adjusted by schools and colleges which have their own culture, internal organisation and goals. If we adopt this line of reasoning,

Davies notes, then it becomes clear that selection is not the only issue of importance to the policy-makers. 'Even for *them* education is not only about occupational selection but also about moral values, research, and the transmission of knowledge . . . it would be rash indeed to argue that all of these can ultimately be reduced to selection.'[48] In other words, education is about more than selection.

Davies also points out that, if we are to discuss selection in education seriously, then we need to consider such things as the class structure and rates of mobility. For example, if there was little mobility, then selection would not be that important. Also, we should look at economic changes and the patterns of recruitment to jobs, where in-service training should be taken into account as this influences occupational selection. Similarly, selection is influenced by such things as family size and parental attitudes. When we place educational selection in this wider context of the total selection process in society, we may find that the part that education plays is not so significant as Hopper suggests.

The whole of Davies's attack on Hopper is aimed at showing that the emphasis on selection is misplaced and the typology that Hopper develops is too simplistic to be of great value in generating further understanding and research. Davies wants to suggest that a more important and fruitful area of investigation should be the management of knowledge. We will treat this topic shortly (see p. 89), but for the moment we wish to follow the debate that Turner and Hopper have begun by looking briefly at the ideas of Dennis Smith.[49]

Dennis Smith

Smith challenges many of Davies's criticisms, suggesting that he has misunderstood the intention of Hopper's paper. Hopper was trying to outline a typology which could be used to compare and contrast educational systems in various countries. He was also trying to produce a framework which would allow further questions about the organisation of education to be raised and researched. Hopper chose to look at the issue of selection (which he recognises is not necessarily a central one) but does not thereby assume a neat fit between educational selection and the needs of the economy. Indeed, one area for investigation which Hopper's framework throws up, is the impact of various economic systems on the organisation of selection. Hopper's central point is a fair one, thinks Smith. All industrial societies have the common problem of the need for people in 'positions in the various hierarchies of power' to 'justify their position to themselves and others'.[50] What Hopper does is to produce a typology of possible ways of organising selection that a country may adopt and to suggest the possible ideologies that may be used to justify how selection is organised and who is chosen. These ideologies can act independently of the structure of selection although there is a strain to consistency. The ideologies might also influence the content of what is taught in education. (Here we assume that Smith is suggesting that, for example, an aristocratic ideology — which justifies selection of people with diffuse skills on the basis of their individual right to elite status — will influence the training and education that the selected group receives by a concentration on diffuse skills.)

Some of the confusion in Hopper's and Davies's work can be resolved, Smith believes, by a clearer definition of the notion of selection. We can think of selection as involving three levels.

First level:	selection and allocation to routes in education
Second level:	selection and allocation into routes plus instruction and certification
Third level:	selection and allocation plus instruction and certification plus recruitment to an occupation.

Davies is correct in pointing to the complex nature of selection in society, says Smith, but this may not invalidate Hopper's point. Davies seems to be dealing with selection in sense three, while Hopper may be talking about selection in the other two senses. However, neither author is altogether clear as to which level he is referring.

The assumptions implicit in Hopper's work are not unreasonable, Smith adds. They are: (1) certificates obtained in education are the main method of recruitment to jobs; (2) children are evaluated for skills and ability prior to selection at level one; (3) decisions taken at the first and second levels influence selection at the third level; (4) people are aware of these facts; (5) norms used in the third level will influence selection at the lower levels; (6) ideologies will be used to justify the process of selection at the various levels. According to Smith, then, Davies has misinterpreted Hopper's assumptions.

Where Hopper does fall down, says Smith, is in failing to say from where the various ideologies come, and in assuming consensus on ideologies. Of course, this is not very different from Davies's view, and like him Smith goes on to point out the importance of an analysis of power. Another criticism Smith makes is that Hopper fails to distinguish official and formal selection from informal selection. Smith raises other points of detail which are interesting in themselves but which need not detain us here.

We have given an outline of the ideas of Turner and Hopper and traced the debate that has followed from their writings. We wish at this stage to make one or two initial comments on these ideas and the debate.

Both Turner and Hopper adopt the functionalist perspective which takes as its main concern the way that order is maintained in society and the problems that society must solve if it is to remain stable. This pre-occupation, combined with the moral and economic issues we touched upon earlier, has led the authors to look at the issues of social mobility and selection. Turner attempts to contrast the English and American solutions to the problem of recruitment to elite positions and the allied problem of ensuring the loyalty of the non-elites. He stresses the importance of the 'organizing folk norms' which he assumes most people within the society accept. These norms are put into practice in the organisation of elite recruitment within the two educational systems. Of course, Turner's work is dated in relation to England because of the introduction of comprehensive schools. However, on the basis of his general argument it might be thought that England is moving towards a 'contest norm'. We wonder though to what extent this is true. The existence of streaming and informal selection in schools would suggest that a sponsored norm exists and is still powerful. Possibly the prime example of sponsorship is to be found in the public schools where pupils are clearly selected early and given a privileged educational experience in a separate educational context. However, as Halsey notes, public schools have little to do with facilitating mobility; their chief function seems to be the maintenance of elite positions. They are involved in 'status differentiation'[51] rather than in mobility. Indeed, when we look at the amount of mobility in England, we are led to suggest that education is much more concerned with the maintenance of social stratification than the improvement in mobility, no matter what the policy-makers wish. This leads us to believe that Davies and Smith are correct in drawing our attention to the distinction between official statements and what happens in practice, and of the need to explain any differences between the two. We would also note, in passing, that, if Turner's ideas were correct, then we would expect our class structure to become more open like that of the United States as we move towards a 'contest' system. However, there is no evidence to suggest any such movement.

Hopper, in developing Turner's ideas and trying to generalise them, has produced a framework which he thinks will allow comparison between education in all industrial societies. He, too, sees selection as the crucial function of education. Like Turner he also seems to assume some sort of consensus on 'ideologies' which ensures the efficient operation of educational selection. It is precisely this point that Davies and Smith contest. They argue that power is an important variable and that we cannot assume that there exists agreement among society's elites. Davies wants to suggest that the concentration on selection limits our understanding of the role of education in society; Smith has more sympathy with Hopper's view of its crucial importance. What we find particularly interesting, though, is the way that both Davies and Smith seize upon Hopper's statement about the problems faced by elites in justifying their position. This leads us to believe that the debate is about far more than the adequacy of Hopper's framework for the comparative analysis of education. What we are seeing, we suggest, is a fundamental difference of theoretical approach. Hopper normally talks about 'society's' problems. The idea that elite groups have problems in maintaining their position of power belongs to a different theoretical framework. This framework sees society as composed of different groups of people, each with its own interests and aims, possessing different degrees of power, and each trying to get the educational system to do as it wishes. The selective process in education is, therefore, the outcome of the relative influence of these groups at any one point of time, and is subject to modification as power shifts or interests change. For Davies and Smith, then, selection is a social product.

We feel that it is important to stress at this point that Davies and Smith are adopting a different theoretical approach from that of Hopper. To some extent they are influenced, we suspect, by the ideas of Max Weber and of Peter Berger and Thomas Luckmann. This rejection of the functionalist approach by Davies and Smith reflects the criticisms which were being levelled at functionalism at this time within the discipline of sociology. We will examine these criticisms in more detail in Chapter 5. For the moment we wish to look at Davies's attempt to redefine the major function of education as the management of knowledge.

THE MANAGEMENT OF KNOWLEDGE

Ioan Davies, as we have noted, suggests that the concentration on the selective function of education limits our understanding of the part that education plays in society. 'Selecting people for jobs is one of education's latent functions: its *manifest* function is the management of knowledge.'[52] Education, Davies argues, is concerned with the moulding of the reality-images of young people. Values, norms *and* knowledge have to be examined and the relationships between these three aspects of experience need to be clarified. We have to look at the way that education transmits knowledge and at the influence of norms and values on the content and organisation of what is transmitted. We also need to look at the way that pupils receive the knowledge offered by education and incorporate it into their own experiences.

Peter Berger and Thomas Luckmann

Before we look in more detail at Davies's ideas, we feel that an understanding of the background upon which his ideas are based may help. The publication of the book *The Social Construction of Reality* by Peter Berger and Thomas Luckmann in 1966 had a major impact on the sociological world. These authors argue that social reality is a construct of the activity of people. Society is a human product. If we assume that human beings are born with little instinctive programming, then it is clear that people themselves must make up the rules of behaviour that constitute society.

Berger and Luckmann develop their argument as follows. They say that, if we reflect on some ordinary, everyday activity, we can recognise how many decisions are being made. Consider, for example, going to work in a car. We have to make decisions about which route we should take, about how fast to drive, which gear we should be in and what position on the road we should adopt. However, we don't feel that we are making so many decisions because we have become familiar with our route and how to drive the car. We go to work in an almost automatic or instinctive way. The psychological effort of making thousands of decisions is reduced because we are able to self-programme. This can be stated in a slightly different way by saying that we tend to act habitually. Furthermore, in an activity like driving to work it is comparatively easy to change an habitual action, because only one person is involved. So we can decide to drive more slowly or take a different road.

In our relations with other people we also tend to interact habitually. However, in social relationships the situation is more complex and less easy to change. The creation of the habitual action is something that is done with others; it is a joint construction. Suppose that we join a car-sharing scheme in which we drive some colleagues to work for a week and they take it in turns to drive us. In this situation the route we have to follow is more determined by the need to pick up our colleagues. The time we leave the house is also restricted by the need to get them to work on time. Even if we feel rather ill, we still feel some obligation to go to work so that we can satisfy our side of the agreement. In the same way our colleagues' activity is constrained because they are in the car-sharing scheme. What has happened, then, is that by developing a joint activity each individual has become constrained by the relationships he helped to form. This process of constructing relationships with others and being constrained by that which we make is part of everyday reality. Berger sums up the process by saying that we jointly construct reality with others. This reality becomes objectivated; that is, it faces us as something we cannot wish away. The objectivated reality must then be taken into consideration when we act.

Berger and Luckmann use a model of people marooned on a desert island to elaborate their ideas. In such a situation people slowly come to establish joint patterns of activities — which we call roles. Roles may evolve in which men do some jobs, women others. Language will develop; it will be jointly and slowly constructed. Once in existence it will be binding on the participants, who now *have* to speak the new language to be understood. At the same time knowledge will grow and come to be shared: knowledge of how to do various activities, knowledge of what activities are appropriate to what sort of person such as male and female. Indeed, knowledge is involved in the social construction of reality from the beginning.

With the advent of the next generation of children, the situation changes radically. The child has no experience of the construction of the society, he is born into a 'real' world that seems to be an objective fact. He has to learn to speak the language that others have constructed, and has to come to understand who he is and what is expected of him. At the same time, the older generation has to develop explanations for why things are as they appear to be. When faced with the question, for example, of why it is that boys have to hunt when girls don't, answers may be given in terms of the aggressive nature of the male and the passive nature of the female. In other words, a new set of 'knowledge' is evolved on the basis of the patterns of activity that have been established. At a later date this knowledge may be further elaborated into theology (women are linked to the sun god who is the source of fertility in nature and like the sun must be kept warm by the camp fire so that they may be fertile), or psychology (the survival of the species has led to the development of different innate and natural abilities and aptitudes in the different sexes). The development of this 'higher order knowledge' both maintains the social structure that has been developed and leads to changes in social behaviour. In our example, the women may be expected to wear lots of clothes to keep warm and fertile, whilst the men periodically undergo rituals to prove their aggressiveness. The interplay between the way people act, the norms and values of the group and the 'knowledge' that develops is thus very complex.

Furthermore, these socially constructed aspects of society are internalised in the process of socialisation so that the individual's identity and way of thinking about self and society are moulded. The male and female come to 'know' the difference between them, know what is expected of them, what masculine and feminine emotions and attitudes are, and know why the male and female are as they are.

Berger and Luckmann thus provide a model in which 'reality' is socially constructed, is socially maintained by the activity of people, and may be changed by the activity of people. But 'reality' attains the quality of an object that cannot be willed away by the individual. This reality contains what is taken as knowledge, that which 'makes sense' of the world to the members of the society. This knowledge, therefore, also attains the status of an object which cannot be wished away. In addition, the socially produced reality becomes part of the individual's consciousness through the process of socialisation when he or she is given an identity.

Ioan Davies

These ideas, we believe, are basic to Davies's analysis of education, the major function of which is the management of knowledge. According to Davies the central question concerning the management of knowledge is: 'What part does it play in the creation of social consciousness?'[53]

Davies says that the term 'management of knowledge'

has three meanings: it refers to the social structures and procedures which generate knowledge-as-discipline; it further refers to the ways that educational institutions control the discipline–knowledge imparted and the world views of the members of institutions; and it finally refers to the ways in which individuals and collectivities manage the tensions which arise out of the conflict between their own world-view and the discipline–institutional conceptions of knowledge.[54]

If we take each of these items in turn, we will be able to get a more detailed understanding of Davies's ideas. The first aspect of the management of knowledge demands that we discover the origins of the 'national cultural styles' which give a shape to the curriculum. Davies also refers to 'national intellectual styles' which he seems to think is a more or less synonymous term. As examples of these styles he mentions the possibility that Russian and American managers may be given different training for what appears to be the same job. He also points out that 'French anthropology is logical and metaphysical; British is empirical'.[55] The detail he provides of these cultural or intellectual styles is skimpy. However, we think that Davies is right to point to national differences in the basic approach to the selection of knowledge for education.

It may well be that in general the French adopt a philosophical approach to study and the British adopt a more empirical approach. Pierre Bourdieu, for example, an author we will be dealing with in Chapter 7, suggests that in French education the emphasis is on style and flair, sometimes to the exclusion of content. Similarly, P.W. Musgrave, reporting a survey in 1963, says

> It was found that a far greater proportion of [6th Form, British] boys whom their headmasters considered capable of gaining first-class honours degrees chose careers in pure science as opposed to careers in technology . . . in Sweden the most able boys appeared to take courses in applied rather than in pure science; in Holland proportions were more equal; in West Germany, though more able boys went to pure science courses, the proportion was in no way as great as in Britain.[56]

This could be taken to be an indication of different intellectual styles in the sciences. In the area of sociology, Coulson and Riddell contrast the content of textbooks used in various countries. They state that American books tend to

> orient their approach to sociology around the concept of *culture* . . . But if we look at European textbooks, we find them giving much less emphasis to the idea of culture, and emphasising much more the idea of *structure*. Similarly, in most American, and in a number of British textbooks, the idea of social change is given a very subordinate place . . . whereas all Eastern European textbooks give a central place to the concept of change.[57]

Here there seem to be major differences in what are considered to be central issues in what is nominally the same subject or discipline.

In order to get at the origins of such differences in intellectual style, Davies suggests we need to look at the history and the structure of the societies in question. An important consideration, in this respect, will be the study of the educational systems. We must understand the power-structures in both society and education, and the way that institutions organise the knowledge that is to be transmitted. Ideology must be studied in this context as it may have an impact on the way that new knowledge is incorporated into the discipline areas.

The second aspect mentioned by Davies is that of the schools. We must consider such things as the organisation of the school, the curriculum it develops and the emphasis given to different types of knowledge. Involved in this will be a consideration of the common-sense knowledge of the teachers, the values and ethos of the school (is it secular or denominational, for example), as well as consideration of the sorts of pupils it receives.

Thirdly, we need to look at what the pupils do with the knowledge to which they are exposed. The subcultural values, the peer group's attitudes, and the experiences of the pupils both in and out of school will all affect the way they relate to the knowledge and values transmitted.

Davies sums up his ideas in a simple statement. ' "Look what they've done to my brain, ma." Ultimately that is what the sociology of education is all about.'[58]

COMMENTS

We feel that Davies has done a great service in redirecting the emphasis of the sociology of education. We do, however, agree with Smith,[59] who points out that the rejection of selection as a central theme has itself led Davies to take a partial view of education. Selection is involved in the decision as to who shall receive what type of knowledge. The knowledge of the upper-stream child, and the reality-images thus formed, will be different from that of the lower-stream child. This may even be true when pupils are nominally taking the same subject as Keddie suggests.[60]

In this chapter we have looked at examples of the functionalist approach to education. The essence of this approach is to consider the major functions of education, that is, the ways that education helps in the maintenance and development of society. We have examined the work of Turner and Hopper which, in different ways, embodies the functionalist approach. The ideas of Davies and Smith, however, show something of a new emphasis. Davies, basing his ideas on the work of Berger and Luckmann, suggests another function for education besides selection, namely the management of knowledge. Smith sees the management of knowledge as implying selection. Both Davies and Smith, however, challenge the assumption of consensus which is one of the main characteristics of the functionalist approach. They both point to the need to look at the power structures of society and the educational system and to the need to examine the 'definitions' of the situation held by the participants in education. The educational system, with its structure of knowledge and its processes of selection, is now seen as the outcome of the interaction of parties, both inside and outside education, who hold different degrees of power. Consequently, the routes that pupils take in education, the type of knowledge to which they are exposed and the sort of future life they will attain are seen to be constructed through interaction. Such an approach, we believe, is the way to progress in the study of education and society.

We have already noted a number of criticisms that have been levelled at the functionalist perspective from within sociology. So far in our exposition, however, we have included only criticisms about detail and have left the attack on the basic theoretical framework in abeyance. It is now necessary to look at the adequacy, or lack of it, of the theory itself.

NOTES

1. T. Parsons, *The System of Modern Societies* (Prentice-Hall, Englewood Cliffs, 1971).
2. T. Parsons, 'The School Class as a Social System' in A.H. Halsey, J. Floud and C.A. Anderson (eds.), *Education, Economy and Society* (Free Press, New York, 1961).
3. On this point see C. Wright Mills's 'translations' of Parsons in Chapter 2 of *The Sociological Imagination* (Oxford University Press, New York, 1959).
4. Parsons, *The System*, p. 98.
5. Ibid., p. 95.
6. Parsons, 'The School Class', p. 445.
7. A. Comte, 'The Positive Philosophy' in K. Thompson and J. Tunstall (eds.), *Sociological Perspectives* (Penguin, Harmondsworth, 1971), p. 21.
8. P.H. Partridge, *Consent and Consensus* (Pall Mall, London, 1971).
9. Parsons, *The System*, p. 98.
10. Ibid., p. 99.
11. Parsons, 'The School Class', p. 453.
12. Ibid., p. 434.
13. Sometimes he speaks of a fourth system, the 'behavioural organism'. In our view, however, this fourth element plays a minor part in his general theory and for that reason we omit reference to it here.
14. See, for example, T. Parsons, 'An Outline of the Social System' in T. Parsons *et al.* (eds.), *Theories of Society* (Prentice-Hall, Englewood Cliffs, 1971), p. 34.
15. T. Parsons and E. Shils (eds.), *Toward a General Theory of Action* (Harper and Row, New York, 1962), p. 23.

16. Ibid., p. 190.

17. Ibid., p. 191.

18. T. Parsons, *Societies: Evolutionary and Comparative Perspectives* (Prentice-Hall, Englewood Cliffs, 1966), p. 9; 'An Outline', p. 38.

19. Parsons and Shils (eds.), *Toward a General Theory*, p. 172. The choices concern what Parsons calls the 'pattern-variables'.

20. Ibid., p. 148.

21. Parsons, 'An Outline', p. 39.

22. Mills, *The Sociological Imagination*, p. 31.

23. Parsons and Shils (eds.), *Toward a General Theory*, p. 150.

24. Parsons, 'The School Class', p. 437.

25. Ibid., p. 440.

26. Ibid., p. 449.

27. See, for example, R. Davie and Neville R. Butler, *From Birth to Seven*, Second Report of the National Child Development Study (Longman, London, 1972).

28. R. Rist, 'On Understanding the Process of Schooling: The Contributions of Labelling Theory' in J. Karabel and A.H. Halsey (eds.), *Power and Ideology in Education* (Oxford University Press, New York, 1977), p. 298.

29. See, for example, A.H. Halsey, A.F. Heath and J.M. Ridge, *Origins and Destinations* (Clarendon Press, Oxford, 1980).

30. For example, P. Bourdieu, 'Cultural Reproduction and Social Reproduction' in R. Brown, *Knowledge, Education and Cultural Change* (Tavistock, London, 1973), p. 98.

31. R. Turner, 'Sponsored and Contest Mobility and the School System' in E. Hopper (ed.), *Readings in the Theory of Educational Systems* (Hutchinson, London, 1971).

32. J. Westergaard and H. Resler, *Class in Capitalist Society* (Penguin, Harmondsworth, 1975).

33. *Social Trends* (HMSO, 1978).

34. J.H. Goldthorpe, *Social Mobility and Class Structure in Modern Britain* (Clarendon Press, Oxford, 1980).

35. Halsey *et al.*, *Origins and Destinations*, p. 203.

36. Turner, 'Sponsored', p. 76.

37. Ibid., p. 77.

38. Ibid., p. 83.

39. Ibid., p. 86.

40. In Hopper (ed.), *Readings*, p. 92.

41. Ibid., p. 95.

42. Ibid., p. 99.

43. Ibid., p. 292.

44. Ibid., p. 298.

45. P.W. Musgrave, *The Sociology of Education* (Methuen, London, 1965), p. 175.

46. I. Davies, 'The Management of Knowledge: A Critique of the Use of Typologies in Educational Sociology' in Hopper (ed.), *Readings*, p. 113.

47. Ibid., p. 115.

48. Ibid., p. 121.

49. D. Smith, 'Selection and Knowledge Management in Educational Systems' in Hopper (ed.), *Readings*.

50. Ibid., p. 142.

51. A.H. Halsey, 'Theoretical Advance and Empirical Challenge' in Hopper (ed.), *Readings*.

52. Davies, 'Management', p. 124.

53. Ibid., p. 126.

54. Ibid., p. 130.

55. Ibid., p. 131.

56. P.W. Musgrave, *The Sociology of Education* (Methuen, London, 1965), p. 181.

57. M.A. Coulson and C. Riddell, *Approaching Sociology* (Routledge and Kegan Paul, London, 1970), p. 2.

58. Davies, 'Management', p. 133.

59. Smith, 'Selection'.

60. N. Keddie, 'Classroom Knowledge' in M.F.D. Young (ed.), *Knowledge and Control* (Collier-Macmillan, London, 1971).

5 AN ASSESSMENT OF THE FUNCTIONALIST APPROACH

We now turn to an assessment of the functionalist view of society and education.

CONSENSUS

As we have seen, the functionalists argue that societies are held together by a consensus of values. This view is clearly false if it implies that social stability cannot be maintained by other means. A value consensus is, in fact, only one possible solution to the problem of order and it is by no means the most usual. More frequently a powerful group uses the police and army to impose order on a population by terror or threats. In such regimes there is little in the way of 'socialisation' into a 'common culture' in order to get people to do what is required of them. Rather, the dominant group rules in its own interest and simply coerces or eliminates any opposition. Not only have such regimes been common throughout history; they are also frequently found in the modern world. Furthermore, these societies are quite stable — witness, for example, the level of international investment in some third world military dictatorships.

Of course, we recognise that, sometimes, a value consensus is the basis of social cohesion. Even so, the functionalist view of the nature and origin of such a consensus is grossly inadequate. It fails to see that social stability may be a result of a 'manipulated' or 'false' consensus. The most obvious form of such a manipulated consensus is probably to be found in totalitarian states where a tiny minority control the beliefs and values of vast numbers of human beings through propaganda, the mass media, education and outright coercion. Some writers claim that, in so far as there exists a consensus in contemporary Western societies, it, too, is 'engineered'. They argue that the dominant group or class in society seeks to secure its privileges by getting the rest of the population to accept beliefs and values which maintain and legitimate the dominant group's position. Once again this is done by means of the mass media, education, etc. The various ways in which such value systems are transmitted has been well summarised by Barrington Moore in the following, much-quoted sentence:

To maintain and transmit a value system, human beings are punched, bullied, sent to jail, thrown into concentration camps, cajoled, bribed, made into heroes, encouraged to read newspapers, stood against a wall and shot, and sometimes even taught sociology.[1]

In addition to the idea of a manipulated consensus, there is another conception of consensus which has received little attention in recent sociological literature. It is the view that in modern Western society there exists a 'procedural' rather than a 'substantive' consensus (whether 'genuine', as in functionalist theory, or engineered). Advocates of the notion of a procedural consensus take the view that the conflicts of values, beliefs and interests typical of the pluralistic societies of the West do not produce disruption and chaos because they are held in check by an agreement to settle such differences by means of agreed 'procedures'. Social order is maintained in the face of a *dis*sensus on values by an acceptance by all parties concerned to use one set of rules rather than another in resolving disputes. As one writer has put it: 'we may think of modern nation states as communities whose basic consensus is restricted to agreement on the procedures for maintaining order and settling disputes.'[2] Ralph Miliband, a Marxist writer, has characterised this notion of procedural consensus quite well in a brief description of what he calls the 'liberal view of politics'. He writes:

> In the liberal view of politics, conflict exists in terms of 'problems' which need to be 'solved'. The hidden assumption is that conflict does not, or need not, run very deep; that it can be 'managed' by the exercise of reason and good will, and a readiness to compromise and agree. On this view, politics is not civil war conducted by other means but a constant process of bargaining and accommodation, *on the basis of accepted procedures*, and between parties who have decided as a preliminary that they could and wanted to live together more or less harmoniously. Not only is this sort of conflict not injurious to society; it has positive advantages. It is not only civilized but also civilizing. It is not only a means of resolving problems in a peaceful way, but of producing new ideas, ensuring progress, achieving ever-greater harmony, and so on.[3]

Another author, Graeme Duncan — in a book concerned with the *Two Views of Social Conflict and Social Harmony* of the nineteenth-century writers Karl Marx and John Stuart Mill — has argued that such an agreement on the procedures and processes for settling conflicts has been one reason why a revolution of the sort Marxists hope for and predict has not occurred in Western societies. As he says:

groups have been satisfied, or have been willing to act peacefully within the system, because of the growth of political and judicial institutions which appear to give their claims reasonable attention. Social conflict itself has provoked the search for new means of negotiation and interaction, with the aim and effect of channelling and controlling the antagonisms and hostilities . . . In the course of this process of socialisation, class claims and demands have been modified and their character altered . . . There is general acceptance of, or acquiescence in, the broad features of the institutional system within which conflict and change occur. Even where particular decisions have been rejected, the dissatisfied groups have normally preferred, where possible, to work for more acceptable settlements through parliaments, pressure groups and arbitration courts, while seeking in some cases to reduce their bias, rather than to reject the whole system of negotiation, or the whole society of which these institutions are an integral part.[4]

Clearly, there is much more to be said in elucidating such a notion of procedural consensus, and we shall take up certain points in our evaluation of the Marxist perspective on education in Chapter 9. Now, however, we must consider the implications of these criticisms of the functionalist notion of substantive consensus for our view of education.

Many of the criticisms we made of Durkheim in Chapter 2 obviously apply to the functionalists. We suggested there that in Britain, for example, it is difficult to find any values common to all members of society, and that British society can be seen as a series of social groups, each having its own system of values. There may well be some overlap of values, but there are no values common to all. If that is so, then clearly education cannot, as Parsons suggests, transmit such values. It may, of course, transmit the values of the dominant group within society and help to sustain a manipulated consensus — a consensus which legitimates the power and privileges of such a group. But this is a radically different view of the function of education from the one advanced by Parsons and others.

Similarly, if a person accepts the idea of a procedural consensus, his view of the role of education changes considerably. Procedural consensus, as we have seen, rests on the notion of a conflict of values, beliefs and interests within society. Such conflicts will, in all probability, be reflected in the educational system. Consequently, no one set of values will be transmitted by schools and colleges. Rather, the different views which exist in society about what education ought to be doing — views which largely stem from different conceptions of the way society in general ought to be organised — will manifest themselves in the educational system. Some of these differences are evident in contemporary debates concerning, for example: (1) the existence of a private sector in British education; (2) 'traditionalism' versus 'progressivism'; (3) the pursuit of equality as opposed to the pursuit of quality or excellence, which involves some form of selection; (4) education as 'training' or as something valuable for its own sake. Furthermore, these competing views of the aims and purposes of education are reflected in practice. Local education authorities and headteachers in this country enjoy considerable freedom and autonomy with respect to the curriculum and organisation of their schools, resulting in a wide variety of educational provision. For example, schools such as Summerhill exist alongside Eton and Harrow; and those with an emphasis on academic excellence, selection and formal teacher–pupil relationships coexist with schools where the stress is on rather more 'social' aims, mixed-ability teaching and an 'open', informal atmosphere. This is not to say, of course, that one particular conception of education will not become dominant in practice — there are obviously 'fashions' in education and traditions die hard. Furthermore, educational theories, as we noted above, often derive from, or are an element of, more general social and political ideologies. As these rise or decline in importance in a particular society, changes will often occur in the structure of the educational system and in the typical pattern of educational provision.

There is obviously much more that could be said on these matters. For the moment, however, we must turn to a consideration of other criticisms of functionalist theory.

CHANGE

Functionalism has often been criticised for its inability to deal with the issue of social change. If we accept their model of society as a more or less integrated whole, we must ask, how is it possible for change to occur? Only two answers appear to be forthcoming: (1) change comes about through something happening outside the society, that forces change within it — for example, a war or an international economic collapse; (2) change results from a failure in the socialisation process on a massive scale. However, there are problems for functionalist theory with both answers. The second answer is incompatible with some of functionalism's central premises concerning the crucial role of socialisation into a society's common culture. On the other hand, the first answer is unacceptable on empirical grounds. It suggests that change is never initiated 'internally'. But clearly changes do occur from within a society, as is evidenced by, let us say, the women's movement.

A further problem arises when considering the idea of change caused by external factors. Functionalism, as we have seen, argues that the institutions of society are interrelated. The economy is related to the educational system and the family, which in turn are connected to the economy. Supposing a change occurs in the economy — say as the result of an international economic collapse — then this will affect the family and the educational system. But a change in the family will also *independently* affect the educational system, and a change in the educational system will, likewise, independently affect the family. These changes in the family and in education will also, in turn, have an impact on the economy. Thus once change starts, the theory seems to imply a sort of continuous chain reaction with all parts changing all others continuously. This seems to be at odds, however, with the functionalist idea of society as a stable entity, in which everyone has a clear conception of their role in the various social institutions. For, if these institutions are subject to continuous change, then roles and role-expectations will alter accordingly and the socialisation process will rapidly become an inadequate preparation for such roles. The very admission of change, then, by the functionalists brings major problems for the theory.

Functionalists could respond to such a criticism by suggesting that in any social system there will be a 'strain towards equilibrium', that is, a tendency for things to readjust to a state of functional stability. But if we ask why this happens, functionalists seem to say either that some 'societal force' or 'unseen hand' is responsible (which really takes us no further), or they are forced to admit that it is people themselves who bring things under control because they do not want too much change in their lives. In this case, however, they are obliged to step outside the functionalist framework, for they are now describing the needs and wants of *individuals* rather than the needs of 'society'. And if they are to assert that it is people themselves who produce resistance to change, they ought, in consistency, also to argue that social stability in general is brought about by what people do rather than by some societal 'need' for it. In other words, they ought to adopt a different theoretical perspective.

In much the same vein, some critics believe that the functionalists' difficulty in providing a satisfactory theory of social change is linked to the inadequacies of their theory of social stability. As Percy Cohen says:

> The truth of the matter is that if the functionalists have not produced adequate theories of social change this is largely because they have not produced adequate theories of social persistence . . . What has been wrong with functionalism is that it has simply asserted that

social systems or certain types of system tend to persist without giving more than a hint of why this occurs.[5]

Put differently, functionalism asserts, as a sort of dogma, that there is a 'law of order' in society.

TELEOLOGY AND DETERMINISM

Another difficulty with the functionalists' theory is logical in nature. It is often said that the explanations the theory produces are 'teleological'. What this means is that functionalism asserts that an institution comes into existence to solve some societal problem or problems. Thus education exists to solve the problems of socialisation, selection and the management of knowledge. The cause of the existence of education is thus the function it serves. Cohen puts the point as follows:

> a teleological explanation in sociology consists in showing that religion exists in order to sustain the moral foundations of society, or that the State exists in order to coordinate the various activities which occur in complex societies. In both these cases, a consequence is used to explain a cause; the end conditions of moral order and coordination are used to explain the existence of religion and the State. It is as though one were to say: X produces Y, therefore the occurrence of Y, which is desirable, must explain the occurrence of X. Critics rightly argue that this type of explanation defies the laws of logic, for one thing cannot be the cause of another if it succeeds it in time.[6]

In addition, functionalism provides us with a deterministic view of the relationship between man and society. Society, especially culture, shapes and moulds the individual, but, in the functionalists' view, society and culture are not, in turn, shaped and moulded by individuals. A vitally important dimension of social life is thus ignored. For it is essential to recognise that society both creates and is created by us — otherwise one is left with a distorted image.

The point applies not just to society as a whole but to all its component institutions. J.S. Mill put it as clearly as anyone over a hundred years ago; it is a pity that the message has been 'forgotten' by some contemporary social scientists. Speaking of political institutions he says:

> Let us remember, then, in the first place, that political institutions (however the proposition may at times be ignored) are the work of men; owe their origin and their whole existence to human will. Men

did not wake up on a summer morning and find them sprung up. Neither do they resemble trees, which, once planted, 'are aye growing' while men 'are sleeping'. In every stage of their existence they are made what they are by the human voluntary agency. Like all things, therefore, which are made by men, they may be either well or ill made . . .[7]

With regard to educational institutions, it may be true that at certain times in the history of a society the younger generation is socialised into a particular set of values in the process of the creation of a 'false' consensus. But if that is the case, then it is because certain individuals and groups concerned with education at various times and places have made it so. Also, of course, once made educational institutions can be remade, that is, changed or transformed; the power of inertia, custom and unreflecting habit may be great, but it is not overwhelming. We need only to glance at the history of education in Britain in the last two hundred years to recognise that.

Of course, economic and other conditions set limits to what people can do. Even so the limits are frequently quite wide, and the freedom of action of individuals and groups considerable. Clearly, some people are better placed than others to influence the course of events. For example, a headteacher can more readily bring about changes in a school than can a young probationary teacher; and the Secretary of State for Education has more power than a clerk in a local education authority office to transform the whole course of educational policy. However, despite such differences of power, the point is that men *generally* are responsible for society being the way it is. We are not, as Parsons would have it, mere players of roles; we also create and modify the roles we play. Indeed to think in terms of man as primarily a role-player, and therefore of society as a stage and social life as a drama — concepts and images so central in Parsonian and functionalist sociology — is highly misleading.[8] For, as a character in E.M. Forster's *Howard's End* says: 'Life is sometimes life and sometimes only a drama, and the difficult thing is to distinguish t'other from which.' In functionalist sociology, however, life is considered as nothing but a drama. As a consequence, it is blind not only to the different domains of existence, but also to the true nature of role-playing itself.

APPROVAL-SEEKING

The functionalists' notion of society as a structure of roles is, of course, very much tied to their view of man as an approval-seeker. Individuals, in their view, play the roles assigned to them not only because they are committed to society's shared moral standards, but also because they want the approval and esteem of others: not to do what is expected of them brings disapproval and thus loss of 'gratification'.

Once again we would say of the functionalists that they only give us part of the story. Certainly approval-seeking is an important human motive. Teachers of very young children, for example, know how much such children want to please their teacher, and they act accordingly in the classroom. To say this, however, is to recognise that young children are often very different from older children. Older children are not so dependent on the good opinion of their teachers. Indeed, they may be indifferent to it in the way that adults are so often unconcerned about the opinions of many of their fellow men. Older children and adults only want the approval of those that are important or significant to them — those whose opinions they value or respect. In their dealings with the rest other motives predominate. One such motive is, of course, fear. Secondary school pupils may do what is expected of them, not because they want the teacher's approval, but because they wish to avoid punishment or ridicule. Similarly, they may work hard and be well behaved in class, not because they seek the teacher's approval, but because they enjoy the work, are interested in learning, and want to 'get on'. The teacher's approval may accompany such conduct, but it is not the primary motive for acting this way. For example, Peter Woods in his chapter on 'Pupil Adaptations' in the book *The Divided School* points out that many pupils comply with the school's demands upon them because they accept and identify with the goals of the school and the means the school uses to attain these goals. This is especially true of two groups of pupils: (1) those in the early years of the secondary school where 'many pupils beginning a new school have an air of hope and expectancy'; and (2) those 'in the upper school [where] pupils on examination routes are coming within sight of their examinations and [where] many seem to have a very clear perception of what they are doing and why'.[9] Similarly, Furlong found that the pupils he studied behaved well and conformed to the school's discipline when their teachers 'were "good" and were seen as being able to teach well'. He concludes that, for the pupils, 'their behaviour was always rational, logical and based on careful and continual assessment of their teachers'.[10] In other words, it was nothing to do with approval-seeking.

In the case of those pupils who disrupt a class because they are only interested in 'having a laff' or 'mucking about' — the subject of a good deal of recent attention in the sociology of education[11] — the functionalist notion of approval-seeking might seem to be nearer the mark. For in many such cases one major aim is to impress their classmates, i.e. gain the approval of their peers. But rather than confirming the functionalists' analysis, this example raises another problem for their theory, namely that in such cases there exist *conflicting* expectations for conduct. Such pupils cannot gain the approval of *both* the teacher and their peers, for teachers require one form of behaviour and fellow pupils another.

Such a situation of conflicting expectations is quite a common occurrence in society generally. If we do what one set of people expect of us, we must disappoint, and risk the disapproval of, another set. Also, of course, the person with an independent mind, determined to 'be his own man', will disappoint everybody — family, friends, teachers and so on. But the functionalists never consider such possibilities, because of their assumption of a consensus of role-expectations in society, and because of their narrow view of human nature.

To consider human beings as merely approval-seekers is, in the words of Dennis Wrong, 'an extremely one-sided view of human nature'.[12] Developing the argument, Wrong says that:

Modern sociology, after all, originated as a protest against the partial views of man contained in such doctrines as utilitarianism, classical economics, social Darwinism, and vulgar Marxism. All of the great nineteenth century and twentieth century sociologists saw it as one of their major tasks to expose the unreality of such abstractions as economic man, the gain-seeker of the classical economists; political man, the power-seeker of the Machiavellian tradition of political science; self-preserving man, the security-seeker of Hobbes and Darwin; sexual or libidinal man, the pleasure-seeker of doctrinaire Freudianism; and even religious man, the God-seeker of the theologians. It would be ironical if it should turn out that they have merely contributed to the creation of yet another reified abstraction in socialized man, the status-seeker of our contemporary sociologists.[13]

Furthermore, Wrong considers that this limited view of human motivation is bound up with a selective view of the basis of social order and social stability. As he says: 'The assumption of the maximization of approval from others is the psychological complement to the sociological assumption of a general value consensus,' and 'The oversocialized view man . . . is a counterpart of the overintegrated view of society . . . '[14]

SUMMARY

These criticisms are clearly sufficient to cast doubt upon the whole functionalist analysis of education. Functionalism has no causal adequacy and it is unfortunate that later authors failed to recognise, as Durkheim had, that functional and causal explanation are quite different. However, while functionalist theory gives us no causal explanation, it may still be usefully employed to provide us with an initial framework. This is to repeat the point made by Max Weber when he says:

> For purposes of sociological analysis two things can be said. First this functional frame of reference is convenient for purposes of practical illustration and for provisional orientation. In these respects it is not only useful but indispensable. But at the same time if its cognitive value is overestimated and its concepts illegitimately 'reified', it can be dangerous. Secondly, in certain circumstances this is the only available way of determining just what processes of social action it is important to understand in order to explain a given phenomenon.[15]

When applied to education, Weber's point of view may be taken to mean that a functionalist analysis may be used to suggest certain functions for education and to specify certain relations between education and the other parts of society. However, a causal explanation of why these functions exist must be given in terms of the aims of individuals and groups and the power that they have to impose their ideas. Functionalism, therefore, can have some part to play in our understanding of education by providing us with a starting-point.

The rejection of functionalism as the dominant theory in the sociology of education allowed other approaches to come to the fore. An explosion in theoretical speculation and research followed. It is possible in retrospect to see these developments as following a number of different theoretical lines.

A number of authors rejected the oversocialised conception of man implicit in functionalism and argued that it was people in interaction who made society. If one wanted to understand society or any part of it then it was necessary to begin by observing the interaction of people and discovering how they thought and felt. In the sociology of education this involved looking at teachers' and pupils' definitions of such things as learning, the good and bad pupil, intelligence and so on. The method of discovering such definitions was by observing face-to-face interactions or being involved in such interactions.

The work of Berger and Luckmann focused attention on 'knowledge' and this led to the development of what has been called the 'new' sociology of education. We will deal with this approach in Chapter 11.

Marxist sociologists took over many of the ideas of the functionalists but adapted them to their own conception of society. Selection, socialisation and the management of knowledge, became seen as mechanisms for the maintenance of the unequal and unjust capitalist system.

There appears to be an affinity between functionalism and some Marxist views of education, despite many other differences. Both approaches attempt to explain how education contributes to the maintenance of the status quo. They both tend to deal with the relationship of education to the wider society, especially the economy. Finally, in our view at least, they both tend to neglect the importance of the actors' definitions of the situation. It is for this reason that we will be treating Marxist analyses of education before those we have called interpretive.

NOTES

1. B. Moore, *Social Origins of Dictatorship and Democracy* (Penguin, Harmondsworth, 1969), p. 486.

2. E. Haas, *Beyond the Nation State* (Stanford University Press, Stanford, 1964). Quoted in P.H. Partridge, *Consent and Consensus* (Pall Mall, London, 1971), p. 92.

3. R. Miliband, *Marxism and Politics* (Oxford University Press, Oxford, 1977), p. 17 (emphasis added).

4. G. Duncan, *Marx and Mill: Two Views of Social Conflict and Social Harmony* (Cambridge University Press, Cambridge, 1973), p. 303.

5. P. Cohen, *Modern Social Theory* (Heinemann, London, 1968), p. 58.

6. Ibid., pp. 47–8.

7. J.S. Mill, *Considerations on Representative Government* (1861) (Dent, London, 1910), p. 177.

8. This is not to say, however, that the image of society as a drama is exclusively functionalist in nature. It has been used in a different way by other, non-functionalist, writers. For example, by P. Berger in *Invitation to Sociology* (Penguin, Harmondsworth, 1969).

9. P. Woods, *The Divided School* (Routledge and Kegan Paul, London, 1979), p. 72.

10. V. Furlong, 'Anancy Goes to School: A Case Study of Pupils' Knowledge of Their Teachers' in P. Woods and M. Hammersley (eds.), *School Experience: Explorations in the Sociology of Education* (Croom Helm, London, 1977), p. 183.

11. See, for example, P. Willis, *Learning to Labour* (Saxon House, Farnborough, 1977), and, again, Woods, *The Divided School*. We shall discuss Willis's work in Chapters 8 and 9, and that of Woods in Chapters 9 and 11.

12. D. Wrong, 'The Oversocialised Conception of Man in Modern Sociology' in L. Coser and B. Rosenberg (eds.), *Sociological Theory* (Collier-Macmillan, London, 1966), p. 117.

13. Ibid., p. 118.

14. Ibid., pp. 117–18.

15. Max Weber, *The Theory of Economic and Social Organization* (Free Press, New York, 1964), p. 103.

PART II

THE MARXIST PERSPECTIVE

6 THE MARXIST PERSPECTIVE — AN INTRODUCTION

Our purpose in this chapter is to provide an introduction to the main ideas and issues within Marxist theory as a basis for an understanding of the Marxist perspective on education.

Marxist theory can be divided into two parts. First there is the theory of society and history that is usually referred to as 'historical materialism'. It is a conception of how society changes and how the various parts of society are related to one another. Second there is the Marxist concept of man or human nature, which is interwoven with a theory of the 'good society'. The notions of 'alienation' and 'communism' are here central.

HISTORICAL MATERIALISM

The starting-point of a Marxist analysis is the view that it is what people do to keep alive or maintain themselves in existence that really matters. The basic fact about society is how men and women produce the means to live. It is therefore economic activity, or production in a wide sense of the word, that is fundamental. Everything else that people do and that goes on in society is in some way related to or derived from this. Hence Marxists see society as composed of two major parts: (1) the economic structure or 'base' or 'foundation' and (2) the 'superstructure' of other social institutions and practices such as politics, education, religion, family life, and men's ideas, beliefs and values.

However, over and above this short statement one enters into areas of controversy. For, as Kolakowski points out: 'There is scarcely any question relating to the interpretation of Marxism that is not a matter of dispute.'[1] In what follows we shall explore some of these disputes.

Base and Superstructure

First there is the 'base/superstructure' issue and the related controversy of 'determinism versus voluntarism' in Marxist thought. For, although Marxists believe that everything that goes on in the superstructure of society is in some way related to economic activity (or the base), they differ in their views as to the nature of that relationship. On the one hand there are those who believe that the economic base *determines* the superstructure in the sense that, for example, a society's educational system, or its form of government, or the type of family prevalent at any particular time is a direct consequence of the nature of its economic system. Furthermore, as the economic base changes, so too do these other social, political and cultural institutions. As Marx himself says: 'With the change of the economic foundation the entire immense superstructure is more or less rapidly transformed.'[2] For example, the transition from the feudal to the capitalist 'mode of production', it is argued, brought with it a change in the nature of the political system. Monarchy and aristocracy were replaced by a liberal–democratic form of government and state, which was more in keeping with the capitalist economic base. Similarly, the extended family gave way to the nuclear family as the structure of the latter was more compatible with the demands of the new industrial system. Moreover, a society with little provision for formal education was transformed into one where mass schooling became a central feature.

This 'economic determinist' conception is challenged, however, by those who see Marxism as granting rather more 'independence' and 'autonomy' to the various parts of the superstructure of society. They argue that, although the economic base certainly *conditions* the superstructure, it is, in turn, *conditioned by it*. There exists, they say, an interaction, or a dialectical relationship, between the 'mode of production' and other social and political institutions, which is a process of reciprocal influence. Economic forces certainly have an impact upon, for example, the political or educational system; but the latter also help to shape and change the economic base. Those who interpret Marxism in this way usually add, however, that 'in the final analysis' it is economic forces which are dominant. The superstructure, they say, has only 'relative autonomy'. And here they like to quote Engels who once said that 'the whole vast process goes on in the form of an interaction — though of very unequal forces, the economic movement being by far the strongest, most primordial, most decisive'.[3]

This theory of 'relative autonomy' (as it is now usually called) has been widely adopted by Marxist writers in the twentieth century. It is subscribed to by Marxists as different as, for example, Louis Althusser and his followers on the one hand, and Ralph Miliband on the other.[4] Furthermore, there is a tendency among such people to claim that this conception of Marxism is derived from the writings of Marx himself. They argue that a proper reading of the texts shows that Marx was not an economic determinist and that, in Miliband's words, 'Marx's own cast of mind was strongly anti-determinist'.[5]

We would argue, however, that this is a very selective and one-sided reading of Marx. For although Marx, and Engels, certainly do advance an 'interactionist' view in their work, they *also* put forward an economic determinist conception of society and social change. *Both* positions are to be found in the texts and one cannot say of either that it is the correct interpretation and that any comments by Marx and Engels to the contrary are mere aberrations or slips of the pen. We believe, in other words, that Marx and Engels were inconsistent and that their writings contain contradictions (although some Marxists who recognise this prefer to speak of 'tensions' — which is odd in light of the fact that the term 'contradiction' has such a central place in the Marxist vocabulary). Each side in the dispute has, therefore, a valid claim to call themselves followers of Marx.

In order to substantiate our view that Marx and Engels are, at times, economic determinists, we want now to quote some of the relevant passages from their work. First, however, we must say something about the meaning of the unfamiliar terms they use. For Marx and Engels the economic base of society has two components: the 'forces' of production and the 'relations' of production. Forces of production are also referred to as the 'means' of production and 'instruments' of production. By forces of production is meant the tools and machines that are used in the productive process, and the resources, skills and methods involved in production. In effect, the forces of production refer to the level of technological development of a society. Relations of production is a rather less straightforward concept.[6] On the whole, however, it refers to the system of ownership and control of the property involved in the production process (such as land, buildings and machinery). But as for Marx such property is the basis of social class, the relations of production are, to a great extent, synonymous with social class relations.

Marx and Engels as Determinists. With this as a background we now turn to a consideration of those parts of Marx and Engels's writing which provide evidence for an economic determinist interpretation of historical materialism. An examination of these will also, of course, enable us to 'fill out' and develop our account of the theory.

In *The Poverty of Philosophy* Marx wrote:

In acquiring new productive forces, men change their mode of production, and in changing their mode of production, their manner of gaining a living, they change all their social relations. The windmill gives you society with the feudal lord; the steam mill with the industrial capitalist.[7]

Similarly in *Wage Labour and Capital* he says:

These social relations into which producers enter with one another
. . . will naturally vary according to the character of the means of
production . . . the social relations within which individuals produce,
the social relations of production, change, are transformed, with the
change and development of the material means of production, the productive forces.[8]

Or again in the famous Preface to *A Contribution to a Critique of Political
Economy*:

At a certain stage of their development, the material productive forces
of society come in conflict with the existing relations of production,
or — what is but a legal expression for the same thing — with the
property relations within which they have been at work hitherto. From
forms of development of the productive forces these relations turn into
their fetters. Then begins an epoch of social revolution. With the change
of the economic foundation the entire immense superstructure is more
or less rapidly transformed.[9]

Finally in *The Communist Manifesto* we find Marx and Engels saying that:

The bourgeoisie cannot exist without constantly revolutionising the
instruments of production, and thereby the relations of production,
and with them the whole relations of society.[10]

According to the view presented here it is the character of the forces
of production which determine the nature of the relations of production
and, thereby, the nature of society more generally.

Forces of Production → Relations of Production → Superstructure.

Economic Base

And it should be noted that this stress on the importance of the forces
of production means that historical materialism is not only a form of
economic determinism but also a species of technological determinism.
It is saying that a social system is shaped by its level of technological
development and that technological advance brings about wholesale social
and political change.

However, Marx and Engels do not consistently take this view. Whilst
remaining within an economic determinist framework they sometimes

argue that it is the relations of production which are the basic determinant of the nature of society and social change, and that technological development flows from the changes in a society's productive relations. This view tends to predominate when Marx and Engels are providing a historical analysis of the rise of capitalism (whereas the technological determinist view is generally to be found in those parts of their work where they are supplying a general statement of their theory). It is difficult to find short, succinct statements by Marx and Engels to illustrate this view, but John Plamenatz perceptively summarises this aspect of their thought as follows:

> If we look at Marx's account of the rise of capitalism, we find him admitting readily enough that property relations [relations of production] have a powerful influence on productive methods [forces of production]. A considerable part of the first volume of *Capital* is taken up with explaining how the decay of the feudal relations of production made possible the development of new productive methods. There is no question there of the methods of production peculiar to capitalism being born in the womb of feudal society and then gradually transforming it into a capitalist society as feudal relations of property, now become fetters on these methods, give way to other relations more in harmony with them. As Marx describes the transformation, capitalist methods of production could only emerge because feudal relations of property were already giving way to others. There were no limbs to break the fetters until the fetters were broken.[11]

Represented diagrammatically this view states that:

Relations of Production → Forces of Production → Superstructure.

Economic Base

Of course, whichever view is taken — whether it is the forces or the relations of production which are given primacy — the theory still remains a form of economic determinism. The whole of the superstructure of society derives its nature directly from the operation of economic forces upon it.

Among other things this means, of course, that the free action of human beings has no impact upon the course of events. Like all deterministic theories of society and history, historical materialism therefore denies that individuals (either singly or collectively) can play a role in controlling their destiny. Whatever we, as individuals, seek to achieve, whatever principles and ideals we try to live by, these are determined for us by the working out of certain objective or impersonal forces or processes. Our ends and purposes and subsequent action have no influence on these forces. Whatever our illusions to the contrary, we are the creatures and not the creators of such objective processes.

For many determinists, including Marx, an important implication of this view is that the social world can be studied in much the same way as the world of nature. They believe that, just as natural scientists search for and discover the 'causes' of events and 'laws' of nature, so the social scientist can formulate certain 'laws' of society and social change. These laws, they feel, will make clear to us not only what is happening in society, but also what is going to happen. They will both explain the present and predict the future. Marx himself — like so many nineteenth-century social scientists — thought that he could do for the science of society what Newton had done for physics and Darwin for biology. As they had provided us with the laws of nature and of biological evolution, so Marx felt he had been able to discover the laws of social evolution.

A very clear statement by Marx of this point of view is to be found in the Preface to the first German edition of *Capital*. It is worth quoting at length, not only because it provides indisputable evidence that Marx was, in some of his work, a determinist, but also because it helps us to understand what a 'science' of society involves. Marx says that in *Capital* he is setting out 'the natural laws of capitalist production . . . these tendencies working with iron necessity towards inevitable results'. He continues:

> And even when a society has got upon the right track for the discovery of the natural laws of its movement — and it is the ultimate aim of this work, to lay bare the economic law of motion of modern society — it can neither clear by bold leaps, nor remove by legal enactments, the obstacles offered by the successive phases of its normal development. But it can shorten or lessen the birth-pangs. To prevent possible misunderstanding, . . . here individuals are dealt with only in so far as they are the personifications of economic categories, embodiments of particular class-relations and class-interests. My standpoint, from which the evolution of society is viewed as a process of natural history, can less than any other make the individual responsible for relations whose creature he socially remains.[12]

Furthermore, in an Afterword to the second German edition where Marx is considering the response in the press to views stated in *Capital*, he approvingly quotes a lengthy passage from a Russian journal in which, he feels, his 'dialectical method' has been presented in an accurate and 'generous way'. The reviewer says that: 'Marx treats the social movement as a process of natural history, governed by laws not only independent of human will, consciousness and intelligence, but rather, on the contrary, determining that will, consciousness and intelligence.'[13]

On the view presented here then, individuals can do nothing to change the course of events which follow a necessary path to inevitable conclusions. No political decisions or efforts of the human will can overturn the natural process of development. All that people can do is to 'shorten or lessen the birth pangs'. The gynaecological analogy is an interesting one (it is also Marx's favourite analogy). For, as with the process of childbirth, the end result is predetermined: all one can do is to facilitate a natural process by a correct understanding of what is happening and by acting accordingly.

Structuralist Marxists. Among contemporary Marxists it is the 'structuralists', such as Louis Althusser and his followers, who are the most notable exponents of this determinist conception of historical materialism. In Chapter 7 we examine the ideas on education of Althusser, and also of Stuart Hall who, in his Review of the Open University's *Schooling and Society* course, cogently presents a structuralist determinist analysis of education. Here, however, we want to draw attention to one important feature of this Althusserian position, namely that it combines a determinist (as opposed to voluntarist) view of the social process, with an 'interaction' view of the relationship between the base and superstructure. Althusserians, in other words, believe that society is what it is not because human beings (collectively or individually) make it so, but as a consequence of the operation of certain objective 'structures and processes'. These structures and processes, however, are not just economic in nature. Superstructural factors play a part, even if the economic forces are dominant 'in the last analysis'. A consideration of the Althusserian position, then, shows that the 'base/superstructure' issue and the 'determinism/voluntarism' issue, though interlinked, are nevertheless separate disputes.

Voluntarist Marxists. Apart from the work of the 'structuralist' Marxists, however, the dominant interpretation of historical materialism in the twentieth century has been voluntarist in nature. The work of the Italian Marxist Antonio Gramsci is an example of this. In Gramsci's view it is wrong to think of Marxism (or the 'philosophy of praxis' as he often calls it) as a 'science of society' which takes natural science as its model. To seek 'the laws of the evolution of human society in such a way as to predict that the oak tree will develop out of the acorn' is an infringement of the 'dialectical principle'.[14] Such a deterministic or 'fatalistic' conception of historical materialism may, says Gramsci, have served a useful purpose in an earlier period of history. In this respect, he says, it is similar to the theory of predestination in religious thought where men would cry 'it is God's will' in order to explain or justify a certain course of events. However, this sort of fatalistic theory has had its day. For Gramsci, economic changes and crises provide only the necessary not the sufficient conditions for a change to a different and superior form of society. As he says: 'It may be ruled out that immediate economic crises themselves produce fundamental historical events.'[15] Similarly, Gramsci argues that, although technological developments are of great importance, they do not directly lead to major social changes.[16] Such changes only occur when certain 'subjective' conditions also prevail. Men must consciously intervene at favourable moments in history and grasp the opportunity which economic progress provides to create a new morality and superior type of social and political system. On this view, then, economic development 'ceases to be an external force which crushes man, assimilates him to itself and makes him passive; and is transformed into a means of freedom, an instrument to create a new ethico-political form and a source of new initiatives'.[17]

Gramsci, therefore, attempts to steer a course between what he sees as two equally untenable positions: a deterministic or 'mechanistic' view, and an excessively voluntaristic position. The latter, he believes, fails to take into account at all economic forces which, as he says, are 'objective, independent of human will' and constitute a 'refractory reality'.[18] The former does not allow for the influence of ideas on the course of history and neglects the impact of human will. Kolakowski sums up Gramsci's position here by saying that: 'He believed that the human will was not governed by any historical necessity, but he naturally did not regard it as completely unfettered.'[19]

The sort of human will that Gramsci has in mind was that exercised by the mass of the people, guided and led by a revolutionary party who have an understanding of the historical process. He believes that there must be a profound change in the consciousness of ordinary men and women before a revolution can take place. They must develop a clear view of their social conditions and of the possibilities open to them, and in this they will be assisted by intellectuals who are an integral part of a revolutionary party.

A second important voluntarist interpretation of Marxism is to be found in the 'critical theory' of the Frankfurt School. One of the main concerns of the critical theorist is with the 'positivism' of the social sciences; that is, the tendency to think that there exists 'laws' of society akin to the laws of nature. For the critical theorist this is a form of 'false consciousness' which 'reifies' what are really humanly alterable processes. (Positivism also, they believe, endorses the status quo and helps to maintain various forms of social domination.) Some contemporary critical theorists, however, recognise that Marx himself, for all his greatness, at times adopted a 'positivist' or determinist conception of society and social change. Albrecht Wellmer, for example, in his *Critical Theory of Society*, writes at length about Marx's 'latent positivism' saying that Marx conceived of his social theory 'as a "science" in the same sense as the natural sciences', and refers to one of the passages from *Capital* that we quoted above as evidence of this.[20] And Wellmer goes on to state that there is, in fact, an 'unresolved contradiction'[21] in Marx's work between such a determinist and more voluntarist (or critical) interpretation of social life.

Wellmer's conception of critical theory continues and builds on the work of other members of this school of thought such as Adorno, Marcuse and Habermas. Its aim is with the development in men of that critical consciousness or awareness which enables them actively to seek their emancipation from repression. In Wellmer's words, it is the 'insight into the history and meaning of experienced social bondage and constraint at which critical theory aims as the precondition of a process of collective emancipation'.[22] But, in addition to drawing attention to the importance of consciousness and ideology, Wellmer, like his contemporary Habermas, considers the sphere of politics to be of crucial significance in the contemporary world. In their view the political system or the state is one of the main determining forces in modern society, perhaps outweighing the economic structure in importance. Indeed, political decisions are now central to the functioning of the economic systems of the industrialised world. As a consequence, critical theorists such as Wellmer and Habermas do not look to technological progress as a basis for emancipation, but to the political activity of individuals enlightened as to their true interests. In Wellmer's summary: 'Since history itself has thoroughly discredited all hopes of an economically grounded "mechanism" of emancipation . . . the criticism and alteration of the "superstructure" have a new and decisive importance for movements of liberation.'[23]

This emphasis on the importance of the superstructure is, of course, something that critical theorists have in common with Gramsci. James Joll has said of Gramsci that perhaps he went further than any other Marxist thinker in recognising the importance of the superstructure and the force of ideas in producing historical change, as well as seeing the impossibility of establishing any precise correlation between economic circumstances and intellectual developments.[24]

Perhaps he should have added 'with the possible exception of the critical theorist'.

An 'Unresolved Contradiction'. The works of the critical theorists and of Gramsci, then, provide examples of the voluntarist interpretation of historical materialism, in contrast to the determinism of the structuralist Marxists such as Althusser. The question naturally arises: 'Which of these forms of Marxism is most in keeping with the ideas of Marx himself?' On this matter we would support the view put forward by Wellmer. There *is* an 'unresolved contradiction' in Marx's writing between a determinist conception of society and social change, and a voluntarist critical theory or philosophy of praxis. The two exist side by side in his work. Several other writers on Marx and Marxism have drawn attention to this. Alvin Gouldner, for example, has entitled a recent book on the subject *The Two Marxisms*, in which he argues that 'the internal contradictions of Marxism . . . have been with it from the first'[25] — by which he means in the work of Marx and Engels. Furthermore, Gouldner stresses that both the determinist and voluntarist readings of Marxism

> are a true part of Marxism. We are not faced with only a *seeming* contradiction that can be glibly resolved by claiming that one side is false, revisionist, opportunist, misguided, not really Marxist, while the other is the authentic, genuine, dyed-in-the-wool, true revolutionary article[26]

Similarly, Tom Bottomore, in his *Marxist Sociology*, states that it is

> necessary to establish, as a starting-point, that Marx's conceptions were capable of giving rise, in one direction, to a broadly positivist sociology, and in another direction to a style of thought which has generally been referred to as 'critical philosophy'; and that these possibilities existed side by side in his thought from the outset, even though the emphasis in his early writings appears more Hegelian, and in his later writings more positivist.[27]

Naturally, some Marxists, and certain interpreters of Marx, deny this view. Georg Lukács, for example, argues that 'Fatalism and voluntarism are only mutually contradictory to an undialectical and unhistorical mind. In the dialectical view of history they prove to be necessarily complementary opposites.'[28] For Lukács the vital factor is the 'class consciousness' of the proletariat. As he says: 'Class consciousness is . . . the point at which the economic necessity of its struggle for liberation changes dialectically into freedom.'[29] Kolakowski interprets the essence of Marxism in the same way. In the consciousness of the proletariat, he says, 'the opposition of freedom and necessity disappears, for what is in fact the inevitability of history takes the form of a free initiative in the proletariat's consciousness'.[30] Or again: 'In the class-consciousness of the proletariat, historical necessity coincides with freedom of action; the opposition between human will and the "objective" course of events' ceases to exist;[31] in the revolutionary action of the proletariat we find 'a free activity which is nevertheless historically necessary'.[32]

However, we can make little sense of such a view. To claim that an action is both free *and* determined is to infringe a fundamental law of logic, namely the Principle of Non-Contradiction which states that nothing can be both A and not-A at the same time. For example, an object cannot be both wholly red *and* wholly green or wholly yellow (that is, not wholly red). Likewise an action cannot be both free and determined (that is, not free). For if an action is free it means that it is not determined, and if it is determined it means it is not free. We therefore find Lukács's position unintelligible. The only way in which it can become meaningful is if 'freedom' is defined in a very restricted manner, not as 'self-determination' but as 'the recognition of necessity'.

Class Conflict

Finally we must say a word about the role of class conflict in Marxist theory. Our account so far has concentrated on the relationship between the forces and relations of production, the superstructure of society, economic determinism of Marxism, etc. Little mention has been made of the notion of class conflict. And yet, when most people think about Marxism, they probably think of it as predominantly a theory of class conflict; and are perhaps able to call to mind such statements by Marx and Engels as: 'The history of all hitherto existing society is the history of class struggle.'[33] What, then, in the light of our discussion so far, is the role of class conflict in Marxist theory?

Once again one cannot give an unambiguous answer on the basis of an inspection of the writings of Marx. In so far as the concept of the 'relations of production' is defined in terms of social class relations (as we suggested earlier) then, as a constituent of the economic base, class conflict obviously has a central role — as long as Marxism is conceived as a form of economic determinism. However, if superstructural factors are granted a greater autonomy, the role of class conflict in history necessarily subsides. In addition — just to complicate matters further — Marx and Engels sometimes speak as if the relations of production were not synonymous with social class relations. They state that the contradiction within the economic base between the forces and relations of production is 'expressed' in the form of class conflict. For example, in *The German Ideology* Marx and Engels say:

> Thus all collisions in history have their origin, in our view, in the contradiction between productive forces and the forms of intercourse . . . This contradiction between the productive forces and the forms of intercourse, which as we saw has occurred several times in past history . . . necessarily on each occasion burst out in a revolution, taking on at the same time various subsidiary forms, such as allembracing collisions, collisions of various classes, contradictions of consciousness, battles of ideas etc., political conflicts, etc.[34]

On this view, then, class conflict is said to be a subsidiary form of the basic conflict in history between forces and relations of production. The idea is that the clash of economic forces sets in motion class conflict, as well as political conflict etc. Class conflict, then, certainly has an important role but, in this statement of historical materialism, not a central, determining role.

Before we move on to a consideration of the Marxist conception of man and of the 'good society', we should perhaps note that in our account of historical materialism we have largely confined ourselves to exposition. On the whole, we have abstained from any comments on the validity of this conception of society and social change. This is the subject of the first part of the final chapter of this section, Chapter 9. However, if the reader wishes, he or she could now turn to that commentary (p. 198) before moving on to our discussion of other aspects of Marxism.

ALIENATION AND COMMUNISM

Alienation

Central to Marx's critique of contemporary society is the concept of alienation. Marx's classic formulation of the idea is to be found in the section of the *Economic and Philosophical Manuscripts* entitled 'Alienated Labour'. Although the reference here is to 'labour', it soon becomes clear that, for Marx, labour or 'production' are synonymous with 'life activity' or, more simply, 'life'. Alienated labour, therefore, means 'alienated life'.

Marx distinguishes four aspects of alienated labour.

1. Man is alienated from his product. When human beings work their labour is 'embodied in an object and turned into a physical thing'.[35] Such 'objectification' is a normal part of human life. However, objectification is turned into alienation when the object produced by man becomes 'alien to him and . . . stands opposed to him as an autonomous power. The life which he has given to the object sets itself against him as an alien and hostile force'. That which man has created comes to 'dominate him'.

2. Man is alienated not only from the product of labour but also from the process of producing or his work activity. In a famous passage Marx says:

> What constitutes this alienation of labour? First, that the work is *external* to the worker, that it is not part of his nature; and that, consequently, he does not fulfil himself in his work but denies himself, has a feeling of misery rather than well-being, does not develop freely his mental and physical energies but is physically exhausted and mentally debased. The worker, therefore, feels himself at home only during his leisure time, whereas at work he feels homeless. His work is not voluntary but imposed, *forced labour*. It is not the satisfaction of a need, but only a *means* for satisfying other needs. Its alien character is shown by the fact that as soon as there is no physical or other compulsion it is avoided like the plague.

With alienation there is no 'joy in producing and . . . enjoyment of the product'.

3. Man is alienated from his 'species-being', his human or social being. Species-life, according to Marx, is free, conscious activity. It involves the manipulation of nature by man for his own purposes. Through species-activity 'nature appears as his work and his reality . . . and he sees his own reflection in a world which he has constructed'. Under alienation all this is absent. Man's labour is not 'free and self-directed'. His life activity becomes a means to an end, rather than an end-in-itself. It is simply an instrument to be used for keeping alive or

obtaining the necessities of existence, such as food and shelter.

4. 'A direct consequence of the alienation of man from the product of his labour, from his life activity and from his species-life, is that man is alienated from other men. When man confronts himself, he confronts other men.' Alienation is therefore 'expressed' in the relationships between men. In so far as my labour and the product of my labour are alien to me and do not 'belong' to me, they must belong to, or be the property of another man — the capitalist. The capitalist appropriates what I produce and makes it his private property. Through his ownership of the product of labour and his control of the process of producing, he exercises power over the worker. The worker, therefore, is 'under the domination, coercion and yoke' of the capitalist. Thus the basis for social division and class conflict is laid in alienation and private property.

In Chapter 3, we pointed out — following Lukes — that the concept of alienation can only be properly understood if one knows what it is *not* to be alienated. In other words, the meaning of the term only becomes fully clear if one takes into account Marx's conception of the 'good society', that is, his view of the 'healthy' or 'natural' condition of the individual in society. Furthermore, such a conception involves or presupposes a theory of human nature. Hence we must now turn to a consideration of Marx's notion of communism and his view of the nature of man.

Communism

Communism is a crucial category in Marx's work. However, it has often been observed that Marx's descriptions of that condition are extremely thin and are scattered throughout his writing. Indeed, what Marx has to say about communism is rather like what the Bible has to say about heaven, that is, very little.[36] Nevertheless, one can construct a fairly complete picture of Marx's view of the good society without too much difficulty.

Communism involves the complete transformation of human existence. It is a society in which the essential nature of man is fully expressed. Under communism, therefore, alienation and its accompanying features — private property, class conflict and domination — will disappear. As Marx says, in the sort of prose typical of the *Manuscripts*, 'Communism is the positive abolition of private property, of human self-alienation, and thus the real appropriation of human nature through and for man.'[37]

Thus what is *absent* under capitalism will be *present* with the realisation of communism. Men will no longer be alienated from their products, from the process of producing, from their species-being and from their fellow men. This means, in the first place, that the process of objectification becomes a means of 'affirming' the life of man rather than denying it. In the essay 'On James Mill', Marx explains in more detail what this affirmation involves. He writes:

> Supposing that we had produced in a human manner; each of us would in his production have doubly affirmed himself and his fellow men. I would have: (i) objectified in my production my individuality and its peculiarity and thus both in my activity enjoyed an individual expression of my life and also in looking at the object have had the individual pleasure of realizing that my personality was objective, visible to the senses and thus a power raised beyond all doubt. (ii) In your enjoyment or use of my product I would have had the direct enjoyment of realizing that I had both satisfied a human need by my work and also objectified the human essence and therefore fashioned for another human being the object that met his need. (iii) I would have been for you the mediator between you and the species and thus been acknowledged and felt by you as a completion of your own essence and a necessary part of yourself and thus have realized that I am confirmed both in your thought and in your love. (iv) In my expression of my life I would have fashioned your expression of your life, and thus in my own activity have realized my own essence, my human, my communal essence.
>
> In that case our products would be like so many mirrors, out of which our essence shone.[38]

Objectification, therefore, is naturally a form of self-expression and self-knowledge. The objects people create are a manifestation of their personality and evidence of their essential human capacities. Through this process men reveal their nature and attain a sense of their identity. In other words, they come to understand and know themselves by means of the externalisation of their powers.

In addition, the process of production is itself a rewarding experience. Men feel the 'joy of producing'. Labour is no longer toil, but a creative activity in which men find fulfilment and intrinsic satisfaction. It is also a form of self-realisation. Through their work human beings develop their capacities and potentialities. Marx speaks of labour as a process of 'self-creation' whereby men make themselves what they have it in them to be. Through their activity they bring out or make actual what exists in them in potential. Marx in fact stresses that such self-creation occurs not only under communism, but throughout human history. As he says in *Capital*:

> Labour is, in the first place, a process in which both man and Nature participate . . . By thus acting on the external world and changing it, he at the same time changes his own nature. He develops his slumbering powers and compels them to act in obedience to his sway.[39]

However, full human development occurs only under communism. In communist society we find the all-round development of the individual. Men are no longer confined in their work to a single task, as is the case with the narrow division of labour under capitalism. Rather:

> in communist society, where nobody has one exclusive sphere of activity but each can become accomplished in any branch he wishes, society regulates the general production and thus makes it possible for me to do one thing today and another tomorrow, to hunt in the morning, fish in the afternoon, rear cattle in the evening, criticise after dinner, just as I have a mind, without ever becoming hunter, fisherman, shepherd or critic.[40]

Communist man is, therefore, the whole man in whom we witness a many-sided development — 'the evolution of all human powers as such'.[41]

Furthermore, the self-realisation and self-knowledge experienced by the individual under communism is essentially social in nature. It is not confined to the individual concerned. For in developing my capacities and potentialities, I help others to appreciate a human being's capabilities. I 'educate' them in what it means to be human. I provide, therefore, the means whereby they can develop their powers and abilities. And, of course, they do the same for me. Self-development, then, is a co-operative, not a competitive, process. Under communism it involves the 'mutual completion' of individuals, rather than the 'mutual plundering' which is central to capitalist social relationships.[42]

For Marx, then, the good society is one in which there is no essential conflict between the self and others. Individual and social interests do not clash but coincide: the good of the individual *is* the common good and vice versa. Under communism there is no gulf between the individual and society; it is only in a capitalist system that 'species-life itself — society — appears as a system which is external to the individual and as a limitation of his original independence'.[43] With the advent of communism society does not 'confront' the individual, it 'confirms' him. Adapting

Rousseau, Marx speaks of the 'life-giving air of society'.[44] Man under communism is shown to be a social, not an egoistic, creature 'which can develop into an individual only in society'.[45] 'Only in community with others', says Marx in *The German Ideology*, 'has each individual the means of cultivating his gifts in all directions.'[46] Communism involves the full development of human individuality *and* a rich communal life.

Unity and Harmony. Marx's vision of communism, then, is of a society of perfect unity and harmony. It is a society of men at harmony with themselves which is also (and perhaps therefore) a harmonious society. Social integration and solidarity develop spontaneously as individuals identify freely with the social whole. There is no need, therefore, for a government or state whose function is both to protect the individual from the encroachments of others and to reconcile the conflicts of interest between individuals. For such conflict disappears in a society of voluntary unity which answers to the basic requirements of human nature.

This image of society as an organic community which nevertheless promotes individual self-development is, according to Kolakowski, the 'Romantic motif' in Marx's thought. (The idea of man as a self-creator is the 'Promethean' element.) However, the continuity between Marxism and Romanticism is only partial. As Kolakowski puts it:

> Romanticism in its classic form is a dream of attaining social unity by reviving some idealized feature of the past: the spiritual harmony of the Middle Ages, a rural Arcadia or the happy life of the savage, ignorant of laws and industry and contentedly identifying with the tribe. This kind of nostalgia is, of course, the reverse of Marx's viewpoint . . . Unity will be recovered not by destroying modern technology or invoking primitivism or rural idiocy, but by further technical progress . . . The destructive effects of machines cannot be cured by abolishing machines, but only by perfecting them . . . future unity will be obtained not by jettisoning the achievements of social development but by continuing it . . .[47]

Communism, for Marx, is the highly developed technological society of the *future*. The good society, in which the essential nature of man is for the first time fully revealed, is to be found at the end of mankind's process of development, not at the beginning. This means that history is the story of the progress of man towards the perfection of his nature. Furthermore, alienation (and thus private property, capitalism, etc.) are a *necessary* part of this process. They are not 'mistakes' which could have been avoided were it not for human ignorance, or the actions of a few bad men dominating and exploiting the innocent masses. Rather, for Marx, alienation is an inevitable feature of history. It is a necessary condition of the full development of human powers.

At one point in the *Manuscripts*, Marx asks: 'How does it happen that man alienates his labour? How is this alienation founded in the nature of human development?'[48] His answer is that 'The human being had to be reduced to this absolute poverty in order to be able to give birth to all his inner wealth.'[49] Marx's position on this question indicates, we believe, his indebtedness to Hegel. John Plamenatz explains Hegel's view of the necessity of alienation as follows. According to Hegel:

> The self must be thrown back upon itself, it must feel isolated in its environment, detached from it and oppressed by it, if it is to become deeply self-conscious. An intense self-awareness which necessarily takes the form of self-estrangement, must precede the full attainment of freedom . . . [Man] must first feel himself to be a stranger in the world before he can become fully at home in it; he must have a profound sense of his own unworthiness before he can fully appreciate the dignity of man.[50]

This can also serve as a summary of Marx's view. The experience of alienation and self-estrangement is an important formative influence on man's development; it is part of the process of achieving human freedom and self-realisation. As Plamenatz says — this time summarising the ideas of Marx — 'Alienation, of course, is not in itself liberating but it is an experience to be passed through on the way to liberation.'[51]

COMMENTS

Although we want to reserve our criticisms of historical materialism for Chapter 9, the final one of this section of the book, we wish at this point to make some brief comments on the Marxist conception of alienation, communism and human nature.

At the end of his three-volume study of Marxist doctrine, Kolakowski observes that: 'Marxism has been the greatest fantasy of our century. It was a dream offering the prospect of a society of perfect unity, in which all human aspirations would be fulfilled and all values reconciled.'[52] But is there any reason to suppose that all values are reconcilable, and that such unity is either possible or desirable?

Many writers in both the liberal and (non-Marxist) socialist traditions argue that conflicts of values are inherent in any complex form of social life. This is because, in the words of Isaiah Berlin, 'the ends of men are many and not all of them are in principle compatible with each other'.[53] Quite simply, we cannot have everything. Choices between conflicting, and equally ultimate, ends have to be made and compromises established. Kolakowski provides one expression of this viewpoint when he says that:

> If socialism is to be anything more than a totalitarian prison it can only be a system of compromises between different values that limit one another. All-embracing economic planning, even if it were possible to achieve . . . is incompatible with the autonomy of small producers and regional units, and this autonomy is a traditional value of socialism, though not of Marxist socialism. Technical progress cannot coexist with absolute security of living conditions for everyone. Conflicts inevitably arise between freedom and equality, planning and the autonomy of small groups, economic democracy and efficient management, and these conflicts can only be mitigated by compromise and partial solutions.[54]

Marxists, on the other hand, assume that all good things are intrinsically compatible with one another, and that eventually all men will pursue the same ends and share the same view of the world.

But it is not just values that conflict. There are also important conflicts of interest between men. Although some of these derive from economic causes, there are others which have nothing to do with private property and class divisions but have their origin in religious, linguistic, racial and cultural differences. Marxism has always ignored these bases of social antagonism, or else has seen them as rooted in class divisions and a product of alienation. As a consequence, it has always been insensitive to the complex nature of social conflict and to the need for that form of political activity by means of which different interests can be conciliated.

We see no reason, therefore, to accept the view that, with the abolition of private property, the division of labour and the class domination deriving from them, there will be an end to human conflict. Similarly, we find it difficult to believe that evil and suffering will make a sudden exit from the stage of history, and that individual and social purposes will merge. It may well be that men have a greater potential for human sympathy and fellow-feeling than has so far been exhibited in history. But one does not have to be a convinced Hobbesian to take the view that elements of self-love and self-seeking will still remain and that there will be a need for some form of social control in any society of the future. Some degree of coercion and restraint of the individual through law, government and more informal means seems to be a permanent part of the human condition.

Marx's vision of communism, then, is no more than a millennial dream. It is certainly not a serious programme for the reorganisation of society. Nowhere are we told just how alienated men are to become de-alienated. It is merely assumed to be a part of the process of human development and the outcome of a purifying experience of 'revolutionary praxis'. Plamenatz sums up the point well when he says: 'Marx, who had so much that is suggestive to say about alienation, its causes and its symptoms, had very little that is useful to say about how to get rid of it.'[55]

All this should not be taken to mean, of course, that someone who rejects the Marxist conception of the good society and human nature must, therefore, be satisfied with the existing state of affairs. Marxists would often have us believe that this is so. In reality, however, the liberal and non-Marxist socialist traditions of thought display a constant concern for greater economic and social justice, the reduction and elimination of poverty, the maintenance and extension of individual and democratic freedoms in the face of encroachments by state bureaucracy, etc., without being encumbered by the disabling notion of an earthly paradise just around the corner.

NOTES

1. L. Kolakowski, *Main Currents of Marxism* (Clarendon Press, Oxford, 1978), vol. 1, p. vi. And even the above statement would be contested by some writers.

2. K. Marx, Preface to *A Contribution to a Critique of Political Economy* in *Marx and Engels, Selected Works* (Lawrence and Wishart, London, 1968), pp. 182–3.

3. F. Engels, Letter to Schmidt in *Selected Works*, p. 699.

4. See, for example, L. Althusser, *For Marx* (Penguin, Harmondsworth, 1969) and R. Miliband, *Marxism and Politics* (Oxford University Press, Oxford, 1977).

5. Miliband, *Marxism and Politics*, p. 9.

6. On the nature of the relations of production see H.B. Acton, *The Illusion of the Epoch* (Cohen and West, London, 1962), and J.P. Plamenatz, *Man and Society* (Longman, London, 1963), vol. 2, ch. 5.

7. K. Marx, *The Poverty of Philosophy*. Quoted in Plamenatz, *Man and Society*, p. 275.

8. K. Marx, *Wage Labour and Capital* in *Selected Works*, p. 81.

9. Marx, Preface to *The Critique*.

10. K. Marx and F. Engels, *The Communist Manifesto* in *Selected Works*, p. 38.

11. Plamenatz, *Man and Society*, pp. 282–3.

12. K. Marx, *Capital* (Lawrence and Wishart, London, 1974), vol. 1, pp. 20–1.

13. Ibid., p. 27.

14. Q. Hoare and G. Nowell Smith (eds.), *Selections from the Prison Notebooks of Antonio Gramsci* (Lawrence and Wishart, London, 1971), p. 426.

15. Ibid., p. 184.

16. Ibid., p. 163.

17. Ibid., p. 367.

18. Ibid., pp. 180–1.

19. Kolakowski, *Main Currents*, vol. 3, p. 251.

20. A. Wellmer, *Critical Theory of Society* (The Seabury Press, New York, 1974), p. 68.

21. Ibid., p. 70.

22. Ibid., p. 73.

23. Ibid., p. 121.

24. J. Joll, *Gramsci* (Fontana, London, 1977), p. 85.

25. A. Gouldner, *The Two Marxisms* (Macmillan, London, 1980), p. 30.

26. Ibid., p. 34.

27. T. Bottomore, *Marxist Sociology* (Macmillan, London, 1975), p. 11.

28. G. Lukács, *History and Class Consciousness* (Merlin Press, London, 1971), p. 4.

29. Ibid., p. 42.

30. Kolakowski, *Main Currents*, vol. 1, p. 180.

31. Ibid., p. 304.

32. Ibid., p. 232.

33. Marx and Engels, *The Communist Manifesto* in *Selected Works*, p. 35.

34. K. Marx and F. Engels, *The German Ideology* (Lawrence and Wishart, London, 1965), pp. 92–3.

35. This and the quotations that follow are, until otherwise indicated, from T. Bottomore, *Karl Marx: Early Writings* (Watts, London, 1963), pp. 120–34.

36. We are indebted to Michael Jones for pointing this out to us.

37. Bottomore, *Early Writings*, p. 155. Although the notion of communism is never explicitly mentioned in the Marxists' sociology of education, this image of the good society lies behind their criticisms of contemporary education.

38. D. McLellan (ed.), *Karl Marx: Early Texts* (Blackwell, Oxford, 1971), p. 202.

39. Marx, *Capital*, vol. 1, p. 173.

40. Marx and Engels, *The German Ideology*, p. 45.

41. K. Marx, *Pre-Capitalist Economic Formations* (Lawrence and Wishart, London, 1969), p. 84.

42. McLellan (ed.), *Early Texts*, p. 194.

43. 'On the Jewish Question' in Bottomore, *Early Writings*, p. 26.

44. Ibid., p. 34. In the 'Discourse on the Origins of Inequality', Rousseau speaks of 'the health-giving air of liberty' (Dent, London, 1913), p. 146.

45. D. McLellan (ed.), *Marx's Grundrisse* (Macmillan, London, 1971), p. 17.

46. Marx and Engels, *The German Ideology*, p. 93.

47. Kolakowski, *Main Currents*, vol. 1, p. 411.

48. Bottomore, *Early Writings*, p. 133.

49. Ibid., p. 160.

50. Plamenatz, *Man and Society*, vol. 2, p. 160.

51. J.P. Plamenatz, *Karl Marx's Philosophy of Man* (Clarendon Press, Oxford, 1975), p. 154.

52. Kolakowski, *Main Currents*, vol. 3, p. 523.

53. I. Berlin, *Four Essays on Liberty* (Oxford University Press, London, 1969), p. 169.

54. Kolakowski, *Main Currents*, vol. 3, p. 528.

55. Plamenatz, in *Philosophy of Man*, p. 172.

7 THE MARXIST ANALYSIS OF EDUCATION: THEORIES OF DIRECT REPRODUCTION

We shall begin our examination of the Marxist analysis of education by considering, in this chapter, what are sometimes known as theories of 'direct reproduction'. Education, according to this view, helps to 'reproduce' or maintain the capitalist economic system. Some of these direct reproduction theories involve an economic determinist conception of society. Others — for example Miliband's — are more voluntarist in nature, emphasising that the ruling class moulds education to suit its own purposes. Finally, certain theories — notably Althusser's — whilst paying lip-service to the idea of the 'relative autonomy' of education, nevertheless see education as nothing more than an element of the 'state apparatus', the crucial function of which is to perpetuate capitalist relations of production.

In keeping with our aims as stated in the Introduction, we shall not attempt to review all of the direct reproduction literature. Rather, we shall focus on what we regard as the more important examples of the theory, that is, works in which the nature of direct reproduction theory is most clearly and comprehensively formulated, and/or those which have attracted the most attention within the sociology of education.

S. Bowles and H. Gintis

Bowles and Gintis's *Schooling in Capitalist America* is an excellent book with which to start our account of Marxist views of education, both because it contains almost all the major ideas and concepts characteristic of this school of thought and because it is so clearly written. The book is free from the disfiguring jargon and perverse style so characteristic of much of modern sociology.

The fundamental idea of the book is that education cannot be understood independently of the society of which it is a part. Rather, it is tied to society's basic economic and social institutions. This is true, Bowles and Gintis argue, of both the 'capitalist' societies of the West and the 'state socialist' societies of Eastern Europe such as Russia (and they think that in certain respects the economic systems of both capitalism and state socialism are similar, namely 'in their respective mechanisms of social control in the economic sphere').[1] However, the main focus of their attention is Western capitalist society and, in particular, the United States.

Education in the United States, they argue, serves to perpetuate or 'reproduce' the capitalist system. It is one of several social institutions which maintain or reinforce the existing social and economic order. Because of this, education cannot act as a force for social change promoting greater equality and social justice. In this respect, it is similar to the state and government. As Bowles and Gintis say: 'education and state policy are relatively powerless to rectify social problems within the framework of a capitalist economy.'[2] Anyone who thinks that education can contribute to the solution of social problems has an 'incomplete understanding of the economic system'.[3] Indeed, only through an analysis of American capitalism 'can one understand the workings of the U.S. educational system'.[4] 'The Capitalist Economy', says the title of Chapter 3, is 'At The Root Of The Problem'.

THE CAPITALIST SYSTEM: THE NEED FOR REPRODUCTION

Bowles and Gintis think it is necessary, therefore, to describe the main features of the capitalist system; and their main points are well summarised at the beginning of Chapter 3.

'The U.S. economy', they say, 'is a formally totalitarian system in which the actions of the vast majority (workers) are controlled by a small minority (owners and managers).'[5] This contrasts with the political system of the country which is 'formally democratic'. (We shall comment on this identification of 'totalitarian' with 'undemocratic' later in the chapter, see p. 147.) 'The undemocratic structure of economic life in the U.S.', they go on to say, 'may be traced directly to the moving force in the capitalist system: the quest for profits.'[6] The quest for profit, or surplus value as it is also called, involves 'exacting from labour as much work as possible in return for the lowest possible wages'.[7] Naturally, this produces conflict between the two sides of industry. But in this conflict the capitalists, on the whole, have control of the situation. First and foremost, this is because of 'the market and property relations of capitalism' in which one finds 'the severely unequal ownership of productive and financial resources'. Such unequal private ownership bestows control of economic activities on the owners and managers and 'give[s] rise to relations of dominance and subordinacy within the confines of the capitalist enterprise'.[8]

Even so, the power position of the owners and managers is not secure; it can be threatened by the potential unity of the workers. The dominance of capitalists is, however, maintained or reproduced in various ways.[9] First-ly, by the existence of a pool of unemployed labour which weakens the bargaining position of the workers and which is, according to Bowles and Gintis, a further aspect of the 'market and property relations' of capitalism. Education, they argue, helps to maintain this pool. Second-ly, there is 'the direct application of force' through the use of 'the police power of the state' and the passage of anti-trade union legislation. Bowles and Gintis point out, however, that: 'It is precisely against this solution that workers have fought their major battles and won some significant victories over the past century.'[10] But the use of such force can be counter-productive anyway. The long-run success of the system depends on (1) 'a widely accepted ideology justifying the social order' and (2) a set of 'social relationships which both validates this ideology through everyday experience, and fragments the ruled into mutually indifferent or an-tagonistic groups'.[11] In other words, it is not just a matter of people holding certain beliefs about the rightness of the system, but of their being ac-customed to social relationships which reinforce these beliefs or make them seem plausible and realistic.

In the American capitalist system the 'ideology' is provided by the 'technocratic–meritocratic' theory (about which more will be said shortly); and the set of 'social relationships' are the 'social relations of work' to be found in the corporate capitalist system. The main characteristic of such social relations of work is that individuals experience little control over decision-making and work activities. There exists, first, an hierar-chical division of labour, i.e. 'control over work processes is arranged in vertical layers of increasing authority with ultimate power resting nearly exclusively in the top echelon of owners and managers'.[12] Secondly, there is a system of 'bureaucratic authority' whereby 'activities are governed by regulations promulgated by management'.[13] Essentially, this amounts to saying that the control of the production process is not in the hands of the producers themselves but of 'non-workers', i.e. owners and managers.

These then are ways in which 'the class and power relations of economic life' are perpetuated or reproduced. Bowles and Gintis go on to say that they have very important implications (1) for economic in-equality — over and above that so far discussed — and (2) for personal development.

By economic inequality, Bowles and Gintis mean the inequalities in the distribution of income, wealth and job opportunities which, they claim, stem from the class structure or the property and market institutions of capitalism and which, as we have noted, also embody certain crucial inequalities. They argue that access to a job depends on the individual's class, age, sex, race, etc. rather than on talent, ability, qualifications and job experience — facts which run counter to the 'technocratic–meritocratic' ideology. As for personal development, Bowles and Gintis take the view that the capitalist enterprise is inimical to such self-development.

> We suggest [they say] that the nature of work is a fundamental determinant of personal development; a central factor being the degree to which workers have control over planning, decision-making, and execution of production and tasks, as well as sufficient autonomy to express their creative needs and capacities. In capitalist society (due to the operation of the forces outlined . . .) work is largely devoid of these qualities for most people.[14]

Work, therefore, is 'alienated'; and Bowles and Gintis stress that this is not a result of modern technology, but is rooted in the way that modern technology is used in the class-based 'relations of production'.

Education's Contribution to Reproduction

Education fits into the picture in the following way. As we have just seen, the dominance of the capitalist class needs to be maintained or reproduced in the face of potential opposition by a united movement of working people. Education is one of the means by which this is accomplished. As Bowles and Gintis say: 'The educational system is an integral element in the reproduction of the prevailing class structure of society.'[15]

It does this in two main ways: firstly, it justifies or legitimates the class structure and inequality by fostering the belief that economic success depends essentially on the possession of ability and the appropriate skills or education; and, secondly, it prepares young people for their place in the world of class-dominated and alienated work by creating those capacities, qualifications, ideas and beliefs which are appropriate to a capitalist economy. Put differently, the function of education is reproduction and this takes place by means of legitimation and socialisation. (There is an interesting similarity here to Parsons's analysis, where the functions of education are said to be 'socialization' and 'selection'. A major difference, however, between Parsons and Bowles and Gintis is that, whereas Parsons is clearly in favour of the social system for which children are being socialised and selected, Bowles and Gintis disapprove of the society which is being reproduced.)

Legitimation. With regard to the first of these means of reproduction — legitimation — Bowles and Gintis argue that the educational system transmits the 'technocratic–meritocratic ideology' or, as they also call it, the 'ideology of equal educational opportunity and meritocracy'. This ideology has been expounded by, among others, the sociologists Davis and Moore in their article on the functionalist theory of stratification. In Davis and Moore's view, inequalities of income, wealth and status are justified by the fact that the most important positions in society need to be filled by the most talented people. Such people need to undergo a period of training for these positions which requires sacrifices of one kind or another on their part. In order to induce people to undertake this training, society must offer inducements in the form of high income and high prestige; consequently, inequality is both necessary and desirable. As Davis and Moore put it: social stratification — or economic inequality and the hierarchical division of labour, in Bowles and Gintis's terms — 'is thus an unconsciously evolved device by which societies ensure that the most important positions are conscientiously filled by the most qualified persons'.[16]

Bowles and Gintis criticise this view on the grounds that it is an ideological façade. They argue that ability (which they take as synonymous with IQ) is not an important criterion for economic success; rather what matters is a person's socio-economic background.

Socialisation. As for the second method of reproduction — socialisation — the authors argue that this occurs essentially through the shaping of the worker's 'consciousness'. As Bowles and Gintis say:

> it is clear that the consciousness of workers — beliefs, values, self-concepts, types of solidarity and fragmentation, as well as modes of personal behaviour and development — are integral to the perpetuation, validation and smooth operation of economic institutions. The reproduction of the social relations of production depends on the reproduction of consciousness.[17]

Such beliefs, values, etc., they say, develop in a person's social relationships. The relationships encountered at work are very important in fostering these beliefs and values, but so too are those of the family and those found in the educational system. With regard to education, Bowles and Gintis assert that it 'tailors the self-concepts, aspirations, and social class identifications of individuals to the requirements of the social division of labour'.[18] More specifically, 'schools reward docility, passivity and obedience . . . [and] penalise creativity and spontaneity'.[19] Schools try to teach people to be 'properly subordinate'; they seek to destroy initiative and the capacity for self-determination or self-development; and schools attempt to render individuals incapable of acting together so as to control their economic and social activities. Furthermore, they do all this because the capitalist economic system 'requires it': the world of alienated work demands alienated personnel and 'one-dimensional patterns of human development'.

The Correspondence Principle

Bowles and Gintis then go on to consider the question of *how* this is achieved. They argue that it is attained by means of the 'correspondence principle'. They use the term correspondence because of the fact that it appears in Marx's famous Preface to *A Contribution to a Critique of Political Economy*, where he speaks of the 'relations of production' being 'the real foundation on which rises the legal and political superstructure and to which *correspond* definite forms of social consciousness'. They describe the correspondence principle in the following way:

> the educational system operates in this manner not so much through the conscious intentions of teachers and administrators in their day-to-day activities, but through a close correspondence between the social relationships which govern personal interaction in the work place and the social relationships of the educational system. Specifically, the relationships of authority and control between administrators and teachers, teachers and students, and students and their work replicate the hierarchical division of labour which dominates the work place.[20]

In other words, it is through the 'form' of the educational system rather than through its 'content' that the process of socialisation takes place. It constitutes the hidden curriculum of the school.

The correspondence between the social relations of education and those of work has four main aspects. First, students, like workers, have little power: their control of the curriculum is minimal and is similar, therefore, to that of the workers over the content of their jobs. Second, education, like work, is seen as a means to an end rather than an end in itself. Neither are intrinsically satisfying but are undertaken (1) for the sake of 'external' rewards — qualifications and wages — and (2) to avoid unpleasant consequences — educational failure and unemployment. Third, the division of labour at work, which confers on each person a narrow range of tasks and engenders a disunity among the workforce, is repeated in the specialisation and compartmentalisation of knowledge, and in the unnecessary competition between students. Finally, the different 'levels' of education correspond to, and prepare people for, the different 'levels' of the occupational structure. In the secondary school the stress is on 'doing as you are told', i.e. the pupils are expected to comply with the school's rules. As they go into higher education, such 'external' controls become inappropriate: students are now expected to get on with their work unsupervised and be self-directing. In Bowles and Gintis's view they have 'internalised' the demands of administrators and teachers. All this 'corresponds' to the system of authority in industry and commerce. Workers on the shop-floor are closely supervised; upper-level white collar workers, on the other hand, will have internalised the aims and values of the organisation and will work 'independently'.

Bowles and Gintis spend some time trying to substantiate these points by drawing upon various pieces of research which, they claim, show that the same types of behaviour and the same personality traits are rewarded in both education and work, namely those required by the capitalist system. Thus 'creativity' and 'independence' are penalised in school and disapproved of at work; whereas 'perseverence', 'dependability', 'identification with the organization', 'punctuality' and so on, bring approval and are rewarded.

Bowles and Gintis then undertake an examination of certain aspects of US educational history, mainly with a view to filling out our understanding of the correspondence between education and economic life. They stress that

> The fit between schooling and work described in the previous chapters is, in one sense, too neat. The ensuing study of historical change in the U.S. school system reveals not a smooth adjustment of educational structure to economic life, but rather a jarring and conflict-ridden course of struggle and accommodation.[21]

In other words, it may be thought from what has been said so far that the capitalist class has had it all its own way, having been able to impose upon the working class the amount and type of education that has most suited its purposes. But in this section of the book, Bowles and Gintis emphasise that 'the spread of mass education can best be seen as an outcome of class conflict, not of class domination. The impetus for educational reform and expansion was provided by the growing class consciousness and political militancy of working people'.[22] Class conflict, as we have already seen, stems from the pursuit of surplus value by the owners of the means of production, and the attempt by working people to defend themselves against this exploitation. The capitalist class — again as we have seen — maintains or reproduces its position of dominance in a variety of ways including the use of education for the purpose of legitimation and socialisation. We have been led to believe by Bowles and Gintis that they were successful in this. But at this point in the book there is a change of emphasis. Bowles and Gintis now say that they meet with continual opposition (including opposition in the educational system), such that the capitalists have to make concessions. This is not to say that the workers get what *they* demand: Bowles and Gintis are as much against the 'popular demand' theory of education as the 'class domination' theory or, as we would say, the 'conspiracy theory'. Rather, they argue, the two sides negotiate a 'compromise'. As they say: 'The evolution of U.S. education over the last century and a half was the result of a compromise.'[23] But it has been a compromise which enables the capitalists to hold on to their power. As the authors put it:

> In supporting greater access to education, the progressive elements in the capitalist class were not so much giving the workers what they wanted as giving what would minimize the erosion of their power and privilege within the structure of production. Educational change has historically played the role not of a complement to economic reform but as a substitute for it.[24]

Education and the Economic Structure

One final point should be noted about Bowles and Gintis's analysis of historical changes. They argue that in this analysis they have gone beyond just demonstrating a correspondence between education and economic activity, and established 'a strong prima facie case for the causal importance of economic structure as a major determinant of educational structure'.[25] However, even though a causal account is proposed, Bowles and Gintis also say that 'no simple or mechanistic relationship between economic structure and educational development is likely to fit the available historical evidence'.[26] For 'political factors' intervene between the educational and the economic in very complex ways. Furthermore, the authors recognise that, in other countries, the causal relationship does not hold. As they put it: 'In a few areas — such as Prussia and Scotland — where military or religious purposes dominated educational policy, mass instruction was implemented considerably before the impact of capitalist expansion was felt.'[27] Yet Bowles and Gintis do not consider the implication of these statements for their general Marxist thesis. At times they seem to abandon their economic determinist conception of society in favour of a theory of relative autonomy.

In summary, then, Bowles and Gintis's whole theory breaks down into three parts: (1) what education does — reproduction, (2) how it does it — the correspondence principle; and (3) the forces responsible for reproduction — primarily the economic structure.

SOCIALISM AS AN ALTERNATIVE

The final part of Bowles and Gintis's book is a consideration of a 'radical' and 'revolutionary' alternative to the present state of things, an alternative they describe as 'socialism'.

Economic Democracy

The problem with capitalism, as they see it, is the 'undemocratic struc-ture of economic life', namely that a minority owns the productive resources of the community and is thereby able to control the activities of the majority. Socialism would involve, first, the abolition of such private ownership and, second, control of the productive process by the mass of working people. These socialist aims, Bowles and Gintis stress, 'go beyond the achievement of the Soviet Union and countries of Eastern Europe'.[28] (Note their wording here; they do not argue for a fundamen-tally different form of socialism from that found in the Communist bloc; rather for something that 'goes beyond' its 'achievement'.) Bowles and Gintis argue that, whilst these societies have certainly reduced economic inequality (presumably in the sense of differences of income), they have introduced or maintained 'the relationships of economic control, dominance and subordination characteristic of capitalism'.[29] In other words, the abolition of private ownership of the means of production (the first aim of socialism noted above) has not brought with it the control of the production process by working people (the second socialist aim). In effect, there is no 'economic democracy'.

For Bowles and Gintis, 'Socialism is a system of economic and political democracy in which individuals have the right and obligation to struc-ture their work lives through direct participatory control.'[30] Democracy, or the participatory control of one's life, is important in their view because it is the primary means of human self-development and of the fulfilment of capacities and potentialities. *Economic* democracy provides an alter-native to the system of 'wage-labour' found in capitalist societies and eliminates the dominance of one group over another in the economic sphere. (The fact that under Eastern European Communism there is no *political* democracy, let alone economic democracy, is something Bowles and Gintis choose to ignore.) However, they argue that as a consequence of these changes work would no longer be 'alienated', though they do stress that all members of the community will have a 'legal obligation . . . to share equitably in performing those socially necessary jobs which are, on balance, personally unrewarding and would not be voluntarily filled'.[31] So the 'realm of necessity' — in Marx's phrase — will still remain; not all work will be personally rewarding and a means of self-development. Economic democracy also brings with it, they assert, increased economic efficiency and a more equal division of income. It will also make political life in the United States more democratic because 'all of the glaring inadequacies of political democracy in the U.S. are attributable to the private ownership of the means of production and the lack of real economic democracy'.[32] (That the economic inadequacies of contemporary Communism may be due to the complete absence of political democracy is a point which escapes them.) Political functions will remain for there will still be conflicts or disputes between groups and regions, and government will need to act as mediator. Furthermore, economic democracy will 'liberate' education: education will become a genuine means of promoting personal development and equality. There will be a 'democratic and participatory classroom' (the nature of which is not explained), but the preparation of the young for the world of work will continue. Education would, therefore, still have an 'economic function'. As they say, 'An educational system thus freed from the legitimation of privilege could turn its energies towards rendering the development of work skills a pleasant and desirable complement to an individual's life plans.'[33]

The Need for Authority

Another important feature of Bowles and Gintis's conception of the 'good society' is that, although, throughout the book, they criticise the arbitrary authority endemic to capitalist societies, they do not wish to see the abolition of authority as such. On the contrary, they think it is an abiding necessity in human society. This is because of what they see as the inevitable conflict between the individual and the community or society. In this, of course, they are very unMarxian. As we have noted in the previous chapter, Marx takes the view that there is an essential harmony between the individual and society; indeed, that it is wrong to speak of 'society' as something separate from the individual human beings who compose it.

Bowles and Gintis, on the other hand, argue that for the individual there must be 'a submission to the requirements of social life'. Society must reproduce or maintain itself (note that reproduction occurs not only under capitalism) and this is only possible if there are certain 'constraints' imposed upon the individual's freedom, spontaneity and autonomy. This repression of the individual is a preparation for life in the community. Schools, like other social institutions, have an important part to play in this. In a rather Durkheimian way, Bowles and Gintis argue that: 'The teacher is delegated by society to mediate the passage to adulthood . . .'[34] Consequently there is an inevitable conflict (or contradiction as Bowles and Gintis like to say — in Marxist fashion) between teachers and pupils or students. To deny the necessity for such 'social control' and to demand 'a release from the bonds of authority', as some radical teachers do, is to be immune to 'the realities of everyday life'.

Although with respect to the issue of the relationship between the individual and society Bowles and Gintis depart from Marxian orthodoxy, in other respects they follow the traditional line of thought. For example, in the final chapter they consider, once again, the 'contradictions of capitalism' and assert that a basic contradiction exists between — in Marxist terms — the 'forces' and the 'relations' of production. As they put it:

> The power, class and institutional arrangements of capitalist society do not permit the full exploitation of the benefits of those productive forces that the capitalist growth process has brought into being. Modern capitalism is characterised by a set of highly advanced technological possibilities played out in the confines of a backward and retarding set of social relationships.[35]

The result is the familiar crises — familiar, that is, to Marxists — of the capitalist system.

COMMENTS

We will make some further points about Bowles and Gintis's book in the final chapter of this section, Chapter 9, where we consider the validity of the Marxist approach as a whole. However, there are certain points relating specifically to *Schooling in Capitalist America* that it is appropriate to deal with here.

The authors attempt to demonstrate statistically that the belief that economic rewards are based on ability is erroneous. Economic rewards, they argue, are determined more by social class background. To prove

Figure 7.1: Bowles and Gintis's Framework for a Path Analysis

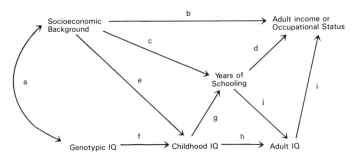

Source: S. Bowles and H. Gintis, *Schooling in Capitalist America* (Routledge and Kegan Paul, London, 1976), p. 133.

their case they construct a 'path diagram' in which the lines of influence are laid out (Figure 7.1), and they calculate the strength of the various influences using survey data. Their statistics reveal that IQ is less influential than background when it comes to determining adult income. However, Coxhead has noted that there is no path between background and adult IQ.[36] Using Bowles and Gintis's data, he calculates it and finds that background is negatively related to adult IQ. In other words, the higher the social class the less effect it has on IQ scores for older people but the more effect it has for young children. As Coxhead says: 'this implies, if the figures are correct, some mechanism whereby, starting with a fixed Child I.Q., Adult I.Q. is differentially reduced for individuals of high social background relative to those of low social background.'[37] Coxhead tries to find other path models and comes up with equally strange results; for example, Child IQ is negatively related to education. This indicates, he suggests, that the original data is suspect, and indeed Bowles and Gintis have combined data from different studies as well as including estimates. Thus Bowles and Gintis have not proved their case; however, these considerations do not disprove their theory that education, by being presented as a ladder for able people, legitimates the social class system — they merely cast doubt upon the evidence used to support the thesis.

There is another methodological criticism we wish to make. Bowles and Gintis argue that the 'personality traits' rewarded by education are similar to those rewarded by the economy. As part of this argument they assert that 'creativity' is not rewarded in education — which in capitalist society is alienating rather than personally fulfilling. Many people, however, would feel that education does foster and reward creativity; yet

Bowles and Gintis's data show that this is not the case. However, when we look at the way that the authors define creativity, we find that the characteristics of 'positive creativity' are defned in the following way: 'Inventive; is always coming up with new ideas; sometimes crazy, unrealistic ones; thinks of unusual (often weird) possibilities for solving problems.' To be negative on creativity is to be: 'Practical-minded; is the most sensible; often comes up with good useful ideas but rarely unrealistic or impractical ideas.'[38] We wonder into which category Leonardo da Vinci would have been placed! It should be obvious that words like crazy and unrealistic indicate a rather different notion of 'creativity' from that normally held. Because of this we must be very cautious in our acceptance of Bowles and Gintis's claim that education rewards the same personality traits as the economy. As a general point, there are always difficulties in interpreting statistical data and it is essential to look at the criteria which are used to locate people into class or personality groupings. Equally, we need to keep in mind when looking at replies to questions that the respondents may place different interpretations on key terms from those intended by the researchers.

A closely related criticism concerns the assertion that different types of school correspond to different levels in the economy. They suggest that predominantly working-class schools tend to emphasise rule following. Bowles and Gintis's assertion, however, is not self-evidently correct, nor do they produce much evidence to substantiate their point. We would suggest, in fact, that it is the more academically orientated schools and streams in which there is more rule following and behavioural control, though admittedly in the pursuit of academic grades. A little later in the book Bowles and Gintis quote Binstock's research in support of their argument. They write: 'Binstock found that institutions that enroll working-class students and are geared to staff lower-level jobs in the production hierarchy emphasise followership and behavioural control.'[39] However, as they note, Binstock's evidence is based on an analysis of college and university handbooks, and there is sometimes a world of difference between the formal rules and regulations of an institution and their implementation in everyday life. Once again, therefore, their evidence is suspect.

Moving on from the methodological criticisms of Bowles and Gintis's work we would note, firstly, that there is little mention of the *content* of education in the book, which suggests that it is unimportant in the process of reproduction. This seems to be a rather odd omission as we would argue that the knowledge transmitted by education, and the ways of thinking which underlie it, are very important contributors to people's views of themselves and their society. Failure to deal with this constitutes a major defect of their work.

Secondly, and as previously noted, Bowles and Gintis use the terms 'totalitarian' and 'undemocratic' synonymously. However, it is quite clearly the case that a society, or particular institutions within a society, can be undemocratic without being totalitarian (although a totalitarian society would necessarily be undemocratic). There are many forms of political system besides democracies and totalitarian states, e.g. autocracies, and any form of tyranny and oppression is not, thereby, totalitarian. Furthermore, totalitarianism is a relatively recent historical phenomenon.

Finally, we want to argue that, with respect to modern 'socialist' states such as China and Cuba, Bowles and Gintis share the illusions of so many contemporary left-wing writers and commentators. In the course of *Schooling in Capitalist America* the authors repeatedly criticise 'liberals' for their misconceptions about Western society; yet their own misconceptions about 'socialist' states run very deep. For these societies possess none of the mechanisms of 'democratic control' which Bowles and Gintis hold so dear. In fact, the available evidence indicates that they are more repressive and bureaucratic than Western capitalist states, and that the individual is subject to a much greater degree of social control by a tiny minority. On their own criteria of what is important and valuable China and Cuba should stand condemned.

Before moving on to a consideration of other examples of direct reproduction theory, we should note that, in an article published in 1981 entitled 'Contradiction and Reproduction in Educational Theory',[40] Bowles and Gintis substantially revise the argument of *Schooling in Capitalist America*. In their earlier work, they say, they saw only a harmonious relationship between education and the economy, whereby education prepares pupils and students to be workers through a correspondence between the social relations of production and the social relations of education. They say that they failed properly to develop the principle of a 'contradiction' between education and the economy, primarily because of their attachment to an economic determinist conception of base and superstructure, which granted no autonomy to the various sections of the latter.

The solution to this difficulty, they continue, is to abandon the base/superstructure model altogether and view society as — and now we come to a form of jargon and verbiage so uncharacteristic of *Schooling* — 'an ensemble of structurally articulated *sites of social practice*'.[41] Modern capitalist society, they say, is composed of three such sites, namely the state, the family and capitalist production, which form a 'contradictory totality'. What this notion seems to amount to is that what happens in one sector of society is often at odds with what is going on elsewhere. As a consequence, it hinders or works against reproduction in those other sectors. Bowles and Gintis provide the following example of this phenomenon. Women and blacks possess formal political equality (in the state site); as a consequence they receive a relatively equal education (education is a 'sub-site' of the state). But capitalist production (also a site) depends upon both groups occupying a subordinate or inferior position. Therefore, there is no 'correspondence' between the social relations of education and those of economic production. Education does not reproduce capitalism but, in this way, undermines it. There exists a 'contradiction' between education and the economy. (In Chapter 8 we shall examine some similar arguments about the 'independence' of education when we consider Marxist theories of resistance, relative autonomy and voluntarism.)

The Open University

We now turn to an examination of certain parts of the influential Open University course *Schooling and Society*. This course had a considerable impact on the development of the sociology of education in the 1970s and constitutes a further important expression of direct reproduction theory.

Some of the sections of the Open University's *Schooling and Society* course very much repeat the earlier arguments of Bowles and Gintis's *Schooling* (and it should be noted that *Schooling in Capitalist America* was a 'set book' for the course). For example, Dale and Esland in Units 2-3 on 'Mass Schooling' assert that the major aims which have been pursued in education are not social amelioration and personal fulfilment — as is claimed by the 'liberal' view. 'Rather,' they say, 'we would argue that the system grew up as a means of maintaining the social hierarchy and controlling the working class.'[42] This conception of the educational system is grounded, they point out, in their view of 'the link between education and the economy, which sees the fundamental function of education as being to serve the economy'.[43] This is not, they stress, what education ought to do: for Dale and Esland share what they take to be the 'liberal' view of the aims of education, namely that it should be 'an instrument for improving social harmony and for promoting greater social equality',[44] and a means of promoting individual self-development. However, as a statement of fact, education has had, and still has, an economic function; and, as the economy in Western societies is capitalist, this comes down to saying that education is an instrument in the service of capitalism.

The remainder of the units on 'Mass Schooling' are an expansion of this view. For example, Dale and Esland say that

> the growth of an education system has been of central importance in reproducing the structures of power and control in society. Not only has it become the main device through which the labour market is provided with differentiated manpower. But it also confers legitimacy on the inequalities which result.[45]

With respect to their view that education has been and is a means of controlling the working class, they point out that, in the nineteenth century, 'The provision of education . . . was closely related to the problem of securing social order. One of the greatest fears was the outbreak of mob rule.'[46] Education was a means of preventing this: 'The labouring classes were seen as the "dangerous classes", and education was regarded as one of the means of containing them.'[47] Dale and Esland here approvingly quote G. Pearson who, in *The Deviant Imagination*, asserts that 'the nineteenth century did not speak of "deviance", it spoke of "paupers", the "dangerous classes" . . . "vagabonds" '.[48]

Now in our view this is to suggest that, for a Marxist, the labouring or working classes are what other non-Marxists in the nineteenth century called the 'dangerous classes' and what, in the twentieth century, have been termed 'deviants'. Yet it should be noted that Marx himself distinguished between the labouring or working class and the 'dangerous classes'; and that in so doing he condemned the latter. For example, in *The Communist Manifesto* Marx and Engels say that: 'Of all the classes that stand face to face with the bourgeoisie today, the proletariat alone is a really revolutionary class. The other classes decay and finally disappear in the face of Modern Industry.'[49] There then follows a brief description of these other classes beginning with the 'lower middle class', but moving on to 'the "dangerous class", the social scum, that passively rotting mass thrown off by the lowest layers of the old society . . . [whose] conditions of life . . . prepare it . . . for the part of a bribed tool of reactionary intrigue.'[50]

So Marx makes a clear distinction between the labouring or working classes and the 'dangerous class'. The former are the proletariat, the latter the 'lumpenproletariat'. In his essay 'The Eighteenth Brumaire of Louis Bonaparte', Marx describes the members of this class in terms as unfavourable as the descriptions Pearson, and Dale and Esland, attribute to nineteenth-century commentators generally. As Marx puts it:

> Alongside decayed *roués* with dubious means of subsistence and of
> dubious origin, alongside ruined and adventurous offshoots of the
> bourgeoisie, were vagabonds, discharged soldiers, discharged jailbirds,
> escaped galley slaves, swindlers . . . pickpockets, tricksters, gamblers
> . . . brothel keepers, porters, *literati*, organ-grinders, rag-pickers, knife-
> grinders, tinkers, beggars — in short, the whole indefinite disintegrated
> mass.[51]

And he concludes this description by calling them 'this scum, offal, refuse
of all classes'. No doubt Marx would have been as much in favour of
the 'control' of such groups — by education or other means — as were
the nineteenth-century supporters of the bourgeois system. Furthermore,
he would, we feel, have been distinctly unimpressed by the romantic image of deviance in much contemporary sociology.

There are two further points worth noting about Dale and Esland's
account because of the similarity to the views of Bowles and Gintis. First,
they argue that the educational system has not been imposed from above,
but has developed 'from a continuous struggle between those representing the needs of capitalism and those seeking to use schooling as a means
of social and personal improvement'.[52] In Bowles and Gintis's terms,
education has been developed as a result not of 'class domination' but
of 'class conflict'. Yet, as with *Schooling in Capitalist America*, Dale and
Esland pay little attention in the course of their discussion to this class
conflict, and the reader is left with the impression that the educational
system is a result of class domination. In other words, the conclusions
and the main body of the text are at odds with each other. Second, Dale
and Esland also condemn the practice of Russian Communism saying
that the organisation of production is basically similar to that found in
capitalist societies. However, they hold the same illusions as Bowles and
Gintis about Communist China, asserting that it is committed to 'quite
different conceptions of socialist economic and political practice from
those of the Soviet Union'.[53]

RALPH MILIBAND AND THE STRUCTURALIST MARXISTS

In our discussion of Bowles and Gintis's *Schooling in Capitalist America*,
we pointed out that their thesis breaks down into three parts: (1) what
education does — reproduction; (2) how it does it — the correspondence

principle; and (3) the forces responsible for reproduction — the economic structure. In the next part of this chapter we want to examine the third of these issues in more detail by considering the debate between Ralph Miliband and some of the structuralist Marxists (Poulantzas, Stuart Hall, Althusser). Miliband takes the view that education's role in the reproduction of capitalism is a consequence of the active attempt by society's ruling class to maintain their position of dominance, whereas the structuralist Marxists argue that reproduction occurs not as a consequence of the actions of individuals but as a result of the operation of objective economic forces.

Ralph Miliband

Ralph Miliband's discussion of education appears in the book *The State in Capitalist Society* as part of a larger analysis of the organisation of modern Western society. He draws upon research in Britain, France, Japan and the United States, and incorporates it into a Marxist framework in an impressive way.

A Dominant Economic Class

In the book Miliband is concerned to present an alternative to what he regards as the prevailing theory of society and the state, namely pluralist–democratic theory (although today it would probably be no exaggeration to say that, within sociology at least, Marxism holds that position). According to this theory, contemporary Western society is an arena of competing interest groups with no one group powerful enough to be able to dominate the rest. Each group seeks to bring pressure on the state in order to achieve the satisfaction of its demands. The state, 'subjected as it is to a multitude of conflicting pressures from organised groups and interests, cannot show any marked bias towards some groups and against others: its special role, in fact, is to accommodate and reconcile them all'.[54] Miliband's aim is to show that this theory 'is in all essentials wrong' and that one group, or rather one class, is dominant in society. Moreover, the state is not a neutral arbiter; rather its 'main purpose is to defend the predominance in society of a particular class'.[55]

The advanced industrial societies of the West are still capitalist in nature, says Miliband. Despite the existence of a public sector, 'the largest part of [the] means of economic activity is under private ownership and control'.[56] There is a very uneven distribution of wealth and a high concentration of private ownership of productive resources. Miliband points out that, in Britain in 1960 '1 per cent of the population owned 42 per cent of personal wealth . . . 5 per cent owned 75 per cent and 10 per cent owned 83 per cent';[57] the remaining 17 per cent of the country's wealth is unevenly distributed among 90 per cent of the population. (By wealth is meant such things as the ownership of land, houses, artistic treasures, consumer durables, and the holding of financial assets such as government securities, building society deposits and company shares.) With respect to the ownership of company shares,

> only 4 per cent of the adult population held any shares in commercial or industrial companies in the mid-1960's, while in 1961 1 per cent of the adult population owned 81 per cent of privately owned company shares and almost all the rest was owned by the top 10 per cent.[58]

The existence of a very wealthy stratum cannot, therefore, be denied; but that does not necessarily mean that it constitutes a 'dominant class'. In fact, it has been argued that a 'managerial revolution' has separated ownership from control of the economy, with the latter now in the hands of managers. Miliband, however, rejects the idea that private ownership is of diminishing significance. He argues that the control of large companies by the individuals and families that own them is still quite common, and that 'managers are often large stockholders in their enterprises'.[59] Moreover, the background of the managerial group is predominantly upper middle class, with something like 64 per cent of managers in large companies having a public school education. In addition, managers, as much as owner–entrepreneurs, must 'submit to the imperative demands inherent in the system of which . . .[they are] both master and servant'.[60] For all these reasons, managers should not be considered as a 'new class'; rather owners and managers together constitute one class — the economically dominant class. Furthermore, they are very much a 'class-for-itself', i.e. aware of their common interests and purposes, and they exhibit a high degree of cohesion and solidarity.

A Ruling Class

Having established the existence of a dominant economic class in modern Western society, Miliband turns to the question of whether it is also a 'ruling class'. The existence of the state — the government, the civil service, the military and the police, the judiciary and parliamentary assemblies — could lead us to conclude that this is not so. And quite clearly, says Miliband, the dominant economic class does not rule or govern directly: businessmen are not in a majority in government or cabinet, although in Conservative governments they are usually well represented. The 'capitalist class' is not, therefore, a 'governing class', comparable to pre-industrial, aristocratic and landowning classes. If then it is a ruling class, it must be so in some other sense of the term. Miliband uses a variety of expressions to try to make it clear what that sense is. A ruling class, he says, is a dominant economic class 'which is able, by virtue of the economic power thus conferred upon it, to use the state as its instrument for the domination of society'.[61] Or, there is a ruling class where 'an economically dominant class rules *through* democratic institutions',[62] or, where it has a '*decisive* degree of political power . . . [and] control of the means of political decision-making'.[63] Finally, there exists a ruling class where 'the holders of state power . . . are the agents of private economic power'.[64] In addition, Miliband quotes Kautsky's formulation that a ruling class 'does not govern' but 'contents itself with ruling the government'.[65]

Now we would argue that, although Miliband brings forward a great deal of evidence in an attempt to show that there is such a ruling class, he is, in fact, unsuccessful in this. He does *not* demonstrate that there is a ruling class as defined. He does *not* show that the dominant economic class 'uses' the state as its 'agent', etc. What he does do is to argue that the state elite — the cabinet, and the heads of civil service departments and the nationalised industries — think and act in such a way that, for them, the national interest and the interests of businessmen are identical. Consequently, while not representing any narrow interest, decisions made in the national interest are rarely incompatible, in the long run, with business interests — although on particular short-term issues there may be disagreement. Furthermore, the state elite tends to be recruited from a narrow sector of society. The educational system works in such a way that those with qualifications for, and interest in, high office mostly come from the upper middle class. Thus the state elite has an outlook and 'ideological dispositions' favourable to the maintenance of the capitalist system and, thereby, to the economic power and privileges of the dominant class. The state elite is conservative in its approach to problems, and is prepared to leave the basic economic and social structure unchanged.

This state of affairs is not substantially altered when social-democratic or left-wing governments are in power: they have tended to maintain the 'foundations of society', which includes the capitalist system. The welfare state has humanised capitalism but not changed it, and nationalisation has meant that the state has taken weaker industries under its control and then run them on capitalist lines. As with government, so with the administrative elites in the civil service: according to Miliband such elites are 'expected to dwell within a spectrum of thought of which strong conservatism forms one extreme and weak "reformism" the other'.[66] Consequently, while affirming their political neutrality, the inclination and advice of top civil servants tend towards maintaining the basic structure of society.

Miliband's argument that the dominant economic class is also the ruling class is, in our view, ultimately unconvincing. For, if the dominant economic class 'rules', even indirectly, then its influence on the state elite has to be demonstrated. One must go beyond merely showing that the decisions of the state elite benefit one group more than any other, and prove that this group has itself ensured that such decisions are made. Yet this is what Miliband fails to do.

The Process of Legitimation

Miliband continues his argument by saying that the capitalist class, despite having the general support of the state elite, must, nevertheless, secure the acquiescence or support of the 'subordinate classes'. These classes, he writes, 'have to be persuaded to accept the existing social order and to confine their demands and aspirations within its limits'.[67] The capitalist class must involve itself, therefore, in justifying and legitimating the existing social and economic order. To put it differently, it must engage in the process of the 'engineering of consent' and in the creation of a 'conservative consensus'. That they are reasonably successful in this is shown by the electoral victories of the Conservative Party. However, Miliband feels that it is necessary to explain why working people act against what the Marxist considers to be their true interests. The beginnings of an answer, he thinks, are to be found in Marx's formulation that 'the ideas of the ruling class are in every epoch the ruling ideas', and that 'the class which is the ruling material force in society, is at the same time, its ruling intellectual force'.[68] Which is to say that the ideas of the ruling class are widely propagated and ideas opposed to their interests tend to be suppressed or ignored. As a consequence, all aspects of life and thought come to be influenced by their principles.

The Role of Education. Many agencies or institutions are involved in the process of legitimation, including political parties, the church, the press, radio and television. But the one that obviously concerns us here is education. According to Miliband, schools and teachers, unlike for example the press, do not generally engage in party-political indoctrination; but they cannot avoid being involved in a broader form of 'political socialisation'. 'Educational institutions at all levels', says Miliband, 'generally fulfil an important conservative role and act, with greater or lesser effectiveness, as legitimating agencies in and for their societies.'[69] Public schools in Britain have always done this quite openly and, until recently, the schools for the 'masses' had, as their purpose, 'to instil . . . a submissive acceptance of the social order'.[70] The position of such state schools has now changed with the growth of the labour movement and political rights, but they still help to maintain the existing social and economic order. This is done in three interrelated ways.

Firstly, schools perform a class-confirming role for the majority of working-class children. There are exceptions to this process, of course, but these tend to reinforce the sense of personal inadequacy of many lower-class children. Because some of their peers are educationally successful, these children tend to assume that their own failure is due to some deficiency in themselves. Secondly, education transmits 'middle-class values', i.e. it imposes on working-class children 'an alien culture, values and even language'.[71] Thirdly, education also instils in its pupils what Durkheim called society's 'fundamental values'; but the fundamental values that the school transmits are, for Miliband, the ones sanctioned by the 'dominant forces in society'.

Universities, as well as schools, are engaged in this legitimation process. They encourage — one may be surprised to find — a conformist mode of thought, largely as a consequence of the pressures on them from the state and the business world. But it is not just a matter of external pressure, for Miliband thinks that universities are quite conservative in their outlook: they have a 'quite autonomous suspicion and hostility towards certain forms of intellectual or political unorthodoxy'.[72] For example, a Marxist economist is unlikely to obtain a university post because academics are liable to believe that such a person could not conceivably be a 'good economist'. Again, this may come as a surprise to some readers, given the intellectual hegemony of Marxism in a number of university departments. Clearly, Miliband is exaggerating.

COMMENTS

While Miliband's statement on education is short, it does clearly indicate the way Marxists approach the study of education in modern society. By arguing that education can be interpreted as a process whereby the inequalities in society are maintained and in which subordinate groups are brought to accept their situation, the Marxists challenge the strongly held assumption that education acts as a means of developing a more equal society. In the same way, the widely held view that education has a culturally enriching function, or that it widens children's horizons, is also challenged. That education does tend to have a class-confirming role cannot be doubted — the statistical data are clear on this point — and, as has been recently stated, educational reform, including the 1944 Education Act, seems to be powerless to change the advantages that the higher social classes bestow on their children in the educational race.[73] However, the other statements that Miliband makes about education, namely that it leads to a feeling of inadequacy among working-class pupils, imposes an alien culture, and teaches principles that are acceptable to the dominant class, are by no means obviously true.[74]

In the same way, we feel that more evidence is needed to substantiate Miliband's assertion that it is the power of groups outside education (the economic and administrative elites possibly), combined with the conservative attitude of teachers, which accounts for the legitimating function of education. There is, we shall argue, some truth in what he says, but the picture is more complex than he indicates. Furthermore, even if we accept that education does legitimate inequalities and ensures that people accept their positions in society, this does not show — as we have already noted — that the groups that benefit from this have engineered it. Miliband's analysis also gives the impression, at times, that the subordinate group are so powerless or so socialised that they are incapable of any positive action on their own behalf. In terms of education, the relationship of teacher and pupil and the accommodation that teachers make towards pupils is ignored. Power is seen as flowing from the top downwards and there is no consideration of the power of the lower orders or, in education, of the influence of pupils over teachers.

Nicos Poulantzas

One of the major critics of Miliband's ideas from within a Marxist framework has been Nicos Poulantzas. While Poulantzas offers many criticisms of *The State in Capitalist Society*,[75] the one that is important for our understanding of Marxist interpretations of education is that directed at Miliband's supposed preoccupation with the 'motivation' of government officials and administrative elites. According to Poulantzas, the interests and purposes of these people are of less importance than the fact that they hold particular positions in society. Translated into educational terms, this would mean that the motivation of teachers, or their conservative attitude, is of less significance than the fact that they hold the position of teachers. As we noted earlier, Marx argues that in the course of production men enter into relationships which are imposed on them and are independent of their wills. In much the same way Poulant-zas argues that the attitudes and actions of individuals are determined for them because of the positions they hold in social institutions. Like Althusser, he assumes that the economy is the basic unit in society and that, while other institutions have a 'partial autonomy', they are deter-mined 'in the last analysis' by the economy. Consequently, these other institutions have objective functions in relation to the economic base: func-tions of direction or repression, of reproduction or legitimation. In terms of education, this would mean that the teacher, no matter what his background or purposes, is bound to act in such a way that the system functions to reproduce and legitimate the social relations of production. Should the teacher refuse, then, on Poulantzas's argument, he or she would presumably be sacked.

It is undoubtedly true that any job makes certain demands on people. In teaching there are the constraints of the timetable, class size, the de-mand for examination success and the like that make some initiatives im-possible to carry through. These constraints operate whether the teacher likes them or not and whether the teacher notices them or not.[76] But Poulantzas and, as we shall see, Althusser, seem to suggest that there is no alternative but for people to be functionaries in the system. Thus all notions of struggle and conflict between individuals and the system are ruled out — ideas which are at the heart of Marx's analysis of society.

Stuart Hall

A point of view similar to that of Poulantzas is taken by Stuart Hall in his Review of the Open University's *Schooling and Society* course (Unit 32). Like Poulantzas, Hall is an Althusserian (a follower of Althusser) and argues that one cannot understand society or any particular aspect of it, such as education, by focusing on the purpose or intentions of the individuals or 'social actors' involved. With respect to education, this is a criticism, says Hall, of both the 'liberal' view and the 'conspiratorial' Marxist view. The former sees the development of education in terms of the humane intentions of various groups of individuals: they have sought to provide a good quality education for all children and, thereby, pro-mote human self-development. The latter sees the course of educational change as the result of the actions of wicked men who, under the guise of furthering the development of human capacities, have really been concerned to keep children in their places and maintain an unjust and dehumanising society. Hall argues that both explanations are opposite sides of the same coin: 'Both belong to the same *order* of explanation, which is to reduce social processes to the intentions — whether good or bad — of the social actors involved.'[77]

Such a form of explanation is inadequate, in Hall's view, because unconscious rather than conscious motives shape education. Men's intentions and purposes, and the explanations they give of what they are doing, are unimportant to the direction and course of educational and social change. Rather, such change takes place 'behind men's backs'. Furthermore, it is not human beings, either individually or collectively, who determine the nature of social institutions or society; on the contrary, it is society which determines the nature of the human beings that compose it. As Hall puts it, 'it is society which produces individuals, not the other way around'.[78] We must, then, analyse the effects on individuals of the 'structures and processes' which are the real elements or components of society, and think of individuals as no more than — in a favourite phrase of the Althusserians taken from Marx's *Capital* — the 'bearers of social relations'.

The 'structures and processes' which are of primary importance in society are, naturally enough, economic in nature. As Hall says: 'it is the nature of a society's economic structures and relations . . . which forms the principal determining force over all other aspects of society, and gives them their general character.'[79] Education, then, must be understood in its relation to society's economic base. And Hall, like the other Marxist writers we have considered, takes the view that education in modern capitalist society 'has the critical effect of sustaining and reproducing the fundamental class relationships of capitalist societies'.[80] But where Hall, and the Althusserians generally, differ from such writers as Bowles and Gintis, and Miliband is in the explanation they give of this process. Although the latter writers do not ignore, in Miliband's phrase, the 'imperative demands inherent in the system', they stress the importance of the action taken by the members of the dominant class(es) to maintain their position. But the Althusserians and Hall emphasise that 'education is changed and shaped by the overall logic of the structures of the society in which it operates'. Moreover

> so long as the fundamental social and economic relationships of a society remain intact, education will tend to obey the 'logic' of that system. Education will tend to be harnessed and made to conform, by means

of certain specific mechanisms, not simply to the interests of particular groups and classes, but to the dominant tendencies *of the whole system*.[81]

Change in education takes place because the capitalist system 'requires' it, not as a consequence of the 'activity of men in pursuit of their ends'.

We shall consider the validity of this sort of 'structural determinism' in the final chapter of this section, Chapter 9, together with further commentary on the other Marxist ideas that we have so far examined. Now we must turn to an analysis of Althusser's writings on education.

Louis Althusser

Althusser's discussion of education is a very brief one and is found principally in his essay 'Ideology and Ideological State Apparatuses'.[82] To understand it one needs to know very little about his general theory of man and society — his 'structuralism'; all one requires is some introduction to Marxist thought.

EDUCATION AS A STATE APPARATUS

Althusser's analysis is very much along the lines of that of Bowles and Gintis, although inferior in both scope and depth. Althusser ascribes to education a 'reproductive' function: education maintains and reinforces the capitalist relations of production which, of course, are relations of exploitation. Where he differs from the American writers is in asserting that education is part of capitalist society's 'State apparatus'. Indeed, for Althusser all components of the superstructure of society are said to be elements of the 'State apparatus'. In traditional Marxist theory, on the other hand, the state is just one part of society's superstructure.

The 'State apparatus' of capitalist society is divided into two parts, namely the Repressive State Apparatus (or RSA) and the Ideological State Apparatuses (or ISAs). The RSA is what, in conventional Marxist theory, is simply known as the state and is composed of the legal system, the police, the army, the government and administration. The basic function of the RSA is to intervene on behalf of the ruling class in the class struggle, and to do so primarily by means of force. However, no ruling class can rule by means of force alone. As Althusser puts it, 'no class can hold state power over a long period without at the same time exercising its hegemony over and in the Ideological State Apparatuses'.[83] According to Althusser, the following institutions can be regarded as Ideological

State Apparatuses: (1) the religious; (2) the educational; (3) the family; (4) the legal (although, as we have seen, this also belongs to the RSA); (5) the political; (6) trade unions; (7) communications, that is press, radio and television; (8) the cultural, that is literature, art and sport. Together with the RSA, the ISAs maintain the capitalist system of exploitation. The reproduction of the relations of production is, as Althusser says, 'secured by the exercise of State power in the State apparatuses, on the one hand the (Repressive) State Apparatus, on the other the Ideological State Apparatuses'.[84] But, whereas the RSA operates mainly through the use of force, the ISAs operate by disseminating the ruling ideology.

The ISAs at first sight seem to be rather diverse and complex, including institutions like education which is clearly largely state controlled, the family which is not, and religion which is officially related to the state in some societies but not in others. Yet Althusser argues that all these institutions are unified. As he puts it:

If the ISAs 'function' massively and predominantly by ideology, what unifies their diversity is precisely this functioning, in so far as the ideology by which they function is always in fact unified, despite its diversity and its contradictions, *beneath the ruling ideology*, which is the ideology of 'the ruling class'.[85]

The terms 'if' and 'in so far' make this statement rather ambiguous. It is not clear whether, for example, we are to regard the family and education as ISAs *only* if they propagate the ruling ideology. If, say, we found families which did not propagate the ruling ideology, would they be regarded as ISAs? Alternatively, Althusser could be saying that all these institutions *must* propagate the ruling ideology or else the ruling class would abolish them. If this is what Althusser means, then existing institutions, by definition, propagate the ruling ideology.

There is a further point. Althusser seems to assume that the ideologies of the separate ISAs are all compatible with each other (as well as being compatible with the ideology of the ruling class). But if this is the case, how are we to explain the not uncommon phenomenon of families who pass on to their children sets of ideas, beliefs and values which are not compatible with those transmitted by the educational system? If Althusser is correct in thinking that all ISAs are 'unified beneath the ruling ideology', such conflict should not occur.

In disseminating the ruling ideology the educational ISA, says Althusser, has a central place — more important even than the political ISA. 'I believe', he writes, 'that the ISA which has been installed in the *dominant* position in mature capitalist formations . . . is the *educational ideological apparatus*.'[86] In feudal society this central place was occupied by the Church, but a long period of political and ideological class struggle led to its replacement by education. The predominance of the educational ISA in contemporary Western society does not mean that the other ISAs do not play a part in maintaining the capitalist system. On the contrary, each of them contributes something. For example, the political ISA reinforces the existing social and economic order by subjecting individuals to one brand or another of the 'democratic ideology'. The communications apparatus performs its function by 'cramming every "citizen" with daily doses of nationalism, chauvinism, liberalism, moralism, etc., by means of the press, radio and television. The same goes for the cultural apparatus (the role of sport in chauvinism is of the first importance) etc.'[87]

However, because children are bound by law to go to school during their formative years, the role of education is of paramount importance. It performs its function in various ways. First, it teaches the skills and techniques appropriate for the child's future job. Second, it imparts the 'rules of good behaviour' or the attitudes suitable for the child's later economic role. For future wage-labourers, Althusser suggests, it fosters 'modesty, resignation and submissiveness'; for future capitalists and managers it instils 'cynicism, contempt, arrogance, self-importance, even smooth-talk and cunning'.[88] Third, it teaches children the ruling ideology of capitalist society both indirectly and directly. Education, says Althusser, 'drums into them, whether it uses new or old methods, a certain amount of "know-how" wrapped in the ruling ideology (French, arithmetic, natural history, the sciences, literature) or simply the ruling ideology in its pure state (ethics, civic instruction, philosophy).'[89]

While it might be possible to argue that civic instruction, literature and ethics could be used to propagate the ruling ideology, how this could possibly happen with a subject such as arithmetic is quite simply beyond us!

Of course, continues Althusser, this whole class-maintaining process is concealed from public view by the 'universally reigning ideology of the school'. This ideology simply obscures the fact that the educational system plays this role. It suggests that the school is a neutral environment, free of the sort of ideological influence just described, and that the teachers respect the freedom of conscience of the children, and so on. But Althusser does not want to blame the teachers for all of this; on the contrary, he argues that they are at the mercy of the system and are forced to perform the functions outlined.

It is easy to criticise Althusser both for the way in which he writes and, more importantly, for the overall view of society which he develops. As we have previously noted, the whole of the superstructure of society is incorporated, by Althusser, in the state, as either a repressive or an ideological apparatus. But we see little point in calling the various parts of the superstructure such as education, religion and communications, etc. *state* apparatuses. In social and political theory, as well as traditional Marxist theory, a distinction is usually made between the state and these institutions, and Althusser gives us no grounds for changing our normal practice. What one has in Althusser's essay is, quite simply, the over-use of the word 'state' — which can easily lead to confusions of thought. In addition, Althusser speaks only of capitalist societies and is silent about contemporary Communist states. If his ideas and his terminological changes have any substantial application, it is, we believe, with respect to these Communist societies. For in these countries the legal system, radio, press and television, the trade unions, literature, art and sport are very much controlled and dominated by those who hold state power. Such institutions can properly be considered to be extensions of the state and can rightfully be labelled as such. But in Western democracies such a link is much more tenuous. Indeed, in Western societies these institutions often have a great deal of independence from the state and are frequently in a position to exert pressure upon it — as much, at least, as the state is in a position to exert pressure upon them. No such independence, however, can be attributed to these institutions under contemporary Communism.

With respect to his view of education, Althusser sees no need to investigate the perceptions of teachers or pupils. His picture of education, as Erben and Gleeson point out,[90] resembles, in many respects, the functionalist views of Durkheim and Parsons. This is particularly evident in the implicit assumption that the socialisation process is successful. Creativity, or any form of independent response by those involved in education, is relegated to the sidelines in the analysis. In face of massive pressure from the state there is little, it would appear, that men can do but grin and bear it.

Althusser, like many Marxist writers, shares with Durkheim and Parsons a basic concern with explaining the existence of social order. Marxist writers arrive at this position, we feel, in an attempt to explain why the predicted revolution has not taken place. Consequently, instead of emphasising the importance of struggle and the factors which lead to social change, they concentrate on reproduction, that is, on how social order is maintained in capitalist societies. Education is then seen in terms of the way in which it contributes to the maintenance of the status quo. While there are clearly differences between Marxist and functionalist writers, there are also, when they analyse education, vast similarities. This is especially true of the assumption that education is successful in its socialisation and legitimation functions. The criticisms we have made of Durkheim and Parsons can also be directed at Althusser. In particular, we would note the way that he 'reifies' the state, his oversocialised conception of man, and his failure to provide any means of conceptualising change or struggle.

Pierre Bourdieu

Finally, we want to examine one more variation on the theme of reproduction, namely the work of Pierre Bourdieu. Bourdieu differs from the theorists we have so far considered in the emphasis he places on the importance of 'cultural' processes in the maintenance of existing social and economic structures. Furthermore, his ideas have had a considerable impact on the thinking of sociologists concerning the nature and role of education in modern society. Pierre Bourdieu's main concerns in the sociology of education are, first, to discover the 'laws' which explain why structures tend to reproduce themselves; and, second, to examine how education acts as a system for transmitting knowledge and ideas. His conclusion that education tends to reproduce and legitimate inequalities in wealth and power is hardly new; such conclusions are frequently found. His suggestion that education is not independent of the wider social and political structure has, likewise, been advocated by others. If he has a contribution to make, we would suggest that it is in the area of how students are evaluated: the criteria used by staff to label some students as 'excellent', others as 'weak'.

Bourdieu seems to think that, as long as a theory is logically coherent, it is, in some sense, accurate and correct. He has little regard for the 'facts', preferring to act like a mathematician and produce axiomatic theories. In certain crucial stages in his argument he disregards the implications of the statistical evidence he presents. His style of writing, assuming the translations from the French accurately reflect his style, is convoluted, vague and jargonised, and tends to mask what few interesting things he has to say. Too often he coins new terms when other ones would be perfectly adequate; he tends to take as fact findings and ideas which are still being hotly debated. Given the opacity of his writing, it is with some trepidation that we attempt to translate his ideas into intelligible prose.

Bourdieu's two basic conclusions are, first, that education helps to maintain and legitimate an unequal and class divided society; and, second that, if education is supposed to function as a system for passing on ideas and knowledge, it is unsuccessful. The steps to his conclusions can be given in a number of statements. (1) Some children progress better in education than others. (2) Progress in education is strongly influenced by the culture that the child gets from his family. (3) Families in the dominant classes give their children 'cultural capital' which allows them to do well in education. (4) The culture of education is similar to the culture of the dominant classes. (5) The culture of the dominant classes defines the criteria by which students are labelled good or bad. (6) Education does not explicitly teach what it examines. (7) Education is granted apparent autonomy from outside interference because it legitimates the power and culture of the dominant classes. Bourdieu's ideas are much more complex than this outline suggests and so we must attempt to flesh out these bones.

CULTURE AND CULTURAL CAPITAL

Cultural Arbitraries

Bourdieu's theory begins with the notion of 'cultural arbitraries'. Certain aspects of culture, he maintains, cannot be accounted for by logical analysis nor do they develop out of the nature of man. An example may help to clarify the point. In Britain we have a form of marriage which is monogamous; in other societies a man or woman may have many marriage partners. There is no logical reason to have monogamy, nor is monogamy a natural state; other societies manage well enough with polygamy. In Britain the father has authority over his young children, in other societies the mother's brother has parental authority. Again there is no logical or natural reason to adopt our style of authority. These then are 'arbitrary', but not accidental, features of our culture.

All cultures contain arbitrary features. Consequently, when we acquire a culture through socialisation, we also acquire cultural arbitraries, without realising it. In a class-based society different cultures exist, consequently different cultural arbitraries exist. The educational system has its own cultural arbitraries, which are, Bourdieu suggests, variants of the cultural arbitraries of the dominant classes. When education goes about educating, it is trying to impose the cultural arbitraries of the dominant classes on the children who come from other cultures. The consequences of this are that the children of the dominant classes find education intelligible and show flair and excellence, that the culture of the dominant classes is shown to be superior and, finally, that an act of 'symbolic violence' is perpetrated on the children of the lower classes by this attempted imposition.

Bourdieu now traces the implication of the idea of the cultural arbitrary for teaching. All teaching, in school or in the home, rests on power. This becomes obvious only when the taught refuse to accept the teacher's authority. On the whole the teacher's authority is accepted. But authority is not something which exists of itself, it is derived from two sources. Firstly, like the authority of the father mentioned above, all authority rests on some cultural arbitrary. For example, the authority of Parliament to make laws rests on the cultural arbitrary of the 'will of the people' manifested in the ballot box. In the same way a teacher's authority is based on the cultural arbitraries that certify he is competent to teach. The second source of authority is having a willing audience. People must accept the right of the person in authority to do or say things or else authority vanishes. So, in schools, pupils — or a substantial number of them — must accept the teacher's right to tell them what to study.

Bourdieu now traces the implications of these ideas for the teacher. Since the teacher's authority rests on some cultural arbitrary and a willing audience, limits are imposed on what he may legitimately teach. Should he move outside these limits, he will lose his authority. For instance, if the Pope were to say that there was no God, he would lose his authority. He would have gone outside the limits of the 'cultural arbitrary' of Catholics and would lose his audience. In the same way, if a primary school teacher were to say that reading and writing were of no importance to children, he would have gone outside the cultural arbitrary of education and would lose his authority. The recent cases of Terry Ellis in William Tyndale Junior School, or of Michael Duane in Risinghill Comprehensive School, could be given as examples of straying beyond the limits of the 'cultural arbitraries' of education.[91]

Since, in Bourdieu's view, the cultural arbitraries of education are those of the dominant classes, then it is the case that the dominant classes determine what is within the limits of legitimate education, not in a conspiratorial manner, but through the domination of their culture. At the same time, the authority of the teacher is delegated to him by the dominant class. Education, then, is in no sense an independent judge of pupils; the criteria for judging pupils is given by the culture of the dominant classes, modified to some extent by the educational system. Further, children raised in the culture of the dominant class are clearly advantaged

in education; they have been given 'cultural capital' which they can spend
to acquire qualifications.

Socialisation

The next stage in Bourdieu's argument is to look at the idea of socialisation, for it is in the process of socialisation that families give their children
culture. Socialisation gives to the child values, norms, ways of thinking
and perceiving. Of particular importance to Bourdieu are the 'master-
patterns', language, and relation to culture and language that are also acquired during socialisation.

Master-patterns seem to be similar to Bernstein's concept of codes;
they are analogous to the rules of a game (like chess) which allow different combinations of moves to take place. When we acquire the master-
patterns of thinking or speaking, we are given the basic rules of the game;
they are like blueprints which help the individual to shape his reality.
On the basis of the master-patterns, Bourdieu says, 'by an "art" of invention similar to that involved in writing music, an infinite variety of
individual patterns directly applicable to specific situations are
generated'.[92] Different cultures have their own master-patterns, as does
the educational system.

Of particular importance, Bourdieu thinks, for organising our thinking is language. As he puts it, quoting Whorf: 'Thinking . . . follows
a network of tracks laid down in the given language, an organization which
may concentrate systematically upon certain phases of reality, certain
aspects of intelligence, and may systematically discard others featured
by other languages.'[93] Here Bourdieu seems to accept as given the very
much debated view that language determines thought. It is an example
of ignoring the debate when the ideas fit with the overall theory. Bourdieu suggests that different classes have their different languages and that
education also has its own language. The language of education is closer
to that of the dominant classes than to that of other classes.

The final, and most difficult, aspect of socialisation that Bourdieu looks
at is the idea that, as we acquire a culture, we also acquire a relationship
to language and culture. It is not obvious what Bourdieu means by this;
our best guess is that he is indicating that, when we acquire our culture,
we learn to adopt attitudes to cultural things like opera, religion,
patriotism. When we acquire language, we learn the appropriate style
to use in different situations. The language of the lecture is not appropriate
when chatting to students in the bar. Bourdieu gives us some examples
of different relations to language. Students were asked to define the non-
existent word '*gérophagie*'. The types of reply were as follows: ' "I don't

know the definition." (Male, Working Class, Provinces.) "Means nothing to me." (Female, Middle Class, Provinces.) "The etymology seems to indicate the eating of the old." (Female, Middle Class, Provinces.)' Bourdieu then remarks:

> These responses, expressing either lucidity or scholastic prudence, or more precisely the desire to 'do one's best', to make use of one's knowledge within the bounds of scholastic prudence, contrast with another phraseology, peremptory, arrogant, off-hand or recherché. 'The etymology is as follows . . . Gerophagy is therefore the custom of eating the aged among certain non-Promethian clansmen.' (Male, Upper Class, Paris.) 'If *gero* comes from geras, an old man, then gerophagy designates a form of anthropophagy oriented towards the older elements of population X.' (Female, Upper Class, Paris.)[94]

These are examples of two types of relation to language, one lucid (I don't know) and prudent (The etymology seems to indicate . . .), the other off-hand and arrogant. But Bourdieu's contention seems to be that it is the latter relation to language which is preferred and rewarded by education. It is also the language style of the upper classes. Given Bourdieu's own style, one is tempted to agree!

The Dominant Classes

Having laid the foundations by looking at socialisation, Bourdieu suggests that the children of the dominant classes have acquired a culture which is similar to that of education. They have been given 'cultural capital'. This can be seen, he indicates, from the statistics of entry into higher education where the upper classes and Parisians dominate. It can also be seen from the entry into the academically prestigious subjects of French and philosophy, where again the upper classes predominate.

Having cultural capital, which is defined by one commentator as 'linguistic and social competencies and such qualities as style, manners, know-how as well as aspirations and perceptions of the objective chances of success',[95] is one explanation of the statistics. We can estimate a family's cultural capital, suggests Bourdieu, by such things as the frequency of theatre-going, listening to classical music, visiting art galleries, reading non-professional books, reading *Le Monde* and *Le Figaro* and not having a television set.[96] Being cultured, in the sense of high culture, is a measure of cultural capital.

Bourdieu is careful to point out that cultural capital is not the only explanation of educational success. Many factors have to be considered.

'It is therefore impossible to take any one of the characteristics defining an individual or a category at any one point in his career', he says in his complex style, 'as the ultimate explanatory principle of all characteristics.'[97] He notes that, while the working class does provide some successful students, they are in the minority. Many of the working class inflict upon themselves 'convictions by default or suspended sentences'.[98] Working-class parents, for example, choose non-academic courses for their children. This is hardly surprising, thinks Bourdieu, since in the experience of these parents the chances of educational success are very slim. Why encourage your child to do what is, in actual fact, almost impossible? The history and experiences of the working class in education affects the decisions of parents about their children's education and perpetuates, in part, working-class educational failure.

With regard to other students, Bourdieu maintains that the middle class achieves some success by hard work and tenacity, which are characteristics typical of the middle-class culture. However, lacking cultural capital, they fail to show elegance and flair in their work. They are conscious of having to 'hang on' at all stages.[99]

Having said that cultural capital is not the only factor, Bourdieu places great stress upon it. For example, when dealing with the successful working-class students, he says: 'sons and daughters of industrial workers, who make up respectively 5 and 9 per cent of the successful candidates, come from families which differ from the rest of their class by having a relatively high cultural level.'[100] In other words, they have some cultural capital.

To review the argument so far, Bourdieu has suggested that the children in the dominant classes are given master-patterns, linguistic codes and relations to language and culture which allow them to be successful in education. Other factors affect educational success, but cultural capital appears to be the most important. The reasons why socialisation into the culture of the dominant classes gives cultural capital and thus educational success are 'the culture it [education] transmits is closer to the dominant culture and . . . the mode of inculcation to which it has recourse is less removed from the mode of inculcation practised by the family'.[101] Saying this does not, of course, make it true; evidence is needed and seems to be somewhat lacking. We could quote the statistical evidence which suggests that upper-class children do relatively well in education, but there are many possible explanations for this, for example the use of private schools. What Bourdieu tries to do, in a way similar to Bernstein (whom we discussed in Chapter 3), is to base his argument on language differences.

In France, Bourdieu states, one can detect two forms of language, bourgeois parlance and common parlance. The former verbalises feelings and judgements while common parlance has 'the tendency to move from particular case to particular case, from illustration to parable or to shun the bombast of fine words'.[102] These differences in language patterns are a reflection of the experiences of different classes when they come into contact with the facts of life associated with their class.

University French is closer to the language of the dominant classes (bourgeois parlance) than to that of any other class. The literate tradition in education assumes that all experiences can be turned into a literary exercise where style and form of expression are important. For children trained in bourgeois parlance that is an easy exercise; they have linguistic capital. These students produce excellent work. But there are many others who are judged to produce mediocre essays with ill-digested theories presented in over-generalised ways. These latter students lack linguistic capital.

If Bourdieu's ideas about language differences and the linguistic demands of education are correct, and there are considerable arguments about that, then it would add substance to the overall theory. However, the theory suggests that the dominant classes possess linguistic and cultural capital; we must ask if all members of the dominant classes possess this capital. Bourdieu's own evidence suggests that this is not the case. On the basis of his investigations he says: 'the structure of economic capital is symmetrical and *opposite* to the structure and distribution of cultural capital — that is to say, in order, heads of industry and commerce, professionals, managers, engineers and lastly civil servants and teachers.'[103] The implication of this is that those with economic power have little cultural capital. If this is so, how can Bourdieu suggest that the culture of education is closer to the culture of the *dominant classes* when, by his own words, he says that many of the people in the dominant classes don't have much in the way of the precious cultural capital? Commenting on Bourdieu's statistics, Musgrove suggests that the data fail to provide any support for the general thesis.

> It is not the rich and the powerful (who are so efficiently 'reproduced') who consume culture and read philosophy and eighteenth-century novels. Culture in the main is consumed by people who are well educated but relatively poor and weak — notably teachers.[104]

These findings must lead us to rethink the Bourdieu thesis. The most Bourdieu can claim is that *educated* parents provide their children with cultural capital. In different words, educated parents equip their children for a successful career in education. How the children of the other members of the dominant class succeed in education is left unanswered, if indeed they do succeed. More importantly, the implication that somehow the culture of education is dependent upon the culture of the dominant classes and serves to legitimate the position of the dominant classes has no substance. It should hardly be surprising that teachers and civil servants have a culture similar to education's culture; they are usually well educated. It would be more reasonable to say that it is the culture of education that has formed the culture of the teachers and civil servants, than that the culture of education is dependent on the culture of the dominant classes.

THE EDUCATIONAL SYSTEM

If we accept that some parents, not necessarily in the dominant classes, do provide their children with cultural resources which allow them to be successful in education, we can ask why it is that the school does not educate all its pupils by giving them the cultural resources they need. Bourdieu thinks that the school does not do so. 'By doing away with giving *explicitly* to everyone what it implicitly demands of everyone the education system demands of everyone alike what it does not give.'[105] At first sight this seems a strange statement — but could be one of Bourdieu's more perceptive remarks. If we recall that culture contains the basic master-patterns of thought and perception, the basic patterns of language and the relation to language and culture, then what Bourdieu is suggesting is that education never explicitly teaches these basics. At best, the educational system exposes pupils to these master-patterns and the 'brighter' pupils latch on to them. But, for Bourdieu, some pupils have already been given the master-patterns through family socialisation. An example of what Bourdieu has in mind may be taken from the subject English. It could be that we teach the rules of spelling and punctuation to pupils in an explicit way but that, when marking an essay, more weight is given to style, characterisation and what we call creativity. But do we tell pupils explicitly the rules of good style, or how to get good characterisation, or what we mean by being creative? To the extent that we place emphasis on these features and do not explicitly teach pupils how to develop their skills, then Bourdieu is correct. Another example may be taken from higher education where we find that a number of markers agree that a paper is of high quality, but cannot say precisely what it is that gives it the quality. For Bourdieu, we think, the explanation would be that the paper exhibits the style that shows that the student has the 'right' relation to the subject or has mastered the basic master-patterns of the discipline.

It is Bourdieu's contention that, in French higher education, style dominates content. This is particularly so in the mass lecture, where the lecturer, faced with a large and varied audience, uses rhetoric and style to maintain his authority. 'Language can ultimately cease to be an instrument of communication and serve instead as an instrument of incantation.'[106] If this is so, then very little communication is taking place in the lecture. Bourdieu adds, 'Transmitting in a language which is little or not at all understood, the professor logically ought not to understand what his students send back to him.'[107] But some students do show 'ease', 'facility' and 'naturalness' in the estimation of the staff; others relate to the subject in 'pedantic' and 'vulgar' ways. Bourdieu's explanation is that some students, who have linguistic and cultural capital, can decipher the message and respond in the correct code. These students are mostly from the upper classes — a point we have already contested strongly. The educational system fails, in Bourdieu's eyes, explicitly to teach the pupils how to decipher the linguistic code it uses or what is the proper way to relate to the subject. We will comment on this part of Bourdieu's thesis shortly, for we do consider that it has some merit.

The final point of importance that Bourdieu makes is that the educational system seems to be autonomous. Indeed it resists attempts from outside to change it. This is particularly surprising in the case of higher education, where so little is actually taught. Why then is the system allowed such autonomy? The answer is that it is only partially autonomous, all teaching authority is delegated. In his view (but not ours), it is delegated from the dominant classes. In fact the educational system's main function is not to transmit knowledge, he argues, but to act as a mechanism of selection and to legitimate inequalities in society. The very autonomy that education is given in devising its own criteria of excellence hides the fact that the criteria benefit the upper classes. The educational system remains autonomous so long as it remains within the cultural arbitraries of the upper classes.

So it has to be asked [Bourdieu writes], whether the freedom that the educational system is given to enforce its own standards and hierarchies, at the expense, for example, of the most evident demands of the economic system is not a quid pro quo of the hidden service it renders to certain classes by concealing social selection under the guise of technical selection [selection by ability] and legitimating the reproduction of social hierarchies.[108]

Bourdieu's language, as may be clear from some of the quotations, is complex and convoluted. It is true that his writing transmits little to the people who do not possess the 'cultural capital' of which he makes so much. This may be a deliberate use of style to demonstrate his thesis, but it also serves to mask his ideas.

The thesis put forward by Bourdieu suggests that the independence of education from other aspects of society is never total but partial. The French experience may be different from that in Britain, for we would argue that very few people would consider either the content or structure of British education to be independent of outside influence. A brief reading of the newspapers or a look at the history of education would clearly indicate the partial dependence of education on social and political structures. Bourdieu's argument suggests that education reproduces and legitimates the class structure by conferring status on the children of the dominant classes. There is a general belief that the people who excel in education are clever or bright, but Bourdieu suggests that excellence in education is brought about by being socialised in the family into a culture which is basically similar to that of education. It is the children of the dominant classes who enjoy this socialisation process and are given cultural capital. The culture of education is essentially similar to that of the dominant classes. Indeed, it would appear that the cultural arbitraries of the dominant classes, determine the basic structure of educational knowledge and that the teacher's authority is delegated from the culture of these classes. If this is the case, then it is easy to see how the children of the dominant classes will succeed and those of other classes will struggle. But, as we have pointed out, Bourdieu's evidence shows that it is not the case. It is the relatively powerless, educated, teachers and civil servants who give their children cultural capital, not the powerful managers and directors. This part of Bourdieu's argument fails. The best he can claim is that the culture of education is similar to the culture of the educated classes.

Implicit in the thesis is the view that children from homes lacking in cultural capital will be unsuccessful in education. This view has been strongly contested by Halsey, Heath and Ridge. After studying the replies from 8,529 men born between 1913 and 1952 they make the following point.

Eighty per cent of those at technical schools came from what may be crudely termed 'uneducated' backgrounds and two-thirds of those at

Grammar School. This is a striking result. It means that state schools (much more than private schools) were doing far more than merely reproducing 'cultural capital'; they were creating it too. They were bringing an academic or technical training to a very substantial number of boys from homes that were not in any sense educated.[109]

To be fair to Bourdieu, he does acknowledge that children from in-dustrial workers' families do gain qualifications. His point is that they come from families with more cultural capital than other workers. Halsey's data assume that lack of cultural capital is the same as lack of formal education. While there are good reasons to think this is Bourdieu's view, he does not state it. Consequently it could be argued that Halsey's data are not adequate to evaluate Bourdieu's thesis. Having said this, we think it unlikely that all the pupils from 'uneducated' homes had cultural capital to begin with. We would tend to go along with the view that education does create cultural capital and not merely reproduce it. Halsey's data cast considerable doubt on this aspect of Bourdieu's thesis, but do not totally disprove it.

The most interesting of Bourdieu's ideas, we feel, is that education implicitly examines what it does not teach. Many pupils and students do not have the cultural background or linguistic competence to translate the messages that are sent to them by staff. In higher education staff em-phasise rhetoric and style when lecturing or examining. This view raises two issues; that of teaching and that of evaluating students.

Bourdieu maintains that style seems to dominate content; very little gets through. It is undoubtedly true that there are lecturers and authors who adopt a convoluted style and jargonised language. There is a temp-tation in lecturing to large and diverse audiences to entertain rather than to teach. With some lecturers it is difficult to understand what is being said, with others there is little content. These are bad lecturers but not, we suggest, in the majority in Britain. In academic subjects there are problems of jargon and terminology — strange words like verb, adjec-tive, infinitive, hypothesis and socialisation. The good teacher tries to be aware of the difficulties and the complexity of language he is using. At this level most staff, we think, are aware of the problems of being explicit. There is, however, the more basic problem of being explicit about the master-patterns of thought involved in different disciplines and in education generally. Anyone who has struggled to get on the 'wave length' of philosophy or sociology will recognise this. It is interesting to see the way that students from different academic disciplines respond to a new subject. We have found that students of biology, sociology, English or economics think in different ways, for example, about class and educational attainment. This is more than biologists giving explanations based on innate factors or economists stressing economic factors in the provisions of schools, but differences in approach to conceptualising the problems and explanations offered. English students tend towards the search for meanings, biology students look to develop laws and graphs to show more 'objective' relationships. We would suggest that there are these different master-patterns involved in disciplines and could accept that there are some basic patterns to education in general.

We would also accept Bourdieu's contention that the basic forms of thought are not explicitly and fully described by teachers. We would also suggest that the basic rules of our language are not fully and explicitly described. Yet children, by being exposed to the language, are able to master rules which are as yet incapable of description. The point we would raise here is that the master-patterns of language or academic disciplines may not be capable of explicit formulation; that we acquire the master-patterns by exposure to books and teachers who use them. Bourdieu himself suggests that acquiring a 'habitus' (a term he uses for being socialised) can only happen in family socialisation. The family does not explicitly define the rules of language or thinking when it socialises. Socialisation into the master-patterns of education may then be of a similar form to family socialisation. The human mind intuits the master-patterns from the 'surface' patterns to which it is exposed. Bourdieu may be correct in what he is saying, but the implication that things could be otherwise may be mistaken.

In terms of evaluation Bourdieu does make some interesting points. He suggests that style and relationship to culture are the important things. This is worthy of further investigation, we suggest. Certainly the style of presentation either in written work or oral discussion does seem to be an important element. Some subjects explicitly demand a particular literary style; science demands the passive impersonal form — 'a beaker was filled' rather than 'I filled a beaker'. This was not the style of Charles Darwin. Certainly a lot may be gained by looking at the styles demanded by academic disciplines. The extent to which the way that something is said can influence the assessment of examiners is worthy of consideration.

Bourdieu, then, does have some interesting notions buried in his thesis. We would suggest that the major idea that education serves to legitimate and reproduce social hierarchies remains unproved, and that the thesis that the upper classes dominate education by providing their children with cultural capital is, quite simply, wrong.

In this chapter we have examined the more important formulations of direct reproduction theory. In doing so we have drawn attention to the differences as well as the similarities in the views of the authors considered. However, no matter what variations one finds amongst the writers concerned, the central theme remains the same, namely education directly maintains or reproduces capitalism.

NOTES

1. S. Bowles and H. Gintis, *Schooling in Capitalist America* (Routledge and Kegan Paul, London, 1976), p. 57.
2. Ibid., p. 20.
3. Ibid., p. 53.
4. Ibid., p. 53.
5. Ibid., p. 54.
6. Ibid., p. 54.
7. Ibid., p. 54.
8. Ibid., p. 55.
9. The reproduction process is defined by Bowles and Gintis as those mechanisms which 'maintain and extend the dominant patterns of power and privilege', Ibid., p. 126.
10. Ibid., p. 55.
11. Ibid., p. 55.
The concept of *ideology* is one of the most widely used and complex terms in the Marxist vocabulary. Unfortunately, there are so many meanings associated with the term that it is not always clear which ones are being used. Sometimes, for example, the word is used to indicate a more or less coherent set of ideas about society as a whole, or about some part of it. More often, the term carries the implication that the ideas serve the particular interest of a group or class in society. On other occasions it is implied that the picture of the world represented by an ideology is inadequate. This inadequacy works in the interest of a group or class. One interpretation of the notion of inadequacy is to suggest that ideologies reveal something true about society but also hide something which is equally true. For example, to describe Britain as a free society with the individual's civil rights protected by the law, is true; but this picture neglects to mention that employers have a great deal of power over workers and that the law also supports an owner who sells his property and puts people out of work.

Because of the variety of uses of the term, the statement that ideologies determine education can take on widely different meanings. Similarly, when Marxists say that education transmits ideologies, it could mean as little as 'education passes on ideas', or that 'education gives an inadequate and class biased picture of society'.

Perhaps the most interesting notion associated with ideology is the dialectic relationship of ideas and society. Ideologies, it is argued, are created on the basis of people's experiences of life. But experience is structured by ideologies. The most important aspect of life, in Marxist thinking, is the relationships people enter into in production. In capitalist society many aspects of a worker's life are dictated by the owner. Owners organise working practices according to their own ideology. Because of this the worker's everyday experience is moulded by the employer's ideology. The owner's ideas are made real in everyday activity and may become a part of the common sense of the worker. Educational ideologies contain notions of man and society that are a product of class relations in capitalist society. These views, arising from the base, limit the sorts of developments that education might take. The concept of ideology can thus provide a way for Marxists to argue that the economic base determines the educational system, if not in detail at least in general terms.
12. Ibid., p. 61.

13. Ibid., p. 61.

14. Ibid., pp. 68–9.

15. Ibid., pp. 125–6.

16. K. Davis and W.E. Moore, 'Some Principles of Stratification', *American Sociological Review*, vol. 10, no. 2 (1945), p. 243.

17. Bowles and Gintis, *Schooling*, p. 127.

18. Ibid., p. 129.

19. Ibid., p. 42.

20. Ibid., pp. 11–12.

21. Ibid., p. 151.

22. Ibid., pp. 239–40.

23. Ibid., p. 240.

24. Ibid., p. 240.

25. Ibid., p. 224.

26. Ibid., p. 179.

27. Ibid., p. 160.

28. Ibid., p. 266.

29. Ibid., p. 266.

30. Ibid., p. 266.

31. Ibid., p. 267.

32. Ibid., p. 268.

33. Ibid., p. 267.

34. Ibid., p. 273.

35. Ibid., p. 275.

36. P. Coxhead, 'Some Comments on Bowles and Gintis', Appendix to Unit 13 of E202, *Schooling and Society* (Open University Press, Milton Keynes, 1977).

37. Ibid., p. 71.

38. Bowles and Gintis, *Schooling*, p. 300.

39. Ibid., p. 134.

40. S. Bowles and H. Gintis, 'Contradiction and Reproduction in Educational Theory', reprinted in R. Dale *et al.* (eds.), *Education and the State*, Vol. 1, *Schooling and the National Interest* (Falmer Press, Lewes, 1981).

41. Ibid., p. 49.

42. R. Dale and G. Esland, 'Mass Schooling', Units 2–3 of E202, *Schooling and Society*, p. 3.

43. Ibid., p. 4.

44. Ibid., p. 10.

45. Ibid., p. 31.

46. Ibid., p. 37.

47. Ibid., p. 37.

48. Ibid., p. 37.

49. K. Marx and F. Engels, *The Communist Manifesto* in *Marx and Engels. Selected Works* (Lawrence and Wishart, London, 1968), p. 44.

50. Ibid., p. 44.

51. Ibid., p. 138.

52. Dale and Esland, 'Mass Schooling', p. 10.

53. Ibid., p. 22.

54. R. Miliband, *The State in Capitalist Society* (Weidenfeld and Nicolson, London, 1972), p. 4.

55. Ibid., p. 3.

56. Ibid., p. 7.

57. Ibid., p. 25.

58. Ibid., p. 26. According to Inland Revenue Statistics, in 1982 1 per cent of the population owned 17 per cent of the UK's personal wealth and 10 per cent owned 43 per cent.

Between 91 and 95 per cent of personal wealth was accounted for by only half the adult population (reported in *The Times*, 30 October 1984).

59. Ibid., p. 35.

60. Ibid., p. 34.

61. Ibid., p. 23.

62. Ibid., p. 22.

63. Ibid., p. 48.

64. Ibid., pp. 54–5.

65. Ibid., p. 55.

66. Ibid., p. 123.

67. Ibid., p. 178.

68. Ibid., pp. 180–1.

69. Ibid., p. 239.

70. Ibid., p. 240.

71. Ibid., p. 242.

72. Ibid., p. 256.

73. See A.H. Halsey, A.F. Heath and J.M. Ridge, *Origins and Destinations* (Clarendon Press, Oxford, 1980).

74. Alternative suggestions are made by:

1. Paul Willis, who argues that some working-class children reject school's 'ideal-pupil' image as being inappropriate for them — there is no sense of personal inadequacy on the children's part. See *Learning to Labour* (Saxon House, Farnborough, 1977).

2. David Hargreaves, whose work on delinquescent sub-groups suggests that, while the school may teach middle-class values, it is not obviously successful in getting them inculcated. Rather, pupils form their own sets of values in contradiction to those of the school. See *Social Relations in a Secondary School* (Routledge and Kegan Paul, London, 1967).

3. The critics of Bernstein's work on class, language and education. See A.D. Edwards, *Language in Culture and Class* (Heinemann, London, 1976) and L.A. Jackson, 'The Myth of the Elaborated and Restricted Code' in B.R. Cosin *et al.* (eds.), *School and Society* (Routledge and Kegan Paul, London, 1977).

Clearly, then, we cannot accept Miliband's statements as beyond dispute.

75. See N. Poulantzas, 'The Problem of the Capitalist State' in R. Blackburn (ed.), *Ideology in Social Science* (Fontana, London, 1972).

76. R. Sharp and A. Green, *Education and Social Control: A Study of Progressive Primary Education* (Routledge and Kegan Paul, London, 1975).

77. S. Hall, 'Review of the Course', Unit 32 of E202, *Schooling and Society*, p. 11.

78. Ibid., p. 12.

79. Ibid., p. 13.

80. Ibid., p. 17.

81. Ibid., p. 25.

82. Originally published in L. Althusser, *Lenin, Philosophy and Other Essays* (New Left Books, London, 1971). A substantial extract can be found in B.R. Cosin, *Education, Structure and Society*, 2nd edn. (Penguin, Harmondsworth, 1972).

83. Cosin, *Education*, p. 254.

84. Ibid., p. 256.

85. Ibid., p. 254.

86. Ibid., p. 258.

87. Ibid., p. 259.

88. Ibid., p. 261.

89. Ibid., p. 260.

90. M. Erben and D. Gleeson, 'Education as Reproduction' in M. Young and G. Whitty (eds.), *Society, State and Schooling* (Falmer Press, Lewes, 1977).

91. R. Auld, *William Tyndale Junior and Infants School Public Enquiry* (ILEA,

London, 1976). L. Berg, *Risinghill, The Death of a Comprehensive School* (Penguin, Harmondsworth, 1968).

92. P. Bourdieu, 'Systems of Education and Systems of Thought' in R. Dale, G. Esland and M. MacDonald (eds.), *Schooling and Capitalism* (Routledge and Kegan Paul, London, 1976), p. 194.

93. Ibid., p. 196.

94. P. Bourdieu and J.-C. Passeron, *Reproduction in Education, Society and Culture* (Sage, London, 1977), p. 135.

95. M. MacDonald, 'The Curriculum and Cultural Reproduction', Unit 18 of E202, *Schooling and Society*, p. 49.

96. P. Bourdieu, 'Cultural Reproduction and Social Reproduction' in R. Brown (ed.), *Knowledge, Education and Cultural Change* (Tavistock, London, 1973), pp. 72–5.

97. Bourdieu and Passeron, *Reproduction*, p. 89.

98. Ibid., p. 157.

99. P. Bourdieu and M. de Saint-Martin, 'Scholastic Excellence and the Values of the Educational System' in J. Eggleston (ed.), *Contemporary Research in the Sociology of Education* (Methuen, London, 1974), p. 355.

100. Ibid., p. 340.

101. Bourdieu in Brown (ed.), *Knowledge*, p. 80.

102. Bourdieu and Passeron, *Reproduction*, p. 116.

103. Bourdieu in Brown (ed.), *Knowledge*, p. 89.

104. F. Musgrove, *School and the Social Order*, (Wiley, Chichester, 1979), p. 26.

105. Bourdieu in Brown (ed.), *Knowledge*, p. 80.

106. Bourdieu and Passeron, *Reproduction*, p. 110.

107. Ibid., p. 111.

108. Ibid., pp. 152–3.

109. Halsey, Heath and Ridge, *Origins and Destinations*, p. 77.

8 THE MARXIST ANALYSIS OF EDUCATION: RESISTANCE, RELATIVE AUTONOMY AND VOLUNTARISM

In the Marxist sociology of education in recent years, theories of direct reproduction have been superseded by conceptions of education which stress the importance of 'resistance' within education to the process of the reproduction of capitalism. The idea of the relative autonomy of education has also been given serious attention; and both concepts have been combined with an analysis which is more voluntarist in nature.

Michael Apple

The work of Michael Apple is a case in point. In *Education and Power* (1982) Apple says that in his earlier book, *Ideology and Curriculum*, he held a simple, mechanistic view of the relationship between education and the economy. There he thought only in terms of a 'functional correspondence between what schools taught and the "needs" of an unequal society'.[1] Industry requires docile workers and the schools produce them. In particular, the bottom layers of pupils get a hidden curriculum that prepares them to fit into and accept their place on the lower rungs of the economic ladder. In short, he says, he held schools to be a mirror of society.

In *Education and Power* and *Cultural and Economic Reproduction in Education* (also 1982), Apple offers a modified conception of the educational process. He argues that it is too simple to think only in terms of schools reproducing the social relations of production. Although reproduction certainly takes place, the concept does not do justice to the 'complexity of school life', and ignores 'the struggles and contradictions' that exist in the school (and in the workplace and the state).[2] Schools are not institutions where what is taught 'inexorably moulds students into passive beings who are able and eager to fit into an unequal society'.[3] The hidden curriculum is not absorbed directly, rather it is 'mediated' by the class culture of the pupils. Like workers in industry, pupils possess a culture containing values and norms at odds with those of the dominant culture of the wider society. This not only enables them to see through the capitalist ideological façade to the reality of inequality at its base;

179

it also provides pupils with a means of challenging the system of control in their schools.

In working-class schools, then, it is likely that there will be at best partial acceptance, and often outright rejection, of both the formal and hidden curriculum. Such schools are 'sites' of 'resistance', conflict and struggle. Drawing upon the work of Gramsci and Erik Olin Wright, Apple says that pupils, and to some extent teachers, constitute an oppositional tendency and countervailing pressure within the school system. However, having said this, Apple stresses that we must not develop an 'overly romantic outlook'. We need to remember that, despite resistance, power is still unequally distributed. 'Struggle and conflict may indeed exist; but that does not mean it will be successful.'[4]

Nevertheless, though the outcome of resistance may be uncertain, the very presence of it indicates that what pupils do is not necessarily determined by economic and social forces. Pupils are not mere 'bearers' of the ideology which the school is attempting to transmit. Rather, because culture is a 'lived' process, pupils are 'creatively acting in ways that often contradict these expected norms and dispositions which pervade the school'.[5] Apple provides the following example of such 'creative' action. He says that:

> Large numbers of [pupils] in inner-city and working-class schools, to say nothing of other areas, creatively adapt their environments so that they can smoke, get out of class, inject humour into the routines, informally control the pacing of classroom life, and generally try to make it through the day. In these same schools many students go even further. They simply reject the overt and hidden curricula of the school. The teacher who is teaching about mathematics, history, careers, etc., is ignored as much as possible. Also, the covert teaching of punctuality, neatness, compliance and other more economically rooted values is simply dismissed as far as possible. The real task of the students is to last until the bell rings.[6]

With these notions of resistance and creative adaptation, Apple is seeking to develop a more voluntaristic form of analysis. He wants to abandon the view that education is determined by the economy, and is urging us to see the school and the culture of the pupils as relatively autonomous. Not only, he feels, is such a perspective more in accord with the facts. It also, and more importantly in his opinion, provides some hope for the transformation of the education system. For the theory of direct reproduction breeds a very pessimistic view of the role of schools: that they only reflect and are powerless to change the larger society.

Henry Giroux

Henry Giroux also stresses the voluntaristic nature of resistance theory, as well as the basis which it offers for challenging the more repressive features of schooling. In his article 'Theories of Reproduction and Resistance in the New Sociology of Education: A Critical Analysis',[7] Giroux points out that reproduction theory has played down the importance of human freedom and self-determination in the education system. Schools, he says, 'are often viewed as factories or prisons, teachers and students alike act merely as pawns and role bearers constrained by the logic and social practices of the capitalist system'. Because of this, 'The idea that people do make history, including its constraints, has been neglected.'[8] Theories of resistance, on the other hand, 'restore a degree of agency and innovation'[9] to the subordinate classes and groups. Furthermore, the culture of such groups is 'constituted as much by the group itself as by the dominant society. Subordinate cultures, whether working class or otherwise, partake of moments of self-production as well as reproduction.'[10] What pupils do within such cultures, therefore, is not merely the result of external forces operating on them, but, in part, derives from their own decisions and actions. As Giroux expresses it:

> One of the most important assumptions of resistance theory is that working-class students are not merely the by-product of capital, compliantly submitting to the dictates of authoritarian teachers and schools that prepare them for a life of deadening labour. Rather, schools represent contested terrains marked not only by structural and ideological contradictions, but also by collectively informed student resistance.[11]

Schools, therefore, are 'sites' for ideological struggle and for competition between competing class cultures.

The life of pupils in schools, according to Giroux, is not totally dominated by the wider economic and social system as the theorists of direct reproduction would have us believe. They have some autonomy. Indeed, schools as a whole possess some independence from the capitalist system. As he says in the book *Ideology, Culture and the Process of Schooling*, 'schools often find themselves at odds with the needs of the dominant society'.[12] In addition, they are subject to conflicting demands from different sections of the community. For example, some elements of the middle and upper classes want schools to produce scientists and technicians, whilst other elements want a broad-based integrated curriculum. 'Conflicting claims on schools', continues Giroux, 'also come from competing ethnic, religious and racial groups.'[13]

However, such independence is only partial. Schools possess only a relative autonomy. They operate within conditions and limits set by the wider society, even though they also shape those conditions and limits. In the end, the economy is 'the ultimate determinant'.[14]

Many other Marxist writers, besides Apple and Giroux, now stress the importance of resistance and relative autonomy. For example, Madan Sarup in his *Education, State and Crisis* concludes that 'schools not only reproduce the social relations of production, they also reproduce forms of resistance. Many pupils develop a characteristic resistance to the overt aims of schooling.'[15] To provide support for their theoretical arguments these Marxists invariably draw upon the detailed empirical studies of schools by Marxist ethnographers. In particular, they refer to Paul Willis's *Learning to Labour*,[16] Angela McRobbie's 'Working Class Girls and the Culture of Femininity' (which we shall discuss in Chapter 9),[17] Paul Corrigan's *Schooling the Smash Street Kids*,[18] and the research of Robert Everhart.[19] Here, we shall concentrate on Willis's work as it is the most important and influential of the ethnographic studies.[20]

Paul Willis

Willis says that the existence of anti-school cultures in schools with a working-class catchment area has been the focus of much attention in recent years, for example, in the work of David Hargreaves (whose writings we discuss in Chapters 3, 9 and 10) and of Colin Lacey.[21] However, he believes that there has been a tendency to consider such cultures in isolation from their wider social context. His argument falls into two parts.

Firstly, counter-school cultures, involving as they do resistance and opposition to authority, are an aspect or manifestation of working-class culture generally. In particular, they closely resemble 'shop-floor' culture. Counter-school culture, therefore, is one expression (shop-floor culture is another) of certain basic working-class attitudes and values. This has important implications, Willis believes, for education. Whatever schools do to mitigate the effects of their 'disruptive minority' (Willis's quotation marks) — such as de-streaming and mixed-ability groupings, or a more personal and friendly approach by the teachers — will ultimately be in-effective. Resistance and an oppositional culture will always emerge in one form or another because of the pupils' working-class roots. As Willis puts it, 'there is an undoubted sense in which working-class values and feelings . . . work against the school'.[22]

Secondly, as a consequence of the similarity between anti-school and shop-floor culture, the transition from school to factory work is relatively easy. The cultural background of such pupils prepares them for it. They readily 'choose' to enter the world of the shop-floor, and thereby accept their 'subordinate roles' in the existing system. In this process there is an element of 'self-damnation' which contributes both to the maintenance of working-class underprivilege and to the reproduction of the capitalist social order.

We shall now examine these arguments in greater detail.

Counter-school Culture

The counter-school culture is strikingly similar to shop-floor culture and both are aspects of the larger culture of the working class.

Willis's work is based mainly on a case study of a group of twelve non-academic working-class boys who attended a secondary school in a small Midlands town. At the outset of his account of their anti-school culture, Willis says that: 'The most basic, obvious and explicit dimension of counter-school culture is entrenched, general and personalised opposition to "authority".'[23] The 'lads', as they are called, possess 'an essential belief that the teachers' authority is arbitrary'.[24] Their resistance to the school and their rejection of what it stands for derives from this belief.

This opposition to authority expresses itself in numerous ways. We find truancy, smoking, drinking and a non-conformist style of dress among the 'lads'. But they also engage in vandalism, violence and theft. The members of the school counter-culture have been responsible for breaking into the school, throwing boulders on to a train from a bridge and stealing from handbags. Speaking of their attitude to stealing, Willis says that: 'In some way a successful theft challenges and beats authority.'[25] And of their attitude to fighting he states that: 'It breaks the conventional tyranny of "the rule" . . . It is the ultimate way of breaking a flow of meanings which are unsatisfactory, imposed from above.'[26] During school hours their resistance is principally manifested in a struggle to do as little work as possible, and in an attempt to distance themselves from normal school activities and attitudes. Among the 'lads', says Willis, 'there is an aimless air of insubordination', and they 'specialise in a caged resentment which always stops just short of outright confrontation'.[27] They are, therefore, engaged in 'continuous guerilla warfare'.[28] In their attitude to other pupils they display a contempt for what they themselves call the 'ear-oles' and Willis terms 'conformists', that is, pupils who are not members of the school counter-culture and who, to some extent, identify with the aims of the school in that they want to get on with their work. The 'lads', on the other hand, display a disdain for knowledge and qualification. What matters to them is 'knowing a bit about the world' and 'having your head screwed on'. They think only about the here and now and are dedicated to 'having a laugh'. Furthermore, they persistently engage in a searching out of weakness in others and are deeply racist and sexist.

In moving to a consideration of Willis's conception of shop-floor culture, we find him immediately drawing our attention to the basic similarity with school counter-culture. In so doing he identifies what he considers to be the essential features of both. He writes:

> The really central point about the working-class culture of the shop-floor is that, despite harsh conditions and external direction, people do look for meaning and impose frameworks. They exercise their abilities and seek enjoyment in activity, even where most controlled by others. They do, paradoxically, thread through the dead experience of work a living culture which is far from a simple reflex of defeat. This is the same fundamental taking hold of an alienating situation as one finds in counter-school culture and its attempt to weave a tapestry of interest through the dry institutional text.[29]

More specifically, he says that one of the main characteristics of shop-floor culture is 'the massive attempt to gain a form of control of the work process'.[30] Sometimes, this means that the men actually run production. The same thing occurs in the school. As Willis says:

> Again this is effectively mirrored for us by working-class kids' attempts, with the resources of their counter-culture, to take control of classes, insert their own unofficial timetables, and control their own routines and life spaces . . . Of course, there is the obvious difference that the school informal organization is devoted to doing nothing, while in the factory culture, at least, 'the job's done'. But the degree of opposition to official authority *in each case* should not be minimized, and production managers in such shops were quite as worried as deputy heads about 'what things were coming to'.[31]

Furthermore, in both cases the attempts to control their situation are based on the informal group, which Willis regards as 'the fundamental unit of resistance in both cultures'.[32] In summary, he says that in both cultures one finds 'specific working-class themes: resistance; subversion of authority; informal penetration of the weaknesses and fallibilities of the formal; and an independent ability to create diversion and enjoyment'.[33]

Preparation for the Factory

The cultural background of the pupils of the school counter-culture prepares them for the world of the factory. It thereby facilitates both the reproduction of working-class culture (cultural reproduction) and of Western capitalism (social reproduction).

Pupils of the school counter-culture readily move into unskilled and semi-skilled jobs because they provide a working situation in keeping with their already developed attitudes and values. According to Willis, apprenticeships for skilled manual work are unattractive to the 'lads': 'Such jobs seem to offer little and take a lot.'[34] Similarly with non-manual work. As far as the 'lads' are concerned, it demands too much and encroaches on their independence. For the 'lads', says Willis, mental work 'carries with it the threat of a demand for obedience and conformism. Resistance to mental work becomes resistance to authority as learned in the school.'[35] Mental work is also regarded as essentially feminine and a threat to their masculinity.

However, Willis believes that this whole process ultimately helps to maintain the existing economic and social system. He argues that, whilst the school counter-culture and working-class culture in general contain the potential for liberation, they also, and predominantly at the present time, contribute to the continued enslavement of working-class people.

Willis develops the argument in the following way. The counter-school culture he believes possesses an important insight into ('penetration' of) the conditions of working-class life. The 'lads' understand — even if they cannot articulate it — that the pursuit of educational achievement and the competition for qualifications produces benefits for the few but leaves the majority of their class where they are. They see that: 'A few can make it. The class can never follow.'[36] At school, therefore, they are not interested in trading respect and obedience for knowledge and hoped for qualifications. This Willis regards as a 'radical act: it refuses to collude in its own educational suppression.'[37] It also indicates that the school counter-culture contains a latent demand for a new form of society.

Working-class culture, on the other hand, is also 'fundamentally limited'.[38] 'It is quite wrong', says Willis, 'to picture working-class culture or consciousness optimistically as the vanguard in the grand march towards rationality and socialism.'[39] The 'moving spirit' of working-class culture encourages an accommodation to the existing system, rather than a rejection of it and an attempt to change it. It accepts that there will always be a 'them' and 'us' and does not challenge the rights of management. For all its opposition to authority, therefore, the working class ultimately consents to the prevailing set of power relationships. Thereby, they collude in their own domination.

The result of the whole process is that capitalist social and economic structures are reproduced. However, for Willis, as for other resistance theorists, this does not occur without a struggle. Reproduction is not of the simple, direct kind, with external economic forces impinging upon passive subjects. Willis objects to structuralist accounts of reproduction. As he says: 'Social agents are not passive bearers of ideology, but active appropriators who reproduce existing structures only through struggle, contestation and a partial penetration of those structures.'[40]

The Centre for Contemporary Cultural Studies (CCCS)

Finally, we shall examine two publications by Birmingham University's Centre for Contemporary Cultural Studies (CCCS), namely 'Social Democracy, Education and the Crisis' in the volume *On Ideology*, and *Unpopular Education: Schooling and Social Democracy in England since 1944.*[41]

CCCS's theoretical stance in these two works is not dissimilar from that of the writers examined so far — in fact Willis, at the time of the publication of *Learning to Labour*, was a Research Fellow at the Centre. CCCS protests against the pessimistic determinism of much of direct reproduction theory and emphasises the importance of human will and agency in history, which nevertheless operates within certain structural constraints. It recognises the importance of the idea of reproduction, but states that certain formulations are far from adequate. As it puts it: 'One of the weaknesses of some versions of the theory, Althusser's for instance, is that they appear to have little place for that capacity for resistance which may be exercised by children and teachers in schools.'[42] In its view, schools do not *simply* respond to the demands of the economic system, rather they possess a relative autonomy. However, 'the needs of capitalist industry do exercise a *major influence* on the character and structure of the educational system'.[43] The *extent* of that influence, though, depends upon the strength of the opposing forces. In the end, however, CCCS takes the view that 'schooling is more determined than determining; that schooling plays a role in winning the consent necessary to run a divided society; and that schooling *plays a part* in the reproduction of labour power'.[44]

In all of this, as we have said, CCCS does not differ greatly from writers such as Apple and Giroux. But, whereas Apple and Giroux confine themselves to such theoretical considerations, CCCS goes on to provide a substantive account of developments in the English educational system during the present century (and, more especially, since 1944). Its account merits close and careful attention, and it is to this that we now turn.

THE IDEOLOGY OF SOCIAL DEMOCRACY

The main argument of CCCS is that, in the period 1944–70, educational policy was based upon the ideology of 'social democracy'. This ideology was part of the post-war 'consensus' in British society, and was constructed by three social groups who formed a coalition or alliance. These were: first (and foremost), the Labour Party; second, educationalists working in the areas of sociology and economics; third, the teaching profession.

The Labour Party's commitment to social democracy, says CCCS, has a long history. (The term 'social democracy' does not, therefore, refer to the policies of the recently formed Social Democratic Party.) It can be traced back to the inter-war years, when some of the key features of Labour policy were formed. These features are: first, 'the commitment to educational progress through state policy and the neglect of a more direct, popular educational connection';[45] and second, a concern with 'access' to education and a neglect of matters of 'control' and 'content'.

Commitment to State Policy

From its earliest days, according to CCCS, the Labour Party has been trying to achieve socialism by means of working through the existing political system. This attachment to parliamentary democracy is based on the belief that the state can be used as a neutral instrument for the promotion of the benefit of all sections of society. (For Marxists, on the other hand, the state is an instrument of class domination: as society is capitalist in nature, the state must be a capitalist state and operate in the interests of capitalism.)

Given this attachment to the existing political system, the Labour Party has always felt that the educational interests of working-class children can be furthered through (Labour) government policy initiatives and the system of state schools. The Labour Party, therefore, 'began as and remained an educational *provider for* the popular classes, not an educational *agency of* and *within* them'.[46] It did not 'set out from the cultural and educational resources of working-class communities', that is, from the 'tradition of working-class self-education'.[47] Instead of taking as its starting-point the sort of independent, working-class educational organisations that, according to CCCS, had sprung up at times during the nineteenth century, the Labour Party organised education from the 'top downwards'. Instead of 'popular' education, therefore, it imposed a non-popular, that is an 'unpopular', form of schooling. Working-class radicals in the 1830s and 1840s feared such a type of educational provision. They viewed it as an attempt to teach 'down' to the popular classes and, says CCCS, 'saw provided education of all kinds as a tyranny or, at best, as a laughable irrelevance'.[48] They demanded, therefore, independent educational forms subject to democratic self-control in a system organised from the 'bottom upwards'. The Labour Party, however, failed to adopt such an educational objective and concentrated on the provision of state schooling.

In this they were supported by a second member of the social-democratic coalition, namely the academics working in education-related disciplines. According to CCCS, the 'basic standpoint' of their research was 'the orientation towards reform via the state, rather than to popular knowledge and agitation'. Such research operated, it continues, 'through personal advice to potential governments, to persons with power within the educational apparatus and, especially, to Labour Ministers of education'. The pattern, therefore, was that of 'elite politics revolving more around the private salon than the party branch. It lacked contact with popular educational experiences.'[49]

Access to Education

The second major feature of Labour Party policy — the concern with 'access' to education rather than the 'content' and 'control' of it — comes out clearly, CCCS argues, in the writings of R.H. Tawney, whom they describe as 'the most important "philosopher" of British Social Democracy'.[50] (We shall also discuss Tawney's work in Chapter 12.) Tawney's main work on the subject was *Secondary Schools for All* (1922), the very title of which sums up Labour Party policy in the inter-war years. That policy was to abolish the old system of elementary schools for the majority and secondary schools for the few, replacing it with universal access to secondary education. 'This meant', says CCCS, 'the reorganization of all schools into primary or secondary, the abolition of fees in secondary schools, the increase of maintenance allowances, and an expansion of secondary school places.'[51]

In the post-war period, this concentration on access developed into a concern with the *form* of secondary education. The issue was a comprehensive versus a tripartite system. It was here that the research of the sociologists of education became important. They drew attention to working-class underachievement in education and the wastage of ability. Thereby, they helped to move the Labour Party in the direction of non-selective schools.

Questions of 'control' and 'content', on the other hand, were largely neglected. Confining ourselves here to the discussion of content, CCCS argues that 'social democracy possessed no conception of the nature and purposes of education which could be said to be its *own*'.[52] Tawney, for example, was certainly opposed to a narrowly vocational conception of education. However, 'No positive conception of education was forthcoming to place in opposition to capitalist imperatives, only a conception of culture, which Tawney inherited from Matthew Arnold, which was presented as being outside or above classes.'[53] The idea that popular education should be concerned with 'really useful knowledge' was absent.

The idea of 'really useful knowledge', says CCCS, was something that developed in the nineteenth century. 'This view of education was typical among those who had gained an educational experience of a positive kind through politics, and in the oppositional cultural worlds of popular radicalism, socialism and feminism.'[54] It consisted, we are told, of 'a knowledge of everyday circumstances, including a knowledge of why you were poor, why you were politically oppressed and why, through the force of social circumstances, you were the kind of person you were, your character misshapen by a cruel competitive world'.[55] This conception of education also refused to accept the distinction between 'truth' and 'usefulness', believing that these things were identical. (A mistake in our view. For, even if you were to accept that what is true is useful — and this is by no means obvious — it certainly does not follow that what is useful is true. For example, it may well be useful for a society's ruling group to have their subjects believe that 'free competition' produces universal well-being. Yet few people — including Marxists — would thereby conclude that a *laissez-faire* doctrine was true.)

It was not only Tawney, however, who was at fault concerning the content of education. The Labour Party itself, we are told, avoided such questions and left it to the third member of the ideological coalition, the teachers, to fill the gap. It was they who, in the 1950s and 1960s, 'supplied the content' and provided 'the missing centre of social democratic policies'.[56] In large part this derived from the teachers' pursuit of professional status, which involved a demand for autonomy and the control of the curriculum — demands which the Labour Party was happy to accept.

THE POLICIES OF SOCIAL DEMOCRACY

These, then, are the two key features of the social democratic approach to education of the Labour Party and its allies. CCCS goes on to say that this concern with access to education through state provision was fundamental to the Party's policies whilst in government in the 1960s. It is revealed, for example, in its programme of expansion of further and higher education, and in the raising of the school-leaving age to 16. It then argues that underlying these policies were certain basic *assumptions* or *goals*, namely, the pursuit of *equality of opportunity* on the one hand, and *equality* on the other. We must now look in some detail at these two aspects of Labour's 'dual repertoire'.

Equality of Opportunity

Equality of opportunity, says CCCS, is the 'Fabian' or 'liberal' element of Labour's social-democratic ideology. Central to it is the idea of 'careers open to talent'. It involves the notion that any artificial barriers to social mobility should be removed and that ability, not class background, ought to determine economic position and material rewards. The aim, therefore, is 'a more efficient and fair selection and reward of talent', as well as a more rational form of social organisation.[57]

In the opinion of CCCS, equality of opportunity is best understood as an economic goal involving, as it does, notions of competition, individualism and the market. Within this framework, education in the 1950s and 1960s was regarded as a 'form of investment'. One influential statement of this point of view was by the economist John Vaizey, who 'played a part in the development of bodies of knowledge . . . that provided the basis for the practical common sense of the 1960s policy-makers'.[58] For Vaizey, education was a major cause of economic growth, and investment in 'human capital' was, therefore, a way of meeting the requirements of the economy for skilled and flexible manpower. However, the notion of education as an investment was not thought of as being incompatible with the idea of education as a means of developing individual potentialities and capacities (education as a form of 'consumption'). The 'manpower perspective', say Vaizey and Debeauvais, 'is not an anti-humanistic point of view. On the contrary a high level of general culture — as well as being the ultimate end of educational activity — is necessary for the adaptation of the working force to the new economy.'[59] The same theme occurs, says CCCS, in the speeches of Labour politicians such as Harold Wilson. Wilson and others claimed that economic and humanistic ends could be reconciled and that, therefore, teachers could, in the words of CCCS, 'concentrate on doing their best for the child with the assurance that it would benefit him or her in the most obvious material ways too'.[60]

Equality

The pursuit of equality, and not just equality of opportunity, is the 'egalitarian' — as opposed to the Fabian or liberal — element of Labour's social-democratic ideology. CCCS points out that Tawney and, more recently, Anthony Crosland in *The Future of Socialism* stress that equality of opportunity by itself is an inadequate socialist goal. It needs to be supplemented by a concern with the greater equalisation of rewards and conditions. Crosland probably best summed up the argument — though CCCS does not quote this particular passage — when he said that:

> equality of opportunity and social mobility . . . are not enough. They need, not to be played down, as some sociologists would have us do, but to be combined with measures above all in the educational field, to equalise the distribution of rewards and privileges so as to diminish the degree of class stratification, the injustice of large inequalities, and the collective discontents which come from too great a dispersion of rewards.[61]

In this passage, Crosland gives us some idea of why he thinks equality valuable. CCCS says that, in common with like-minded egalitarians, he sought social cohesion and the minimisation of divisions and resentment, the creation of social harmony, a 'common culture', and fraternity.

CRITICISM OF SOCIAL DEMOCRACY

Having set out what it sees as fundamental to the ideology and policies of social democracy, CCCS turns to *criticism*. It makes a number of points.

Contradictory Goals. It argues that the pursuit of the dual goals of equality of opportunity and equality involves a contradiction. 'It is a commonplace of social philosophy', it says, 'that the two kinds of equality represent different positions and point to contradictory outcomes.'[62] The pursuit of equality involves challenging the idea and the fact of advantage and privilege. The principle of equality of opportunity, on the other hand, is concerned that there should be an open and fair competition for economic rewards and social privileges — the equal opportunity to become unequal.

The Inadequacy of State Policies. Secondly, it maintains that Labour has consistently believed that class-based disadvantages can be removed by political means or through 'social policy solutions'. It fails to see, therefore, that class inequalities are rooted in social relations of production of capitalism; and that one cannot achieve equality by educational reform in a society 'still structured by unequal relations of class, gender and race'.[63] For CCCS, the only solution to the problem lies in the transformation of capitalist society. Such a solution is unacceptable to the Labour Party, however, as its Fabian/liberal element 'has been centrally concerned with the mission of managing and reforming a capitalist society'.[64]

Equality as Harmony. Thirdly, even the egalitarian strand in Labour's policy has brought problems. Too often equality has been thought of as a means to an end, such as social cohesion and harmony, rather than an end in itself from which social order will follow. Furthermore, although in the pursuit of equality Labour has sought to represent popular, that is working-class, interests, it has always thought that such interests are best served through capitalist economic growth. In CCCS's judgement, therefore, the Labour Party 'has always served two masters', and assumed a basic harmony of class interests. 'This project of the harmonization of class interests', adds CCCS, 'is what, in the end, warrants the term "social democracy"'.[65]

The Fabian Emphasis. However, Fabian/liberal goals have been dominant in the period 1950–70. This can be seen, argues CCCS, in the case of comprehensive schools. 'Comprehensive schools', it says, 'did remove forms of separation, to some degree; they did allow a greater autonomy of teachers and pupils. Yet they were not encouraged even to begin to implement stronger definitions of equality.'[66] This also comes out in the Labour Party's 'elitist', non-popular approach to education. Reform of the educational system has been made from 'above' by professionals. The working class has been the object of policy, not its author.

Class Inequality and Educational Failure. Indeed, working-class people have been seen by Labour politicians, under the influence of their academic advisors, as 'problems' — 'bearers of educationally disadvantaged behaviour'.[67] Working-class failure and underachievement in education have been explained in terms of deficiencies in home background and parent culture.

> We are told, over and over again, that working-class people are more or less materially deprived, lack cultural resources and so do not

encourage their children at school. But *why this is so* (in so far as it is so) remains perpetually obscure.[68]

CCCS argues that sociologists of education and, subsequently, Labour politicians — partners in the social-democratic coalition — have failed to see the connection between underachievement at school and the nature of the wider society. As CCCS puts it: 'The class character of educational backgrounds was not related to the class organization of the society as a whole and especially to processes of class domination.' The concentration on home background — and, for that matter, on the 'labelling' practices of teachers — 'displaced attention and blame away from an unequal society and on to the principal sufferers'.[69] Working-class failure must be seen, therefore, as a direct consequence of inequalities and divisions that are intrinsic to a capitalist and patriarchal society. Similarly, working-class opposition and resistance to schooling has to be set in this context. The working class has an ambivalent attitude to schooling and gives it a low value. CCCS regards this as a 'sensible (if pessimistic)' response,[70] given that the working class is destined for a life of routine labour in the workplace and home.

The 1970s

CCCS continues its account by saying that, in the 1950s and 1960s social-democratic ideology went virtually unchallenged. In the 1970s, however, the 'educational settlement' of those years came under attack. One of the main reasons for this was the failure of education to promote economic growth. As CCCS puts it: 'Education had been regarded as a prime mover of economic development in the 1965 National Plan. Now, the economic maelstroms of the 1970s seemed to have quickly demolished these notions with the "return" on such investments looking palpably poor.'[71] Despite a considerable investment in education, it was felt that it was not providing industry with the skilled, adaptable workforce that it required. In addition, education was failing the very children it was specifically intended to help. In CCCS's words:

> from viewing the schools as *the* means of solving a problem, namely working-class failure and its economic and cultural consequences, the emphasis is now one which charges the schools with failing to do this, despite the resources which have been invested.[72]

Furthermore, these two types of criticism of the educational system often went hand in hand. A typical example was to be found in *The Financial*

Times where it was said that 'industry is suffering from an undereducated workforce, while many working-class children are being given the added disadvantage of a non-education on top of all their other burdens'.[73]

During the 1970s, says CCCS, there was in fact widespread concern about falling standards and indiscipline, which came to something of a head in the William Tyndale affair. Consequently, the idea that what went on in schools could be safely left to the teachers was called into question. In 1976, the then Labour Prime Minister, James Callaghan, initiated the 'Great Debate' on education when, in a speech at Ruskin College, Oxford, he stated that there must be a full discussion of the following issues: the methods and aims of informal instruction; the case for a core curriculum of basic knowledge; the proper way of maintaining the use of resources in order to achieve a good national standard of performance. This, says CCCS, marked an important shift in Labour policy. The demand was now for a closer external control of teaching and teachers, and for a greater public accountability of schools — a position similar to that of right-wing, Black Paper authors. Also at this time, continues CCCS, Labour was coming to see education essentially as a means of training young people for their place in the world of work. 'Schooling and its social purposes were to be politically subordinated to the perceived needs of a capitalist economy in the throes of crisis.'[74] This comes out particularly in the work of the Manpower Services Commission which, CCCS says, is 'the best single condensation of Labour's educational politics in the 1970s'.[75] In effect, therefore, the relative autonomy of the educational system in the 1960s has disappeared, and been replaced by 'a closer conformity between the educational system and the necessities of production'.[76]

Since the 1979 General Election victory of the Conservatives, 'the challenge to social democratic orthodoxies . . . has become wholesale demolition'.[77] This is worrying for CCCS because, despite its critical attitude to social democracy, 'Modern Conservatism is even more inimical to popular education than its social democratic rival.'[78] 'Populist Toryism' is, therefore, to be distinguished from 'popular' education and politics — though they do not succeed in making clear the distinction. What is clear, however, is that popular education and politics involve active participation by the majority of the people at grass-roots or local level. Control must be in their hands, and not those of the experts or professionals. We must move away, therefore, from a concern with state and parliamentary politics, and develop a commitment to 'non-statist forms of socialist practice'.[79] This involves a conception of education in its 'socialist and feminist definition'; though they add — in typical Marxist fashion — that 'this does not simply exist waiting to be "realized": it will not be easy to form, its shape can only be known at later stages in a long process'.[80]

In summary we can say that, for the group of writers we have just considered, 'resistance' to the demands of the capitalist economic structure is a fundamental feature of the educational system. The idea that schools simply mould their pupils to fit the 'needs' of contemporary society ignores, they believe, the existence of oppositional cultures within the educational system. Indeed, they regard such opposition as a manifestation of attitudes and values to be found in working-class culture generally. Furthermore, they reject the structuralist Marxist view that human beings act as they do because of the operation of impersonal economic forces. History, according to the resistance theorists, is made by men not through them. Human will and agency, as well as structure, are important. As a consequence, they see pupils as creatively adapting to the environment in which they find themselves. Moreover, schools are said to possess a relative autonomy from the demands of the wider society. Even so, reproduction still takes place; but for these writers it occurs 'indirectly' rather than 'directly', that is, alongside or through the process of resistance.

At this point we leave behind our exposition of the Marxist perspective and turn to an assessment of this theory of education and society.

NOTES

1. M. Apple, *Education and Power* (Routledge and Kegan Paul, London, 1982), p. 24.

2. M. Apple, *Cultural and Economic Reproduction in Education* (Routledge and Kegan Paul, London, 1982), p. 8.

3. Apple, *Education and Power*, p. 14.

4. Ibid., pp. 83–4.

5. Ibid., p. 95.

6. Ibid., p. 96.

7. H. Giroux, 'Theories of Reproduction and Resistance in the New Sociology of Education: A Critical Analysis', *Harvard Educational Review*, vol. 53, no. 3 (1983), pp. 257–93.

8. Ibid., p. 259.

9. Ibid., p. 260.

10. Ibid., p. 261.

11. Ibid., p. 260.

12. Giroux, *Ideology, Culture and the Process of Schooling* (Falmer Press, Lewes, 1981), p. 100.

13. Ibid., p. 100.

14. Ibid., p. 102.

15. M. Sarup, *Education, State and Crisis* (Routledge and Kegan Paul, London, 1982), pp. 113–14.

16. P. Willis, *Learning to Labour* (Saxon House, Farnborough, 1977).

17. A. McRobbie, 'Working Class Girls and the Culture of Femininity' in CCCS, University of Birmingham, *Women Take Issue* (Hutchinson, London, 1978).

18. P. Corrigan, *Schooling the Smash Street Kids* (Macmillan, London, 1979).

19. See, for example, R. Everhart, *Reading, Writing and Resistance (sic)* (Routledge and Kegan Paul, London, 1983).

20. The following account will also draw upon Willis's articles: 'The Class Significance of School Counter-Culture' in M. Hammersley and P. Woods (eds.), *The Process of Schooling* (Routledge and Kegan Paul, London, 1976); 'Cultural Production and Theories of Reproduction' in L. Barton and S. Walker (eds.), *Race, Class and Education* (Croom Helm, London, 1983).

21. D. Hargreaves, *Social Relations in a Secondary School* (Routledge and Kegan Paul, London, 1967); and C. Lacey, *Hightown Grammar* (Manchester University Press, Manchester, 1970).

22. Willis, *Learning to Labour*, p. 73.

23. Ibid., p. 11.

24. Willis, 'The Class Significance', p. 195.

25. Willis, *Learning to Labour*, p. 40.

26. Ibid., p. 36.

27. Ibid., pp. 12–13.

28. Ibid., p. 19.

29. Willis, 'The Class Significance', p. 189.

30. Ibid., p. 189.

31. Ibid., p. 190.

32. Ibid., p. 190.

33. Willis, *Learning to Labour*, p. 84.

34. Ibid., p. 126.

35. Ibid., p. 103.

36. Ibid., p. 128.

37. Ibid., p. 128.

38. Willis, 'The Class Significance', p. 198.

39. Willis, *Learning to Labour*, p. 122. A similar conclusion is to be found in Corrigan, *Schooling the Smash Street Kids*. Corrigan says that, whilst they engage in resistance and struggle, 'at no stage do they ever display anything but a *subordinate* consciousness in the struggle' (p. 147).

40. Willis, *Learning to Labour*, p. 175.

41. D. Finn, N. Grant and R. Johnson, Centre for Contemporary Cultural Studies (CCCS), University of Birmingham, 'Social Democracy, Education and Crisis' in *On Ideology* (Hutchinson, London, 1978) and CCCS, *Unpopular Education: Schooling and Social Democracy in England Since 1944* (Hutchinson, London, 1981).

42. CCCS, 'Social Democracy', p. 145.

43. CCCS, *Unpopular Education*, p. 31 (emphasis added).

44. Ibid., p. 248.

45. Ibid., p. 34.

46. CCCS, 'Social Democracy', p. 150; *Unpopular Education*, p. 46.

47. CCCS, 'Social Democracy', p. 150.

48. CCCS, *Unpopular Education*, p. 34.

49. Ibid., p. 88.

50. CCCS, 'Social Democracy', p. 152.

51. CCCS, *Unpopular Education*, p. 43.

52. CCCS, 'Social Democracy', p. 156.

53. CCCS, *Unpopular Education*, p. 44.

54. Ibid., p. 34.

55. Ibid., p. 37.

56. CCCS, 'Social Democracy', p. 170.

57. CCCS, *Unpopular Education*, p. 72.

58. Ibid., p. 75.

59. Quoted in CCCS, *Unpopular Education*, p. 78.

60. CCCS, *Unpopular Education*, p. 97.
61. C.A.R. Crosland, *The Future of Socialism* (Cape, London, 1964), p. 169.
62. CCCS, 'Social Democracy', p. 182.
63. CCCS, *Unpopular Education*, p. 182.
64. Ibid., p. 97.
65. Ibid., pp. 97–8.
66. Ibid., p. 129.
67. Ibid., p. 164.
68. Ibid., p. 137.
69. Ibid., p. 138.
70. Ibid., p. 157.
71. Ibid., p. 172.
72. CCCS, 'Social Democracy', p. 188.
73. Quoted in CCCS, *Unpopular Education*, p. 216.
74. CCCS, *Unpopular Education*, p. 220.
75. Ibid., p. 228.
76. CCCS, 'Social Democracy', p. 185.
77. CCCS, *Unpopular Education*, p. 7.
78. Ibid., p. 243.
79. Ibid., p. 265.
80. Ibid., p. 260.

9   AN EVALUATION OF THE MARXIST PERSPECTIVE

In our evaluation of the Marxist perspective we shall first provide a critique of the theory of society and social change (historical materialism) which forms the basis of the Marxist analysis of education (see Chapter 6). For, clearly, if the general theory is faulty, this has important implications for our view of the Marxist perspective on education.

In turning to the Marxist analysis of education, we shall begin with an assessment of direct reproduction theories (as discussed in Chapter 7) by considering the views of Reynolds and Hickox.

Next we shall move to an examination of the ideas presented in Chapter 8, starting with the theory of relative autonomy. Here we shall draw upon the work of Andy Hargreaves. There then follows a sustained critique of the idea of resistance in education. In particular, we discuss Willis's highly influential *Learning to Labour*. In this section of the chapter we also examine the claims made by writers such as Johnson that there is a continuity between the oppositional behaviour of school counter-cultures and the resistance of the working class in the nineteenth century to the demands of capitalism. Finally, we spend some time considering the arguments of CCCS concerning 'social democracy' and education by looking at alternative conceptions of society, state and education in the writings of Crosland, Galbraith and the 'pluralists'.

HISTORICAL MATERIALISM — A CRITIQUE

Our basic criticism of historical materialism is that, if it is a theory of economic determinism, then, quite simply, it is false; whereas, if it is a theory of relative autonomy, proposing that there is an interaction between base and superstructure in which economic forces condition but are conditioned by the superstructure, then it is a truism, a mere commonplace, and as a consequence Marxism cannot be distinguished from many other types of social and political theory.

A Theory of Economic Determinism

That Marxism as a theory of economic determinism is untenable is perhaps indicated by the move away from such a conception of historical materialism by many Marxists in the twentieth century. They have probably come to recognise that historical and social analysis will not support such a view. Important in this respect has been the example of Soviet Russia. For the great transformation of Russian society which has occurred since the revolution of 1917 has not been a result of economic developments in the Marxist sense. The major changes in Russian society have not been a consequence of the forces and relations of production coming into conflict with one another and producing a new social form. The events of 1917, for example, were not preceded by a period of technological advance. Rather what mattered in the Russian Revolution was that a group of individuals, imbued with a particular ideology, saw their opportunity and seized power. And, having gained control of the state, they set about transforming society (especially the economy) in accordance with the idea they had of a superior way of life.

On this question of the role of ideas and their relation to economic circumstances in Soviet Russia, Karl Popper has written:

> In a fight against tremendous odds, uncounted material difficulties were overcome, uncounted material sacrifices were made, in order to alter, or rather to build up from nothing, the conditions of production. And the driving power of this development was the enthusiasm for an *idea*. This example shows that in certain circumstances ideas may revolutionize the economic conditions of a country, instead of being moulded by these conditions.[1]

In other words, it was 'superstructural' factors — especially ideology and political power — that were crucial in transforming a semi-feudal society into a highly industrialised nation. There is, then, as Popper states, a 'glaring contrast' between the development of the Russian Revolution and Marx's economic determinism. The men involved were not the 'bearers' or 'personification' of economic forces, subject to an 'economic law of motion' working with 'iron necessity towards inevitable results' — to quote again from *Capital*. Rather they were the creators of a new economic base. It is ironical, then, that the history of Marxism itself furnishes an example that clearly falsifies economic determinism.

A similar point, although made more generally, is to be found in Isaiah Berlin's discussion of Marx. Speaking of Marx's work he says that:

> It set out to refute the proposition that ideas decisively determine the course of history, but the very extent of its own influence on human affairs has weakened the force of its thesis. For in altering the hitherto prevailing view of the relation of the individual to his environment and to his fellows, it has palpably altered that relation itself; and in

consequence remains the most powerful among the intellectual forces which are today transforming the ways in which men act and think.[2]

It is also worth noting, whilst considering the role of ideas in history, and especially the impact of Marxist theory upon the development of Soviet society, that such considerations indicate that the concept of 'Marxism–Leninism' is a contradiction in terms. The reason for this comes out very clearly in Plamenatz's discussion of the ideas of Lenin and Trotsky. Speaking first about the ideas of Trotsky as early as 1905 he states:

> Trotsky believed with Marx that socialism cannot exist except in an advanced industrial economy: he therefore believed that the Russia of 1905 would need to be greatly changed before she could be made socialist. What he imagined in 1905 became one of the essential tenets of Communism; he imagined that the workers, led by the party of their class, might first make a revolution and then use political power to create the advanced industrial economy which is alone (according to Marx) compatible with socialism. Like Lenin in *Two Tactics*, he placed *after* the revolution what, in the opinion of Marx and Engels, should come *before* it. This simple inversion, which makes nonsense of historical materialism, is the essence of Bolshevism.[3]

A Theory of Relative Autonomy

We now turn to a consideration of the criticism that, in so far as historical materialism is not a form of economic determinism, then it is a mere truism, a banal commonplace. This point has been made by a number of writers. For example, in his book *The Politics of Democratic Socialism*, the British socialist Evan Durbin says that, if Marxism takes the view that economic factors are just one among a number of factors that can influence the course of history, then there is no case against the theory — because it would be very odd indeed if this were *not* true. Marxism, he continues,

> must attribute a determining or solitary influence to economic causes, for otherwise there is little interest in the theory. No one would be greatly moved by the doctrine that economic causes were only one type of cause active in history — one among many such types — because who would wish to deny such a view?[4]

Who indeed! Certainly not the vast majority of non-Marxist sociologists who also believe that society is made what it is because of the operation of a 'plurality' of factors — political, religious, ideological, cultural, as well as economic. At any particular time, one of these factors may, of course, be of decisive importance. But that is to be determined by empirical investigation and historical analysis.

A similar point is made by Kolakowski. He writes:

> It would seem that to say there is an interaction between the relations of production and the 'superstructure' is to utter a truism which all would accept and which has nothing particularly Marxist about it. Historic events — wars, revolutions, religious changes, the rise and fall of states and empires, artistic trends and scientific discoveries — can be rationally explained by many circumstances, not excluding technology and class conflicts: this is a matter of common sense and would not be denied by a religious believer, a materialist, or any philosopher of history unless he were a fanatical champion of some 'unique factor' or other. That books and plays cannot be understood without knowledge of the historical circumstances and social conflicts of the time was known, long before Marx, to many French and other historians, some of whom were conservative in politics. We must ask then, what exactly is historical materialism? If it means that every detail of the superstructure can be explained as in some way dictated by the demands of the 'base', it is an absurdity with nothing to recommend it to credence; while if, as Engels's remarks suggest, it does not involve absolute determinism in this sense, it is no more than a fact of common knowledge. If interpreted rigidly, it conflicts with the elementary demands of rationality; if loosely, it is a mere truism.[5]

In much the same vein, Sidney Hook, in his *Revolution, Reform and Social Justice*, argues that in recent decades the 'original' Marxist doctrine of economic determinism has been 'watered down' by 'common sense' imbibed from the English scene. As a consequence, it is no longer an imposing but simplistic monism.[6]

All three of these writers agree, therefore, that, if historical materialism is a form of economic determinism, it is a bold, coherent, but untenable theory; whereas, if it asserts that not just economic, but many other factors, are responsible for making society what it is, then, although it is no longer open to such an objection, it loses its distinctiveness as a form of social analysis. In other words, if Marxists adopt the latter interpretation of the doctrine, they make the theory immune to criticism; but in the process it becomes trivialised. As Durbin comments, what is now being said is not worth discussing. Or, as the great philosopher Edmund Burke put it in another connection, 'by a miserable subterfuge, they hope to render their proposition safe by rendering it nugatory'.[7]

The traditional way out of this unhappy dilemma is, as Kolakowski points out, for Marxists to remind us that the 'interaction' view of the relationship between base and superstructure nevertheless emphasises that economic factors are dominant 'in the final analysis'. But this formula does not take us any further, for, as Kolakowski says,

> the additional vague statement about 'determination in the last resort' has no meaning whatsoever in historical explanation as long as we are not able to define what are the *limits* of this 'ultimate determination' and, similarly, the *limits* of the 'relative autonomy' granted to the other domains of social life.[8]

Likewise, Hook stresses that Marxists employing this notion need to assign different weights to the different factors. Yet this is what they signally fail to do. Rather, what we are left with is a vague and imprecise theory which can be all things to all men. It enables Marxists to have their cake and eat it too. It permits them to agree that, say, political factors or ideology are sometimes of decisive importance in the course of social change; but also to claim that 'ultimately' economic forces are dominant. Any fact whatsoever can be fitted into the theory, which can therefore explain everything and anything. No conceivable observations can contradict it, and the formula explains whatever occurs. As Popper points out, the theory is therefore unfalsifiable and self-confirming. Consequently, it is not a scientific theory. For the hallmark of such scientific theories is that it is possible to refute them. Bryan Magee summarises Popper's point when he says that, according to Popper:

> A scientific theory is not one which explains everything that can possibly happen: on the contrary, it rules out most of what could possibly happen, and is therefore itself ruled out if what it rules out happens. So a genuinely scientific theory places itself permanently at risk.[9]

But the theory of 'relative autonomy' and 'determination in the final analysis' does not place itself at risk in this way. On the contrary, whatever occurs is regarded as a confirmation of the theory. There is no way in which it can be falsified. Against this sort of theory you just cannot win.

THEORIES OF DIRECT REPRODUCTION IN THE MARXIST ANALYSIS OF EDUCATION

Similar criticisms to these have been made of the Marxist analysis of education. In this section we shall look at the theories of direct reproduction.

David Reynolds

In Chapter 8 we saw that many Marxists themselves now reject an economic determinist conception of education. They believe, for example, that resistance as well as reproduction goes on in schools, that pupils are not the helpless victims of an economic system but also active agents, that schools have some autonomy from the demands of the economy, etc. This notion of the relative autonomy of the educational system has been further developed by David Reynolds in his 'Relative Autonomy Reconstructed'.[10] But in the course of his essay he provides a sustained critique of reproduction theory which is worth examining in some detail.

Reynolds argues that it is difficult to see any close 'correspondence' between the capitalist economic base and the educational system. He maintains that various sorts of empirical evidence support this conclusion.

Education and the Economy. There is only a limited fit between education and the 'needs' of the economy. Reynolds argues that it is difficult to see how British capitalism is served by an educational system in which there is so much anti-social conduct. Furthermore, 'The amount of resistance, of rejection of the mental and of searching for the manual is clearly more than is functionally necessary for the recruitment of the number of workers needed to form the unskilled working class population.'[11] In addition, there is little correspondence between the curriculum of the schools and the requirements of the economic system. As Reynolds says:

> The survival in schools of a liberal, humanities-based curriculum, the emphasis upon the acquisition of knowledge for the purposes of intellectual self-betterment rather than collective material gain, the limited swing to science within higher education, the continuing status of 'pure' disciplines as against work-related applied knowledge, the decline in commercially important foreign language courses at sixth form level and the continuing presence in schools of a 'cultural' world

of sexist practices that effectively isolates many able girls from doing industrially relevant courses in science and technology all suggest a lack of correspondence.[12]

This lack of fit between education and the requirements of the economy, continues Reynolds, is in large part due to the structural fact of the autonomous nature of education in British society. Britain, he says, has 'a heavily decentralised locus of power in the education system that is rare in a European context, where central government intervenes more in the areas of both pedagogy and curriculum content'.[13] This results in a considerable variation between schools which are outwardly subject to the same pressures — a variety which derives from the substantial autonomy which LEAs and headteachers possess within the present system. But it is not just structural factors alone which promote the autonomy of education. Very often the people who exercise that autonomy possess an 'anti-industrial bias'. As Reynolds puts it:

> The large number of radicals who have been attracted into teaching, the presence among many of them of a liberal, educational orientation rather than a training orientation, the attraction of teaching to those with high autonomy needs and the ways in which schools are a refuge for those with high security needs (Derr and Delong, 1982) do not suggest an overwhelming orientation amongst those in education to generate in their schools crucibles in which industrially relevant skills and characteristics are forged.[14]

In addition, the very autonomy of the educational system has been used by the teaching profession to promote its own class and status interests in ways which are not necessarily functional for the capitalist economic enterprise.

Education and Capitalist Values. Capitalist economic values are not central in British culture and have not penetrated key institutions such as schools and government. Reynolds says that recent research by Weiner, for example, in his *English Culture and the Decline of the Industrial Spirit*, shows that public schools in the nineteenth century 'actually aimed to "civilise" children . . . away from holding "capitalist" values about the importance of science, technology, business and commerce'.[15]

Schools' Independence. There is a growing body of knowledge which draws our attention to the independence of the school. Schools, Reynolds says, possess the freedom to develop in their pupils the sort of qualities which they deem desirable. As a consequence, pupils are often unsocialised into the mainstream values of capitalist society.

M.S.H. Hickox

Further criticisms of direct reproduction theories are made by M.S.H. Hickox in his article 'The Marxist Sociology of Education: A Critique'.[16] Hickox's main argument is that no real evidence has been offered to support the view — advanced, for example, by Bowles and Gintis in *Schooling in Capitalist America* — that education reproduces the class structure by means of (1) legitimation and (2) socialisation.

Legitimation

As we have seen in our account of direct reproduction theories, Marxists argue that the educational system transmits the ideology of equal opportunity and meritocracy. This, they believe, helps to legitimate existing inequalities in the 'hierarchical division of labour' because it spreads the view that economic success depends on ability and educational qualifications.

Hickox argues that, because in most modern industrial societies there is very little connection between educational attainment and occupational position, it is difficult to see how the possession of educational qualifications can provide a legitimation for economic inequalities. However, we feel that here, to some extent, Hickox misses the point. Marxists do not say that educational qualifications actually correlate with economic position, only that there is a widespread belief that they do, and that it is this belief which helps legitimate the division of labour. For Marxists, it is socio-economic background not educational qualifications which determines occupational position.

Where Hickox is on stronger ground, however, is when he points out that there is some evidence which seems to indicate that 'the industrial working class accords relatively little legitimacy to educational qualifications'. In Scase's study, for example, only 2.5 per cent of English workers thought educational credentials were an important determinant of social class. They accorded much greater importance to family background and economic factors. Hickox comments that: 'This might seem to imply that the average member of the working class shares the educational sociologists' perception that the effect of education is merely to confirm pre-existing social status.'[17] It also implies, of course, that the average member of the working class shares the viewpoint of Marxist reproduction theorists, and hence it undermines their argument about legitimation.

Socialisation

According to direct reproduction theories, the maintenance of capitalism is also accomplished by means of the socialisation of pupils in schools. The educational system, it is said, shapes their values, beliefs and aspirations in such a way that they readily fit into the existing relations of production. This is achieved principally through a 'correspondence' between the social relations of production and those of work with respect to matters of authority and control.

Hickox points out that correspondence theorists typically see the introduction of mass schooling in the nineteenth century as being closely linked to capitalism's need for a passive and disciplined workforce. Education, it is said, was a way of imposing 'appropriate' attitudes towards work and authority on working-class children. But Hickox asks if there is any evidence to show, first, that capitalists actually viewed education in this way and, second, that mass education performed and performs such a socialisation function?

With respect to the first of these questions, Hickox points out that Marxist historians themselves often fail to make a good case. For example, in Richard Johnson's study of working-class education in Britain before 1850, the evidence tends to suggest that 'in the main factory owners were more impressed by the need to preserve child labour and to conserve resources than by the hypothetical benefits to be derived from subsidizing working class education'.[18] As for the idea that education instils appropriate work attitudes and values, Hickox argues that in England there was a considerable gap between the onset of industrialisation and the provision of mass schooling — suggesting that the capitalists got along quite well for many years without any socialisation through education. Furthermore, the amount of money spent on working-class education in the nineteenth century, when it did come along, was very small — indicating again that not too much importance was attached to it as a means of promoting appropriate attitudes and values. Concerning the present-day role of education, Hickox says that 'there is remarkably little evidence to support the view that the experience of formal education has been an important formative influence on the work attitudes and expectations of the working class in capitalist societies'.[19] Indeed, he continues, 'the values of working class subculture itself have been far more important in shaping working class attitudes to work than the experience of formal education'.[20]

The relative ineffectiveness of formal education in the socialisation of young workers is brought out very clearly, says Hickox, in the studies by Willis and Frith. Frith, for example, points out that the demand for 'mature' and 'responsible' young workers is a recent phenomenon, reflecting changes in the labour market in the 1970s. Prior to that time it was always expected that mature attitudes to work would only develop as a consequence of marriage and of setting up a household, and that the young worker would be largely irresponsible. Thus, says Hickox, it is only after a century of mass schooling that education is being asked to perform the function which correspondence theorists believe has been with it from the first.

THE THEORY OF RELATIVE AUTONOMY IN THE MARXIST ANALYSIS OF EDUCATION

Andy Hargreaves

In the first part of this chapter we examined the criticisms of relative autonomy theory made by such writers as Durbin and Kolakowski. A similar type of critique has been developed by Andy Hargreaves with respect to theory of the relative autonomy of education. (Note we are speaking of Andy, not David, Hargreaves. There are two 'Hargreaves' in the contemporary sociology of education.) Hargreaves says that these Marxists claim to be offering a subtle and sophisticated analysis of the relationship between education and capitalist production. He believes, however, that 'the attempt to explain the simultaneous dependence and independence of schooling . . . has been responsible for widespread incoherence in the explanations that have been advanced'.[21] Quite simply, they want to have it both ways, maintaining that education is both determined and not determined by economic factors. Their arguments, therefore, are unclear and contradictory. Furthermore, they lie beyond the realm of proof and disproof. As a consequence, says Hargreaves, in relative autonomy theory, 'anything goes'.

In addition, argues Hargreaves, it is difficult to see what is specifically Marxist about an approach which stresses both the independence and dependence of education in relation to economic forces. In these circumstances, he says, it would be better to abandon Marxist categories altogether and employ a pluralist or Weberian approach. (We shall have more to say about such perspectives on education, later in this chapter (p. 224), and in Chapter 13.)

THE THEORY OF RESISTANCE IN THE MARXIST ANALYSIS OF EDUCATION

Hargreaves also provides a critique of the idea of resistance in the Marxist sociology of education. However, we should like to approach our consideration of this notion through a sustained commentary on Willis's *Learning to Labour*.

Paul Willis

SCHOOL COUNTER-CULTURE: AN EXTENSION OF WORKING-CLASS CULTURE?

The central question to ask concerning Willis's thesis is whether there is any evidence to support his view that school counter-cultures (involving, as they do, a resistance and opposition to authority) are, in fact, an extension or reflection of working-class culture generally.

Willis's Evidence

In the first place, the evidence which Willis himself supplies in *Learning to Labour* is unconvincing. For in the school that he studied *all* of the pupils — 'conformists' as well as members of the school counter-culture — have a working-class background. He tells us that the school is set in an essentially working-class town at the heart of an inter-war council estate and is 'exclusively working class in intake'.[22] The conformists, therefore, are just as much working class as the 'lads'. One of Willis's reviewers — Val Burris — has clearly seen this point. She notes

> Willis's tendency to generalize from the behaviour of the lads to sweeping statements about the working class as a whole. Even as he emphasizes a radical discontinuity between the lads and the majority of working class conformists, Willis speaks as if these particular students somehow typified the most basic and widespread features of working class adaptation to school and work.[23]

Indeed, given that the conformists are in the majority in the school, it is they, rather than the 'lads', who ought to be considered representative of working-class values and attitudes (in so far as one can speak of working-class culture as a unity).

Furthermore, in the article 'The Class Significance of School Counter-Culture', Willis claims that there is a basic similarity between the outlook of the central figure in the school counter-culture and the attitude to work of the boy's father. Willis's statement is worth quoting in full. He writes:

> Here is a foundry-man talking at home about his work. In an inarticulate way, but for that perhaps all the more convincingly, he attests that elemental, essentially masculine, self-esteem in the doing of a hard job well — and to be known for it.
>
> 'I work in a foundry . . . you know drop forging . . . do you know anything about it . . . no . . . you have the factory know the factory down in Bethnall Street . . . I work there on the big hammer . . . it's a six-tonner. I've worked there 24 years now. It's bloody noisy, but I've got used to it now . . . and it's hot . . . I don't get bored . . . there's always new lines coming in and you have to work out the best way of doing it . . . You have to keep going . . . and it's heavy work, the managers couldn't do it, there's not many strong enough to keep lifting the metal . . . I earn 80, 90 pounds a week, and that's not bad is it? [mid-70s] . . . it ain't easy like . . . you can definitely say that I earn every penny of it . . . you have to keep it up you know. And the managing director, I'd say "hello" to him you know, and the progress manager . . . they'll come around and I'll go "all right" (thumbs up) . . . and they know you, you know . . . a group standing there watching you . . . working . . . I like that . . . there's something there . . . watching *you* like . . . working . . . like that . . . you have to keep going to get enough out.'
>
> Here is Joey, this man's son, in his last year at school, and right at the heart of the counter-culture:
>
> 'That's it, we've developed certain ways of talking, certain ways of acting and we've developed disregards for Pakis, Jamaicans and all different . . . for all the scrubs and the fucking ear-'oles and all that . . . There's no chivalry or nothing, none of this cobblers you know, it's just . . . if you'm gonna fight, it's savage fighting anyway, so you might as well go all the way and win it completely by having someone else help ya or by winning the dirtiest methods you can think of like poking his eyes out or biting his ear and things like this.'
>
> There's a clear continuity of attitudes here . . .[24]

We find the claim for continuity here quite remarkable — it almost takes our breath away! For what is striking about these extracts, in our view, is the sharp difference of outlook between Joey and his father. Joey's father obviously takes a pride in his work and derives considerable self-respect from it. He finds it an interesting and challenging job, which requires not only physical strength and stamina, but also a considerable degree of initiative for its proper performance. He clearly enjoys the recognition by management that he is doing a demanding job well and has a good, friendly relationship with them. Furthermore, whilst he seems to accept the authority of senior management, he is in no way servile or submissive. Joey, on the other hand, is devoid of such qualities. Unlike his father, he is not on good terms with members of other social groups and classes (management for the father; conformists, teachers and ethnic minorities for the son); rather, he displays a contempt for anyone who is not part of his own small world. In addition, it is difficult to see how Joey's capacity for gratuitous violence and brutality is equivalent to his father's ability to undertake tough, demanding work. Certainly both require considerable strength and effort, but the purpose and meaning of each is entirely different.

Angela McRobbie

A similar criticism can be made of another piece of Marxist ethnography, namely Angela McRobbie's 'Working Class Girls and the Culture of Femininity'. Like Willis, McRobbie studied a group of working-class pupils who had developed an anti-school culture. Again, like Willis, she claims to have discovered a basic continuity between this culture and that of the working class generally. For example, she says of the girls of the counter-culture that their 'class instinct' is 'expressed' in that culture.[25] However, McRobbie then proceeds to give an example of the way in which the working-class parents of one of the girls want her to work hard at school, take an interest in things, get on in life, etc. That is, they display attitudes and values which are at odds with those that are central to the school counter-culture.

This difference of outlook between members of the school counter-culture and working-class parents is not uncommon in our view. The attitudes of the parents in McRobbie's study are fairly typical, we believe, of many working-class people. We would argue, therefore, that there is often no continuity between the counter-school culture and the parent culture: the former is not a manifestation of the latter.

David Hargreaves

Support for this view can be drawn from a number of sources. Take for example David Hargreaves's 'classic' study *Social Relations in a Secondary School*.[26] On the face of it Hargreaves's study might seem to provide evidence for the Willis/McRobbie thesis as the research indicates the presence in Lumley Secondary Modern of a substantial delinquent sub-culture. The members of this sub-culture display both anti-school attitudes and, when away from school, engage in the sort of delinquent activities typical of the 'lads'. However, one of Hargreaves's central points is that the school is roughly divided down the middle in two sub-cultures: the delinquents or 'delinquescent' and the 'academic'. The boys of the academic sub-culture, Hargreaves tells us, tend to belong to the top two streams in the four-stream year group. In stream A the pupils are committed to the school and what it stands for. They put a premium on academic achievement and, as a consequence, are well motivated and work hard. Hargreaves says that these pupils are 'concerned to get the most out of their lessons',[27] and are critical of teachers if lessons are inadequately prepared. As well as being intolerant of teacher incompetence, they dislike fellow pupils who 'mess about' in class and hold back progress in their work. They also express resentment at having to mark time whilst waiting for these other pupils to catch up. Furthermore, they value good teacher–pupil relations and are proud of the fact that teachers can trust them to work unsupervised.

Whereas A-stream pupils regard academic work as 'valuable for its own sake', those in the B stream see it as a means to an end. The boys in the B stream work in class in order to obtain the Local Leaving Certificate which, they feel, will be a means to a better job. This 'instrumental' orientation, however, means that, besides working hard, the B-stream pupils also like to 'mess about' and 'have fun'. But Hargreaves stresses that these two elements coexist: the latter does not supersede the former. 'Playing the fool', he says, 'is seen more as a *relief* from hard work, not a *replacement* of it.'[28] In the lower stream, though, it is a different matter. Here 'messing about' dominates. Consequently, there exists a genuine anti-school culture — the focus of resistance theory.

At this point it must be stressed that, according to Hargreaves, the boys of *both* the academic and the delinquescent sub-cultures are working class in origin (for too readily it is assumed that the former are middle class). Hargreaves tells us that 97 per cent of the school population come from a working-class background, that is, their fathers are in manual as opposed to non-manual occupations.[29] Clearly, then, the values of the boys from the academic sub-culture are as much working class in nature as those of the delinquescent group. Furthermore, the values of the academic group reflect the values of their parents. Hargreaves points out that the high-stream boys tend to come from homes where there is an attachment to the values of achievement, hard work, the importance of getting on in life, good manners, individual responsibility and resourcefulness, respect for property, etc.[30] Unfortunately, Hargreaves insists on calling such values 'middle class' in spite of his recognition of the fact that many working-class people accept them as valid. However, Hargreaves is clear on the really important matter, namely that the values of the academic sub-culture are in keeping with, or a reflection of, the values of a substantial section of the working class. Consequently there is no support in his study for the view which identifies the values of the school counter-culture with those of the working class as a whole.

Resistance: A Working-class Tradition?

It should also be noted that the attachment of many working-class people to the values just listed has a long history. It is not a recent phenomenon — a product of post-war affluence or 'embougeoisement' or whatever. Rather, such values have been part of the very texture of working-class life for perhaps a century or more. We can find little evidence to support the view, advanced by some Marxists, that the sort of conduct displayed by the 'lads' is a traditional part of working-class life. For example, Richard Johnson (of CCCS) sees a continuity between the oppositional behaviour of school counter-cultures and the acts of working-class resistance to the demands of capitalism in the nineteenth century.[31] However, we would argue that large sections of the working class have traditionally demonstrated support for the values so conspicuously rejected by school counter-cultures.

For example, in Chapter 8 we saw that the 'lads' are contemptuous of mental work and even find the prospect of apprenticeships unattractive. Willis would have us believe that this is typical of working-class people. Richard Hoggart gives us a different view.

Richard Hoggart. In his famous account of working-class life in the present century — *The Uses of Literacy* — Hoggart draws our attention to the respect of working-class parents for 'booklearning'. He also stresses their concern that their children 'get on in life'. This stems, he says, not from a sense of snobbery but from a desire to reduce the troubles associated with poverty. Apprenticeships are also highly valued. As Hoggart puts it:

> It is still important to 'have a trade in your hands', and this not merely because a skilled tradesman has, until recently, almost always earned more. The skilled workman can say more firmly than the unskilled labourer that he is 'as good as the next chap'. He is out of the ruck with those who receive the first shock of large labour cuts . . . Fathers who are anxious to 'do right' by their boys still try to have them apprenticed.[32]

And concerning apprenticeships and 'booklearning', we see no reason to suppose that the attitude of working-class parents has changed much since Hoggart wrote these words.

Bill Williamson. Similarly, in Bill Williamson's biographical study of mining in the north-east of England in the latter part of the nineteenth and the early years of the present century, there is an emphasis on the importance, in the mining community, of attitudes and values which are absent in the school counter-culture. Williamson points out that the miners of his grandfather's generation all shared the same social and economic position. 'Claims to be different', therefore, 'had to be based on more abstract qualities such as respectability, bearing, honesty, integrity and learning.'[33] Speaking of his grandfather, Williamson says: 'He took great care in his work and enjoyed seeing jobs done properly with precision.'[34] 'As a pit man,' he adds, 'my grandfather valued men who would "pull their weight". Doing what was expected of him at work was for him a positive value and he expected others to do the same.'[35] Consequently, says Williamson: 'There were some men my grandfather would not work with because he considered them too lazy or unreliable.'[36] Such an attitude naturally carried over into other areas of life. Williamson notes his grandfather's dislike of 'scivers'. Among the miners generally, he continues, it was normal, if a son followed his father into the pit, for the father to be responsible for the boy's basic work discipline. This involved obeying the rules and giving their full effort.

We find little in this description of Williamson's grandfather and the north-east mining community to remind us of the 'lads' of the school counter-culture. For example, the words 'honesty', 'integrity', 'learning' are quite inappropriate when describing Joey and his friends — although 'lazy', 'unreliable', 'scivers' are certainly closer to home. We can see little continuity here between the two cultures.

Robert Roberts. The same conclusion can be drawn from an examination of Robert Roberts's *The Classic Slum*. Roberts says of Salford life in the first quarter of the present century that: 'Despite poverty and appalling surroundings parents brought up their children to be decent, kindly and honourable and often lived long enough to see them occupy a higher place socially than they had ever known themselves: the greatest satisfaction of all.'[37] Honesty was also greatly prized. As Roberts says: 'the stigma for filching even the smallest object remained real.'[38] (In Hoggart's Hunslet we are also told that parents strove to prevent their children from 'getting into bad ways'.) Furthermore, Roberts draws our attention to a feature of working-class life which is dramatically at odds with what Willis, for example, has told us is the central characteristic of both the school counter-culture and working-class culture generally, namely the attitude to authority. For, as we have seen, Willis believes that resistance to authority is central to the world of the 'lads', and that subversion of authority is a 'specific working class theme'. Roberts, on the other hand, in keeping with other commentators on working-class culture, points to a long tradition of *deference* to authority. He argues that the working class in Salford had a deep-seated respect for their social superiors. Parents, for example, treated their children's teachers with awe. To a large extent, he continues, these attitudes were a product of people's social and economic position. The threat of the workhouse and prison, for example, 'played a major role in keeping the poor profoundly deferential before any kind of authority'.[39] Also, the attempt to 'stave off that dreaded descent into the social and economic depths' brought not just deference towards, but fear of, authority. 'Under the common bustle', says Roberts, 'crouched fear. In children — fear of parents, teachers, the Church, the police and authority of any sort; in adults — fear of petty chargehands, foremen, managers and employers of labour.'[40]

Nevertheless, Roberts adds, such fear was combined with the feeling that these people were their 'betters'. Speaking of the majority of unskilled workers, he states that:

> It was their belief, widely expressed at election times, that the middle and upper classes, with their better intelligence and education, had a natural right to think and act on behalf of the rest, a right that one should not even question . . . In all, then, before 1914, it is true to say that a poor man knew his place: he wanted that place recognised, however humble, and he required others to keep theirs.

In sum, says Roberts, there existed:

> Apathy, docility, deference: our village as a whole displayed just those qualities which, sixty years before, Karl Marx had noted, stamped the poor industrial workers — qualities which convinced him that the English proletarian would never revolt of his own accord.[41]

Furthermore, Roberts quotes Engels to the same effect. Writing at the time of a major strike in 1889, Engels said that: 'The repulsive thing here is the Bourgeois "respectability" which has grown deep into the bones of the workers.' He also speaks of the way in which the working class has developed an 'inborn respect for its "betters" and "superiors"'.[42]

Engels on Authority. At this point it is worth noting that although Engels — like Marx — was obviously unhappy about the respectability of the working class and their general deference to those in authority, Engels was not opposed to the existence of authority *as such*. Resistance theorists such as Willis, on the other hand, not only imply that the school counter-culture's opposition to authority is a valid response in present conditions; they also tend to suggest that that authority itself is in some way illegitimate. When Willis, for example, lists the 'specific working class themes', the 'subversion of authority' appears alongside 'the independent ability to create diversion and enjoyment' — and a note of approval is sounded in each case. One has the impression from Willis's work, therefore, that he is suspicious of all authority. In this respect he is perhaps not untypical of many of the more radical and egalitarian writers on society and education of the last decade or so who tend to condemn all forms of unequal relationships, including relationships of authority. (Although we have already noted in Chapter 7 that Bowles and Gintis do not share this attitude.)

Engels's position is different. In a fascinating article entitled 'On Authority', Engels observes that: 'A number of Socialists have latterly launched a regular crusade against what they call the principle of authority.'[43] Authority, he says, means 'the imposition of the will of another upon ours; on the other hand, authority presupposes subordination'. Having defined the term, Engels goes on to pose the central question:

> Now, since these two words sound bad and the relationship which they represent is disagreeable to the subordinated party, the question is to ascertain whether there is any way of dispensing with it, whether — given the conditions of present-day society — we could not create another social system, in which this authority would be given no scope any longer and would consequently have to disappear.

Engels's basic answer to this question is that modern industry and agriculture *requires* the exercise of authority (and, therefore, the existence of subordination). He argues that the complexity of the industrial process demands the co-ordination of many workers. Someone, he says, has to undertake this task and be responsible for making decisions when problems and difficulties arise. To those who oppose the principle of authority, Engels replies: 'Wanting to abolish authority in large-scale industry is tantamount to wanting to abolish industry itself.' Furthermore, this would be as true of a communist as of a capitalist economy. Some socialists, Engels says, argue that in a communist society those who take decisions will be the 'elected delegates' of the workers and that, properly speaking, they will not therefore exercise 'authority'. Engels's response to this view is to say that: 'These gentlemen think that when they have changed the name of things they have changed the things themselves.'

A SIMPLE DICHOTOMY

At this point we must move on to a consideration of other criticisms of resistance theory generally and Willis's work in particular.

In their discussion of school life, Willis and others tend to think in terms of a simple dichotomy: conformists versus the 'lads'. As far as they are concerned, the educational system is composed of just two groups of pupils, namely those who comply with the demands of the school, and those who resist or reject its fundamental purposes. They fail to see, therefore, that there exists a much greater variety of pupil responses to education and schooling.

Willis's Argument

Willis, for example, seems to accept at face value the 'lads' ' view that the conformists in the school cannot, at the same time as being involved in their school work, also take an interest in some of the things that are at the centre of the world of the 'lads' — music, clothes, the opposite sex, drink, etc. There is no recognition by Willis, therefore, that someone might be a 'conformist' in some respects — that is, might be interested in the world of knowledge and ideas, care about getting an education (and not just about 'getting on') — *and* have 'outside' interests. At least the resistance theorist Everhart recognises the existence of such a pupil. He points out that, in the school he studied, the pupils who were most highly regarded by their peers were those who could *both* get good grades and have a good time. And David Hargreaves, as we have already seen, points out that in one section of the academic sub-culture at Lumley the pupils work hard *and* have fun. Furthermore, Willis does not seem to appreciate that 'conformist' pupils who value the educational experience of the school may also 'rub up' against school authority, from time to time, in what they regard as some of its more unreasonable or trivial manifestations. In other words, such pupils may identify with the aims of the school academically, whilst rejecting some of its other demands — and in this respect they are probably no different from some teachers.

The problem with Willis's analysis is that he would have us believe in a one-dimensional world in which there are those who want an education, and those who enjoy life. It never seems to occur to him that these pursuits can be combined, and that the person who takes an interest in his or her education is not, thereby, dull, obsequious and a social conformist. Nor does he seem to appreciate that such a person has more of a life than the members of the school counter-culture whose world revolves around gratuitous violence, theft, vandalism, sexism, racism and general nihilism.

At just one point in the book, however, Willis does qualify his position. He says that:

> Any school year is, of course, a complex mixture of individuals ranging from 'lads' to 'ear-oles' . . . In large working class comprehensive schools the situation is likely to be more confused and diversified as the chances increase of a phalanx of working class kids trying to achieve something academically whilst keeping their dues paid up with 'the lads'. Furthermore, in schools where a sizeable proportion of working class kids are properly upwardly mobile and going on to university, the option of being something of an 'ear-ole' might be seen somewhat differently. All of these things may well act to blunt the starkness of the opposition we have uncovered . . . between the conformists and non-conformists, and to make the social map more complex.[44]

Yet Willis never explores the implications of this important qualification for his general argument: he just goes on talking about conformists and non-conformists in the same old way, and continues to assert that the 'lads' are the representatives of the working class. His basic thesis remains unaffected by his admission. As it stands, it appears to be an afterthought, and he certainly does not let it interfere with the subsequent development of his argument.

Andy Hargreaves

Andy Hargreaves also draws our attention to the way in which resistance theorists ignore 'the immense diversity and complexity' of pupils' responses to schooling. He believes that this is because any such recognition would call into question 'the very applicability of the category "resistance" to vast and diverse areas of pupil conduct'.[45] Jean Anyon's work, says Hargreaves, is a case in point. Anyon, he says, 'appears to credit pupil actions with the status of "resistance" not after scrutinising her data, but by arbitrary designation'. She does not carefully distinguish the frequency of the occurrence of resistance, as compared with other pupil responses, in the schools she studied because 'she barely acknowledges other modes of pupil response at all'.

> Much of the explanation for this failure [continues Hargreaves] is to be found in her somewhat indiscriminate application of the category 'resistance' to almost all pupil actions that do not count as absolute and willing compliance to teachers' demands . . . As a result, some particularly strange things are cited as examples of resistance. Alongside the 'obvious' cases of arson and vandalism, for example, Anyon includes putting a bug (insect) in a pupil's desk as a form of active resistance, and counts withholding enthusiasm and failing to respond to teachers' questions as a form of passive resistance.[46]

Hargreaves goes on to say that, by contrast, some other, non-Marxist writing 'draws much more subtle distinctions between different types of pupil activity',[47] and in particular mentions the work of Peter Woods in *The Divided School*.

Peter Woods

We shall be looking at the work of Woods in some detail in Chapter 11 when we consider 'interactionist' studies of teachers and pupils. Here we would just like to note that Woods distinguishes a *number* of modes of pupil response to schools.

'Conformity', he says, takes on several forms: (1) 'Ingratiation' is the extreme response which involves 'sucking up' or being the teacher's 'pet'. (2) 'Compliance' is a more moderate response which takes two forms, 'optimistic' and 'instrumental'. The distinction here is very similar to that made by David Hargreaves between pupils who regard academic work as valuable for its own sake, and those who see it as a means to an end. (3) 'Ritualism' is where a pupil simply accepts school as a fact of life and does what is asked of him, but shows no real identification with the goals of the school. (4) 'Opportunism' involves a basic conformity, but the pupil is also experimenting with other modes of adaptation.

In addition to these four types of conformism, Woods also identifies: (5) 'Retreatism', where school is felt to be a 'waste of time', empty and boring. Such pupils pass their time by 'mucking about' and 'having a laugh'. (6) Colonisation, where the pupils accept that they have to come to school, but seek to make the best of it by establishing a 'relatively contented existence' and 'working the system'. Finally, and at the other extreme to conformism, a (7) 'intransigence' and (8) 'rebellion'. There intransigent displays considerable antipathy to the school and is very awkward to handle. The rebel is less so, as he or she 'replaces' the goals of the school with his own. As a consequence, such pupils spend a lot of time discussing 'outside' interests.

In his later book, *Sociology and the School*, Woods makes it clear that he believes this model of 'pupil adaptations' is a more refined instrument for discussing pupils' responses to school than the simple notion of pro- and anti-school cultures. Referring to the argument of *Learning to Labour*, he says that: 'Not all working class boys "rebel" in the style of Willis's lads. No doubt some are intransigent, but equally many will be practising ritualism, colonizing and even conformity.' And he concludes: 'This would have implications for Willis's thesis about the connection between the lads' culture and social class.'[48]

Henry Giroux

The resistance theorist Henry Giroux has recently made an attempt to respond to this line of criticism. He says that 'the current use of the concept resistance by radical educators suggests a lack of intellectual rigour and an overdose of theoretical sloppiness.' If it is to be more than a catchword, it is imperative that Marxists 'be more precise about what resistance actually is and what it is not'.[49] In particular, says Giroux, they have to recognise that not all 'oppositional behaviour' is resistance. We must make a distinction between 'forms of oppositional behaviour that can be used for either the amelioration of human life or for the destruction and denigration of basic human values'. Only the former category should be described as 'resistance'. Thus understood it involves a commitment to 'freedom and emancipation' and to the 'struggle against domination and submission'.[50]

To illustrate his meaning Giroux provides the following example:

> Recently, I heard a 'radical' educator argue that teachers who rush home early after school are, in fact, committing acts of resistance. She also claimed that teachers who do not adequately prepare for their classroom lessons are participating in a form of resistance as well. Of course, it is equally debatable that the teachers in question are simply lazy or care very little about teaching, and that what in fact is being displayed is not resistance but unprofessional and unethical behaviour.[51]

Much the same can be said of course of Willis's 'lads'. Most of their behaviour is at best uncouth and rude, at worst immoral and unethical. In general, it involves that 'destruction and denigration of basic human values' to which Giroux refers. In which case it is difficult to understand why Willis seems to admire the lads so much. For the tone of his account — with the possible exception of the description of their racism and sexism — is one of approval. This is particularly strange in light of his Marxist standpoint, as Marxism involves the idea that socialism or communism will bring with it a higher form of morality. Yet the conduct of the 'lads' falls well below that which is typical of the majority in capitalist or bourgeois society.

Stan Cohen

Stan Cohen has made a similar point in his discussion of the type of subcultural theory emanating from the Birmingham Centre — which includes, of course, *Learning to Labour*. He says that in such studies:

> The subculture is observed and decoded, its creativity celebrated and its political limitations acknowledged — and then the critique of the social order constructed. But while this critique stems from moral absolutism, the subculture itself is treated in the language of cultural relativism. Those same values of racism, sexism, chauvinism, compulsive masculinity anti-intellectualism, the slightest traces of which are condemned in bourgeois culture, are treated with a deferential care . . . when they appear in the subculture.[52]

Cohen also points out that these sub-cultural theorists, unlike their predecessors, wish to stress the political and historical significance of such things as counter-school cultures, football hooliganism, punk fashions and concerts, etc. But for Cohen 'most delinquency is numbingly the same and has never had much to do with those historical "moments" and "conjunctures" which today's students of working class youth cultures are so ingeniously trying to find'.[53] In the same vein we would argue that Willis's claim that the 'lads' have 'penetrated' the façade of an unequal society in their refusal 'to trade conformity for qualifications' is a gross exaggeration. Their attitude can be explained much more simply: school has no relevance for them, they just want to get to work. In *this* respect they are perhaps typical of a *section* of the working class for whom schooling has never been particularly important. Williamson, for example, notes that in his grandfather's generation 'doing well at school or doing badly were not things that mattered much'.[54] Such an attitude, however, does not necessarily involve intransigence; it is readily expressed in ritualism, colonisation etc. Indeed, these would be its more normal manifestations.

Sub-cultural Theory

Besides displaying considerable sympathy for the life-style of their sub-jects and seeing historical significance in their actions, Willis and other sub-cultural theorists also seem to find them an inexhaustible source of interest. Such fascination with their subjects is not uncommon among many students of deviance and sub-cultures. It is to be found, for exam-ple, in the work of Howard Becker. In his review of Becker's work, Alvin Gouldner points to Becker's implicit critique of the respectable world of the middle class, which is combined with a romantic attitude towards deviance. Becker's school of deviance, he says, 'expresses the satisfac-tion of the Great White Hunter who has bravely risked the perils of the urban jungle to bring back the exotic specimen'.[55] Furthermore, such sociologists frequently identify with the world of the underdog. Speak-ing of the research of Becker and his colleagues in the 1950s and 1960s Gouldner says that:

> theirs is a school of thought that finds itself at home in the world of hip, drug addicts, jazz musicians, cab drivers, prostitutes, night peo-ple, drifters, grifters and skidders: the 'cool world'. Their identifica-tions are with deviant rather than with respectable society. For them orientation to the underworld has become the equivalent of the pro-letarian identifications felt by some intellectuals during the 1930's. For not only do they study it, but in a way they speak on its behalf, affir-ming the authenticity of its style of life.[56]

The similarities here with the work of Willis and other resistance theorists are too obvious to require comment. The only difference bet-ween them is that now the life of the underworld and underdog is iden-tified with that of the proletarian. Proletariat and lumpenproletariat become synonymous.

SOCIETY, STATE AND SOCIAL DEMOCRACY

In Chapter 8 we examined at some length the criticism by CCCS of 'social democracy'. It is now time to take an independent look at the theory of social democracy as it provides us with a critique of, and an alternative to, the Marxist conception of society, state and education.

C.A.R. Crosland

In particular, we want briefly to examine the ideas of C.A.R. Crosland in *The Future of Socialism* where an attempt is made to refute the Marxist analysis of modern British society. Indeed, right at the beginning of the book, Crosland states that 'in my view Marx has nothing to offer the contemporary socialist, either in respect of practical policy, or of the correct analysis of our society, or even of the right conceptual tools or framework'.[57]

Crosland rejects the claim, made by many Marxists, that the ownership of productive resources has a determining effect on the social structure. Summarising the argument of *The Future of Socialism* in a later essay, Crosland says that the 'revisionist' thesis of the book 'maintained, contrary to the Marxist doctrine, that the ownership of the means of production was no longer the key factor which imparted to society its essential character'.[58] In his view, therefore, the extension of public ownership in industry — the 'abolition of private property' — is not necessarily a solution to society's problems. In industry there has been a managerial revolution: managers rather than owners now control production. There has also been a growth in the power of organised labour. But, in addition, the capitalist class has lost much of its power to the state.

Changes in the Balance of Power

In the nineteenth century, the capitalist class controlled not only industry but also the state. Crosland believes that Marx was right when he asserted that the government was nothing but an executive committee for managing the affairs of the bourgeoisie. However, there has been a change in the balance of power. The state today has an enormous influence on the operation of private business as a consequence of accepting responsibility for the economy. It also directly controls a much larger share of business decisions by virtue of employing a considerable number of the working population and having responsibility for a large amount of investment. As a consequence, it is much the most powerful force in all industrial societies. Crosland quotes the Marxist Harold Laski as saying that: 'Whatever the forms of state political power will, in fact, belong to the owners of economic power.' He argues, however, that, if we are to think in terms of simple formula, it would be much better to turn Laski's statement on its head and take the view that 'whatever the modes of economic production, economic power will, in fact, belong to the owners of political power. And these today are certainly not the pristine class of capitalists.'[59]

Britain, therefore, is a very different society today from what it was a hundred years ago. Crosland maintains that it is no longer accurate to call Britain a 'capitalist' society. The term 'capitalism' applies to a society such as existed in nineteenth-century Britain and/or where the private ownership of the means of production determines all else. However, 'our society is now different in kind from classical capitalism',[60] and today 'the ownership of the means of production decides much less than the character of the political system'.[61] It is misleading, therefore, to go on talking about 'capitalism'. However, there is no accepted new terminology. The 'mixed economy' and the 'welfare state' have gained acceptance, but neither satisfactorily describe contemporary Britain.

The Aims of Socialism

Crosland then turns his attention to an analysis of the aims of socialism — indeed, the bulk of the book is concerned with this issue. Space prevents us from examining his important and interesting arguments, except to note that his discussion compares very favourably with that of Marxists. For Crosland provides us with a detailed analysis of socialist principles and policies, including the contribution by and the implications for education. He offers a clear account and assessment of the options before us, and, even if one does not ultimately agree with him, one at least knows what one is disagreeing with. The same cannot be said of Marxist writers who usually rest content with a vague, cloudy notion of socialism. For example, we have already seen in *Unpopular Education* that CCCS takes the view that 'education in its fullest sense, in its socialist and feminist definition . . . can only be known at later stages in a long process'.[62] We regard such an attitude as irresponsible. It is also open to certain logical objections. For, if you do not know what a socialist education in a socialist society consists of, then how can you know that it is going to be any different from, or better than, what we have at present? And if you are not clear about the nature of your objective, then how can you ever know that you have attained it? You cannot pursue an end, or move towards its attainment, if you do not know where you are going.

J.K. Galbraith

Some of Crosland's arguments concerning the shift in the balance of power in modern Western societies are, of course, supported by other writers. For example, in his recent book *The Anatomy of Power*, J.K. Galbraith argues that there has been a considerable change in the role of the state in the last hundred years. In the nineteenth, and early decades of the twentieth, centuries, the government was certainly the servant of capitalist economic interests.

> The state [says Galbraith] was an extension of the instruments of enforcement of industrial capitalism: it did for industrial capitalism what industrial capitalism could not do for itself. That the United States government or that of Britain might be regarded as an enemy of business, a commonplace conception today, would not have entered anyone's mind in the middle of the last century.[63]

The Marxist thesis, then, is certainly valid as far as the nineteenth century is concerned. However, it does not accurately describe the present state of affairs where, in Galbraith's words again, 'a conflict between government and industry' is normal.[64]

Furthermore, in the nineteenth century the capitalist class had little competition from other organised groups in its pursuit of power: 'both directly and through the state it was *the* power.'[65] Today, says Galbraith, that situation has radically altered:

> A striking feature of the age of organization [Galbraith's way of describing contemporary society] is the huge number of organized groups — trade unions, trade associations, political action committees, farm organizations — that seek to appropriate the instruments of power of the state for their own purposes. And also the greater number of organizations within the structure of the state itself — departments, agencies, authorities, public corporations, the armed services — that have become original sources of power.[66]

The Pluralists

With regard to the first of these points — the growth of a large number of organised groups competing for power — Galbraith's position is similar to that of many *pluralists*. For pluralists argue that modern society has to be understood as an arena in which a 'plurality' of such groups act politically to promote and protect the interests of the individuals whom they represent. Such groups are in contention for power: their interests clash, they do not coincide. Yet no one group is able permanently to dominate the rest or the government. Power is not concentrated, therefore, in the hands of the capitalist class, but is spread or dispersed among these organised groups. The power of any one group is counter-balanced by that of the others.

According to some pluralist writers, the state's role in all of this is a 'negative' one. It is to 'hold the ring' and ensure that the competition takes place within the established ground rules that structure group conflict. More frequently, however, pluralists give the state a more 'positive' role. The government's job is to try to reconcile the conflicting interests and to find a compromise which, to some extent, is acceptable to them all. The state, however, remains an independent force. It is not 'in the pocket of' any single group.

Raymond Aron once summarised the pluralist position in the following way. He said that,

> democratic societies, which I would rather call pluralistic societies, are full of the noise of public strife between the owners of the means of production, trade union leaders and politicians. As all are entitled to form associations, professional and political organizations abound, each one defending its members' interests with passionate ardour.

And in such circumstances, 'Government becomes a business of compromises.'[67]

Robert Dahl

What are the implications of the pluralist conception of society and the state for our view of education?

To date, there is very little in the way of a pluralist account of education. However, one major pluralist writer, Robert Dahl, has incorporated an analysis of education into his study of the power structure of a local community. Dahl — echoing Crosland and Galbraith — found that in New Haven, Connecticut, there had been a major change in the social and political system in the last hundred years. In the nineteenth century there was one social and economic elite — a ruling class — that dominated the life of the whole town. During recent decades, however, this has been replaced by a plurality of elites who have only limited spheres of influence. That is, one group exercises power in one area of social life, a second in another area, and so on. Dahl studied three such areas — education, urban redevelopment and political nominations — and found that the people taking decisions in each case were different. The power of each elite, therefore, was found to be restricted rather than broad in scope, and the competition between them ensured that they did not come together to form an integrated elite or unified ruling class.

Dahl stresses, however, that the power of such elites is not only limited by the competition between them. It is also restricted by democratic political procedures. The citizens of New Haven, says Dahl, exercise considerable 'indirect' influence through the electoral mechanism. Although political elites possess enormous 'direct' influence as a consequence of their ability to initiate or veto proposals for policy, the people generally also possess power because such elites are often 'involved in tireless efforts to adapt their policies to what they think their constituents want'.[68] Political leaders are subject to the 'law of anticipated reactions'. That is, they try to anticipate what the voters will support or tolerate. Their behaviour is guided by how they expect the electorate to react at the next election. Whilst such elites certainly try to *shape* the 'preferences' of the citizens, they also *respond* to their 'preferences'.

For example, in New Haven there was considerable dissatisfaction among teachers and parents about existing educational policies. Teachers' salaries were low and the school building programme was quite inadequate. One group of politicians promoted the cause of the teachers and parents and, as a consequence, this helped to get them elected to political office. Subsequently, numerous changes and improvements were made in the educational system: a major survey of educational provision was conducted, a new director of education was appointed, school expenditure went up, teachers' salaries were raised, and two new schools were constructed. Dahl comments that these political leaders did not *create* this important political issue or shape the attitudes of the electorate with regard to the problem of education. Rather, they *responded* to the underlying feelings of resentment towards existing policies and 'helped to activate and channel discontent'.[69] This case illustrates, then, the nature of the power and influence exercised by the people in a modern pluralist democracy.[70]

SUMMARY

In this chapter we have considered a wide range of criticisms of Marxist theory. This has been necessary, of course, because Marxists themselves, whilst pursuing a common theme, have nevertheless produced a number of variations on that theme. In conclusion we want to try to tie the ends together by briefly summarising our major points.

In the first place we argued that Marxists are faced with something of a dilemma. An economic determinist conception of society is untenable, but a theory of relative autonomy reduces historical materialism to the level of a banal commonplace, as well as making the theory unfalsifiable.

We also noted that this line of criticism has been carried over into the sociology of education. Reynolds, we saw, argues that the empirical evidence will not support a theory of 'correspondence' between the organisation of education and the demands of the capitalist economy. Britain, for example, has a decentralised educational system in which schools and LEAs possess considerable independence. Similarly, Hickox maintains that the Marxist claim that education reproduces the class structure through the processes of legitimation and socialisation is not borne out by the facts. The ideology of 'equal opportunity and meritocracy' is not subscribed to by a large section of the population; and education has not played an important role in shaping working-class attitudes to work. As far as the theory of the relative autonomy of education is concerned, Andy Hargreaves contends that it is difficult to see what is specifically Marxist about an approach which stresses both the independence and dependence of education in relation to economic factors.

In our assessment of resistance theory we focused particularly on the work of Willis because of the impact it has had within the sociology of education. We pursued a number of lines of criticism. In the first place, we argued that Willis's own evidence provides weak support for his thesis. Secondly, we maintained that other empirical research does not substantiate the view that school counter-cultures are a reflection of wider working-class attitudes and values. We also questioned the view that resistance has been an important feature of working-class culture throughout the nineteenth and twentieth centuries. We argued that Hoggart, Williamson and Roberts draw our attention to characteristics of working-class culture which are at odds with the attitudes and values found among the members of the school counter-culture. In particular we noted the importance of deference, rather than resistance, to authority. Returning to Willis, we went on to argue that pupils' responses to school are more complex and varied than he would have us believe. We also suggested that resistance theorists generally should take account of Giroux's distinction between oppositional behaviour which promotes, and that which leads to the destruction of, basic human values. We concluded this section of the chapter by noting, with Cohen, that some sociologists often see too much significance in delinquent behaviour. We also pointed out that such writers seem to feel considerable sympathy for the deviant and the underdog, vindicating the authenticity of their style of life.

Finally, we turned our attention once again to certain broader issues within Marxist theory. Following Crosland and Galbraith, we argued that there has been an important change in Western society in the last hundred years. The state is now no longer subservient to the capitalist class (as Marxists would have us believe); on the contrary, it is now much the most powerful force in all industrial societies. Furthermore, contemporary society has witnessed the growth of a large number of organised groups competing for power. According to the pluralists, no one of these groups is able to dominate the rest or the government. Power is therefore dispersed, not concentrated. We also noted that, to date, there is little in the way of a pluralist analysis of education, except in the work of Robert Dahl who points out that, in the community he studied, the group taking decisions concerning education was different from the groups taking important decisions in other areas of social life. Furthermore, the people generally had some 'indirect' influence and power through the electoral process. In other words, there was no ruling class controlling education.

NOTES

1. K. Popper, *The Open Society and Its Enemies* (Routledge and Kegan Paul, London, 1962), vol. 2, p. 108.

2. I. Berlin, *Karl Marx* (Oxford University Press, London, 1963), p. 284.

3. J. Plamenatz, *German Marxism and Russian Communism* (Longman, London, 1954), pp. 284–5.

4. E.F.M. Durbin, *The Politics of Democratic Socialism* (Routledge and Kegan Paul, London, 1940), p. 166.

5. L. Kolakowski, *Main Currents of Marxism* (Clarendon Press, Oxford, 1978), vol. 1, p. 364.

6. S. Hook, *Revolution, Reform and Social Justice* (Blackwell, Oxford, 1976), pp. 4–5.

7. E. Burke, *Reflections on the Revolution in France* (Penguin, Harmondsworth, 1968).

8. L. Kolakowski, 'Althusser's Marx' in R. Miliband and J. Saville (eds.), *Socialist Register, 1971* (Merlin Press, London, 1971), p. 121. Our emphasis.

9. B. Magee, *Popper* (Fontana, London, 1973), p. 43.

10. D. Reynolds, 'Relative Autonomy Reconstructed' in L. Barton and S. Walker (eds.), *Social Crisis and Education* (Croom Helm, London, 1984).

11. Ibid., p. 292.

12. Ibid., p. 293.

13. Ibid., p. 293.

14. Ibid., p. 294.

15. Ibid., pp. 295–6.

16. M.S.H. Hickox, 'The Marxist Sociology of Education: A Critique', *British Journal of Sociology*, vol. 33, no. 4 (1982).

17. Ibid., p. 571.

18. Ibid., p. 572.

19. Ibid., p. 572.

20. Ibid., p. 573.

21. A. Hargreaves, 'Resistance and Relative Autonomy Theories: Problems of Distortion and Incoherence in Recent Marxist Analyses of Education', *British Journal of Sociology of Education*, vol. 3, no. 2 (1982), p. 115.

22. P. Willis, *Learning to Labour* (Saxon House, Farnborough, 1977), p. 4.

23. V. Burns, 'Review of *Learning to Labour*', *Harvard Educational Review*, vol. 50, no. 4 (1980), p. 526.

24. P. Willis, 'The Class Significance of School Counter-culture' in M. Hammersley and P. Woods (eds.), *The Process of Schooling* (Routledge and Kegan Paul, London, 1976).

25. A. McRobbie, 'Working Class Girls and the Culture of Femininity' in CCCS, University of Birmingham, *Women Take Issue* (Hutchinson, London, 1978), p. 104.

26. D. Hargreaves, *Social Relations in a Secondary School* (Routledge and Kegan Paul, London, 1967).

27. Ibid., p. 14.

28. Ibid., p. 30.

29. Ibid., p. 141.

30. Ibid., p. 168.

31. Johnson also claims that 'there is no reason to suppose that children in the nineteenth century were any less creative in their forms of resistance in school than children are now' ('Notes on the Schooling of the English Working Class, 1780-1850' in R. Dale *et al.*, *Schooling and Capitalism* (Routledge and Kegan Paul, London, 1976), p. 5).

32. R. Hoggart, *The Uses of Literacy* (Penguin, Harmondsworth, 1958), p. 80.

33. B. Williamson, *Class, Culture and Community* (Routledge and Kegan Paul, London, 1982), p. 68.

34. Ibid., p. 85.

35. Ibid., p. 90.

36. Ibid., p. 89.

37. R. Roberts, *The Classic Slum* (Penguin, Harmondsworth, 1973), pp. 24–5.

38. Ibid., p. 36.

39. Ibid., p. 71.

40. Ibid., pp. 87–8.

41. Ibid., pp. 167–8.

42. Ibid., p. 30.

43. F. Engels, 'On Authority' in *Marx and Engels: Selected Works* (2 vols., Progress Publishers, Moscow, 1955), vol. 1. This and the following quotations are from pp. 635–8. We refer here only to Engels's views. Marx did not write directly on the subject. However, we are not aware of him ever having disagreed with Engels's published views.

44. Willis, *Learning to Labour*, pp. 84–5.

45. A. Hargreaves, 'Resistance and Relative Autonomy Theories', p. 112.

46. Ibid., p. 113.

47. Ibid., p. 113.

48. P. Woods, *Sociology and the School. An Interactionist Viewpoint* (Routledge and Kegan Paul, London, 1983), p. 90.

49. H. Giroux, 'Theories of Reproduction and Resistance in the New Sociology of Education. A Critical Analysis', *Harvard Educational Review*, vol. 53, no. 3 (1983), p. 289.

50. Ibid., p. 290.

51. Ibid., pp. 290–1.

52. S. Cohen, 'Symbols of Trouble', Introduction to the new edition of *Folk Devils and Moral Panics* (Martin Robertson, London, 1980), p. xxvii.

53. Ibid., p. v.

54. Williamson, *Class, Culture and Community*, p. 26.

55. A. Gouldner, 'The Sociologist as Partisan' in *For Sociology* (Allen Lane, London, 1973), p. 37.

56. Ibid., pp. 29–30.

57. C.A.R. Crosland, *The Future of Socialism*, revised edn. (Cape, London, 1964), pp. 2–3.

58. C.A.R. Crosland, 'Socialism Now' in *Socialism Now and Other Essays* (Cape, London, 1975), p. 17.

59. Crosland, *The Future of Socialism*, p. 10.

60. Ibid., p. 34.

61. Ibid., p. 41.

62. CCCS, *Unpopular Education: Schooling and Social Democracy in England Since 1944* (Hutchinson, London, 1981), p. 260.

63. J.K. Galbraith, *The Anatomy of Power* (Hamish Hamilton, London, 1984), p. 128.

64. Ibid., p. 144.

65. Ibid.

66. Ibid., p. 145.

67. R. Aron, 'Social Structure and the Ruling Class', *British Journal of Sociology*, no. 1 (1950), pp. 10–11.

68. R. Dahl, *Who Governs?* (Yale University Press, New Haven, 1961), p. 101.

69. Ibid., p. 162.

70. As Plamenatz says, the power of the electorate is to decide 'who shall have power and roughly on what terms' ('Electoral Studies and Democratic Theory', *Political Studies* (1958)).

PART III

THE INTERPRETIVE APPROACH

10 THE MICRO INTERPRETIVE APPROACH — AN INTRODUCTION

Macro–Micro Approaches

Most of the work we have dealt with in Parts I and II have been what is usually called 'macro' in focus. Functionalist and Marxist authors seem to share a number of assumptions, at least when they look at education. It is thought that education can only be understood by locating it within the wider society. The everyday activity of teachers, pupils and administrators is seen to be dominated by such things as: society (Durkheim); the needs of society (functionalists); the economy, class system or ideology (Marxists). The outcome of education is therefore predictable, leading as it does to the maintenance of the status quo.

Such approaches have been subject to considerable criticism, as we have seen. Perhaps the most significant criticism has been that macro approaches often regard human beings as little more than products of socialisation. Human creativity seems to be ignored, human freedom non-existent. A second and important criticism has been that these macro approaches tell us little about the richness and complexity of human life: they fail to grasp the reality of life in schools and do not help us understand what makes teachers and pupils 'tick'. At best they give us a general framework with which to analyse education, but one that is of little use in day-to-day classroom encounters. It's all very well to say that pupils and teachers are alienated and that we must change society, but this hardly helps us to get through Friday afternoon.

The twin problems of unacceptable assumptions and lack of relevance have led to the development of 'micro' sociological approaches. Martyn Hammersley has suggested that the differences in micro and macro approaches are usually thought of in the following ways:

1. In sociological research, should one assume determinism [macro], or free will [micro]?
2. Is the goal of sociology to produce generalised explanations which abstract from the details of social phenomena [macro], or is it to document the process of social life in all its detail and complexity (its 'richness', if you like)? [micro]
3. Can theories be tested against empirical data [macro], or can one only

judge them by their internal coherence since all data are theory-laden [micro]?

4. Do sociologists produce scientific theories which document what is 'really' going on while participants' views are simply myth or ideology? [macro] Or must sociologists' accounts in some sense build upon the interpretations of participants [micro]?

5. Can social events best be explained as the product of the structure of national (or international) society [macro], or can valid explanations be provided which appeal to the features of relatively small-scale organisations and groups or even the characteristics of individual people [micro]?[1]

Generally speaking these micro, interpretive, approaches begin from very different assumptions from the theories which we have so far examined. We will outline some of these assumptions and then, in the remainder of this chapter and in Chapter 11, look at the work that has been produced by authors who adopt these views.

ASSUMPTIONS OF MICRO APPROACHES

Everyday Activity. Everyday activity is the building block of society. Ultimately every aspect of society can be traced back to the way people act in everyday life. What keeps the educational system going is the day-to-day activity of teachers, learners, administrators, inspectors and the like. Changes in education or in society are brought about by changes in such activity. If we want to understand education, we must begin by looking at everyday activity.

Freedom. Everyday activity is never totally imposed; there is always some autonomy and freedom. This is not to say that there are no constraints on the way we act; nor does it imply that people are uninfluenced by their background. What is insisted upon is that people can and do create their own activity to some extent; everyday life is produced by people acting together and producing their own roles and patterns of action.

Meaning. To understand everyday activity we must grasp the *meanings* that people give to their behaviour. Unfortunately, in interpretive theory the term 'meaning' is complex and often undefined. It seems to include such notions as aims or intentions (so we can ask what a teacher aims to do in a lesson, or what a pupil's intentions are). It also seems to include the idea of significance (so we can ask what the teacher or pupil sees as significant in the lesson). Moreover, the notion of reasons is included (allowing us to ask what reasons does the teacher or pupil give for the activity).

It is assumed that the meanings are personal to the actor; they are not given by culture or society, rather they are constructed from culture by the actors involved.

Interaction. Everyday activity rarely involves a person acting in isolation, rather it consists of interaction with other people. Consequently, as well as giving meaning to our own action, we also give meaning to the activity of others. Put differently, we interpret the behaviour of other people with whom we interact. For example, let us consider the situation of a teacher asking a question and the pupils putting up their hands. The teacher has to interpret what a pupil means when raising a hand. Does it mean the pupil knows the answer? Is the pupil trying to avoid detection? Does it mean the pupil does not want to appear stupid? Any of these interpretations is possible. It is, of course, equally true that the pupils are interpreting the teacher's behaviour when deciding to put up their hands or not.

A number of important points follow from recognising that we interpret others' activity. Firstly, subsequent action depends on our interpretations. In our example, suppose the teacher decides that the pupil is trying to avoid detection, he may well ask him for the answer. Secondly, and more importantly, our interpretation of the other person's activity depends on 'what we already know' about him. This will include such things as age, sex, race, intelligence, motivation and the like. To return to our example, suppose the teacher 'knows' the pupil to be intelligent and well motivated, this will affect his interpretation of his action. To use the terminology, we have 'typifications' of people which we use in interpreting their behaviour.

Other elements play a part in our interpretation of action. We divide activity up into various categories, like 'working' or 'messing about'. When we make this categorisation of activities, we bring into account a set of assumptions about what constitutes 'working' and 'messing'. Often these assumptions are regarded as common sense; they are not examined but are taken-for-granted. However, a full understanding of how a person comes to act in the way he does demands an investigation into the realm of the common-sense assumptions that are being used.

Negotiation. An analysis of action must include a study of the actors' meanings and interpretations. However it would be incorrect to think that meanings and interpretations remain static and unchanging. It is clear that people do modify their views. Interpretive sociology tends to suggest that over time actors come to have shared understandings and interpretations. The sharing is brought about through a process of 'negotiation' of meaning. Negotiation is seen as a continuous process, not something that happens once and is finished. It occurs in subtle ways, with modification to the actors' understanding of what is going on. Shared assumptions develop. It should be stressed that the term negotiation does not imply that all parties have the same power at their disposal.

Subjectivist Approach. The final point we wish to make at this stage concerns how we are to get at the actors' meanings. The interpretive approach demands that we adopt what is called a 'subjectivist' method. That means that we have to try to get inside the actors' heads and see how they define the situation. The problem is that we have our own assumptions and categories. It is quite possible that, when we report what we have observed, we will give our own interpretation rather than that of the actors. It should be clear, for example, that if we observe interaction with preconceived ideas, such as that teachers are producing 'factory fodder', then we will misinterpret the actors' meanings. Similarly, if we observe behaviour having notions of 'work', 'messing', 'ability' and 'motivation', we are liable again to misinterpret what is happening. It is argued that to avoid this we should 'bracket out' our own assumptions and typifications and observe as a stranger. We should be careful to elicit the actors' views uncontaminated by our own. In this way we can be true to the meanings and understandings of those we observe. Peter Woods puts it well when he writes:

> Of course we shall never be able to get into another's mind to see exactly how it is working . . . and indeed it is often difficult to analyse our own thoughts and actions. But close observation and sympathetic interviewing over a lengthy period — a popular time span is a year — and in a variety of contexts can bring us close to an appreciation of that interpretive work, that construction of meanings that is at the heart of social life.[2]

The problem of observer bias is a very difficult one to deal with. We will be suggesting that it is impossible to enter any situation without preconceptions or assumptions. Indeed, it is the function of theory to sensitise us to certain aspects of the actors' subjective make up. We will suggest that in order to understand behaviour we, the observers, must categorise and classify types of outlook. We believe that it is the sociologists' job to give meaning to the actors' meanings by locating them within the wider context of society. We will try to show that in fact the observer cannot remain as a mere describer of activity but is inevitably drawn into some form of structuring of the data which he presents.

VARIATIONS WITHIN MICRO APPROACHES

So far we have dealt with the common assumptions of the micro approach but we should note that there are variations in emphasis within it.

Interactionist authors tend to see the relationship of teacher and pupil as a situation of conflict in which teachers and pupils have different goals which they want to achieve. Strategies are developed by the parties in an attempt to impose their particular definition of the situation on the other. It is accepted that the teacher has more power than the pupils, but this domination is never total. Consequently negotiation takes place and the classroom is thought of as negotiated order.

Phenomenologists tend to concentrate on eliciting the actors' knowledge of the situation, particularly their knowledge of the other people involved. In coming to 'know' others, actors have a set of categories which they use to interpret each other's behaviour. A teacher, for example, may interpret a pupil's behaviour as clever or dull. It is necessary to discover the process by which the title clever or dull is bestowed on the child. Terms like 'clever' or 'dull' are part of the taken-for-granted language of teaching but must, phenomenologists argue, be examined and the implicit meanings revealed. It is in this way that the actors' definitions of the situation can be adequately revealed.

Ethnomethodologists take a somewhat different line of approach. They are interested in discovering the procedures which actors use to make the world intelligible. The world may be thought of as a chaotic, unrelated series of events, but this is not how it is perceived. People have therefore imposed order on chaos to make it intelligible to themselves. The ethnomethodologist tries to unravel the processes whereby people make their everyday world intelligible.

While there are differences in emphasis within micro interpretive approaches, there is much common ground, especially between interaction and phenomenology. For this reason, we have not distinguished between the two in our exposition. We have devoted a small section in Chapter 11 to outlining an ethnomethodological position which is, in our view, a rather extreme form of the micro approach.

David Hargreaves

David Hargreaves's very influential and excellently written book *Interpersonal Relations and Education*,[3] provides an example of the micro approach. The book is divided into two parts, a statement of theory and a discussion of its applications. The central notion in the book is 'the self' and the theory to be adopted is called 'symbolic interactionism'. The self, according to this theory, is not something we are born with, it is something that develops through interaction with others. As Hargreaves says: 'The central idea, in short, is that a person's self develops in relation to the reaction of other people to that person and that he tends to react to himself as he perceives other people reacting to him.'[4]

Hargreaves follows the ideas of G.H. Mead on the development of the self and traces the implications of these for the analysis of the relationship of teacher and pupil. Since many other authors have followed a similar approach, we will spend some time in elaborating these ideas, whilst basing our account primarily on Hargreaves.

SYMBOLIC INTERACTIONISM

The Self

Communication, particularly language, is of fundamental importance in understanding the symbolic interactionist stance. When we communicate, we try to elicit a reaction in another. To say 'I am hungry' is to try to get a response of food or sympathy from another. But to say 'I am hungry' is to say something to myself as well; it allows me to understand a physical feeling within myself, and to give myself food or sympathy. As Hargreaves puts it: 'So if I make a request of another person I arouse in myself the very response I am trying to evoke in him.'[5] This capacity means that people are capable of 'rehearsing possible courses and consequences of action'[6] without actually doing anything. I can hold an internal conversation: 'If I do or say this, he will do or say that.' I can, therefore, plan my actions. But in planning I am making a judgement about how the other person will respond; that is, I am looking at myself from another person's point of view. In Mead's terms, I am taking the 'role of the other' to look at myself. This recognition leads to the idea that the self is a reflexive thing; as Hargreaves puts it:

> The self has an important reflexive quality: it is both subject and object. In interaction a man learns to respond to himself as others respond to him . . . He acquires a self by putting himself in the shoes of others and by using their perspective of him to consider himself.[7]

The most significant influence on the development of the self is usually the parents. The child looks at himself by taking over the role of the parents, often in play, and judging himself from their point of view. He starts to get some notion of what he is like, but he also takes over the attitudes and values of the parents in judging himself. Not only that, but in learning about himself he also learns about society. To say 'I am a male child' is to have learned that society distinguishes between the sexes and that age is an important factor. It involves learning that there are the roles of father, mother and children. The discovery of self and society go hand in hand. As Hargreaves says:

> The child's conception of 'reality' — what society, social institutions, his fellow men are like, what is 'important' or 'proper' or 'good' or 'right' — all this is socially mediated to the child, and in the first instance by taking over his parents' attitudes.[8]

As the child grows older he encounters more people and comes to recognise that certain values and attitudes are held by all. Eventually the child attains the notion of the 'generalised other' where some values are regarded as universal and where the 'self' is seen as a stable entity which is carried from one encounter to another.

The self is thus seen as a product of thinking about oneself from the viewpoint of others, not something bestowed in a mechanical way. We play a part in moulding ourselves, but others are involved in so far as we 'take their roles'. In interaction with others, Hargreaves thinks, 'a person's behaviour is influenced not by the acts of the other as such but by the meaning (intentions, motives, etc.) which the person assigns to the other's acts'.[9]

The essence of the Meadian legacy is that the individual 'does not merely respond to those forces that play upon him from inside or outside. The person thus constructs and chooses what he does; his acts are not predetermined responses.'[10] But, we must note, the person's responses are not completely divorced from the influence and impact of the wider society.

Perceiving People

Hargreaves develops his ideas further by noting that people give meaning to objects in the world. 'The object', he thinks, 'acquires its meaning in relation to a person's goal or plan of action.'[11] Thus the meaning given to a piece of chalk depends on whether we want to write on the board or throw it at a pupil. Meanings, though, are not private since we obtain a set of readymade meanings or interpretations from our ancestors. One important set of interpretations is the system we use to categorise other people. Finally, Hargreaves reminds us that, when we interact, we interact with other people. We recognise that others have goals, have their own ways of interpreting the world and some freedom.

> Each member of the interaction, then, has to interpret the conduct of the other before he can react to it. Each has to interpret the goals and intentions of the other, and then evaluate them for his own goal or plan of action, and then construct his own responding action in that light.[12]

Hargreaves further notes that one important aspect of interaction involves how we perceive the other people. Perception is more than just seeing, it involves organising impressions and drawing conclusions. For example, when we meet someone we usually notice his or her age, sex, race, accent, clothing; we give these factors our attention and draw conclusions about the other person which we take into account when interacting with him. Other things about him, the colour of his eyes or hair, are given less significance. Why 'age' should be more significant than 'eye colour' seems to depend on what Schutz has called 'interpretive schemes'. We have developed, or learned from others, ways of organising our impressions or paying attention to some aspects of what we see and ignoring others. When we focus on age rather than eye colour, we assume that age is more important for understanding others; it tells us more about them and is more significant in our interaction with them. The 'interpretive scheme' we use may be shared by all people in our society, it may be associated with only one group, or it may be purely personal. Our perception of the other person is influenced also by our own goals or the roles we occupy. For example, our perception of a girl kissing a boy will change when we realise that the girl is our daughter or is the person that our son intends to marry. When relating our perception of the other person to our goals and roles, we use what Hargreaves, following Schutz, calls a 'system of relevance'.

Over time we develop a 'conception of other' which provides us with a stable and intelligible picture of what the other is like; we attribute personality traits (moody, affable), attitudes and abilities to the other person and thus come to know him or her well. This 'conception of other' has been built up through a continuous process of perception in which interpretive schemes and relevance structures have been involved.

Hargreaves also notes that we make use of stereotypes, that is 'a set of characteristics which are held to be common to members of a category'.[13] Stereotypes can be useful to us in anticipating how we might react to other people, but they can be dangerous in leading us to false assumptions about them.

Roles

So far Hargreaves has documented the complexity involved in understanding interaction in which the 'self' engages in the perception of others and in the construction of responses to them. In addition, he says that we must realise that, when we act, we do so within a social situation. If we wish to explain action and interaction we have to look at the social structure which provides the context for action. Here Hargreaves introduces the idea of role.

Society, says Hargreaves, is a complex structure of inter-related positions such as child, parent, teacher, doctor and so on. A role is defined by Hargreaves as the 'behavioural expectations associated with a position'.[14] In other words, because we are in the position of teacher, we are expected to do certain things, have certain attitudes, dress in a certain way. Moreover, to be in the position of teacher is to be related to others' positions such as pupil, fellow staff, parents, headteacher, HMI and the like. We are involved in a 'role set', the members of which have expectations of us. By the same token, we have expectations of the other members of the role set: we expect certain behaviour and attitudes from colleagues and pupils. To be in a role is thus to be subjected to expectations and to have expectations. Very rarely do expectations define everything that we do; quite often they provide a general guideline or set of rules inside which we operate. There are very few aspects of the teacher's role that all members of the role set agree upon. Indeed, there may well be different expectations coming from parents, headteacher, colleagues and pupils. This can cause role 'conflict' or 'strain'. The main point that Hargreaves wants to make is that being in a role puts us within a fairly loose framework of expectations which gives some rough shape to our actions. However, we still have to create our role in detail within this framework.

We do this by bringing our self-conception, our view of our role, as well as our interpretations of the role of others, into account. The actor is involved in a considerable amount of decision-making when he acts in a role.

Interaction is thus a dynamic process involving continuous interpretation and decision-making by all the parties concerned. But interaction would not even begin unless there were some shared definition of the situation. Because we experience the same, or similar, situations as our role set, we develop an intersubjective (or shared) understanding of the situation. This is not to say that our definitions and those of our role set are identical but that, over time, we negotiate a shared definition of the situation that all regard as reasonable. This shared definition tends to be a 'working consensus', a sort of compromise which the parties accept for the moment and out of which they can get some satisfaction. The negotiation of the 'working consensus' is an ongoing process and requires the parties concerned to indicate their initial definition (by words, gesture and by generally presenting a 'front') and continuously to modify it in the course of the interaction.

Hargreaves's exposition of the symbolic interactionist approach thus highlights the complexity of the interaction process, and the amount of knowledge that is needed by the sociologists to understand it.

CLASSROOM APPLICATIONS

The Teachers

When applying this theory to teacher–pupil relations, Hargreaves first sets the scene. Pupils are compelled to come to school, where the teachers have the power to determine and enforce their definition of the situation on them. Because of this power we must begin our analysis of classroom applications by looking at the teachers' definitions of the situation. Hargreaves says: 'Obviously the teacher's first step is to define the situation . . . in a way he regards as adequate. His definition of the situation must be congruent with his conception of his classroom role.'[15]

In a later chapter Hargreaves tentatively suggests that we can discern three general types of self-conception. These he calls 'liontamers', 'entertainers' and 'romantics'. For the 'liontamers', education is a process of civilising pupils who are regarded as wild and untamed. Pupils have to be driven to learn whatever the teacher regards as good for them. The teacher is an expert in the subject who has to defend standards and bring pupils up to the required level. The pupils' role is to absorb the knowledge set before them. Discipline is firm, testing frequent. The 'entertainer' is rather different. He, too, does not believe that pupils want to learn, but feels that the best method of inducing learning is to make the material interesting. He tends to prefer themes to subjects, uses carefully contrived 'discovery methods' and a variety of audio-visual techniques. Much of his time is spent in going round the classroom checking that the pupils are engaged on their topics. Relations with pupils tend to be friendly and informal. The 'romantic' begins from a different point of view. Pupils naturally want to learn, learning is part of the human condition. The teacher's role is to facilitate learning, and pupils must be free to choose what they should learn. The curriculum should be constructed by the teacher and pupils together, either individually or in small groups, rather than being predefined for the pupil by the teacher. The relationship between teacher and pupil must be based on trust. There is a suspicion of marks and grades, for what is important is for the pupil to 'learn how to learn'.

Hargreaves insists that these three types of teacher are stereotypes and constitute only the beginnings of an analysis. He acknowledges that all teachers are unique in certain ways. As he says of his three 'types':

> They are *artificial* constructions, derived from actual teachers, but the types are not to be found in this form in the real world. Each is thus a collection of fragments of real teachers, *but it would be a disastrous mistake to think that the teaching profession can be divided neatly into three groups.*[16]

So the analysis of classrooms begins by looking at the teacher's role or self-conception. However, there are two sub-roles which Hargreaves thinks all teachers must fulfil — the 'disciplinarian' and 'instructor' subroles. The sub-role of disciplinarian includes such things as the teacher's responsibility for organising activities within the classroom, dividing the class into groups, the timing of activities and movement within the classroom, as well as defining and enforcing rules. The sub-role of instructor covers determining what should be learned, how it should be learned, and what is to be regarded as proof of learning. In practice, says Hargreaves, these roles fuse together. Furthermore, whilst these sub-roles refer to all teachers (and presumably are taken into account when the teacher defines his or her role), he suggests that 'there are great variations in the ways in which teachers interpret and perform the two basic sub-roles'.[17]

Hargreaves's discussion of sub-roles is, we believe, significant, as it suggests that the teacher cannot define his role as he wishes: there are constraints and expectations which force the teacher to include disciplining and instructing in his self-conception. While there may be some freedom to define or interpret how he is going to perform these sub-roles, failure to incorporate them in the teacher's conception of the role would lead to exclusion from the profession. The point we are stressing is that the individual's *conception* of his role is only part, albeit an important part, of what has to be considered in understanding the interaction of teacher and pupil. The teacher is not totally free to define the situation as he wills; the situation must be regarded, in some sense, as independent of and limiting to the individual's definition. We make this point because the interpretive approach sometimes seems to suggest that definitions could be different and that, if only teachers would adopt a different definition of the situation, life for the pupils would be far better. While it is true that teachers can change their definition of the situation in some respects, they cannot change it in all respects, certainly not when acting as individuals.

The second significant point that Hargreaves makes follows from the idea that we must begin by looking at the teacher's self-definition. He writes:

> Implicit in the teacher's definition of his own role is a definition of the pupil role. The teacher cannot specify how he intends to behave without at the same time specifying how he intends the pupils to behave . . . The teacher's expectations of the pupils will derive from, and be congruent with, his conceptions of his own role.[18]

We feel that there is a certain ambiguity in this view which comes from the notion of 'expectations' as used in the above statement. We agree that, when we define a role for ourselves, we also define an *ideal* role for our partners. If we define ourselves as 'romantics' or 'liontamers', we also imply an ideal pupil role, one that, as Hargreaves notes, is congruent with and supports our own self-definition. However, we may not *expect* our pupils to conform to our ideal pupil; indeed we may expect them *not* to conform. Furthermore, we may find ourselves being forced, by the way that pupils respond to us, to adopt a role that is quite different from our ideal. Consequently, we think it is important to distinguish our ideal self-conception as teachers; our conception of the ideal pupil role; our realistic expectations of pupils; our actual role conception.

Hargreaves says that, when pupils accept the ideal role we define for them, the pupils are seen as 'good' and teaching becomes a satisfying experience. Pupils are judged in terms of their conformity to the disciplinary and instructional aspects of the teachers' sub-roles, and it is likely that 'good pupils' will be given preferential treatment, even if the teachers are unaware that this is happening. Clearly, pupils who fail to conform will be regarded as 'bad' and teaching will become unsatisfying.

In summarising Hargreaves says:

> we can say that the teacher defines the situation in terms of his own roles and goals, especially as they relate to his instructional and

disciplinary objectives, and assigns to the pupils roles and goals that are congruent with his own. He selectively perceives and interprets pupil behaviour in the light of his definition of the situation. On the basis of further interaction with the pupils and repeated perceptions of them, he develops a conception of individual pupils (and classes) who are evaluated, categorized and labelled according to the degree to which they support his definition of the situation. He then responds to the pupils in the light of these evaluative labels.[19]

The Pupils

Having looked at the teachers' definitions of the situation, Hargreaves turns his attention to the pupils. Pupils have a complex attitude to school which is little understood and is difficult for teachers to recognise. It appears that most pupils like school and accept that the teachers define the situation for them. The stereotype that emerges from investigations into the pupils' conception of the 'ideal teacher' is that the teacher should be strict and fair (the disciplinary role), should be clear and interesting (the instructional role) and should also be pleasant and understanding. How pupils feel about individual teachers was not known at the time Hargreaves wrote *Interpersonal Relations and Education*, but more work has been done recently.

Hargreaves suggests that the most important thing, from the pupils' point of view, is 'pleasing the teacher'. This involves finding out what the teacher wants, concealing what displeases the teacher and balancing the need to please the teacher with the need to gain approval from friends. Giving the teacher what he wants all the time can lead to being known as a 'show off' or 'creep'. Considerable skills are required to get the balance right, especially as every teacher is different. As Hargreaves puts it:

> the pupil needs the ability to recognise what is expected of him, a set of skills to meet these expectations, a set of strategies which will allow him to depart from these regulations without incurring disapproval or to give the impression that he is meeting the expectations when he is unable or unwilling to do so.[20]

Hargreaves gives the impression that pleasing the teacher is something the pupils feel they have to do rather than something they want to do. Furthermore, because teachers want the pupils to be enthusiastic, they often fail to see that the pupils are, in fact, putting on a 'front'. Indeed, Hargreaves notes that the expression of real feelings, especially boredom and frustration, is discouraged by teachers, who tell the child to 'pay attention' or 'stop messing about'. One of the most important ways of pleasing teacher is to give the right answer. Quite often though this involves finding a formula or recipe which does not involve 'real' learning. For example, in maths the pupils may not understand a problem but they develop ways of getting the right answer.

There are alternatives, though, to pleasing the teacher. The delinquent for example, finds that pleasing the teacher is unprofitable and substitutes the goal of annoying the teacher. However, the delinquent tries to avoid incurring severe penalties and, generally, only 'plays up' with the weaker members of staff. In other situations, he adopts an attitude of 'expedient compliance'. Another alternative for pupils is what Hargreaves calls 'indifference', where the pupil is unconcerned about pleasing the teacher, but will do so to avoid trouble.

Interaction

Having examined the definitions of teachers and pupils separately, Hargreaves brings the teachers and pupils together in his analysis of their interaction. Where teachers' and pupils' definitions are congruent, a state of 'concord' exists. When the definitions of the two parties are incompatible, then a state of 'discord' exists. Most classrooms exhibit a state of 'pseudo-concord' where the definitions of the situations are partly compatible. Since pupils have some power, they can resist the imposition of a definition incompatible with their own. What results is a state of negotiation, 'whereby teachers and pupils each go halfway with respect to some demands and whereby in other areas the teacher withdraws or moderates his demands on the pupils in return for conformity to other teacher demands'.[21]

Both teachers and pupils use a variety of strategies to try to foster their own definition or to modify the other's views. Among the teachers' 'negotiative techniques' are: the use of promises and threats, modifying what were anyway excessive demands, appeals to higher authority ('what will the Head say'), divide and rule, and so on. Pupils use: appeals to justice, attrition, appeals to higher authority ('my mum says'), etc. The end product of the interplay of strategies is a reasonably orderly classroom and the development of a shared understanding of what is going on.

In suggesting that the 'pseudo-concord' is the typical situation, Hargreaves seems to imply that the process of negotiations is a continuous one. He also says quite explicitly that he regards classrooms as a place where conflict, but not open war, is happening. The parties in the interaction are both trying to impose their definitions of the situation on

the other, both using what techniques or strategies they can devise to maximise the chances of achieving their own goals.

COMMENTS

There are a number of points of issue which are raised by Hargreaves's
analysis which we will mention briefly here and develop in Chapter 11.
Firstly Hargreaves does not tell us where the teachers' self-conception
comes from or why teachers adopt the definitions that they do. He uses
the concept of role-expectations to explain why there is a certain similarity
among all teachers. However, we are not told why some teachers approx-
imate to 'liontamers' or 'romantics'. Secondly, Hargreaves, in *Interpersonal Relations*, fails to give sufficient weight to teachers' and pupils'
knowledge, although he does rectify this in his later work.[22] Finally it
should be noted that Hargreaves uses a 'conflict model'. The impression
given is of a continuous battle or struggle between the teachers and pupils,
each holding different definitions of the situation and each seeking to
find ways of winning over the other party or imposing their own views.
We feel that this model is more appropriate to secondary schools, and
to certain years within them, than it is to primary schools or higher
education.

In spite of these comments we feel that Hargreaves has provided a
clear, intelligible and interesting approach to the analysis of teacher–pupil
relations. The interpretive approach can be used to develop an understanding of the classroom and school we suggest. However, it is necessary
to clarify the role of the sociologist in the analysis of interpersonal relations. Is he to regard himself as a detached, unbiased observer? Indeed,
is it possible to describe without interpreting? Secondly, we feel that it
is necessary to show how the relation of education to such things as the
economy is brought about in the interaction process. Too often, in our
view, the micro interpretive approach seems to be content to describe
what is happening without tracing its significance for the wider society.

NOTES

1. M. Hammersley, 'Some Reflections on the Macro–Micro Problem in the Sociology
of Education', *Sociological Review*, vol. 32, no. 2 (1984), pp. 317–8.

2. P. Woods, *Sociology and the School. An Interactionist Viewpoint* (Routledge and
Kegan Paul, London, 1983), p. 17.

3. D. Hargreaves, *Interpersonal Relations and Education*, Student edition (Routledge
and Kegan Paul, London, 1975). In his later work Hargreaves has adopted a Durkheimian
approach to education, as we have noted in Chapter 3, The Modern Durkheimians.

4. Hargreaves, *Interpersonal Relations*, p. 5.
5. Ibid., p. 6.
6. Ibid., p. 7.
7. Ibid., p. 7.
8. Ibid., p. 10.
9. Ibid., p. 7.
10. Ibid., p. 15.
11. Ibid., p. 14.
12. Ibid., p. 15.
13. Ibid., p. 31.
14. Ibid., p. 46.
15. Ibid., p. 116.
16. Ibid., p. 163.
17. Ibid., p. 120.
18. Ibid., p. 124.
19. Ibid., pp. 129–30.
20. Ibid., p. 151.
21. Ibid., p. 133.
22. D.H. Hargreaves, S.K. Hester and F.J. Mellor, *Deviance in Classrooms* (Routledge and Kegan Paul, London, 1975).

11 MICRO INTERPRETIVE APPROACHES: SOME STUDIES OF TEACHERS AND PUPILS

Since the seminal work of David Hargreaves in 1972[1] there have been many studies of teachers and pupils which have used the interpretive approach. Some of these studies try to elicit the teachers' definition of the situation or that of the pupils; others try to conceptualise the interaction of teachers and pupils through the use of the concepts of 'strategy' or 'negotiation'. It is not our intention to try to give a summary of all these researches; rather we will include the work of authors who have had a major impact on the development of the interpretive approach to education. In addition we include articles which seem to us to bear upon or illustrate a particular theoretical point.

A MODEL OF INTERACTION

At this point it is appropriate to outline briefly the model of interaction which has been used as a basis for this chapter. This is presented in diagram form in Figure 11.1.

Teachers operate inside a system of constraints and expectations which limit their freedom of action. Within these parameters teachers develop, by experience: a fairly stable conception of their own roles; a view of the nature of pupils and how they learn; ideas about the knowledge that they are transmitting. These constitute one important element of the teachers' definition of the situation which we call 'self-conception'. Teachers also have 'knowledge' and expectations of their pupils. Some expectations are derived from stereotypes about such things as age, sex, race, home background and possibly stream in the school. Stereotyped expectations are those which teachers have before they encounter pupils. Teachers also get knowledge and expectations from observing and interpreting pupils' actions in class. However, to be able to interpret an action, teachers must have a system of categories — a filing system — into which pupil action may be interpreted. For example, the category of 'ability' is one that teachers use constantly; pupil behaviour is 'interpreted' into this category so that pupils become known as 'bright' or 'dull', 'good at maths' or 'bad at spelling', and so on. Individual pupils, or indeed classes, may be interpreted into categories of motivation, discipline and personality. This experiential 'knowledge' gives rise to expectations about pupils. Teachers' knowledge and expectations constitute a second

249

Figure 11.1: A Model of Teacher–Pupil Interaction, Constraints and Expectations

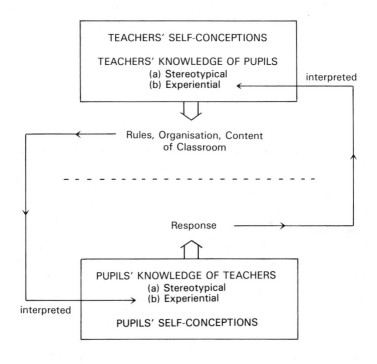

dimension in the teachers' definitions of the situation.

We hold that the teachers' knowledge of pupils combines with their 'self-conceptions' to generate the rules, organisation and content of the classroom. Put differently, teachers create the classroom situation for pupils.

Pupils, like teachers, have their own self-conceptions and their own 'knowledge' of teachers. These elements combine to generate the pupils' 'reponses' to the demands and expectations placed on them by their teachers. Teachers interpret these various responses and develop their experiential knowledge of pupils. Such new 'knowledge' may lead to a modification of the demands and expectations made on pupils, and can lead to a change in the teachers' self-conception. Just as teachers are expanding their knowledge of pupils, so pupils are developing their 'knowledge' of teachers. Increased knowledge can thus lead to the modification of pupils' responses to the new demands and expectations of their teachers.

The organisation of this chapter follows to a large extent from this model. We look firstly at the ideas about teachers' self-conceptions, then at some studies of teachers' 'knowledge' of pupils. Pupils' self-conceptions are then considered, followed by their 'knowledge' of teachers. Finally we note some of the ideas about how teachers and pupils interact.

TEACHERS' SELF-CONCEPTIONS

R. Sharp and A. Green

First we want to examine Sharp and Green's study of a progressive primary school.[2] The study seems to be an attempt, at one level, to explain why the school fails to implement the child-centred, individualised learning approach to education that it advocates. At another level, it tries to show that, while teachers actively construct life in classrooms, they are constrained and limited in what they produce. The theoretical implications of this, Sharp and Green believe, involve the rejection of the micro interpretive approach. The sociological study of education, they say, needs to develop in a Marxist direction. We shall return to a discussion of their criticisms later; for the moment we want to look at the way that they analyse the teachers' views of what they are doing.

THE HEADMASTER'S VIEWS

The headmaster's views of the aims of the school, say Sharp and Green, are very important and are therefore given first consideration. Using extracts from interviews, they try to bring out his views, although they acknowledge that the complexity and subtlety of these cannot be adequately documented. The head believes that the first aim of the school must be the welfare of the children and the care shown to the individual. The school must meet the present needs of the child. If this is done, long-term needs will be taken care of. Literacy and numeracy are important but are not the overriding aim of the school. If children are to develop self-confidence, reliability, adaptability and initiative, which are required in a changing society, they must be allowed freedom of choice. Consequently, the school is organised by vertical grouping so that teachers cannot teach the whole class together but must deal with individuals. The integrated day is used to give flexibility to the teaching programme. One of the major problems, given the size of the classes, is to detect and satisfy the needs of the pupils. Teachers are to instigate learning and to organise the child's environment so that learning can take place. Most of the children come from working-class homes, many from unstable ones. Parents tend to be conservative in outlook and are misdirected in pushing their children into spelling and 'sums' at home. Educational aspirations are generally low. Where children fail to take advantage of the school, it is usually because of unstable home backgrounds. The school must treat the emotional needs of the children and compensate for their home difficulties. Since each child is an individual with unique talents and problems, there cannot be any one suitable method or curriculum for all children. The school is successful, pupils' attainment is good in comparison with that of other children and there are no discipline problems.

Sharp and Green note certain 'ambivalences' in the head's account. There is the problem of the need to teach literacy and numeracy contrasted with the desire to look to the welfare of the child as the first aim. Children should be free to choose, but they also need rules to give them a secure structure within which they can overcome their emotional problems. Parents are seen as having low expectations yet clearly help, or try to help, their children at home.

THE TEACHERS' VIEWS

Sharp and Green next turn to the teachers' views, again giving extracts from interviews. Teachers have ideologies which include general ideas about the nature of knowledge and human nature and which entail beliefs about motivation and learning. They also include some notion of society and the place of education in it, as well as ideas about the role of the teacher and the skills required. These ideas have implications for how the teacher is to evaluate both pupils and her own success. 'In short', they say, 'a teaching ideology involves a broad definition of the task and a set of prescriptions for performing it, all held at a relatively high level of abstraction.'[3] We should note that the term 'ideology', as used here, does not carry the Marxist connotations of false or distorted definitions of reality: the concept 'culture' could have been used just as well.

Ideologies are high levels of abstraction, general ideas, and Sharp and Green use the term 'teaching perspectives' to lower the level of generality. However, they add a particular twist to the definition. They define teaching perspective as a 'co-ordinated set of ideas, beliefs and actions a person uses in coping with a problematic situation'.[4] The definition thus includes the notion of action and relates to problematic situations. We are not clear what is to be understood by 'problematic situation'; it seems to mean a situation in which the actor feels there are problems to be overcome, a situation which requires a solution. If this is so, are we to see all encounters between teachers and pupils as problematic situations?

Surely there are encounters that are not defined as problematic by the participants, and, if so, then 'teaching perspectives' are not brought into operation. Perhaps Sharp and Green mean situations in which problems may arise, in which case all teaching is a problematic situation and 'teaching perspectives' are used continuously. It is not clear, therefore, how much of the interaction between teacher and pupil is covered by 'teaching perspectives'.

It is difficult to elicit such a complex thing as the teacher's perspective, and Sharp and Green look at three teachers to find out how they define the situation. They choose to focus on three related aspects: children and their backgrounds, the school and its ethos and, finally, the classroom. What we give here is a summary of their summary of the teachers' views, although we have organised the presentation in a different way from that of Sharp and Green.

Children and Their Backgrounds

Mrs Carpenter. Most of the children, in her view, are deprived either emotionally or materially. They are defined as thick, difficult, peculiar or abnormal. Out of a class of 36 only 3 pupils are normal, 5 are real problems, most are disturbed.

Mrs Lyons. Most homes, she believes, are unstable with immature mothers who are unable to cope. The children are neglected, sometimes hated, sometimes smothered and given what they want. The pupils are typical of those from abnormal backgrounds and are insecure and maladjusted. They are aggressive, find it difficult to form friends and are over-anxious to read. There are signs that they are seeking security.

Mrs Buchanan. The children come from a different culture from that of the teachers, but this is not a problem; they are quite normal. The background is not a good one educationally but quite a few pupils are bright.

The School and Its Ethos

Mrs Carpenter. The school must compensate for the background by providing a stable environment. It should cater for the present needs of the pupils and not particularly concentrate on literacy and numeracy. The informal open pedagogy of the school allows pupils to play out their insecurities and there should be minimal teacher interference.

Mrs Lyons. The school is a therapeutic community and the teacher must be child-centred. There should be informality but children need some discipline and the teacher must be firm.

Mrs Buchanan. The role of the teacher is to get through to the children, but attainment is important. There should be some direction and compulsion, and she is not sure the progressive approach of the school is the right one for these children. She has doubts about her own ability to carry out the philosophy of the head.

The Classroom

Mrs Carpenter. The classroom is fluid and ever-changing with a minimum of direction and structure. How pupils learn is mysterious and different for each child, so a variety of methods must be available. The classroom is divided into activity areas, but there is no clearly articulated curriculum as this may threaten the child. Interest and readiness are important and the children are encouraged to find something to do which will engage them and keep them busy. Reading is organised on a routine basis and records are kept.

Mrs Lyons. The children need a secure environment and so there is a clear framework of rules. Rewards and punishments are used. Children learn when they are ready and she decides when that is. There is flexibility allowed as to what the pupils will do and when, but choices are related to their readiness. Lots of play is allowed, but some work is required too. She spends a lot of time with the brighter pupils.

Mrs Buchanan. The classroom appears to be as open and flexible as any other. She feels constrained to adopt the progressive approach, but finds it difficult. The pupils find it hard to concentrate and there is too much noise and too many discipline problems. There is not adequate time to deal with the pupils properly. It is important that the pupils settle down before they can work and new arrivals are allowed leeway until they settle, which they do naturally. The good teacher needs to find work to suit each pupil and she tries to get the pupils involved in their work. There are planning sessions when work is decided upon, but many pupils cannot think of what to do. Play may be therapeutic but work involves effort and freedom to choose should come after work has been done. Children need pushing to get on with their work and become engaged in their activities. When pupils are engaged in what she considers to be play rather than work, they are left alone and their efforts are admired. Reading is especially important.

We have no more than outlined a complex set of views, but it is sufficient to indicate the variety of perspectives that are held. Sharp and Green
suggest that, given these differences in perspectives, we would expect
to find rather different outcomes in each class. However, they do not find
this: rather there are similarities in all the classes, especially in the way
that pupils are graded. This means, Sharp and Green believe, that a theory
which places so much emphasis on perspectives and the way actors interpret what is going on must be inadequate. Put differently, the micro
interpretive approach cannot fully explain classroom life. We will return
to a detailed consideration of their ideas (see p. 283); for the moment
we want to look at some other attempts to describe and classify the
teachers' views of the situation.

Martyn Hammersley

Whereas Sharp and Green have tried to elicit teachers' perspectives, Martyn Hammersley[5] suggests that teachers' perspectives can be seen to be
composed of five aspects each of which may be further subdivided. A
summary of these 'dimensions' of the teacher's perspective is given in
Table 11.1.

Under the heading of 'definition of the teacher's role',[6] Hammersley
notes that teachers may be placed along a continuum with several dimensions. For example: teachers may, and usually do, consider that there
is a special expertise to teaching which ordinary people do not have
(authoritative role); but some teachers may regard the skills of teaching
as something that all people possess (no distinct role). Teachers may consider themselves as experts either in areas of knowledge (curriculum)
or in teaching method (method). They may see their role as being concerned with teaching a specific skill or subject (narrow) or may think
of it as being concerned with developing or civilising the whole child
(wide). Teachers may consider that they should control many aspects of
pupil behaviour (high control) or may allow a great deal of freedom to
the pupils (low control). All pupils may be judged according to the same
criteria (universalistic) or they may be judged differently in the light of
such things as ability, age or background (particularistic). Finally, teachers
may see knowledge as something akin to a given body of facts which
have to be mastered (product), or they may be chiefly concerned with
the processes of thinking (process).

When looking at the teacher's 'conceptualisation of pupil action'
Hammersley suggests that: teachers may regard pupils as having special

Table 11.1: Hammersley's Typology

1 *Definition of the teacher's role*
(a) authoritative role ⟷ no distinct role
(b) curriculum ⟷ method
(c) narrow ⟷ wide
(d) high degree of teacher control ⟷ low control
(e) universalistic ⟷ particularistic
(f) product ⟷ process

2 *Conceptualisation of pupil action*
(a) licensed child ⟷ apprentice adult ⟷ adult
(b) individualistic ⟷ deterministic vocabulary of motives
(c) pessimistic ⟷ optimistic theory of human nature

3 *Conceptualisation of knowledge*
(a) distinct curriculum ⟷ no distinct curriculum
(b) knowledge objective and universally valid ⟷ knowledge personal and/or tied to particular purposes or cultures
(c) hierarchical structure ⟷ no hierarchy
(d) discipline-bound ⟷ general

4 *Conceptualisation of learning*
(a) collective ⟷ individual
(b) reproduction ⟷ production
(c) extrinsic ⟷ intrinsic motivation
(d) biological ⟷ cultural learning path
(e) diagnosis ⟷ pupil intuition
(f) learning by hearing about ⟷ learning by doing

5 *Preferred or predominant techniques*
(a) formal ⟷ informal organisation
(b) supervision and intervention ⟷ participation and non-intervention
(c) imperative mode plus positional appeals ⟷ personal appeals
(d) class tests ⟷ assessment compared to past performance ⟷ no formal assessment
(e) grouping ⟷ no grouping
(f) grouping by age and ability ⟷ random, friendship or pupil-choice grouping

Source: M. Hammersley, 'Teacher Perspectives', Unit 9 of E202, *Schooling and Society* (Open University Press, Milton Keynes, 1977), p. 37.

rights because they are young, or consider that they are learning to become adults but do not have all adult rights and responsibilities, or they may see them as adults. Children may be understood as having free will and thus being worthy of praise or blame (individualistic) or as being determined by inheritance or background in what they do. Teachers may adopt a pessimistic view of human nature in which pupils need to be forced to learn and behave properly, or they may adopt an optimistic view of human nature.

COMMENTS

Hammersley goes on to develop the typology by outlining the teachers' views of knowledge, learning and techniques. We do not intend to go through the other dimensions, many of which are self-explanatory, and suggest that reference be made to the original work for further detail. We have included this outline of Hammersley's ideas because it indicates the line taken by some micro interpretive sociologists. We should note that Hammersley is trying to elicit the variety of subjective understandings that teachers have about their job; but we should also note that Hammersley feels it necessary to group or organise the views of teachers into sub-headings like 'definition of the teacher's role' and 'conceptualisation of knowledge'. The sociologist thus plays a part in organising the many diverse aspects of the teacher's subjective outlook, as well as describing these outlooks. Of necessity, it appears, the sociologist's job is to make sense of the way the actors make sense of their world and in doing this he must select and shape what he presents while remaining true to the actors' subjective understandings. We reiterate this point because of the debate as to what part the sociologist should play in the interpretive approach. There has been a tendency, as we have noted, to suggest that the observer must make no assumptions about the actors' definitions. However, Hammersley obviously feels that actors' meanings can be clarified by being placed into a typology such as the one he suggests.

We have included Sharp and Green's outline of the teachers' definition of the situation because it provides a good example of the sort of information that can be generated by a sensitive use of the interpretive approach. It shows how much variation can co-exist within a school. One interesting point to note at this stage is that Mrs Buchanan feels constrained to adopt a style of teaching of which she does not approve. We return to other comments about Sharp and Green's ideas on p. 260.

TEACHERS' KNOWLEDGE OF PUPILS

D.H. Hargreaves, S.K. Hester, F.J. Mellor

David Hargreaves *et al.*, in the book *Deviance in Classrooms*,[7] argue that 'typing' pupils is part and parcel of getting to know them. When pupils come into the secondary school, they are not known by the teachers except for those whose records have been studied. Certain pupils stand out initially, possibly because of physical characteristics or because they have brothers or sisters in the school. Teachers also have general expectations of pupils based on their experience with new intakes. Gradually the pupils become known to the teachers. The authors suggest that teachers go through a process, from an initial 'speculation' about what kind of pupil this is, through an 'elaboration' of the initial speculation, to a final stage of 'stabilisation' when the pupil is known and his behaviour and motives are understood and predictable to the teachers. It is possible that pupils can be 'de-typed' and 're-typed' in the elaboration stage and it is also possible, although Hargreaves *et al.* do not mention it, that some pupils in secondary school will not be known beyond the speculation stage.

In the book Hargreaves *et al.* are particularly interested in how some pupils become typed as deviant by teachers. They note that the 'deviant' breaks many rules frequently in many areas, but not necessarily in major ways. Also the future deviant has no saving grace of high ability or pleasant personality. Gradually the pupil becomes known (or 'typed' in their terminology) as deviant, and the teachers' behaviour changes. Any teacher, when observing a breach of the rules by a pupil, has to decide what to do, whether to intervene or not. The decision about intervention seems to depend on the teacher's estimate of what will follow from the intervention. If the offence is regarded as minor without threat to the teacher's authority and does not appear to be likely to spread, then nothing is done. It would not be worth breaking the flow of the lesson. If what the pupil is doing is seen as a threat to authority or likely to spread, then intervention will take place. There is, then, a variable threshold of intervention.

In the case of the pupils known as deviant, the threshold is raised and intervention is put off. This presumably is because previous attempts to curb the pupil have resulted in a lot of wasted time with no real improvement in behaviour. However, the raising of the threshold of intervention can cause the pupil problems which can only be solved by further rule-breaking. If we assume that the pupil wants attention, then the raised threshold means that he does not get it and he has to break more rules to get the attention he seeks. Of course, this further confirms him as a deviant in the teachers' eyes. The term used to describe this form of deviance is 'secondary deviance'.

One of the frustrating things about this account is that, by concentrating on the way that teachers come to define and treat pupils as deviant, the authors fail to explain why it is that some pupils break the rules more than others. This is largely because they take the view that deviance is not something that is intrinsic to the act but is rather the way others respond to the act. Because they accept this view, they do not seem to think it necessary to look at the pupils' definition of the situation and why they break so many rules.

Roy Nash

As we noted at the beginning of the chapter (p. 249), teachers' knowledge of pupils is developed by interpreting their behaviour into a series of categories that exist within the teachers' minds. In order to gain an understanding of how teachers get to know their pupils, it is necessary to discover what categories they use. Basing himself on the ideas of Kelly, Nash[8] adopted a repertory grid technique in his research, which involved asking teachers to distinguish among their pupils. The teacher was given the names of three pupils and asked to say what characteristic distinguished any one of them from the other two. In doing this, the teacher reveals, so Nash thinks, the categories. The process is repeated until no further categories are forthcoming. The constructs of one primary school teacher which emerged from this method were:

vivacious	_____	subdued
mature	_____	immature
demanding attention	_____	undemanding
able to be left alone	_____	unable to be left alone
quiet	_____	noisy
independent	_____	gang member[9]

Obviously this technique does not indicate what is understood by, say, 'well behaved' and elaboration of this would be needed. The method can also be criticised for being context unspecific, that is, it asks the teacher to fill in the context in which the pupils are to be understood. It could be that for one group of three pupils the teacher is thinking of their behaviour in the classroom, for another group about playground behaviour. It is important to recognise that teachers' categories may vary with context. Keddie[10] notes that, when talking in the staffroom about pupils, teachers use what seem to be a different set of categories to those used when teaching in the classroom. Consequently she distinguishes the 'educationist' and 'teacher' categories when discussing the teachers' knowledge of pupils. The repertory grid technique may be insensitive to such variations but could be amended to cope with this. As it stands, it does provide a useful way to begin to elicit the bases of the teachers' knowledge of pupils.

Nell Keddie

One category by which pupils will almost certainly be known relates to 'ability'. Just as Furlong looked at the meaning of trouble for pupils, so Keddie tries to bring out the unexamined assumptions that teachers hold when they describe pupils as 'able'. Keddie thinks that there are social class assumptions involved in the definition of ability, but this is merely stated rather than argued for in her article. Keddie is more successful in revealing the teachers' meaning of ability. When teachers teach, they have some knowledge of what they are talking about. In a lesson, for example, there will be some central point or concept or skill that the teacher wants to get over. The teacher knows why some concepts or skills are important: for example, sociologists know why the concept of ideology is important. But the pupils, who have not yet undergone the education process, have no idea of the significance of such ideas or skills. 'Bright' pupils accept (or appear to accept) on trust what the teacher defines as important. As Keddie says:

> There is between teachers and A pupils a reciprocity of perspective which allows teachers to define, unchallenged by A pupils, as they may be challenged by C pupils, the nature and boundaries of what is to count as knowledge. It would seem to be the failure of high ability pupils to question what they are taught in schools that contributes in large measure to their educational achievement.[11]

It should be noted that Keddie is not saying that the A-stream pupils do not ask questions; what she is saying is that they do not question the importance of what they are set to learn. The C-stream pupils, by their behaviour and reactions, do question the importance of what they are taught. We shall consider Keddie's general thesis about classroom knowledge in some detail in Chapter 12. We use her research here as an example of the attempts that are being made by interpretive sociology to get at the unexamined organising assumptions of actors.

R. Sharp and A. Green

Sharp and Green[12] adopt a somewhat different approach to understanding the way that teachers come to have categories of pupils. Following from their description of the teachers' perspectives, they argue that the similarities of stratification that emerge in the classroom indicate that factors outside the teachers' perspectives are operating.

They note that, while the teachers' ideology regards all children as equal, it is the bright children that get the most attention. In a similar way, the teachers believe that all children should be treated as unique individuals, yet some children are given what they call 'reified identities'. That is, they are put into rigid categories of 'thick' or 'abnormal' and are not known as unique individuals. The essential feature of the 'abnormal' pupils (who, it will be remembered, may be in a majority in the class) is that the teachers' method of teaching does not work with them. Sharp and Green suggest that the teachers have no common-sense understanding of these pupils and do not share with them a common way of looking at things. Such an understanding could develop, but this is difficult given the number of children in the class wanting attention. Indeed it seems that the class size is very important in Sharp and Green's analysis. They note that the progressive philosophy of teaching held by the teachers (or in one case followed rather than held), demands that children should have the right to choose what they learn and that the classroom should be flexible and open. But this immediately gives rise to a management problem — how do you organise so many pupils? Some children, those classified as normal, are biddable and are prepared to be busy. Once they have chosen an activity, they can be left to get on with it without the supervision that the teacher is, in any case, unable to give them. It seems that the criterion of 'busyness' (their word) is what leads some pupils to be defined as normal. The failure of the abnormal pupil to be busy is accounted for by suggesting that they are unstable. The progressive philosophy of the teachers indicates that insecure pupils should not be threatened. Consequently the abnormal pupils can be left alone to work out their problems. This frees the teacher to organise the rest of the class; but what happens is that she is engaged by the 'ideal' pupils. These ideal pupils know what the teacher wants and are able to give it to her; they thus reward the teacher by proving her method of teaching works and that she is competent.

The account we have summarised, and it should be said simplified, suggests that the notion of 'busyness' which is basic to the categorisation of pupils as normal or abnormal, is a construct of teachers who are trying to implement a progressive approach in a situation which creates difficulties for them. This suggests, think Sharp and Green, that the micro interpretive approach is inadequate. There are factors which are outside the actors' consciousness and control which affect the way that the situation is defined. The explanation of the teachers' definitions of the situation must include therefore an analysis of the situation that gives rise to teachers' categories.

COMMENTS

We have now looked at some of the work on the categories that teachers use when they come to know the pupils. We have also examined two attempts to make explicit the assumptions which are brought into operation when children are categorised. Before we move on we would like to make some comments about teachers' 'knowledge'.

As we noted earlier (p. 249), knowledge may be divided into stereotypical and experiential knowledge. There is some evidence that stereotypical knowledge does have an impact on the way that pupils are understood. Nash[13] lists a number of studies that show that the pupils' social class, as perceived by teachers, does appear to influence their perception of the pupils' ability level. The second type of knowledge, experiential, refers to what teachers learn about pupils by interacting with them. The process of getting to know pupils is complex and will be influenced to some extent, we feel, by stereotypical knowledge. However, we do not feel that it is totally limited by it.

This distinction is important when we consider the theory of the 'self-fulfilling prophecy'. This theory suggests that teachers have expectations of the pupils. These expectations are transmitted to the pupils, in interaction, possibly in subtle ways, but also in the explicit demands that teachers make on the pupils. The pupils are led to live up to, or indeed down to, the teachers' expectations and the prophecy is thus made real in the pupils. For example, if the teachers do not expect the pupils to be clever, they do not demand a high level of work from them and, consequently, the pupils learn little and become unintelligent. Now it is fairly clear that the teachers' expectations are based on their knowledge of pupils. If the knowledge is stereotypical, then it is easy to see that teachers may well *create* in their pupils that which they expect. However, if the teachers' expectations of the pupils are based on experiential knowledge, then we would argue that teachers do not create in the pupils that which they expect and the self-fulfilling prophecy has no place. Teachers 'know' that the pupils will not respond to certain demands, because they never have done so.

PUPILS' SELF-CONCEPTIONS

Under this heading we will look primarily at the work of Peter Woods and the criticisms that have been made of his views. We intend to begin, however, by examining an interesting article by A. Pollard entitled 'Goodies, Jokers and Gangs'.[14]

A. Pollard

The article deals with the views and affiliations of a group of girls in the last year of a 8–12 Middle School. Pollard suggests that among these girls there are three fairly distinct peer groups which he calls the Goodies, the Jokers and the Gang. The Goodies are composed of girls of moderate ability who are not good at sport and who see themselves as a small, friendly club. They tend to be deferential to the teacher and prefer quiet activities. They try to avoid displeasing the teacher and getting into trouble, so they put up with boring lessons and prefer well-ordered, predictable classrooms. The Jokers are a large group who are academically able, interested in getting a good education and who also enjoy sport. They try to establish a rapport with the teachers and enjoy joking with them. When faced with a boring lesson they try to redirect it towards something more interesting. They are not above finding some excitement in covert acts such as passing notes around the classroom and will explore the teacher's tolerance while avoiding serious trouble. They dislike being seen to fail academically and are also critical of teachers who 'pick' on them or who are bad tempered. The Gang are academically weak and rather rough. Members spend a lot of time falling in and out of friendship with each other, they tend to oppose teachers and are sensitive to being picked on. They engage in fights and contests with other gangs and hold the Goodies and the Jokers in little regard, using terms like posh, big-headed and privileged to describe them.

Individuals in these three groups have their own self-conceptions which are both shared and supported by the other members. The Goodies see themselves as kind, quiet and friendly; the Jokers think of themselves as clever, good fun, sensible and respectable; the Gang define themselves as tough and rough. Interaction in the classroom is organised, so Pollard thinks, to maintain these self-conceptions in the eyes of the peer group.

Pupils face two social systems in the school, the official one and that of their peers. The Goodies cope by conforming to the official system, the Jokers have the skill and flexibility to bridge both systems and the Gang refer to the peer group. As Pollard says:

> The situation is difficult for children. Some will seek to cope with it by conforming and seeking to 'please the teacher' as much as possible; some will reject the whole experience, treat it as an attack on their self-esteem and resist it; some may try to negotiate their way through the situation by balancing their concerns with those of the teacher.[15]

Interests at Hand

Pollard suggests that we may understand the process better by considering the 'interests at hand' of the pupils and seeing how they cope with the school situation. These interests at hand are defined as:

1. maintaining their self-image;
2. enjoyment (or 'the degree of intrinsic self-fulfilment to be obtained from interaction with other people[16]);
3. the control of stress; and
4. retaining dignity.

Each group of pupils, Pollard found, has a clear self-image which is supported and reinforced by the peer group. The maintenance of this image in the eyes of the peer group takes precedence over the other interests at hand, particularly for the Gang who need to cheek the teachers to show their toughness. With regard to the second aspect, all pupils enjoy interesting lessons, but the chief source of enjoyment for the Gang is in opposing the teacher by 'causing bother' and 'mucking about'. The Jokers get some enjoyment from covert disruption but prefer to have a laugh with the teacher, not at him. The Goodies' chief enjoyment is in having a quiet life. Avoiding stress was the third of the interests at hand. The Goodies use the tactic of avoiding the teacher's anger and keeping out of trouble, because, Pollard thinks, 'their self-image as quiet, studious, and conformist was undercut with few defences if rejected by a teacher "getting mad" with them'.[17] The Gang need stress to show how tough they are but do not actively look for a serious telling off. When it does happen, it is used to support the tough self-image. Jokers quite enjoy the risk of 'getting done' but do not like to be told off as it negated the type of relationship which they tried to develop with the teacher.[18] Retaining dignity is important both from the individual's own point of view and in relation to the peer group. Being unfairly treated or picked on (particularly for the Gang), being teased (particularly the Jokers), and having one's name forgotten are seen as attacks on dignity.

Enabling Interests

It appears then that the interests at hand refer to the maintenance of an acceptable identity by the pupils. Pollard's analysis focuses on the self, the individual's own self-perception. But in the school situation there are two aspects which have to be juggled to maintain an acceptable identity. These are called 'enabling interests' by Pollard. One of these is the peer group, because all pupils need a supportive audience to help them and to offer mutual protection from teachers and other pupils. Pollard suggests:

> Children's concern to be seen as a full and competent member of their peer group can thus be seen as an enabling interest in the context of their primary concern to protect their self and 'survive' the variety of situations at school which they encounter.[19]

The other enabling interest is learning. Teachers and adults expect pupils to learn, but pupils have to count the cost of learning against the amount of interest or boredom they find. The Gang tends to find lessons a waste of time. Their academic failure means that learning has less to offer them in coping with school and maintaining their self-image than for the other groups. Academic success for the Jokers allows them to develop the occasions for relaxing and having a laugh with teachers. The Goodies enhance their reputation as studious girls by putting up with the lessons.

Pollard gives us an interesting insight into the way that the pupils he studied defined the situation. He starts with the assumption that the maintenance of the 'self' is of paramount significance for the pupils and shows how the pupils try to cope with school life in order to maintain their identity. This emphasis on the 'self' is very much in keeping with the line advocated by Hargreaves. Pollard tries to show that 'self-definition' and the desire to maintain an identity once acquired colours the pupils' judgement of teachers and lessons. He does not tell us how the pupils acquired their particular identities but his analysis is an excellent example of the way interpretive sociology can reveal and put together aspects of pupils' experiences of schooling.

Peter Woods

It is of course possible to pile up study upon study of pupils' views of schooling. At some stage we need to try to bring these different pieces of research together in an organised way. This is what Peter Woods has tried to do.

In his book *Sociology and the School*,[20] Woods chooses to focus his work around a number of key ideas, namely:

1. how the context of action is defined;
2. perspectives — 'the frameworks through which people make sense of the world';[21]
3. cultures, that is the distinctive styles of life including values, beliefs, speech patterns and forms of understanding.

He suggests that perspectives derive from cultures and are linked to action through 'strategies' (ways of achieving goals). In the school situation he believes that there is a continuous process of negotiation. As he puts it:

> The persistent properties of the act of identifying, interpreting, reckoning and choosing, maintain a dynamic which, in interpersonal relations of a conflict nature, makes the actual interplay between persons the most important element, as each seeks to maximise his own interests. In schools, therefore, one might expect the whole day to consist of negotiation of one sort or another.[22]

We feel that we should emphasise that Woods is operating with a conflict model of the school in which the teachers and pupils are seen as having rather different personal aims. This view is not new: for example, in 1932 Waller, in *The Sociology of Teaching*,[23] suggested that teachers are engaged in a continuous struggle to control and educate pupils. Similarly Sara Delamont, in her book *Interaction in the Classroom*,[24] deals with the 'protagonists' and then talks about interaction under the heading of 'let battle commence: strategies for the classroom'. Within the 'conflict' framework, Woods suggests that pupils develop cultures which in turn give rise to perspectives.

Woods notes that there have been a number of studies which have identified a pro- and anti-school culture in secondary schools. These cultures seem to be related in some vague way to social class with the middle-class children being mostly in the pro-school group. (We would also add that the studies also show that the pro-school culture is linked to educational success with the upper-stream pupils being pro-school.) There are also gender factors which affect the ways that boys and girls respond to school subjects. But, says Woods, 'individuals do not slavishly follow sub-cultural norms, nor imprint masculinity or femininity upon themselves without reflection. They do have choices.'[25] It is necessary, therefore, to look at pupils' personal interests and find some way of conceptualising these. Woods develops a model of pupil adaptations based on the ideas of Merton and Wakeford. Essentially what is required is to ask in what ways pupils accept or reject the goals of the school. The same questions can be asked of the means that the school offers pupils to achieve its goals. These too will be accepted or rejected.

Forms of Adaptation

As we saw in Chapter 9, Woods suggests eight possible modes of adaptation, namely: ingratiation, compliance — optimistic and instrumental —

Figure 11.2: Woods's Modes of Adaptation

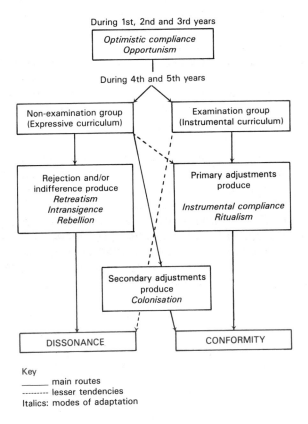

During 1st, 2nd and 3rd years

Optimistic compliance
Opportunism

During 4th and 5th years

Non-examination group
(Expressive curriculum)

Examination group
(Instrumental curriculum)

Rejection and/or
indifference produce
Retreatism
Intransigence
Rebellion

Primary adjustments
produce

Instrumental compliance
Ritualism

Secondary adjustments
produce
Colonisation

DISSONANCE

CONFORMITY

Key
_____ main routes
--------- lesser tendencies
Italics: modes of adaptation

Source: P. Woods, *Sociology and the School. An Interactionist Viewpoint*
(Routledge and Kegan Paul, London, 1983), p. 92.

ritualism, opportunism, retreatism, colonisation, intransigence and rebellion. Woods then produces the chart as shown in Figure 11.2 which he thinks outlines the predominant forms of adaptation.

Woods argues that, in the early years at school, pupils tend to adopt a positive attitude towards both the goals and means which the school offers. For example optimistic compliance indicates that the goals are 'vaguely perceived, but strongly identified with'.[26] Opportunism is another kind of conformity which Woods thinks develops in the second year.

It involves less consistent application to work and frequent but momentary leanings towards other modes. It is a 'trying out' phase before settling into another style, but while experimenting goes on, 'conformity' of one sort or another represents the basic mode.[27]

In the fourth and fifth years pupils are divided into examination and non-examination forms and develop towards either a conformity mode or a dissonance mode of adaptation. On the conformity side of things, pupils may adopt an attitude of an instrumental compliance in so much as they see what they are doing as useful particularly for getting jobs. Another type of conformity is ritualism, where the pupils adopt an identification with the means but an indifference to the goals of the school.

On the dissonance side the pupils may adopt a 'retreatist stance', which involves indifference to or rejection of the means and goals. No replacement is found for the goals of the school and the pupils' life is empty and boring. The problem is how to pass the day, and solutions like wasting time, mucking about and daydreaming are adopted. Intransigence involves indifference to the goals of the school and detestation of the means. The intransigent is disruptive in lessons, a vandal, misbehaves in public and often adopts the styles of a sub-cultural group such as skinheads. Rebellion involves rejection of both goals and means but the substitution of the pupils' own goals. Woods mentions girls who use the school scene to talk about matters relating to the opposite sex and future marriage. They can find aspects of the curriculum absorbing if it relates to their personal interests, such as child-care. They are not such a threat to the school as the intransigent pupils.

The school is likely to make adjustments in the demands it places on its non-examination pupils and quite often these 'secondary' adjustments produce a form of adaptation which Woods calls 'colonization'. This combines indifference to goals and ambivalences to means. The coloniser works the system, volunteering for some jobs to get out of others, giving endless excuses for not participating. 'He accepts the official programme in part, and is concerned about "keeping his nose clean", "getting on", "making the grade", in short, getting what he can out of the system.'[28] He is quite happy to use short cuts, copying homework, copying in tests, or 'lying to avoid punishment'.[29] Staff may turn a blind eye to many of the breaches of the rules by the colonised pupils, seeing it as a better form of adaptation than rebellion or intransigence which are frequently, Woods thinks, the only alternative modes of adaptation. Colonisation 'is possibly the most prevalent mode of adaptation in our schools, and is particularly evident in the middle and later years'.[30]

Woods then goes on to look at the perspectives of the pupils and draws upon many pieces of research to try to elicit the pupils' views of teachers. Since much that he has to say is similar to the work of Furlong which we will deal with shortly, it will be sufficient to quote from the summary to the chapter.

> Pupil perspectives on teachers appear to focus around three major guiding principles — whether they are human, can teach, and keep control . . . For the moment we can say that the evidence suggests that the majority of pupils have a basic orientation towards school which is largely and potentially supportive of the official programme. This is further reflected in their respect for firm (though sympathetic and fair, and not authoritarian) control.[31]

So far we have looked at two examples of attempts to elicit what we call the pupil views of their role, their self-conception. Pollard stresses the importance of the maintenance of an identity by the pupils and uses the notion of 'interests at hand' and 'enabling interests' to clarify the way that pupils defend their identities. He does not, as we have noted, suggest where the identities come from. Woods does take a broader picture, noting the influence of class and gender factors. He tries to explain the various self-conceptions that pupils can develop by looking at their reaction to the official aims and means of the school.

M. Hammersley and G. Turner

The adaptational model of Woods has been criticised by Hammersley and Turner,[32] for failing to recognise the variety of 'official' goals. It may be possible that a pupil will be a conformist with respect to some of the school's goals and intransigent towards others. Teachers may project different images of the required pupil role in different lessons, or indeed within the same lesson. Also there may be different definitions of what constitute legitimate and illegitimate means. Whilst accepting these critical points, it is possible to go somewhat further. Woods says that he is adopting a symbolic interactionist approach. If this is the case, then the nature of the official goals is irrelevant, for the interactionist argues that it is the *perception* of things that matters, not what they are in some sort of objective sense. Consequently, if pupils are to be seen as adapting to the goals of the school, it must be that pupils are adapting to their perception of the goals of the school. In order, then, to categorise modes of-adaptation Woods must first elicit from the pupils their perceptions of these goals. There are two ways then to look at Woods's adaptational model: either he is not enough of an interactionist in his approach, which is essentially Hammersley and Turner's point, or the interactionist approach is itself not adequate to explain what pupils and teachers do; other more 'objective' aspects must be included.

Hammersley and Turner go on to make a number of further criticisms of the adaptational model and then suggest an alternative.

Focusing on the general adaptations of pupils fails, they say, to consider the 'moment-to-moment' changes in the pupils' situation. Analysis of pupil behaviour must begin by identifying 'the intentions, motives and perspectives which underlie it'.[33] Once this is done it will be possible to see the range of possible courses of action that are open to a pupil. 'Each of these lines of possible action will have certain actual and perceived consequences. These consequences will be evaluated as payoffs or costs, in terms of both extrinsic and intrinsic gratifications, including identity implications.'[34] If we accept this argument, it becomes apparent that categorising pupils as simply 'conformist' is overgeneralised. The complexity of pupil response is seen further when we consider that teachers set up what Hammersley and Turner call 'frames', that is 'projected patterns of joint activity which specify the proper behaviour of pupils'.[35] A simpler way of thinking of frames is the set of rules that teachers set up for pupils to follow. Some frames (perhaps referring to make-up, or movement within the school, or uniforms) may be virtually all-pervasive; others, say referring to answering a question, may operate only for a short time. Hammersley and Turner here make reference to Hargreaves *et al.*'s study of deviance.[36] They argue that deviance involves rule-breaking and try to discover what rules operate in schools. Besides the obvious rules, the authors note that lessons tend to go in phases with: an entry phase; a settling phase; a teacher-dominated phase; a pupil-working phase; a clearing up phase, and an exit phase. In each of the phases different rules are in operation, for example, 'keep quiet and pay attention' during the teacher-dominated phase or 'try to answer the question I ask you' during the pupil-working phase.

Teachers tend to indicate which phase is to commence by the use of 'switch-phrases', like 'now get on with your work', but may recall the pupils to a different phase by words like 'pens down, pay attention. You clearly didn't understand what I said.' Given the multiplicity of frames, there are clearly many decisions that pupils have to make, many possible courses of action open to them from moment to moment. Not only that, but pupils may propose their own frames. If we are to talk about conformity or deviance, we must begin by looking at the way that pupils act from moment to moment and not use general categories. Pupils will evaluate the cost of or payoff from conformity, and one feature that will be influential is the way that a pupil sees other pupils and teachers reacting to his actions. Furthermore, pupils have identities, and their actions have implications for how they are seen by others in the school; over time it is possible for a pupil to change identity.

COMMENTS

In this section we have tried to give some flavours of an interpretive approach by looking at the ideas of Pollard, Woods, Hammersley and Turner. Pollard suggests we can understand the pupils' definitions of schools once we understand the way they see themselves. Woods tries to develop a more 'objective' typology but this is criticised by Hammersley and Turner, who seem to suggest that pupils' activity varies from moment to moment so that labels such as 'conformist' are inappropriate impositions by the sociologist.

This raises a major methodological point. Should the observer attempt to classify and define actors' definitions and goals (as Woods does) or should he be content to describe them (as Pollard does). This issue remains unresolved within interpretive sociology. It appears that classification and definition always enter into description either implicitly or explicitly. If this is the case, we would argue that the line adopted by Woods of trying to develop typologies is likely to be more fruitful than the detailed description approach adopted by Hammersley and Turner.

Woods's conflict model of teacher–pupil relations makes sense to many secondary teachers but makes less sense to primary teachers. For those in higher education the conflict often seems to be more with colleagues than with students. We do not wish to suggest that there is no conflict or difficulties in schools, far from it. Rather, we suspect that the notion is overused. Certainly we negotiate with our pupils and students, but we also co-operate. Moreover, there are instances where pupils allow, indeed expect, the teacher to define the situation for them without negotiation. We feel that implicit in many interactionist accounts is the idea of power. It is assumed that teachers are attempting to impose their will on pupils who are unwilling to accept it. But there is an allied concept to power, that of authority, which Weber defined as legitimated power. If a person accepts another's authority, he allows the other to define the situation, or elements of it, for him. Interestingly enough we find that there is little mention of authority in the studies of classrooms, although it is clear that teachers are aware of the need, sometimes, to establish and maintain their authority. At this stage we merely want to point out that the power model of individuals imposing different definitions and negotiating some form of compromise is by no means the only model which can be applied to schools.

PUPILS' KNOWLEDGE OF TEACHERS

Viv Furlong

Viv Furlong argues that the view put forward by David Hargreaves,[37] that pupils can be divided into pro- and anti-school groups, fails to grasp the complexity of the way that pupils behave in classrooms. Hargreaves sees the pupils as developing a culture within the school with specific sets of norms. The pro-school culture stresses such things as working hard, wearing uniform and participating in school activities. The anti-school (or 'delinquescent') norms stress fighting and 'messing about' the non-wearing of uniforms and non-participation in school activities. Furlong suggests that the idea that pupils have a set of norms and values which they use in a consistent manner is false.

> It would be obvious, even to the most casual observer of classroom behaviour, that there is no *consistent* culture for a group of friends. Even the most delinquent pupils will be well behaved in certain circumstances. Teachers do not always invite the same amount of conformity or hostility, and some lessons allow for greater feelings of personal achievement than others. Classroom situations change in the meaning they have for pupils and, as they change, so will the pupils' assessments of how to behave.[38]

What is needed, therefore, is a more sensitive analysis which may be produced by applying some of the ideas of Alfred Schutz. Pupils, says Furlong, construct their subject world; it is not something that is given to them by the school or the society. They do so 'by participating in a socially derived body of knowledge; they impose structure and organisation on their world'.[39]

The common-sense knowledge that the pupils have about school should be regarded as logical. It also 'works'; that is, the view of the world that the pupils have is confirmed by the way that others behave. Pupils produce 'typifications', particularly of teachers, which they use when deciding what action is appropriate, and they also give explanations for their behaviour which make sense to them. If we wish to understand pupils' behaviour, we must look at what the pupils know about school life and the ways that they categorise (or 'typify') their teachers. Further, we should recognise that pupils have what Furlong calls 'interaction sets', sometimes with one other pupil, sometimes with many pupils. What is meant here is that pupils who have similar perceptions of the situation communicate this to each other and define action together. For example, a pupil entering late into the class will be sensitive to the way other pupils define the situation. The pupil may decide to cheek the teacher and the interaction set may support such behaviour through gestures of encouragement; on other occasions such support may be lacking and the interaction set gives no encouragement. The late entrant will tend to modify his or her behaviour accordingly.

In order to try to understand why behaviour varies among pupils Furlong investigated the 'knowledge' of a small number of girls in a London Secondary Modern in 1972/3. These girls were regarded as difficult to teach by staff and they placed a high value on 'mucking about' with their friends. Generally the mucking about was good humoured, but the girls would engage in open rebellion if they felt that they had been unfairly treated. Even when they admitted they were wrong, they regarded being shouted at or being used as an example as illegitimate. The pupils' explanation for their mucking about was to blame the teacher for giving boring lessons, not making them learn, and not controlling the class properly.[40]

Trouble

It becomes clear that the pupils typified teachers according to two dimensions, the 'strict–soft' dimension and the 'good teacher–bad teacher' dimension. Avoiding 'trouble' was a main concern of the girls, but they had their own definition of what constituted trouble. They acknowledged that it was part of the teachers' role to discipline them and would accept punishment when they were caught breaking a rule and when they were forced to admit that they were in the wrong. However, pupils would go to some lengths to avoid admitting they were in the wrong. Also, it appears that the admission of being in the wrong was crucial to their definition of 'fair trouble'. 'Unfair trouble', such as being told off when others were also misbehaving, being shouted at, or having some personal knowledge used against them, led to protests and retaliation. It seems that teachers were assessed as to how much 'trouble' they could make. 'Teachers were seen as either "strict" and their discipline was taken seriously or they were "soft" and their attempts to control the class were fruitless.'[41]

Learning

Although the strict–soft dimension was the most important one, pupils also categorised the teachers in terms of their effectiveness. Here the girls' definition of 'learning' was important and Furlong tried to discover what they understood by the concept. To some extent the girls shared the usual definition of learning as 'understanding something new'.

More often they defined learning as working, as carrying out the tasks they were set, and producing something, be it in cooking, or typing, or taking notes in their books. Feedback was important to the pupils, indicating how well they had learned. Learning, in this sense, seems to have little to do with changing the way that the pupils understood the world. It was concerned with an end product which could be seen by all. The best teacher, in the pupils' view, was the history teacher who adopted the tactic of having the girls copy off the board or work from their textbooks. He marked the work at the end of the lesson, so the girls had continual feedback. The approach was highly structured but allowed the girls to move through the material at their own rate. Other teaching methods, such as projects and discussions, were avoided.

The girls' view of learning was used by them to distinguish good and bad teachers and this categorisation of teachers was added to the strict–soft dimension to determine the sort of conduct the pupils adopted. Some teachers were soft but potentially effective and sometimes the girls worked well in their lessons. Generally though, a lot of time was spent on 'mucking about'. Strict and ineffective teachers seem to have elicited 'going to sleep' in the lessons or 'bunking off'. For the strict and effective teachers the girls worked hard. Nothing is said about the soft and ineffective teachers, but we can guess at the girls' response to them.

COMMENTS

Furlong's work is both interesting and perceptive and we suggest that it 'rings a bell' with a lot of secondary teachers. By looking at the common-sense knowledge of the small group of girls, he is able to elicit their definitions of 'trouble' and 'learning' and show how these concepts are used to typify teachers. Furlong concludes that, on the basis of 'careful and continuous assessment of their teachers', the girls constructed behaviour which to them, was 'rational and logical.'[42]

Furlong does not tell us why the girls held these definitions of trouble and learning, and we are left wondering whether he regards the eliciting of the pupils' definitions of the situation as the first stage in a research process. Once we have understood the definitions we can then go on to explain why these definitions and not others are held, and this would be, in our view, a possible next step. However, as we have noted, some interactionists seem to think that, since action is based on the construction of definitions of the situation by free and creative actors, all we need to know is what definitions are held; to ask why these definitions and not others, is to ask a useless question.

THE INTERACTION OF TEACHERS AND PUPILS

STRATEGIES AND NEGOTIATION

Strategies, Woods says, are the methods which teachers and pupils use to try to achieve their goals.[43] There are always obstructions to the achievement of goals in teaching which arise from the lack of resources, the staff–student ratio, the nature of the pupils, and so on. These obstacles must be taken into consideration and plans of action constructed. The term strategies thus implies the notion of difficulty combined with the actors' subjective appreciation of the situation.

Teachers' and pupils' strategies can be classified in many ways. We could, for instance, talk of motivational strategies, control strategies, identity-maintaining strategies and pedagogical strategies. Pupils can be seen to use 'sussing out' strategies to see where teachers draw the line, strategies to please teachers, strategies to preserve their dignity or maintain their peer-group identity. Rather than giving a list of all the possible strategies available to a teacher, most authors group them into categories. Benyon,[44] for example, sub-divides the 'sussing out' strategies into group formation (which gives the pupils power); jokes and repartee; challenging verbal actions (asking stupid questions and answering back); non-verbal challenges (fiddling with pens or rulers). Woods[45] lists a number of teacher-survival strategies. Teachers, he suggests, become committed to the profession. This may be due to the difficulty of moving to another job or because of the time and effort invested in becoming a teacher. Because they are committed, they have to accommodate to the problems that arise due to lack of resources or pupils' attitudes. In extreme situations survival becomes the important thing and teachers devise survival strategies. Woods mentions a number of such strategies, including 'socialisation', that is getting the pupils to accept their role through the demand for uniforms and deference to staff as well as through the control of movement; 'domination', with physical aggression both official and unofficial as well as verbal abuse; 'negotiation', that is relaxing demands on some things in return for conformity on others; 'fraternisation' through jokes, games in lessons, talking about television with pupils and mild flirting with adolescent girls. Woods mentions other strategies, one of which — morale boosting — we want to describe in some detail. He notes that teachers devise strategies to redefine what they are doing in acceptable terms. 'The greatest danger', Woods suggests, 'is that teachers should doubt what they are doing.'[46] 'Morale boosting' involves the use of laughter and of rhetoric. Rhetoric allows teachers to redefine the survival strategy in acceptable ways. Thus fraternisation becomes thought of as 'treating pupils as people'.

Woods gives an explanation for this line of thought. He adopts the Marxist idea that schools legitimate and perpetuate inequality. It is not the teachers' intention to do this, but, by becoming committed to the organisation, they have to accommodate to the problems they face. The strategies that they develop have the unintended consequence of perpetuating inequality. Woods is clearly trying to relate schools to the wider society. Pupils bring cultures from the wider society into school; constraints from the wider society impinge on teachers. The interaction of teachers and pupils has an impact on the wider society. In trying to relate school and society Woods seems to find it necessary to give meanings to teachers' actions. We would suggest that it is indeed the sociologist's job, with his knowledge of the wider society, to point out the meaning and significance of actions of which actors are unaware. But the actors' own meanings, intentions and definitions must be taken into account as they are the data by which theories must be tested. Put slightly differently, we are suggesting that there may be an interpretive approach which is able to relate the actors' definitions of the situation to the macro issues of the relation of education to society. We will return to this in the comments section after we have considered the idea of 'negotiation'.

> From an interactionist perspective [writes Haralambos] social order results from the interpretive procedures employed by actors in interaction situations. It is a 'negotiated order' in that it derives from meanings which are negotiated in the process of interaction and involves the mutual adjustment of the actors concerned.[47]

The concept of negotiation, then, can be used to explain why so many classrooms are orderly and not chaotic, why many schools function pleasantly and efficiently, and why pupils and staff seem to find some satisfaction in their relationships. This is not to say that everything about schools is easy or pleasant, but most schools and classrooms are reasonable places. The interactionist explanation for this is that teachers and pupils have adjusted to each other so that all can have some degree of satisfaction. For example, teachers may do most of the burdensome work in return for the pupils doing some easy work, rather than none at all. Play, or some form of relaxation such as a film or video, is promised in return for a period of effort. Pupils may negotiate some of the rules in the classroom or the amount of work they have to do in lessons. They can try to achieve an easier life by playing one teacher off against another. Gradually, it is suggested, teachers and pupils come to share a common definition of the situation and an orderly classroom becomes the norm. However, since neither party is fully satisfied, it is possible that the truce may be broken and negotiation begun anew.

AN ETHNOMETHODOLOGICAL APPROACH TO TEACHERS' DISCOURSE

Ethnomethodologists share many of the assumptions of other interpretive sociologists. They recognise the importance of adopting a 'subjectivist' approach and they regard the understanding of meaning as crucial. But there are certain ideas that are peculiar to ethnomethodology.

The theory distinguishes between 'topic' and 'resource'. In the physical sciences the topic is the object of investigation, the resource is the instruments used to observe the object. In the social world the topic is a piece of interaction, the resource is what people use to make sense of interaction. Since the sociologist is a human being and member of society, he will use his own resources to make sense of the interaction he observes. In doing this he may well distort the way that the actors make sense of their interaction. To avoid this the sociologist must try to put to one side his own resources, in order to capture those of the actors.

One method of doing this is to regard every interaction (or 'accomplishment') as a unique event, unrelated to what went before. It is clear that actors do not see every interaction as a unique creation. People link actions together by using their 'methodic practices'. This is analogous to viewing a film in which every frame is a separate event. We see the film as a moving sequence because of our ability to relate separate perceptions together. Ethnomethdologists are interested in the way that actors make sense or link each interaction together to form an intelligible whole. Language is of major importance in this linking process.

Any word has several meanings, any sentence is therefore a collection of ambiguities. What helps to reduce the ambiguity is the actors' understanding of the context. To understand the phrase 'he has gone to see the police', we need to know the context. It could refer to a teenager going to a pop concert or to an irate motorist. This procedure of relating context to meaning is called 'indexicality'. It is necessary for the speaker to give clues which will allow the hearers to 'index' the speech. The hearers use methodic procedures to make sense of the event. Among these procedures are retrospective and prospective methods. In the former the hearers take a present meaning and relate it to remembered past events to make sense of it. In the latter members assume that what follows will clear up any present confusion (or repair indexicality). Another procedure is to relate people to categories that are held in the culture. Associated with categories are rights and duties. Teacher, pupil, policeman and priest are examples of categories. A person may be placed in many categories, so it is necessary for the speaker to 'membership' both himself and his hearers. That is, the speaker must indicate his own category and that of his hearers; the hearers must activate their cultural assumptions to make sense of what is going on.

George Payne

One example of an ethnomethodological analysis of the classroom is that of George Payne.[48] Payne quotes from the first few utterances in a lesson to show how the lesson is accomplished or created. He notes that members share a common culture but points to the way that the teacher's utterances direct pupils to pay attention to (or relate into) aspects of that culture and thereby make intelligible and orderly what is happening.

The first sentence is:

> Teacher: E:r . . . come o:n settle down . . . no one's sitting down till we're all ready.[49]

Membershipping is apparently taking place. The speaker is giving an order ('come o:n'); the hearers are the ones who are to obey. By speaking first in this way the speaker is referring to the cultural categories of teacher and pupil and the relationship between them. These categories exist in the minds of the actors and have no existence outside of this. Hearers have to repair any confusion which may have arisen from interacting with the speaker in a non-teaching context. The utterance ('Come o:n . . . settle down') thus calls into being the teacher–pupil relationship.

The term 'no one' is important too. It could be taken to refer to all people on earth, but clearly is not understood in that way. This word reinforces the membershipping that has already gone on. Sense can only be made of the term 'no one' by recognising that it refers to and creates the category 'pupils'. In the course of thirteen words the speaker has created himself as teacher and his hearers as pupils by membershipping them into cultural categories. But more is involved. Take the phrase 'till we're all ready'. Here the speaker has included himself in the relationship. He has not defined what 'ready' means and, since he has to be ready himself before sitting down can begin, the speaker has given himself the opportunity to decide the next action. The choice of the word 'we' is taken to be a cue to future collaborative action. Here pupils must employ prospective methodic practices (a 'wait and see' procedure) to make sense of what is happening and to link this event with what is to follow.

Payne goes on to look at other utterances, but enough has been said, we feel, to indicate the line taken by ethnomethodologists. Working on the assumption that all events are created by actors, they try to uncover the procedures whereby actors make intelligible their interaction.

In many ways Payne provides an interesting analysis of classroom discourse and does show how sense may be made of the language used by teachers and pupils. However, the ethnomethdological approach, in celebrating human creativity, fails to explain the observable similarities between classrooms. Rather the ethnomethodologist seems to suggest that what makes classrooms similar is the way people make sense of them. The only reality then becomes that created and recreated by the human mind. But this line of approach seems to lead to the question of why so many human minds should make sense of the world in very similar and often depressing ways. We would suggest that the almost solipsistic approach of the ethnos should be modified by recognising that the actors in life's drama are constrained by features which they cannot wish away. Such features, we contend, are socially produced, but they impinge on actors as 'fact'.

COMMENTS

GENERAL COMMENT

We are in many ways very sympathetic to the micro interpretive approach, particularly its attempts to grasp the meanings that actors give to their interactions. The eliciting of the categories and typifications that teachers and pupils use does help us understand what makes people 'tick'. We have suggested some refinements to the notion of 'knowledge' by distinguishing stereotypical and experiential forms which have consequences for the theory of the self-fulfilling prophecy and the way that we understand interaction and changes in the actors' definitions of the situation.

As already noted, we are less happy about the war or conflict analogy which we see as implicit in the notion of strategic interaction. Certainly in secondary schools there does appear to be a conflict situation with many pupils, sometimes hidden, sometimes open. We wonder to what extent the war analogy is applicable to primary schools or higher education. We note that many of the research studies are of secondary schools and disaffected pupils. It may be that another analogy needs to be constructed for studies of other schools. We have mentioned, also, that the notion of strategic interaction gives the impression that actors are constantly trying to maximise their satisfaction at the expense of others; or, put in a slightly different way, that the teachers' and pupils' goals are at odds. This is not, we think, always the case and there can be genuine co-operation and working together. The term strategies could, of course, be used to indicate the attempts of teachers and pupils to devise the best methods of achieving mutually shared goals. When a teacher tries to devise a better method of teaching pupils to read, he or she is clearly using a strategy; but there does seem to be something different when we use the term in this context from the use of the term as applied to imposing one's definition of the situation on others who are resisting. We suggest that the picture generally given of teacher–pupil interaction is a pessimistic one.

THE OBSERVER'S ROLE

There is a second theme that has been running through our discussion of the micro approaches and this concerns the observer's part in the process. The theory seems to suggest that we must get at the actors' definitions of the situation, the goals, intentions, typifications, categories, assumptions and interpretations of others. We must be true to the actors' definitions, we must avoid imposing our own interpretation. However, as we have noted, very few researchers do this. Strategies are suggested, but the term strategy may not figure in the actors' definitions of what is happening. The very use of the term indicates a view of the nature of the interaction. Indeed the attempt to seek out the taken-for-granted assumption seems to us to suggest that these are not part of the actors' ongoing definitions of the situation. Indeed, very few sociologists would argue that we can bracket out our own assumptions.

Theory exists to point us to what we should consider significant. We are told by the theory to look at the actors' meanings or their goals, or their definitions of learning, or their 'knowledge' of pupils. In observing the interaction of teacher and pupil, we are sensitised by the theory to notice some aspects and ignore others. Indeed this is what a theory is for. Put simply, the observer–reporter cannot be a mere describer of the actors' definitions of the situation; interpretation must enter.

We can go on from the above point. Peter Woods, as we have suggested, implies that there are meanings which the actors do not give to their actions, but which are implicit in the action. Woods suggests that teachers use 'rhetoric' as part of the survival strategy of 'morale boosting'. Rhetoric redefines for the actors the strategies they are using, so they are not considered as survival strategies but as ways of treating the pupils as people. The 'real' meaning is disguised by the actors' meaning. We see the sociologist as an observer who has some understanding of the wider picture and is consequently able to see significances which are obscured from the actors when engaged in everyday encounters. This does not imply that we should ignore the attempts to elicit the actors' definitions of the situation; what it does is suggest that we should recognise the active part we are playing in bringing out such definitions.

NARROW FOCUS

Haralambos clearly summarises one criticism of the micro interpretive approach in the following way.

> Interactionists have often been accused of examining human interaction in a vacuum. They have tended to focus on small-scale face to face interaction with little concern for its historical or social setting. They have concentrated on particular situations and encounters with little reference to the historical events which led up to them or the wider social framework in which they occur. Since these factors influence the particular interaction situation, the scant attention they have received has been regarded as a serious omission.[50]

To some extent this criticism is accurate. Furlong, for example, does not explain the origin of the pupils' categorisation of teachers. Pollard also says nothing about the origin of the identities that the pupils are seeking to maintain. Keddie clearly implies that teachers' definitions of ability could, and should, be different.

But it is equally true that some of the authors who see themselves as interactionists do bring into their accounts factors from outside the interaction. Hargreaves notes that, due to the expectations of others, teachers must include the instruction and discipline elements in their definitions of their role. Woods brings in the idea of class culture and gender as an element of the pupils' perspectives. He also talks of pupils and teachers adapting or accommodating to the situation. Clearly these authors are aware that interaction is influenced by factors outside the control of the actors.

Having said this we do feel that the micro interpretive approach has, with some exceptions, neglected to deal adequately with the factors outside the interaction situation which influence what happens. It is clear that the staff–pupil ratio, expectations about examination success, material resources and the expectations of head, colleagues, pupils and parents all influence the teacher. Put differently, action is constrained. A full analysis of interaction must describe the constraints and show how they affect the participants' definitions. Of course, the constraints are socially constructed — they arise from prior interaction. From the teachers' point of view, then, the examination system may be a very powerful constraint, but the examination system itself has been developed and is maintained by individuals and groups with their own goals and definitions of the situation. We can, therefore, adopt an interpretive approach to examine, for example, how the examination system is constructed and maintained.

It is our view that the interpretive approach can be used to explain where the constraints which impinge on the teacher come from. The approach is able to deal with the concept of power[51] and thus explain why the constraints are taken into account when action occurs. Where the approach is weak, we feel, is in tracing the origins of the actors' goals.

FAILURE TO STATE THE ORIGIN OF DEFINITIONS

A second criticism of interpretive sociology is summarised by Haralambos in the following way:

> Similar criticisms have been made with reference to what many see as the failure of interactionists to explain the source of the meanings to which they attach such importance . . . Critics argue that such meanings are not spontaneously created in interaction situations. Instead they are systematically generated by the social structure. Thus Marxists have argued that the meanings which operate in face to face interaction situations are largely the product of class relationships. From this viewpoint, interactionists have failed to explain the most significant thing about meanings: the source of their origin.[52]

Perhaps the most pointed attack on interpretive sociology from this point of view is that of Sharp and Green.[53] They argue that there is a discrepancy between teachers' perspectives and their action in the classroom. They note that in one case the teacher disagreed with the school's philosophy yet there were few observable differences between her classroom and those of others who agreed with it. They further suggest that the important concept of 'busyness' is created by teachers in response to the management problems they face when trying to put the progressive philosophy into practice. They argue that stratification arises in the classroom. This is something that runs counter to the teacher's intentions, but is inevitable in the conditions under which teachers operate. The phenomenological approach which sees actors as free and creative is inadequate to explain how unintended consequences come about. Sharp and Green think that the view of W.I. Thomas — that if something is believed to be true it will be true in its consequences — does not hold. To suggest that all we need to know is the actors' consciousness and how they define the situation is inadequate. Actors are limited in the definitions that they can adopt by actors beyond their control and possibly outside their perception.

We feel that Sharp and Green have failed to notice that micro interpretive sociologists do take factors outside the control of actors into account. However, if Sharp and Green can show that factors which actors do not recognise as constraints influence their definitions of the situation, then an important weakness in the micro approach has been demonstrated. David Hargreaves puts the case well.

> Whether the teachers are or are not aware of these structural constraints is crucial to Sharp and Green's argument. If they are not so aware, and if the consequential nature of such constraints can be demonstrated, then Sharp and Green would be correct in claiming they have exposed one of the limitations of a I/S phenomenological analysis.[54]

Hargreaves goes on to suggest that the authors have failed to show that teachers are unaware of the constraints. They have not asked the right questions of teachers. We would go further. The examples that Sharp and Green give of constraints are such things as: the pupil–teacher ratio; the expectations of the powerful; pupils' attitudes; materials available; the geography of the building. However, when we look at their reports of what the teachers think, we find that some of them are clearly aware of these constraints. They quote from the headmaster in the following way:

> The problems are immense . . . the hard part, I find, is being able to satisfy the needs of so many children . . . how can you satisfy 35–40 children often wanting that number of things at the same time . . . it's done by constantly encouraging children to do it by themselves . . . all the time you are trying to help the children to help themselves, rather like getting a trolley in a supermarket and going round.[55]

Also one of the teachers, Mrs Buchanan, is described by Sharp and Green in the following way:

> If she had a free hand she would be more directive. She would have them all sitting down at certain times of the day making them do reading, writing and number work, but she is conscious of her lack of power to do that. This teacher thinks that she would be disapproved of if she did that and is reluctant to publicly express her lack of sympathy with, and her personal feelings of inadequacy to operate, these very informal methods.[56]

It is obvious from these extracts that the people mentioned are aware of the constraints of pupil–teacher ratio and the expectations of others. Mrs Buchanan is conscious of her lack of power. Given this, it is difficult to see how Sharpe and Green can argue that the micro interpretive approach is unable to recognise that the teachers' consciousness is influenced or possibly limited by the structural constraints. The extracts quoted clearly demonstrate that it is quite capable of this kind of recognition. The extracts also indicate that the teachers are quite conscious of features over which they have no control and to which they have to accommodate. Because of this we would agree that Sharpe and Green's attempt to discredit the utility of the micro interpretive approach fails.

AN ATTEMPTED SYNTHESIS

Andy Hargreaves

On a more positive note Andy Hargreaves[57] has produced an interesting attempt to relate the wider society to interaction in the classroom. He notes that 'how' the teacher organises and evaluates pupils' experience is an interesting topic. 'Why the teacher organises and evaluates the pupil learning and behaviour in one way rather than another would also seem to qualify as a question worth asking.'[58] To link these two aspects together and to relate interaction to its social setting Hargreaves devises the notion of 'coping strategy' and develops a model which we reproduce in Figure 11.3.

Coping strategies are in some sense creative. 'The essence of a model organised around the concept of coping strategy is that all actors . . . act meaningfully and creatively in response to their *experience* world.'[59] But the word 'coping' is used to indicate that 'there are limits to the variety of styles which teachers may adopt in the classroom'. Styles will be generated and sustained only in so far as they enable successful coping with experienced constraints. Put simply, teachers are creative but within the limits of the constraints they *experience*. There are only a limited number of solutions to the problems and dilemmas faced by the teachers.

The constraints, Hargreaves thinks, come from the wider society. In particular they come from the contradictory goals of the educational system which are to foster personal development and equality on the one hand and on the other to prepare the child for his future position in the society. A second important source of constraint refers to the material features of schools which arise from the often *ad hoc* educational planning that goes on. A third source of constraints are the educational ideologies which abound and which may be held by powerful personages who come into contact with the teacher. It is, however, possible for the teacher to put on a 'front' of implementing the ideology while in practice not doing so. These 'societal constraints', Hargreaves says, 'are institutionally mediated'.[60] By this he means that they will be felt differently depending on such things as the age and class background of the pupils.

All teachers are subject to constraints and create coping strategies to deal with them. These strategies are put into operation within the classroom and produce responses from the pupils. The teacher then evaluates the responses and decides whether the strategy is a success or failure. Hargreaves regards coping strategies as 'very generalised definitions of teaching behaviour'.[61] In this sense they are wider than is generally understood by strategies. Strategies give rise to particular decisions within the classroom. It would appear, for example, the common rule of thumb. 'Begin by being strict' is a coping strategy which gives rise to the particular discipline decisions a teacher makes when faced with a new class.

The creation of coping strategies is '*based upon a set of tacitly accepted and taken-for-granted assumptions* about schooling, children and learning'.[62] These assumptions serve to limit the sort of coping strategies that will be developed. From Figure 11.3 it appears that Hargreaves sees the dominant hegemony as having an impact on the teachers' experience, becoming part of their taken-for-granted world.

Figure 11.3: Hargreaves's Coping Strategies

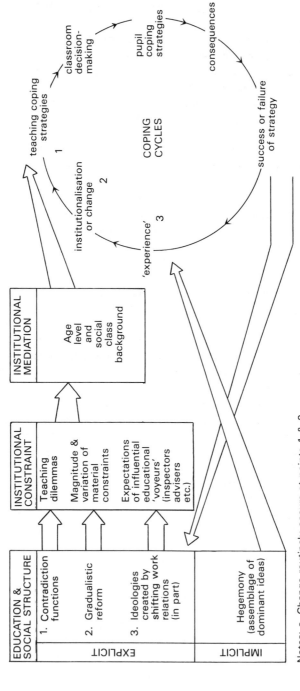

Notes: a. Change routinely occurs at points 1 & 2.
b. Radical change is produced by a reversal of 3.

Source: A. Hargreaves, 'The Significance of Classroom Coping Strategies' in L. Barton and R. Meighan, *Sociological Interpretations of Schooling and Classrooms: A Reappraisal* (Nafferton Books, Driffield, 1978), p. 96.

Hargreaves has attempted to link the insights of micro and macro sociology whilst adopting something of a Marxist orientation. He wants, in his own words to 'provide a framework which might link structural questions to interactionist concerns'.[63] In one sense we think he is successful in that he is able to show that the constraints which teachers experience and the problems they face have their origins within the wider society.

Of particular importance, from our point of view, is the tentative introduction of the notion of ideology and hegemony into the teachers' definition of the situation. The link that Hargreaves forms between ideology and experience may prove to be crucial for the development of the study of education. However, there is nothing within Hargreaves's article to suggest that we *have* to accept a particular Marxist interpretation of the term ideology.

We would accept that people do develop ideas and ideologies and that these become made real (or realised) in organisations and institutions. The progressive ideology may become realised in the organisation of the primary classroom; the ideology of individualism may become realised in the organisation of the secondary school. By becoming realised, these various ideologies come to form the experience of both teachers and pupils. Which ideologies will dominate depends, to a great extent, on who has the power to make them real. The important point for us is that the experience of people is partly shaped by the ideologies of the powerful.

The significance of this relates to what we see as a major problem of the micro interpretive approach. We have already suggested that some micro interpretive sociologists have always recognised the existence of factors beyond the actors' control. We have also suggested that micro interpretive sociology can explain the existence of such factors. The major problem for the micro interpretive approach is to explain why actors pursue some goals and hold certain definitions of the situation, and not others.

Our tentative view is that actors' goals and definitions come from experience. We suggest that actors create goals for themselves in order to make sense of their past and present experience and to project into the future an intelligible, and attainable, plan of life. There is then, as Berger[64] has suggested, a dialectic between the socially constructed society and the consciousness of individual actors and groups of actors. In bringing the wider society into contact with the actors' definition of the situation, the notions of ideology, power and experience may prove fruitful.

288　*Some Studies of Teachers and Pupils*

NOTES

1. D. Hargreaves, *Interpersonal Relations and Education*, Student edition (Routledge and Kegan Paul, London, 1975).
2. R. Sharp and A. Green, *Education and Social Control: A Study of Progressive Primary Education* (Routledge and Kegan Paul, London, 1975).
3. Ibid., p. 68.
4. Ibid., p. 70.
5. M. Hammersley, 'Teacher Perspectives' Unit 9 of E202, *Schooling and Society* (Open University Press, Milton Keynes, 1977).
6. Ibid., p. 37.
7. D.H. Hargreaves, S.K. Hester and F.J. Mellor, *Deviance in Classrooms* (Routledge and Kegan Paul, London, 1975).
8. R. Nash, *Teacher Expectations and Pupil Learning* (Routledge and Kegan Paul, London, 1976).
9. Ibid., p. 21.
10. N. Keddie, 'Classroom Knowledge' in M.F.D. Young (ed.), *Knowledge and Control* (Collier-Macmillan, London, 1971).
11. Ibid., p. 156.
12. Sharp and Green, *Education and Social Control*.
13. Nash, *Teacher Expectations*.
14. A. Pollard, 'Goodies, Jokers and Gangs' in M. Hammersley and P. Woods (eds.), *Life in Schools: The Sociology of Pupil Culture* (Open University Press, Milton Keynes, 1984), pp. 238 ff.
15. Ibid., p. 253.
16. Ibid., p. 249.
17. Ibid., p. 250.
18. Ibid., p. 250.
19. Ibid., p. 251.
20. P. Woods, *Sociology and the School. An Interactionist Viewpoint* (Routledge and Kegan Paul, London, 1983).
21. Ibid., p. 7.
22. Ibid., p. 11.
23. W. Waller, *The Sociology of Teaching* (Wiley, New York, 1932).
24. S. Delamont, *Interaction in the Classroom* (Methuen, London, 1976).
25. Woods, *Sociology and the School*, p. 89.
26. P. Woods, *The Divided School* (Routledge and Kegan Paul, London, 1979), p. 72.
27. Ibid., p. 73.
28. Ibid., p. 74.
29. Ibid., p. 74.
30. Ibid., p. 74.
31. Woods, *Sociology and the School*, p. 62.
32. M. Hammersley and G. Turner, 'Conformist Pupils?' in Hammersley and Woods (eds.), *Life in Schools*, pp. 160–74.
33. Ibid., p. 170.
34. Ibid., p. 170.
35. Ibid., p. 170.
36. Hargreaves *et al.*, *Deviance*.
37. See D. Hargreaves, *Social Relations in a Secondary School* (Routledge and Kegan Paul, London, 1976).
38. V. Furlong, 'Interaction Sets in the Classroom: Towards a Study of Pupil Knowledge' in M. Hammersley and P. Woods (eds.), *The Process of Schooling* (Routledge and Kegan Paul, London, 1976), p. 161.
39. V. Furlong, 'Anancy Goes to School: A Case Study of Pupils' Knowledge of Their Teachers' in P. Woods and M. Hammersley (eds.), *School Experience: Explorations in the*

Sociology of Education (Croom Helm, London, 1977), p. 163.

40. Ibid., p. 166.

41. Ibid., p. 171.

42. Ibid., p. 183.

43. Woods, *Sociology and the School*, p. 9.

44. J. Benyon, ' "Sussing Out" Teachers: Pupils as Data Gatherers' in Hammersley and Woods (eds.), *Life in Schools*, pp. 121 ff.

45. Woods, *Sociology and the School*.

46. Woods, *The Divided School*, p. 166.

47. M. Haralambos with R. Heald, *Sociology, Themes and Perspectives* (University Tutorial Press, Slough, 1980), p. 553.

48. G. Payne, 'Making a Lesson Happen' in Hammersley and Woods (eds.), *The Process of Schooling*, p. 33.

49. Ibid., p. 34.

50. Haralambos and Heald, *Sociology*, p. 551.

51. We follow Max Weber's notion of power as expressed in *The Theory of Social and Economic Organization* (Free Press, New York, 1964). He defines power as the ability to impose one's will, despite resistance. This implies that one person has the resources to penalise or reward another. But a penalty will only be effective if it prevents the other person from achieving something he wants, be it freedom, the absence of pain or a quiet life. If, for example, a child does not want to be in school then the threat to send him home will be ineffective. Power over another is thus related to what that person wants; that is his goals and aspirations. Power over another depends on what the other's goals are; an analysis of power demands an analysis of the actors' goals. Consequently power must be analysed within an interpretive approach.

52. Haralambos, *Sociology*, pp. 551–2.

53. Sharp and Green, *Education and Social Control*.

54. D. Hargreaves, 'Whatever Happened to Symbolic Interactionism?' in L. Barton and R. Meighan (eds.), *Sociological Intepretations of Schooling and Classrooms: A Reappraisal* (Nafferton Books, Driffield, 1978), p. 17.

55. Sharp and Green, *Education and Social Control*, p. 52.

56. Ibid., p. 103.

57. A. Hargreaves, 'The Significance of Classroom Coping Strategies' in Barton and Meighan (eds.), *Sociological Interpretations*.

58. Ibid., p. 75.

59. Ibid., p. 77. Our emphasis.

60. Ibid., p. 88.

61. Ibid., p. 77.

62. Ibid., p. 94.

63. Ibid., p. 74.

64. P. Berger, *Invitation to Sociology: A Humanistic Perspective* (Penguin, Harmondsworth, 1966).

12 THE 'NEW' SOCIOLOGY OF EDUCATION

The 'new' sociology of education, as we pointed out in our introductory chapter, developed in reaction to the tradition of 'political arithmetic' and the dominance of the functionalist approach in the 'old' sociology of education. This approach to education is particularly associated with the volume *Knowledge and Control*[1] and especially the contributions by M.F.D. Young, Geoffrey Esland and Nell Keddie (as well as with some of their subsequent writings). It draws upon the concepts of phenomenological sociology (especially the work of Alfred Schutz) and some of the insights of Berger and Luckmann and Alan Dawe. These are combined, however, with a 'relativist' outlook and the result is a view of education which is sufficiently distinctive to merit separate consideration.

THE BASIC ARGUMENT

The 'new' sociology of education is primarily concerned with the 'content' of education rather than with the 'structure' or organisation of the educational system. The exponents of this approach focus on the curriculum, on the 'educational knowledge' imparted by the school, and on the school's conception of 'what it is to be educated'. They are concerned with the concepts that teachers possess of, for example, 'bright' and 'dull' children, 'academic' and 'non-academic' children, etc., and with examining the distinctions normally made between teachers and taught. As G. Whitty says, the new sociology of education is 'concerned to question the prevailing taken-for-granted assumptions in the world of education'.[2]

The main argument of these sociologists of education can be broken down as follows.

Knowledge Is Socially Constructed

They argue that the school's conception of 'what it is to be educated' is 'socially constructed'. 'Knowledge', for example, is not a 'static entity', something 'out-there' and 'independent of the knower' but a 'social invention'. As for the claim made by philosophers such as Hirst that there are distinct 'forms' of knowledge, Young argues that one must recognise that such forms of knowledge are 'no more than the socio-historical

290

constructs of a particular time'.[3]

In addition, they say, one must explore how the forms of knowledge that make up the school curriculum are related to the interests of particular classes and professional groups; or, more directly, of how the curriculum is a product of pressure from certain vested interests. Furthermore, one must appreciate the class content of education. For the curriculum of our schools is biased in favour of the middle-class child, and this fact helps to explain working-class 'failure'.

Truth and Validity Are Socially Constructed

But it is not just forms of knowledge that are socially constructed; so, too, are our criteria of truth and valid reasoning. These, also, are not absolutes. Norms of truth, says Esland, change. Notions of 'validating the truth of an assertion', 'being scientific' and 'being rational' are all matters of social convention. Both Esland and Young refer for support on this point to an article by the American sociologist C. Wright Mills, and Esland quotes Mills as saying: 'There have been, and are, diverse canons and criteria of validity and truth, and these criteria, upon which the determination of the truthfulness of propositions at any time depends, are themselves, in their persistence and change, open to socio-historical relativization.'[4] Young asserts that our present conceptions of 'being rational' and 'science' are 'dogmas' and that we must start to think in terms of 'alternative thought systems'.

Ability, Knowledge and Educational Failure

Furthermore, the concepts of 'ability' and 'intelligence' are also social products and educational failure can be seen to derive from them. According to Esland, teachers hold unexamined assumptions about a substance called 'intelligence' and these assumptions have a 'self-fulfilling' nature. Lacey's work, he says, 'provides an excellent illustration of the self-fulfilling nature of the teacher's definition of the "good" pupil. The "problem pupils" are so because of the premises on which the differentiation is made.'[5] In other words, educational achievement and failure are a result of the teachers' definition or criteria of ability and intelligence: if these criteria were modified a different pattern of achievement and failure would emerge. Furthermore, this would be one that did not work to the disadvantage of the working-class child for it would be based on the idea of 'cultural diversity' rather than 'cultural deficiency'. In Esland's view, the average working-class child thinks in a different, not inferior, way from his middle-class counterpart.

Nell Keddie. In her article, 'Classroom Knowledge', Nell Keddie considerably elaborates on this view. She argues that many of the proposed remedies for the educational failure of the working-class child — such as de-streaming and an undifferentiated curriculum — will be ineffective if 'hierarchical categories of ability and knowledge' persist.[6] In other words, it is the teachers' notions of 'high and low ability' and their view of the nature of knowledge which are at fault. As she says: 'innovation in schools will not be of a very radical kind unless the categories teachers use to organize what they know about pupils and to determine what counts as knowledge undergo a fundamental change.'[7]

Keddie points out that, at the school she studied, ability is conceptualised in terms of whether or not pupils can manage material or knowledge appropriate to a particular ability band. According to the teachers, A-stream pupils have the ability to 'master subjects'. They can cope with the abstract, intellectual material. C-stream pupils, on the other hand, need more concrete, familiar, illustrative material which is rooted in experience and couched in a language they can understand. Basically they are unable to master subjects and require material which is, so to speak, 'nearer home'.

Keddie's own interpretation of events is rather different from that of the teachers. We should not, she believes, see the differences between A- and C-stream pupils in terms of the one being superior to the other; rather, they have contrasting approaches to knowledge. Of the A-stream pupil's supposed ability to master subjects, she says:

> This is not necessarily a question of the ability to move to higher levels of generalization and abstraction so much as an ability to move into an alternative system of thought from that of his everyday knowledge. In practical terms this means being able to work within the framework which the teacher constructs and by which the teacher is then himself constrained.[8]

This framework or alternative thought system is that of 'expert' as opposed to 'everyday' knowledge. Essentially it involves the process of learning 'what questions may be asked within a particular subject perspective' and 'what is to constitute a problem and what is to count as knowledge'.[9] Such as framework, however, Keddie regards as constraining — as we have already seen. This is because she believes that the structure and language of a subject prevent you from raising certain issues. In one of the examples she provides of social science lessons, Keddie suggests that such subjects cannot accommodate searching questions about, for example, the cruelty and inhumanity of certain practices. Pupils who adopt the framework must therefore often disregard relevant questions about an issue derived from their everyday experience and accept that much of what they learn will be remote from such experience. These A-stream pupils, continues Keddie, become concerned only with the immediate task of 'finding the answer' to the problems set by the teacher within the framework of the subject. They focus their attention on the individual units of study and often fail to grasp the connecting links by which they can see the topic as a whole. Furthermore, these pupils rarely question what they are taught in school. They 'accept their teachers' presentation on trust' and, as a consequence, they become less 'autonomous'.

C-stream pupils, on the other hand, do not operate within the confines of a subject in this way and are primarily concerned with the everyday meaning of an issue. They are also more likely to question the value of what they are taught as opposed to only raising questions within the framework of subject. Consequently, the teacher defines such pupils as unable to master subjects and adjusts her expectations of them accordingly. But such expectations have a major impact on educational achievement, stresses Keddie. As she says: 'It seems likely that it is here that teachers' expectations of pupils most effectively operate to set levels of pupil achievement.'[10] In other words, the teachers create failure.

Keddie, then, offers us a new version of the theory that teacher expectations determine educational achievement. The twist that she gives to the theory is that such expectations are based on the teachers' conception of what counts as 'knowledge' and 'ability', namely subjects and the mastery of them. However, in the tradition of the 'old' sociology of education, Keddie also relates teacher expectations to social class. She suggests that it is the teachers' knowledge of the pupils' background that determines their assessment of the pupils' capacities. As she says: 'Ability is an organizing and unexamined concept for teachers whose categorization of pupils on the grounds of ability derives largely from social class judgements of pupils' social, moral and intellectual behaviour.'[11] So middle-class pupils find their way into the A stream because they are middle class and because they are willing to adopt the teachers' framework of thought. Working-class pupils, on the other hand, are relegated to the C stream because of their background and because teachers do not expect them to be able to master subjects. The fact that their mode of thought is different from that of the teachers, even superior to it, is ignored.

Educational Knowledge and Everyday Knowledge

An important implication of the above is that we should not assume that
the thought systems embodied in the curricula of educational institutions
are superior to common sense. As Young says: 'Formal education is based
on the assumption that the thought systems organized in curricula are
in some sense superior to the thought systems of those who are to be
(or have not been) educated.'[12] The new sociology of education, on the
other hand, starts by

> rejecting the assumptions of any superiority of educational or
> 'academic' knowledge over the everyday commonsense knowledge
> available to people as being in the world. There is no doubt that
> teachers' practices . . . are predicated on just the assumption of the
> superiority of academic knowledge and [it is that] that is being called
> into question.[13]

The new sociologists of education take the view that common-sense
knowledge is just as valid as that found in the curricula of schools. They
also argue that 'educational knowledge' is essentially middle class and,
as a corollary, identify 'everyday' knowledge with that found among the
working class. Finally, and because they reject the notion that 'educational knowledge' is superior to common-sense knowledge, they see no
reason for the existence of a hierarchy between teacher and taught in which
the teacher is conceived as the authority in the classroom transmitting
knowledge to the pupils.

COMMENTS

We have seen that the new sociology of education is concerned to 'question the prevailing taken-for-granted assumptions in the world of education'. Unfortunately, the way these sociologists speak suggests that they
make the questioning of such things synonymous with the rejection of
them. They imply that, as soon as you subject the categories and concepts of teachers to critical scrutiny, they will be shown to be hollow and
worthless, even harmful. It never seems to occur to them that such
categories and concepts may turn out to be quite reasonable ones with
a firm foundation in reality. This should not be taken to mean that we
do not consider it important to examine the nature of concepts such as
intelligence, raise questions about the nature of knowledge and consider
the justification for the inclusion of certain subjects in the curriculum

of schools. However, it must be recognised that at the end of this process of inquiry many existing practices *may* be shown to be well founded.

IS KNOWLEDGE SOCIALLY CONSTRUCTED

Similarly with the claim that knowledge is 'socially constructed': if by this is meant that knowledge is built up by human beings in an attempt to solve problems; that it is not static and unchangeable but is modifiable in the light of experience; and that, therefore, we should regard it as true until further notice, then this is perfectly acceptable. However, when Young tells us that forms of knowledge are *no more than* socio-historical constructs of a particular time, he sounds a relativist note. For he implies that existing forms of knowledge are in some way rather arbitrary, that they are *mere* human inventions. Knowledge, on this view, is a matter of convention — it is no more than what particular groups label as such.

However, we would maintain with David Cooper that: 'There is not the faintest inconsistency in holding both that curriculum subjects are human inventions *and* that the distinctions so produced are rational ones which any sensible curriculum must respect.'[14] Cooper, in this passage, speaks of curriculum subjects. For the moment, however, we want to confine ourselves to a consideration of 'forms' of knowledge and to argue that the distinctions normally made by philosophers between such forms are, indeed, valid ones.

Forms of Knowledge

A particularly clear and short statement on this issue is provided in the dialogue between Isaiah Berlin and Bryan Magee in the book *Men of Ideas*.[15] Berlin and Magee take the view that there are three great branches or forms of knowledge, (i) the empirical, (ii) the formal, (iii) the philosophical, which have resulted from human beings asking three distinct kinds of questions.

The first of these — empirical questions and empirical knowledge — Berlin describes as follows. He says that 'ordinary empirical questions' are

> questions about what there is in the world, the sort of thing ordinary observation or the sciences deal with. 'Are there black swans in Australia?' 'Yes, there are; they have been seen there.' 'What is water made of?' 'It's made of certain types of molecules.' 'And the molecules?' 'They consist of atoms.' Here we are in the realm of verifiable, or at least falsifiable assertions. Common sense works like this too: 'Where is the cheese?' 'The cheese is in the cupboard.' 'How do you know?' 'I've looked.' This is regarded as a perfectly sufficient answer

to the question. In normal circumstances I would not doubt this, nor would you. These are called empirical questions, questions of fact which are settled by ordinary common sense or, in more complicated cases, by controlled observation, by experiment, by the confirmation of hypotheses, and so on.[16]

Of the second type of question (and the second form of knowledge) Berlin says that this is

> the sort of question which mathematicians or logicians ask. There you accept certain definitions, certain transformation rules about how to derive propositions, and rules of entailment which enable you to deduce conclusions from premises. And there are also sets of rules in accordance with which logical relations of propositions can be checked. This gives you no information about the world at all. I am referring to formal disciplines which seem to be entirely divorced from questions of fact: mathematics, logic, game theories, heraldry. You don't discover the answer by looking out of the window, or at a dial, or through a telescope, or in the cupboard. If I tell you that the king in chess moves only one square at a time, it is no good you saying: 'Well you *say* it only moves one square at a time, but one evening I was looking at a chess board and I saw a king move two squares.' This would not be regarded as a refutation of my proposition, because what I am really saying is that there is a rule in chess according to which the king is allowed to move only one square at a time, otherwise the rule is broken.[17]

Berlin stresses that, with regard to both of these two types of questions, 'there are clearly understood methods for finding the answers'. Although you may not know the answer to any particular problem, with both empirical and formal knowledge you most certainly know how to set about finding the answer. With philosophical questions and knowledge it is a different matter. Berlin says of this third kind of question that:

> One of the *prima facie* hallmarks of a philosophical question seems to me to be this: that you do not know where to look for the answer. Someone says to you: 'What is justice?', or 'Is every event determined by antecedent events?', or 'What are the ends of human life? Should we pursue happiness, or promote social equality, or justice or religious worship or knowledge — even if these things do not lead to happiness?' How precisely do you set about answering such questions? Or suppose

someone with an inclination to think about ideas says to you: 'What do you mean by 'real'? How do you distinguish reality from appearance?' Or asks: 'What is knowledge? What do we know? Can we know anything for certain?'[18]

With regard to answering such questions, says Berlin, 'we do what we can'. We would suggest that an example of the sort of thing that can be done is to be found in the sphere of moral and social philosophy. Here we do not strive to verify or falsify propositions — as with the empirical disciplines — but seek the justification of moral and social principles. We do not try to prove, but to make a good case for. In Margaret Macdonald's view, the process is similar to the way in which a good lawyer seeks to defend his client.[19] Moral and political statements, therefore, are not simply expressions of feeling or emotion, but are open to rational investigation. As J.S. Mill said: 'The subject is within the cognisance of the rational faculty . . . Considerations may be presented capable of determining the intellect either to give or withhold its assent.'[20]

What bearing does all of this have on our assessment of the arguments of the new sociology of education? Fundamentally, we feel we need to repeat what we said earlier, namely we regard the distinctions between the three forms of knowledge as valid. The forms of knowledge are certainly human constructions, that is, they have been created by human ingenuity and effort — whoever thought otherwise? — but that does not mean that they are in some way arbitrary.

Knowledge and Group Interests

Next we must examine the new sociology of education's claim that educational knowledge is not only socially constructed but serves certain vested interests.

In assessing this claim it is important to make a distinction between (1) the *origin* and *function* of knowledge, ideas and beliefs, and (2) the *truth* and *validity* of such knowledge, ideas and beliefs. Also, having made the distinction, it is essential to stress that questions of origin and function are quite unrelated to questions of truth and validity. For example, a particular set of ideas may well have their origin in a particular society at a particular time. Also they may serve certain vested interests, that is, help the dominant groups in that society legitimate their positions. A case in point would be the classical economic theory of Smith, Ricardo and James Mill which came into being in the early stages of the Industrial Revolution and was used by the rising bourgeoisie to support a *laissez-faire* economic system. However, the genesis and use of such a body of knowledge is one thing, the assessment of its truth or falsity another. The fact that classical economic theory was employed as a means of legitimating a cruel and unjust economic system is irrelevant to a consideration of the correctness or otherwise of the theory (although an assessment of the social effects of the *implementation* of the theory would, of course, be relevant to any judgement of its truth or falsity). We happen to believe that this theory is erroneous; but this assessment has nothing to do with the fact that it was the product of a particular type of society and served certain vested interests. Similarly with regard to the forms of knowledge which make up the curricula of schools and colleges. No doubt the continued prominence of certain disciplines in the curricula serves particular vested interests. It helps to maintain the job opportunities and the social esteem of graduates in those subjects. Yet the study of such disciplines may, nevertheless, be important and valuable; and judgements about their social functions are irrelevant to judgements concerning their intrinsic value.

Unfortunately, the proponents of the new sociology of education fail to make the distinction between the origin and function of knowledge and ideas on the one hand, and their truth and validity on the other. Naturally, therefore, they are unable to see that the two sets of questions are quite separate.

The importance of keeping these two sets of questions separate can be further appreciated by considering the knowledge and ideas which make up the new sociology of education itself. For the development of this perspective on education can certainly be related to the pursuit of group interests. Were there not careers to be made, for example, out of the new sociology of education? After all, if you create a controversy, you can get an academic living out of it for many years. Yet few would suggest that this was the intention behind the development of this approach to education. Nor should we take the view that, even if this perspective does now serve vested interests in the world of education, this has anything to do with whether or not it is a valid conception of the educational process. To repeat, the function of a body of knowledge is one thing, its truth or falsity another. Whilst maintaining a healthy scepticism towards the curricula of educational institutions, we should not lose sight of this fact.

The sort of scepticism we have in mind is exemplified in the work of Peter Berger. And we can perhaps best bring our discussion of this particular issue to a close by quoting a passage from his work. In an essay on the problem of work he writes:

The world of occupational organizations is one in which a Veblenes-que vision of gigantic conmanship is almost a methodological imperative. This can perhaps be seen most easily in the phenomenon commonly called professionalization, that is, the state of affairs when an occupation is out to convince the public that it is now entitled to the status of the older respected professions (of which medicine and the law are the prototypes). Sociologists have drawn up very serious-looking lists of characteristics that would entitle an occupation to claim professional status for itself. This may be a meritorious task, but we would maintain that one misses the social reality in question unless one grasps the fantastic bamboozling that goes on as these characteristics are acquired or, more accurately, manufactured. The most important of these professional characteristics are, by common consent, the possession of a distinct body of knowledge, transmitted under the auspices of the profession, and a professional ethic, supervised under the same auspices. The ethic is somewhat less of a problem. After all, most occupational groups function within a modicum of ground rules, for their own protection if not that of the public, and these rules can be easily codified. The body of knowledge is where the difficulty enters. What, after all, is the body of knowledge that properly belongs to social work, undertaking, or public relations — to mention three groups with recent but all the more noisy claims to professional status? The general maxim here could be put as follows: 'If a body of knowledge does not exist it must be produced.' It goes without saying that this task is not easy, especially if it involves the construction of a plausible curriculum for the training centres of the nascent profession.[21]

ARE TRUTH AND VALIDITY SOCIALLY CONSTRUCTED?

This brings us to an assessment of the view that criteria of truth and validity are socially constructed and therefore relative. It must be stressed at the outset that this is a much stronger claim than the one just examined. To assert that a body of knowledge and particular ideas and beliefs serve vested interests in society is to put forward what Mannheim called the 'particular' concept of ideology. Ideologies in this sense frequently involve a distorted view of the world, one which is in keeping with the vested interests concerned. The notion that our criteria of truth and valid reasoning are relative, however, belongs to the 'total' concept of ideology. This differs from the former in that it calls into question not just particular ideas and beliefs of one's opponents, but his whole way of thought — his 'total Weltanschauung (including his conceptual apparatus)', in

Mannheim's words[22] — and sees this as being socially determined. Furthermore, whilst the 'particular' conception recognises, again in Mannheim's words, that an opponent is 'distorting or concealing a given factual situation, it is still nevertheless assumed that both parties share common criteria of validity — it is still assumed that it is possible to refute lies and eradicate sources of error by referring to accepted criteria of objective validity common to both parties'.[23] However, this is precisely what the total conception denies. On this view, according to Mannheim, men have 'fundamentally divergent thought systems' which are a 'function of' their different life-situations,[24] and they are the prisoners of such thought systems. We can, therefore, never arrive at objective knowledge or truth because our very criteria of truth are a product of our life situation and vary with that situation. There is only a truth for me and a truth for you. As a consequence, says Mannheim, 'men talk past each other'.

Lukes sums up this idea of the relativity of truth and valid reasoning or logic by saying that it comes down to 'taking seriously Pascal's observation that what is truth on one side of the Pyrenees is error on the other'.[25]

The Self-Referential Objection

The most basic criticism to be made of this relativist position is that the exponents of this view never apply it to themselves, to their own ideas, their own theories, their own knowledge. They are open, that is, to the 'self-referential objection' which states that, if all ideas and ways of thinking are a product of a particular life-situation, then so too is *that* idea, and it cannot, therefore, have any universal validity. Or to state the point a little differently: if there are no universal norms of truth and valid reasoning, if truth and falsity do not exist in any absolute sense, then obviously the thesis about the relativity of all knowledge cannot be true in this sense. Yet Young and his colleagues clearly believe it is true in this sense. The thesis, however, invalidates itself; such writers are hoist on their own petard. Furthermore, in arguing the way they do, these sociologists of knowledge are surely employing the very criteria of truth and valid reasoning which they are claiming are culturally relative. They tell us that norms of truth change, and that notions of a good explanation, being rational, etc., are matters of social convention. But they are themselves using such notions or conventions in saying this. They are, in effect, using reason to try to prove the inadequacy of reason; claiming to provide us with a universally valid explanation of why there is no such thing as a universally valid explanation. Their endeavour is, therefore, self-contradictory.

Writers such as Esland dismiss this sort of argument against them as an instance of 'theoretical conservatism', and he seeks to defend the relativistic position by claiming that the 'dialectic epistemology' of Marx, Durkheim and Schutz does not have a concern for the 'objective'.[26]

We would maintain, however, that writers such as Marx and Durkheim successfully resisted the temptation to see the criteria of truth and logic as relative. Confining ourselves to the case of Marx, we would agree with Parekh's judgement that:

> While appreciating the importance of the socially derived biases, Marx to his credit continues to uphold the traditional concept of objective truth. Indeed it was precisely because he was concerned with the objective truth that he was interested in the phenomenon of ideology . . . For him truth is the highest ideal in the field of theoretical truth, and it is either objective or not truth at all . . . he entered into a sustained debate with the classical economists, and aimed to show why their account of the capitalist society was mistaken. No doubt, he was sometimes not wholly fair to them. The point, however, is that he did not dismiss their economic theories as bourgeois, nor said they were only true for the bourgeoisie. He criticised them, appealed to the universally valid empirical and logical criteria, and accepted whatever in their thought seem true to him . . . Some of his criticisms are perhaps unpersuasive, and his own alternative is not free of grave difficulties. The relevant point, however, is that he was interested in assessing their truth in terms of the universally accepted criteria.[27]

TEACHERS, PUPILS AND EDUCATIONAL FAILURE

Next we turn to an assessment of the view that 'teachers' expectations of pupils . . . set levels of achievement' and that there is a 'self-fulfilling prophecy' at work in teachers' 'definitions' of the good pupil.

Labelling and Description

This, of course, is a familiar thesis within the sociology of education — it is not original to the new sociology of education. But what it ignores is the fact that often teachers' expectations of pupils are firmly rooted in reality. Teachers will define children as able or dull, and expect them to do well or badly, because of their knowledge of the children acquired from regular contact with them over a period of time. Their judgements of children will often be based on their first-hand experience of the children. They are not *labelling* children, therefore, but *describing* them. When teachers say of children that they are difficult or disruptive, the teachers are often not applying pejorative labels but telling us what the children are actually like. In other words, teachers often have good reasons for categorising or 'typifying' children the way that they do. The behaviour of children sets limits to the range of definitions which the teacher can apply.

For example, a class of pupils dedicated to 'mucking about' and 'having a laugh' will be defined as such by the teachers concerned. This can be seen in Furlong's study of a London secondary school. Furlong says of the class he was observing that 'misbehaviour was the norm'.[28]

> The pupils of 4G [he states] spent a great deal of time mucking about; they were always arriving late for lessons, running around the corridors, cheeking teachers, teasing and playing jokes on each other, talking in class when they should be working, and generally misbehaving.[29]

Here, then, we have Furlong's *description* of the class he studied — the description of a trained observer. It was also the teachers' *definition* of the class in question — one shared, incidentally, by the pupils themselves. As Furlong says:

> We have already seen that all the girls mucked about for a lot of their classroom time. *The teachers recognised this in that they characterised the class as 'difficult'*, and from the pupils' perspective mild delinquency was as much a part of normal classroom life as teaching and learning.[30]

In this case, then, the teachers' 'definition' of the situation was well founded, that is, it was a true definition. It was also — as we have seen — in accord with how the pupils saw the situation. And surely such a correspondence between the teachers' perception and the objective nature of the situation is not unusual. All too often those who employ the idea of the 'definition of the situation' overlook the fact that definitions can be assessed against reality and therefore confirmed or falsified by it. Indeed, in so far as such writers systematically adopt a 'phenomenological' perspective, they take the view that there is no 'objective' situation apart from the definition of it by the participants. They believe that there is no external reality to judge a person's definition against, no such thing as reality as opposed to how it is defined. Reality, on their view, is what it is defined to be.[31]

The Self-fulfilling Prophecy

In our view, however, it is foolish to ignore the differences between how people see a situation and the objective nature of that situation. Indeed, the very notion of the self-fulfilling prophecy — which is central to the work of some of the writers we are considering — depends upon us making such a distinction. The idea of the self-fulfilling prophecy derives, in large part, from an essay of the American sociologist R.K. Merton. He defines the idea as follows: 'The self-fulfilling prophecy is, in the beginning, a *false* definition of the situation evoking a new behaviour which makes the originally false conception come *true*.'[32] One of the examples Merton provides to illustrate the idea is that of a 'run' on a bank. If, despite the comparative liquidity of a bank's assets, a rumour of insolvency is believed by enough depositors, the result would be the insolvency of the bank. The prediction of a collapse (the false definition) leads to its own fulfilment (it becomes true).

Note that the whole idea here rests on the distinction between false and true definitions. A definition is false if it does not have objective validity; it is true if it corresponds to the real nature of the situation. On Merton's view, then, the participant's definition of the situation can be assessed against external reality. It can be judged true or false in just the same way that a social scientist's explanations are so judged. As John Rex puts it:

> Just as the social scientist is able to distinguish between those of his own [explanations] which merit retention and those which do not, so he is able to distinguish between those of the observed actors' 'definitions of the situation' which have objective validity and those which do not. He does this by subjecting these interpretations to the same tests as he would interpretations by another sociologist.[33]

And Rex, in more Marxist language, adds that this means we are able to distinguish between true and false consciousness. For the phenomenologist, on the other hand, one way of seeing the world is no better than any other. Furthermore, the explanations of sociologists carry 'no special privileged status', they are no more objective or true than the accounts of anybody else.[34]

Of course, the new sociologists of education do recognise that we can distinguish between true and false accounts of the world. They regard, for example, their own explanations of the educational process as superior to those of 'positivist' sociology. It would seem, therefore, that, in consistency, they ought to be willing to assess the truth or falsity of the actor's definition of the situation. In the case of teachers and their pupils, this would mean being concerned with the extent to which teachers' definitions of their pupils are accurate representations of their behaviour. The new sociologists of education must realise, in other words, that everything has a 'definition' and that what counts is the validity of such definitions.

The Problems of the Labelling Theory of Deviance

There is a further difficulty with the Esland/Keddie line of analysis. As we have seen, Esland takes the view that ' "problem pupils" are so because of the premises on which the differentiation is made' and Keddie argues that educational failure derives largely from the categories of ability and intelligence employed by the teacher. In other words, it is the teacher's view of what counts as a 'problem pupil' or 'ability' that matters, with the implication that, if teachers change their criteria of these things, then 'problem pupils' and educational 'failure' will disappear or be drastically altered.

This view of such matters derives, in large part, from the labelling theory of deviance of Howard Becker. In his book *Outsiders*, Becker says that 'the central fact about deviance' is that

> *social groups create deviance by making the rules whose infraction constitutes deviance*, and by applying these rules to particular people and labelling them as outsiders. From this point of view, deviance is *not* a quality of the act the person commits, but rather a consequence of the application by others of rules and sanctions to an 'offender'. The deviant is one to whom the label has been successfully applied; deviance is behaviour that people so label.[35]

Is this to say, therefore, that, if there were no 'rule' against 'murder', then unjustifiable killing would cease? For if there were no rules, there would be no rule-breaking and thus no deviance in the sense of rule-breaking. Yet presumably people would still go on killing each other unjustifiably (or, in the context of the school, some children would continue to disrupt lessons or bully others — despite the absence of the label 'problem pupil'). The implication of Becker's view is that, with the disappearance of the 'rule', the behaviour which the rule is intended to deter or punish would also disappear. Clearly this is true by definition; however, there would still be people who kill others unjustifiably, and pupils who persistently misbehave.

Another problem with labelling theory — whether applied to education or more generally — is noted by Gouldner. He writes:

> the emphasis in Becker's theory is on the deviant as the product of

society rather than as the rebel against it. If this is a . . . conception of deviance that wins sympathy and tolerance for the deviant, it has the paradoxical consequence of inviting us to view the deviant as a passive nonentity who is responsible neither for his suffering nor its alleviation — who is more 'sinned against than sinning'.[36]

Labelling theory, then, is yet another version of the 'over-socalized conception of man' which we discussed in Chapter 5. It comes down to saying that we are only what other people make us: we are deviants because others make rules and apply them to us. On this view, 'problem pupils' are so because of the way that teachers categorise them — they are in no way responsible for the attitudes of teachers towards them. Such children play no part in the building of their own identity; their behaviour is determined solely by the expectations and definitions of others. In Gouldner's words, they are truly 'passive nonentities'.

EDUCATIONAL KNOWLEDGE AND EVERYDAY KNOWLEDGE

Earlier in the chapter we said that we agreed with those philosophers who take the view that there are three great forms of knowledge. Now we want to take the argument a step further and suggest that the development of these branches of knowledge is a great human achievement, a triumph of the human spirit over ignorance and superstition. Any educational system worthy of its name ought, therefore, to ensure that such knowledge has a central place in the curriculum of its schools and colleges. We should not take the view that 'everyday' knowledge is enough. A curriculum based on the three forms of knowledge will transmit a heritage of inestimable value. It will also provide the basis of future advance, as progress in knowledge and understanding consists of one generation standing on the shoulders of previous generations rather than them starting completely afresh.

Arguments such as these are, of course, commonplace in thinking about education. Writers from a variety of political perspectives subscribe to the view that 'educational knowledge' and the 'thought system' organised in the curricula of educational institutions — to use the terms of Young and his colleagues — are important and valuable. Central to such thinking is the assumption that it would be a great loss to mankind and an enormous step backward if we were to rest content with the sort of everyday knowledge that the new sociologists of education hold in such high esteem.

The Value of Educational Knowledge

R.H. Tawney. If we analyse, for example, some of R.H. Tawney's writing on education, we find him taking the view that education is concerned with 'the knowledge which is the inheritance of the race'.[37] Such an education he considers to be important and desirable for the following reasons.

1. It is intrinsically valuable. The pursuit of knowledge ('educational' not 'everyday' knowledge) is an end in itself. Tawney says that too often in England people think that 'the object of education is not education itself but some external result' such as getting a good job. They do not recognise 'the value of the things of the mind' such as the importance of 'the free exercise of reason' and 'the disinterested desire of knowledge for its own sake'.[38] Nor do they appreciate that subjects such as literature, music and painting are 'concerned . . . with the things which make it worth while to live'.[39]
2. Education is also important for personal development and happiness. A 'humane' education, says Tawney, enables people to develop the faculties which are the essential attributes of human beings. It also provides them with 'spiritual sustenance'.[40]
3. A further major purpose of education is that it should promote 'a reasonable and humane conduct of life'.[41] Tawney sums up his view in the following passage:

> Education, as I see it, though it is much else as well, is partly, at least, the process by which we transcend the barriers of our isolated personalities, and become partners in a universe of interests which we share with our fellow men, living and dead alike. No one can be fully at home in the world unless, through acquaintance with literature and art, the history of society and the revelations of science, he has seen enough of the triumphs and tragedies of mankind to realize the heights to which human nature can rise and the depths to which it can sink.[42]

4. Education also has a social and political purpose. Speaking of the Workers Educational Association, Tawney says:

> It judged the success of its classes, not only by the progress of their members' studies, but also by the degree to which the knowledge gained and habits formed aided fruitful activities in the affairs of daily life. It sought, in addition to making individual students, to awaken working-class movements as a whole to a keener

consciousness both that the promotion of adult education among their younger members and — not less essential — the improvement of public education are of vital importance to the cause for which such movements stand. It regarded education, in short, neither primarily as a hobby or pastime — both excellent things — nor as an avenue to individual self-advancement, but as a social dynamic. In the words of the Statement of Policy appended to our Constitution, it valued adult education 'not only as a means of developing individual character and capacity, but as a preparation for the exercise of social rights and responsibilities'.[43]

Tawney points out that a large number of WEA students are taking courses in Economics, History, International Affairs, Political Science and Sociology and he adds that this is not surprising given 'the daily problems with which the subjects in question deal'.[44] Unlike Keddie, then, Tawney does not see such subjects as in some way separate from 'everyday' issues; nor, in his view, do the disciplines in question involve an 'alternative system of thought'. Rather, such 'educational knowledge' provides an essential means through which 'everyday' problems can be understood and solutions developed. These disciplines, according to Tawney, provide working people with 'enlarged capacities for effective action'. Ordinary men and women, therefore, 'need a humane education both for their personal happiness and to help them mould the society in which they live'.[45]

D. Reynolds and M. Sullivan. Some contemporary writers take a similar view to that of Tawney concerning the importance of 'educational' knowledge. Reynolds and Sullivan, for example, point out that

the new radical perspective in the sociology of education . . . appears to have embraced the theoretical concept of cultural relativism. Those who write from within this perspective appear to be prescribing the replacement of the traditional curriculum, which is seen as a cultural artefact of the bourgeois class, by a curriculum rooted in the pupils' experience of working class culture.[46]

According to Reynolds and Sullivan, this view is considered 'profoundly conservative'[47] by writers within the classical Marxist tradition such as Lenin, Gramsci and Marx himself. Marx, they say, stressed the importance of the role of ideas and of theory in effecting the transformation of capitalism to socialism. He took the view that economic crises alone were insufficient to bring about the transition to socialism. What was also required was political action by the working class based on an understanding of the workings of capitalism and the possibilities for the future. Such an understanding could only be derived, however, from a 'scientific enquiry' into the nature of the existing situation.

'Later Marxists', Reynolds and Sullivan continue, 'have argued that the modes of thought and knowledge base necessary for such an enquiry are those which are labelled as useful or superior by the capitalist educational system.' They quote Lenin as saying that the 'only adequate cultural resource for the development of revolutionary practice was what had served as the content of the traditional humanistic curriculum'.[48] As for Gramsci, Reynolds and Sullivan point out that: 'He argues that a working class denied access to the humanistic rationality of the traditional scholastic mode reinforces the ideological and political hegemony of the ruling class by its incapacity to perceive that the social and economic relations of capitalism can be transcended.' The working class, therefore, needs a form of education which, in Gramsci's words, will develop in it 'the love of free discussion; the desire to search for truth rationally and intelligently'.[49]

Reynolds and Sullivan go on to stress that such a traditional humanistic curriculum is important not only during the transition from capitalism to socialism, but also in a socialist society itself. As they say: 'the education system of an emergent socialist society would of necessity bear more resemblance to the education system as we know it than to the educational visions of the new radicalism.'[50] The present educational system, they point out, is based on the idea of 'the stratification of knowledge', where some forms of knowledge are regarded as superior to others and therefore worth learning. This view, as we have seen, has been disputed by Young and his colleagues. In the words of Reynolds and Sullivan, 'The new sociology of education became characterised by a fundamental questioning of the concept of stratified knowledge and a growing conviction that much of the knowledge base that the schools wished to transmit may not have been worth transmitting.'[51] Reynolds and Sullivan, however, firmly reject this view. They say that some forms of knowledge and thought are today regarded as superior 'because they *are* cognitively and intellectually superior'. A socialist educational system will, therefore, need to be based on such forms of thought in order that their population can be 'excellently educated'.[52] And such an excellent education is important not just as a means to establishing a truly socialist society but also in order 'to maximise the possibility of developing all the intellectual capacities which Marx believed concomitant with the all round development of individuals'.[53]

Liberal Views. It is not just socialists and Marxists, however, who take the view that the curricula of educational institutions should be based on 'superior' forms of knowledge. Many liberals share this conception of the importance of 'educational knowledge'. Matthew Arnold, for example, urges us to study 'the best that has been thought and known' and emphasises that such an education is appropriate for all social classes. In a famous passage he argues that:

> Plenty of people will try to give the masses, as they call them, an intellectual food prepared and adapted in the way they think proper for the actual condition of the masses. The ordinary popular literature is an example of this way of working on the masses. Plenty of people will try to indoctrinate the masses with the set of ideas and judgements constituting the creed of their own profession or party. Our religious and political organisations give an example of this way of working with the masses. I condemn neither way; but culture works differently. It does not try to teach down to the level of inferior classes; it does not try to win them for this or that sect of its own with ready-made judgements and watchwords. It seeks to do away with classes; to make the best that has been thought and known in the world current everywhere; to make all men live in an atmosphere of sweetness and light, where they may use ideas, as it uses them itself, freely, — nourished and not bound by them.[54]

A second nineteenth-century liberal, J.S. Mill, also regards 'educational knowledge' of supreme importance; for, in his view, one of the principal causes of an unsatisfactory life is 'want of mental cultivation'. Mill seeks to justify the importance of an 'excellent education' in the following way:

> A cultivated mind — I do not mean that of a philosopher, but any mind to which the fountains of knowledge have been opened, and which has been taught, in any tolerable degree, to exercise its faculties — finds sources of inexhaustible interest in all that surrounds it; in the objects of nature, the achievements of art, the imaginations of poetry, the incidents of history, the ways of mankind, past and present, and their prospects for the future.[55]

P.H. Hirst and R.S. Peters. Some of these arguments are also central to the thinking of certain contemporary philosophers of education — sometimes dubbed 'liberal'[56] — such as Hirst and Peters. Peters, for example, in his book *Ethics and Education*, takes the view that education is concerned with the initiation of others into worthwhile activities, of which science, literature, history and philosophy are examples. These activities should be central to the curricula of schools and colleges for a number of reasons, of which one of the most important is that they 'illuminate other areas of life and contribute much to the quality of living'.[57] Such disciplines are not divorced from the everyday business of life; rather, if the knowledge of such fields is properly assimilated, 'it constantly throws light on, widens, and deepens one's view of countless other things'.[58] According to Peters, this is because disciplines such as these 'consist largely in the explanation, assessment, and illumination of different facets of life', and someone undertaking the study of them is 'being trained in modes of thought that cannot be tied down to particular times and places'. Consequently, 'A person who has pursued them systematically develops conceptual schemes and forms of appraisal which transform everything else that he does.'[59] In this sense, then, a training in these activities is 'an education for life'.

Socialists, Marxists and liberals alike, then, share a belief in the importance of 'educational knowledge' and its superiority to 'everyday knowledge'. However — as we have seen — this is not to say that the educational and the everyday are unrelated; nor that, in Keddie's words, they form 'alternative thought systems'. For most of the above writers consider educational knowledge crucial for the proper understanding of everyday affairs and an indispensable aid to effective action. Also we must remember Berlin's comments concerning empirical knowledge. In his view common sense ('everyday knowledge') is similar to science: the latter is an extension of the former, dealing with more 'complicated cases'. Both, however, depend upon observation for answering the questions they put: ordinary common sense in the one case, controlled observation, experiment, etc., in the other. (Thus, when the teachers in Keddie's study claim that C-stream pupils cannot 'master subjects', they are probably saying no more than that such pupils are unable to, or unwilling to, extend their everyday experience to a more sophisticated level.)

Our argument here also has implications for our assessment of the new sociology of education's claim that there is no justification for the existence of a 'hierarchy' between teacher and taught in which the teacher is regarded as the authority in the classroom transmitting knowledge to the pupils. On this question we can do no better than to quote some of the words of Hirst and Peters. They write:

the differentiation of knowledge into distinct forms is not an arbitrary matter. There are distinctive concepts, truth-criteria and methodologies which anyone must master who is to have an opinion which is to be reckoned with. There is also a body of knowledge, which has to be mastered, which has been built up by and can be criticized by people who have been trained to work in this form of knowledge. It takes time and considerable experience to master these forms of knowledge, so that a person is in a position to judge and criticize in an informed way. This means that there must be provisional authorities in the different forms and fields of knowledge with which universities and schools are concerned. Their job is to hand on an inheritance in such a way that others can come to criticize it and eventually dispense with their teachers. They must exercise their authority in such a way that another generation can learn to live without them.[60]

For these reasons, then, the 'hierarchy' between teacher and taught is rationally based. Teachers are provisional authorities in the various branches of knowledge. Their aim is not some sort of 'domination' but the development in their pupils and students of that degree of understanding which will enable them to think independently and work autonomously.

Is Educational Knowledge Middle Class?

We now turn to some further comments on the new sociology of education's claim that 'educational knowledge' is in some way 'middle class'.

B. Jackson and D. Marsden. We have seen that it is central to the thinking of many of the writers already considered that such knowledge ought to be available to everybody, to all social classes. A further expression, and development, of this point of view is provided by Jackson and Marsden in their splendid book *Education and the Working Class* — which is an ardent defence of working-class educational interests. In their concluding chapter they quote Matthew Arnold at some length and argue that 'the central culture of our society ("the best that has been thought and known", "the very culture of the feelings", "that spontaneity which is the hardest of all") . . . must be preserved and transmitted'.[61] And it must be transmitted to the working class as much as to the middle class. The problem as they see it is twofold.

Firstly, schools and colleges often confuse such 'high culture' with 'middle-class values' (a problem shared by some sociologists!). They say, for example, that in some schools 'a training in middle-class deportment is still hopelessly mixed up with the transmission of the culture which matters'.[62] Or again:

It seems to us that what we call our central culture and what the teachers call 'middle-class values' are by no means the same thing, and the problem is to disentangle the one from the other in schools which are truly 'open'. When the head-teacher says 'I see grammar school education very strongly as a matter of communicating middle-class values to a "new" population', he is surely not saying something akin to Matthew Arnold's classic statement, but something contrary in spirit, provincial and partisan.[63]

Secondly, because of this 'provincial and partisan' attitude, many able working-class pupils — those who do not accommodate themselves to the prevailing middle-class values and who remain embedded in working-class family and neighbourhood life — leave school before the sixth form. Too often such schools are hostile to the working-class style of life and this leads to a rejection of school by working-class pupils.

In Jackson and Marsden's view the solution to this problem lies in a recognition by the schools of the importance of working-class values whilst getting on with the business of transmitting the culture that matters. As they say: 'The educational system we need is one which accepts and develops the best qualities of working-class living, and brings these to meet our central culture.'[64]

In the course of Jackson and Marsden's book another important point emerges. They say that 'middle-class life transmits within it the high culture of our society';[65] yet it is clear that the middle-class families they studied were not in possession of such a culture. Speaking of such families, they state that: 'They do not, perhaps, have that breadth of cultural interest with which to rouse an intelligent and sensitive child into total adulthood.'[66] In Bourdieu's terms, then, these families do not possess much 'cultural capital'.

Now this point is important when considering the claims that the school is a 'middle-class institution'; that the culture of the school is in keeping with the culture of the middle-class home; and that this fact explains the success of middle-class children and the failure of their working-class counterparts. For, when it comes to 'high culture', it is probably true that many a middle-class home is seriously deficient and that such middle-class children are no better off in this respect than children from homes of manual workers.

Frank Musgrove. Support for this view is to be found in Frank Musgrove's interesting book, *School and the Social Order.* Musgrove says of some of his own research and teaching experience that it pointed to a gap between the values of middle-class parents and those of the school. Middle-class parents, he found, were only concerned that their children should acquire those educational credentials which could be converted into material rewards. For the 'philistine middle-class', as he calls them, 'there was no sense of the school as a place of intellectual culture or even moral values'. Rather school was just 'the anteroom to organisational life with its fat rewards for "fitting in" '.[67] As a consequence, the middle class at the grammar school where he taught 'wanted their sons crammed'. Comparing the attitude of the parents and that of the school, he writes:

> The middle class of northern Nottinghamshire had scant regard for an 'invisible pedagogy'. Many of the 'new' middle class appeared to have obtained professional qualifications through correspondence courses, and the 'model answer' was an apparently foolproof pedagogical strategy which they insistently commended to their sons' teachers. Probably the deepest, most genuinely shared and abiding value that we held as a staff was that 'spoon-feeding' was bad for the intellect and worse for the soul. And more generally 'getting on' was really rather a discreditable preoccupation . . . This was not, in fact, a 'middle-class culture'; it was gentry culture . . . There was no snug fit between the values of middle-class parents and those of the school.[68]

In this sense, therefore, there was no continuity between home and school for the middle-class child, and the school could not be regarded as a 'middle-class institution'. Indeed, Musgrove's experience led him to conclude that, although children from a working-class background experience difficulty with high quality academic schooling, one must recognise 'the still greater disability of having a middle-class home'.[69]

In our commentary on the new sociology of education we have come to the following conclusions. First, that, although the three great branches or forms of knowledge are social constructions, they are not thereby arbitrary. Furthermore, whilst a certain set of ideas may have their origin in a particular society at a particular time and serve certain vested interests, such considerations must be kept distinct from questions of the truth and validity of the ideas. Second, we have suggested that the arguments for the relativity of the criteria of truth and validity are unconvincing. Third, we have argued that it is important to distinguish between true and false definitions, description and labelling, when considering the claim that teachers' concepts of ability and knowledge set levels of pupil achievement. Finally — and drawing upon the work of a number of writers on the subject — we have sought to justify the importance of educational knowledge to all pupils, working class as well as middle class.

NOTES

1. M.F.D. Young (ed.), *Knowledge and Control* (Collier-Macmillan, London, 1971).

2. G. Whitty, 'Sociology and the Problem of Radical Educational Change' in M. Young and G. Whitty (eds.), *Society, State and Schooling* (Falmer Press, Lewes, 1977), p. 33.

3. M.F.D. Young, 'An Approach to the Study of Curricula as Socially-Organized Knowledge' in Young (ed.), *Knowledge and Control*, p. 23.

4. G. Esland, 'Teaching and Learning as the Organisation of Knowledge' in Young (ed.), *Knowledge and Control*, p. 77.

5. Ibid., p. 93.

6. N. Keddie, 'Classroom Knowledge' in Young (ed.), *Knowledge and Control*, p. 156.

7. Ibid., p. 156.

8. Ibid., p. 150.

9. Ibid., p. 151.

10. Ibid., p. 154.

11. Ibid., p. 155.

12. M.F.D. Young, Introduction, *Knowledge and Control*, p. 13.

13. Quoted in G. Whitty, 'Sociology', p. 33.

14. D. Cooper, *Illusions of Equality* (Routledge and Kegan Paul, London, 1980), p. 112.

15. B. Magee, *Men of Ideas* (BBC, London, 1978).

16. Ibid., pp. 22–3.

17. Ibid., p. 23.

18. Ibid., p. 24.

19. M. Macdonald, 'Natural Rights' in P. Laslett (ed.), *Philosophy, Politics and Society* (Blackwell, Oxford, 1970), p. 52.

20. J.S. Mill, *Utilitarianism* (Fontana, London, 1962), p. 255.

21. P. Berger, 'Some Observations Concerning the Problem of Work' in P. Berger (ed.), *The Human Shape of Work* (Macmillan, London, 1964), pp. 230–1.

22. K. Mannheim, *Ideology and Utopia* (Routledge and Kegan Paul, London, 1960), p. 50.

23. Ibid., pp. 50–1.

24. Ibid., p. 51.

25. S. Lukes, 'On the Social Determination of Truth' in *Essays in Social Theory* (Macmillan, London, 1977), p. 139.

26. Esland, 'Teaching and Learning', pp. 70–1.

27. B. Parekh, *Marx's Theory of Ideology* (Croom Helm, London, 1982), pp. 214–15.

28. V. Furlong, 'Anancy goes to School: A Case Study of Pupils' Knowledge of their Teachers' in P. Woods and M. Hammersley (eds.), *School Experience: Explorations in the Sociology of Education* (Croom Helm, London, 1977), p. 175.

29. Ibid., p. 164.

30. Ibid., p. 176 (emphasis added).

31. See, for example, A. Blum, 'The Corpus of Knowledge' in Young (ed.), *Knowledge and Control*, pp. 130–1.

32. R.K. Merton, 'The Self Fulfilling Prophecy' in *Social Theory and Social Structure* (Free Press, New York, 1957), p. 423.

33. J. Rex, 'Thirty Theses on Epistemology and Method' in *Discovering Sociology* (Routledge and Kegan Paul, London, 1973), p. 220.

34. M. Phillipson, 'Theory, Methodology and Conceptualization' in P. Filmer *et al.*, *New Directions in Sociological Theory* (Collier-Macmillan, London, 1972), p. 107.

35. H. Becker, *Outsiders* (Free Press, New York, 1963), p. 9.

36. Quoted in J. Young, 'New Directions in Sub-Cultural Theory' in J. Rex (ed.),

Approaches in Sociology (Routledge and Kegan Paul, London, 1974), p. 166.

37. R.H. Tawney, 'An Experiment in Democratic Education' in *The Radical Tradition* (Allen and Unwin, London, 1964), p. 72. Tawney was here speaking about adult education, but we feel the point has general application.

38. Ibid., p. 80.

39. Tawney, 'The Workers Educational Association and Adult Education' in *The Radical Tradition*, p. 86.

40. Tawney, 'An Experiment', p. 72.

41. Ibid., p. 79.

42. Tawney, 'The WEA and Adult Education', pp. 83–4.

43. Ibid., pp. 85–6.

44. Ibid., p. 87.

45. Ibid., p. 92.

46. D. Reynolds and M. Sullivan, 'Towards a New Socialist Sociology of Education' in L. Barton *et al.*, *Schooling, Ideology and the Curriculum* (Falmer Press, Lewes, 1980), pp. 185–6.

47. Ibid., p. 86.

48. Ibid., p. 187.

49. Ibid.

50. Ibid., p. 188.

51. Ibid., p. 190.

52. Ibid., p. 191.

53. Ibid., p. 190.

54. M. Arnold, *Culture and Anarchy* (Cambridge University Press, London, 1971), pp. 69–70.

55. Mill, *Utilitarianism*, p. 265.

56. See, for example, M. Sarup, *Marxism and Education* (Routledge and Kegan Paul, London, 1978), Ch. 4.

57. R.S. Peters, *Ethics and Education* (Allen and Unwin, London, 1970), p. 159.

58. Ibid.

59. Ibid., p. 160.

60. P. Hirst and R.S. Peters, *The Logic of Education* (Routledge and Kegan Paul, London, 1970), p. 117.

61. B. Jackson and D. Marsden, *Education and the Working Class* (Penguin, Harmondsworth, 1966), p. 243.

62. Ibid., p. 250.

63. Ibid., p. 243.

64. Ibid., p. 246.

65. Ibid., p. 249.

66. Ibid., p. 39.

67. F. Musgrove, *School and the Social Order* (Wiley, Chichester, 1979), p. 11.

68. Ibid., pp. 10–11.

69. Ibid., p. 10.

13 CONCLUSION: THE WEBERIAN PERSPECTIVE

In this book we have examined the principal sociological approaches to education. We have also considered the criticisms that have been made of these theories. In our opinion the response to these criticisms is leading in the direction of a macro interpretive approach similar to that advocated by Max Weber.

THE LIMITATIONS OF OTHER SOCIOLOGICAL APPROACHES

The Functionalist Tradition

As we have seen, functionalist theory provides us with a model of society in which all social institutions, including education, have specific functions. These institutions are divided into sub-systems which in turn are made up of roles. Individuals are socialised into the values of society and into the norms associated with the particular roles to which they have been allocated. By carrying out their roles, members maintain the social and cultural order of society. The functions of education have been identified as socialisation, selection and the management of knowledge. Put differently, education is supposed to inculcate the norms and values of society; to allocate people to their roles, particularly economic ones; and to structure the reality images of the population by the organisation and distribution of 'knowledge'.

There are, as we have noted, a number of unacceptable assumptions and logical problems associated with functionalism. Of particular importance is the 'reification' of society and the consequent belittling of man. Society appears as some sort of entity which has its own wants and desires. People are thought of as programmed puppets with no creativity or free will. No recognition is given to man's capacity to 'make himself' or to change society. The realisation of these limitations has led some authors to suggest that we should see society not so much as a reality in its own right, but rather as a product of the activity of social groups who have their own goals and aims. In this view education is formed by the activity of groups trying to further their aims. This is not to deny that education does have a socialising and selecting function. It does, however, suggest that the account of how and why selection and socialisation takes place has to be couched in terms of actors' goals and the conflicts and negotiations which occur. This is akin to the approach that Ioan Davies employs when he attempts to define the major function of education as the management of knowledge (see Chapter 4). It is an approach that develops from the recognition of the limitations of functionalism.

The Marxist Perspective

The Marxist sociology of education is in some ways similar to that of the functionalists. Both are macro in focus and believe that education cannot be understood independently of the society of which it is a part. Like the functionalists, Marxists seek to explain how education contributes to the maintenance, or reproduction, of the existing social and economic order. They also see this occurring through the process of socialisation and selection. Education, it is said, fosters the qualities and values required by the capitalist economic system, and it allocates people to roles within the hierarchical division of labour. In addition, Marxists believe with Parsons that education helps to legitimate inequalities in society through the dissemination of the ideology of equal opportunity and meritocracy.

We have seen that this view of education and society has been questioned by a number of writers including, more recently, some of those within the Marxist camp itself. The criticisms advanced have, in part, been similar to those made of functionalism, namely that such a view is overly deterministic and takes no account of the way that people shape the social system of which they are a part as well as being shaped by it. In addition, it has been argued that the empirical evidence does not support the idea of reproduction through the processes of legitimation and socialisation. The ideology of equal opportunity and meritocracy is not accepted by the majority of the population, and there is no correspondence between the attitudes and values found in and fostered by the schools, and those required by the capitalist relations of production.

To accommodate these criticisms, the Marxist theory of education has been reformulated. Several authors have suggested that the reproduction process does not go uncontested: there is 'resistance' to the alienating experience of school. Schools cannot simply mould their pupils in accordance with the 'needs' of the capitalist system because of the existence of counter-school cultures which have their roots in more general working-class attitudes and values. In addition, it is said, education has some independence from the wider society. Schools do not simply respond to the demands of the economic system but, in part, control the course of their own development. They possess a 'relative autonomy'.

This modified version of Marxist theory, however, also has major weaknesses. The idea of relative autonomy is vague and imprecise, and it is difficult to see what is distinctively Marxist about an approach which emphasises both the independence and dependence of education in relation to economic forces. Furthermore, when Marxists such as Bowles and Gintis stress, in their revised analysis (see Chapter 7), the importance of political factors in the promotion of a more equal and just society, they adopt an approach which is more in keeping with pluralist or Weberian models of society. Finally the Marxist theory of resistance lacks empirical support: for the majority of pupils from working-class backgrounds are not members of the school counter-culture, and many working-class people themselves possess values and attitudes which are at odds with those found in such sub-cultures.

The Micro Interpretive Approach

The approach which we have called 'micro interpretive' adopts the view that man makes society. Its central concern is to elicit the actors' 'definitions of the situation'. In particular it attempts to investigate: the actors' self-definitions, their aims or goals, their typifications of others and their taken-for-granted assumptions. The interaction of teachers and pupils is conceptualised either as a process of negotiation, or as a series of strategies operated by teachers and pupils. The micro interpretive approach thus celebrates human creativity and freedom, and the criticism that is most frequently made of it is that it fails to take sufficient account of the fact that action is constrained by the situation in which it takes place. The constraints are such that only certain aims, definitions and typifications can be creatively produced by, say, teachers and pupils. What the sociologist must do, therefore, is examine the constraints that impinge upon actors and ask how they are produced and what consequences they have.

WEBERIAN SOCIOLOGY

This recognition that the focus upon the actors' definitions of the situation is inadequate without some analysis of what or who brings about the situation in which action takes place and how the actors' definitions are themselves composed, leads towards an examination of how groups interact to construct, maintain and change the educational system. Such an analysis has been attempted by authors who follow the ideas of Max Weber. We shall devote the remainder of this chapter to a discussion of the Weberian perspective on education by way of a consideration of the work of three major exponents of this approach, namely Ronald King,

Randall Collins and Margaret Archer. In conclusion we shall offer a brief summary of the nature of such a perspective.

Ronald King

In some of his more recent work King has adopted a Weberian perspective. He believes that the importance of a Weberian approach lies in the fact that it does not seek to explain educational change in terms of the operation of certain 'external factors'. Both the functionalists and the Marxists try to find the cause of change in education in the wider society: 'education is explained by something "underneath" or "behind" it.'[1] Neither takes into account the purposeful action and social relationships of those involved in the educational system.

In King's view, no explanation of education is adequate unless the subjectively meaningful action of individuals is examined. We have to consider how social actors see the situation, what they are trying to achieve (their aims and goals), and the consequences (unintended as well as intended) of their action. This is not to say that individuals can do as they please; that they have the sort of complete autonomy attributed to them by some phenomenologists and interactionists. The situation in which individuals find themselves is not of their own making, and it sets limits to what they can do. According to King, Weber 'provided ways of studying and explaining the nature of society which admit its fundamental duality in being constructed and maintained by the actions of people, but also its constraints upon their actions'. And he adds that: 'To regard teachers and pupils as both bound *and* free does not make for simple explanations, but is honest to the experience of what it is to be social.'[2]

King, therefore, believes that Weberian sociology avoids the pitfalls of other sociological perspectives: functionalism and Marxism on the one hand, phenomenology and interactionism on the other. He says that

the study of education using the methods of Weber enables explanations to be made which combine the voluntarism of phenomenology and its important stress on the subjective meaning of social action, with the structural constraints on social action which are emphasised in functionalism and some kinds of Marxism.[3]

A Weberian approach, then, is capable of attending to both micro and macro social processes and of understanding the relationship between them.

ORGANISATIONAL CHANGES

King illustrates the nature of such an approach in his article 'Organisational Change in Secondary Schools'. In 1968–9, King studied 72 secondary schools as part of a research project concerned with the organisation of pupil learning and behaviour.[4] In 1978–9, 45 of these schools were re-surveyed to determine the nature of, and reasons for, the changes that had occurred in their organisation. King found that over the ten-year period there had been a number of important changes, namely: an expansion of examination opportunities for pupils; a decrease in the amount of streaming in favour of mixed-ability teaching, banding and setting; closer monitoring of pupils' work; a decline in the prefectorial system; a reduction in the amount of ritual in school life; and a decrease in sex differentiation with regard to both school work and social activities.

These changes, says King, cannot be explained in terms of developments in the wider society imposing new functions upon education, or by reference to the changing demands of the capitalist economic system. Rather, they must be understood as deriving from the actions of those involved in the educational system, especially those who possess the *power* to create such changes. Of particular importance in this respect are the headteachers. King says that his position 'is not that schools change, but that schools are changed. The organisation of a school is changed by the purposeful actions of those with the power to do so, that is principally the headteacher.'[5] It is headteachers who create and maintain the social structure of the school in keeping with their view of the nature of their pupils (their 'definitions' of pupils) and in line with their understanding of the aims of education (their 'educational ideologies'). According to King, headteachers 'define' their pupils as individuals possessing different abilities, needs and problems — such definitions being partly based on experience. The 'educational ideologies' of the heads centre around: the idea of the school as a community; a view of the nature of ability which believes it to be 'normally distributed'; and an 'educational meritocratic ideology'.

King argues that the changes observed in school organisation can be explained in these terms. For example, he says that the expansion of examination opportunities is largely a result of 'the continued importance of the meritocratic ideology: that opportunities for educational "success" should be provided for children according to their presumed capacity, in their competition for places in the occupational structure'.[6] Similarly, the extension of banding and setting within the schools studied derives, says King, from the adoption by headteachers of a less 'holistic' concept of ability in which 'children are more often defined as having different capacities for different subjects'.[7]

King goes on to stress, however, that, although headteachers are the most powerful force as far as changes in school organisation are concerned, they do not have a completely free hand. What they are able to accomplish is limited by the degree of compliance of both pupils and teachers, by the resources at the head's disposal, and by external factors. With regard to pupils, he says that the evidence suggests that most pupils in secondary schools see the power of heads (and teachers) as legitimate, except for their demands concerning the wearing of school uniform and attendance at assemblies. The authority of school staff is based partly on 'traditional' grounds — school is school[8] — and partly on the strong calculative orientation of many of the older pupils. Sixth-formers, especially the boys, put up with the way their behaviour is controlled because they recognise that doing well at school is often a condition of occupational success.

In his account of the decline of the prefectorial system and of the abolition of school uniform for sixth-formers, King also draws our attention to the sort of power possessed by the pupils themselves with respect to changes in the organisation of the school. He says that headteachers commented on the increasing reluctance of senior pupils to accept the 'policing' role of prefect. There were a number of reasons for this. First, there was the 'increasing maturity' of the pupils; second, they no longer valued the 'privileges of office'; third, their experience told them that there was nothing to be gained from holding such an office in respect of access to higher education or future jobs. As far as the relaxation of uniform requirements was concerned, King points out that the schools were forced into this because of competition for their pupils from the more liberal further education colleges. Had large numbers of pupils 'defected', they would have lost both status and income.

As with pupils, so with teachers. Teachers comply with the demands of the heads partly because they accept the legitimacy of the headteachers' position, and partly on instrumental grounds. Careers depend on the heads' good opinion. But King also draws our attention to the power of the teachers. He says that, ten years on, there had been a 'shift in power' to the teaching staff in the schools surveyed. Subject teachers and heads of department now possessed greater autonomy with respect to when and how much to 'set' pupils. However, King does not tell us whether this was a consequence of 'enlightened' policies by the heads, or a result of teacher pressure which resulted in the headteachers bowing to their demands. In other words, one would have liked to know more about the degree of conflict which existed in the schools and how such conflict was resolved. Such an omission is perhaps surprising in view of the fact that King stresses that a Weberian perspective sees conflict over power, resources, status, etc., as a central feature of social life.

King goes on to emphasise that this discussion of the role and power of heads, teachers and pupils in education should not be taken to imply that a Weberian approach sees school organisation as a 'closed system'. 'Society "outside" a school', he says, 'can and does have consequences for the "inside", through direct relationships with parents, governors, advisors and inspectors, and through indirect, sometimes bureaucratic, ones with employers and representatives of higher and further education establishments.'[9] One such external factor which had an impact on the schools studied was the changed social atmosphere which was both the cause and the effect of the Sex Discrimination Act of 1975. King notes that some of the headteachers responded directly to this greater consciousness of sex differentiation by reducing the separation of boys and girls in the playground, assembly, dinner queue, etc. He also draws our attention to the importance of this factor in his conclusion. He writes:

> It is clear that the specific nature of the organisation of a British school (with one important exception) is not directly determined by any 'external' structure: no professional body or capitalist employer destreams a school or deritualises a prefectorial system. The exception is the legal requirement to provide the same curriculum opportunities for boys and girls in mixed schools.[10]

Randall Collins

At the outset of his article 'Some Comparative Principles of Educational Stratification', Collins asks the question: 'What determines the structures and contents of educational systems?'[11] He says that one influential answer has been provided by a certain type of functionalist theory. This theory takes the view that modern society follows where technology leads, and that, as a consequence, education has developed in response to industrial and commercial demand. In the modern world, it is said, jobs increasingly require higher degrees of skill for their performance and the function of education is to provide the appropriate training in such skills. As the educational requirements of jobs increase, more and more of the population spend longer periods of time in formal education. The expansion of education in modern society, therefore, is a direct result of the development of a technological society.

Collins attempts to refute this view by pointing out that education makes little contribution to economic development, beyond the provision of mass literacy. Also, schools do not supply any specific technical skills; rather these are usually learned on the job. His main argument, however, is that the inadequacies of this theory of education derive from a more basic source, namely the weaknesses of functionalist theory as such. To answer questions about the structure and content of educational systems properly we have to approach them from a different direction. We need to adopt an alternative theoretical perspective such as is found in Weberian sociology.

GROUP CONFLICT AND EDUCATION

For Collins, Weberian sociology concentrates on the processes of conflict and domination in society. It sees social life as an arena in which various groups struggle with and try to dominate each other in an attempt to obtain wealth, status and power. Such groups derive from a number of sources: (1) from differences in property ownership or economic position (Weber's 'class', according to Collins); (2) from differences in cultural position such as ethnic group, religion or education (Weber's 'status'); and (3) from differences in power deriving from positions held in the state or in other organisations and bureaucracies (Weber's 'party'). Class conflict in the Marxist sense is then only *one* form of such group conflict.

Education is used by these groups as one of the means of attaining their ends. It is part of the struggle in society for economic advantage, status and domination. Collins points out that, throughout history, different types of education have been sought by different groups according to the principal ends they have been seeking to achieve. (1) Those who have been concerned with obtaining economic rewards have wanted an education in the form of a training in 'practical skills'. (2) Those making a claim for high social status and cultural integration have usually sought a type of education in keeping with that of high ranking groups. Such an education has normally been literary and aesthetic, and essentially unpractical in nature. (3) Groups seeking political power and control in either the state or large-scale organisations and bureaucracies have not been concerned so much with the content of education as with its structure. They have wanted a formal, meritocratic system with an emphasis on advancement through the acquisition of qualifications through success in examinations. Collins provides a number of examples of this process which help to illustrate its nature.

He says that in China during the T'ang dynasty (AD 618–907) an examination system was used

> as a means of controlling the aristocracy . . . In principle, the system
> was more or less meritocratic; it was to the advantage of the ruler
> to offer opportunities of advancement to everyone rather than to allow
> a small class to monopolise these opportunities and thus grow strong
> enough to become his rivals.[12]

In practice, however, the landed gentry were able to gain control as it
was only they who had the money and the time to acquire the education
necessary for examination success. In Japan in the period 1600–1850 the
Tokugawa regime neutralised the power of the aristocracy

> by requiring its leaders to spend much of their time in court rituals
> . . . and by making education compulsory . . . Thus, potential political
> struggles and military revolt were controlled through a constant focus
> on formalities. The school system operated as a control device both
> by keeping the warrior class under custody for a considerable portion
> of their lives while drilling them in formalities, and by preparing them
> for the bureaucratic routine that made up the substance of govern-
> ment.[13]

In the same period the French and Russian states also used education
as a means of controlling their rivals for power. As Collins says:

> The French state created military and engineering schools so as to
> draw administrators from a source independent of the aristocracy and
> the powerful church-controlled schools. The Russian state, in its ef-
> forts to centralize control, went to the extreme of making aristocratic
> status dependent on government service, which in turn was tied to
> state-defined school qualifications.[14]

With regard to the development of education in the modern industrial
world, Collins thinks that there is some merit in the Marxist view that
education has been used as a means of producing a disciplined labour
force. However, he believes that: 'Historical evidence indicates that mass,
compulsory education was first created not for industrial, but for military
and political discipline.'[15] 'The safer generalization', he continues, 'is that
bureaucratic states impose compulsory education on populations which
are seen as threats to state control, and that those economic classes which
are influential in the state will help define the nature of the "threat".'[16]

However, Collins points out that the modern educational system has also been used by the mass of the population as a way of promoting their *own* ends — principally in social mobility. Education has been viewed by the majority in contemporary society as a means of improving their own economic position and of acquiring status and prestige. Collins concludes that these various pressures upon education — for political control, economic rewards, prestige — mean that education is a kind of marketplace 'in which social actors simultaneously attempt to attain certain goals'.[17]

THE RISE OF CREDENTIALISM

In his book *The Credential Society* Collins expands his analysis of the modern educational system. He begins by quoting Weber's view that in the modern world educational qualifications are being used to 'limit the supply of candidates' for 'socially and economically advantageous positions', and to monopolise such positions 'for the holders of educational patents'.[18] Collins believes that contemporary America has become a society in which the system of educational credentials has developed a stranglehold on occupational opportunities. Educational certificates are being employed by occupational groups to restrict access to the better rewarded and more prestigious jobs. The more lucrative occupations are therefore being monopolised by the holders of the appropriate credentials.

It is useful to note at this point that Frank Parkin, developing Weber's ideas, calls such credentialism a form of 'exclusionary closure'. It consists, he says, of the attempt to close off social and economic opportunities and rewards to 'outsiders'. The other main form of exclusionary closure in modern capitalist societies is property ownership, where the private ownership of productive resources restricts access to the fruits of industrial production. The basis of such closure in Communist states is party membership, and in countries which practise apartheid it is race.[19]

To return to Collins's account: he goes on to consider the rise of credentialism in the United States and points out that it did *not* develop as a consequence of economic changes. The basic structure of the American economy — a controlled rather than a competitive market dominated by a few large corporations — was formed before the rise of credentialism. Credentialism was a later development and arose in a period of multiethnic conflict. The original intention behind the building of a mass school system, he says, was the Anglo-Protestant bourgeoisie's desire to preserve its own culture and protect its social and economic position in the face of the diversity and competition produced by successive waves of immigration. However, the lack of central control within the school system meant that they were unsuccessful in this as the various ethnic/cultural groups used education to suit their own purposes.

Although it may be thought that such a situation would produce a great diversity of educational provision, especially with respect to content, Collins points out that

> the surrounding context would not let any school alone; its students found themselves in a larger world where more and more education was becoming visible in the populace, and higher and higher levels of education were needed for occupational entry. Schools came to imitate one another's programmes; secondary schools in order to enter their graduates in high-prestige colleges, the varieties of colleges and professional schools to make themselves part of the sequence that would allow their students to claim at least a chance of attaining the highest social positions. American schools thus came to form a unified hierarchy.[20]

In this situation, the content of education became less and less important. What mattered, says Collins, 'was the sheer fact of having attained a given level and acquired the formal credentials that allowed one to enter the next level (or ultimately to pass the requirements for entering a monopolized occupation)'.[21]

Having analysed the rise of credentialism, Collins considers the effects of the pursuit of academic and professional qualifications on social stratification. He says that the principal beneficiaries of the credential system have been the professions and those who work in the expanded bureaucracies of industry, government, education and the trade unions. With regard to the professions, Collins takes the view that: 'It has been by the use of educational credentials that the lucrative professions have closed their ranks and upgraded their salaries, and it has been in imitation of their methods that other occupations have "professionalized".[22] As for those who work in modern bureaucracies, Collins believes that such occupations form the 'sinecure' sector of the modern economy. This sector consists of jobs in administration rather than direct production, which are well rewarded, permanent and involve little effort or work. He describes them in the following terms:

> We have elaborated a largely superfluous structure of more or less easy jobs, full of administrative make-work and featherbedding because modern technology allows it and because of political pressures from the populace wanting work . . . Thus we have the enormous structure

of government employment (including education), and the huge work forces of our corporate oligopolies keeping themselves busy seeking new products to justify their jobs. In effect, leisure has been incorporated into the job itself.[23]

The main kind of effort involved in such occupations, adds Collins, is 'the work put into creating or defending conditions to avoid work'.[24]

Occupations of this kind, he continues, were at one time openly bought and sold. In the twentieth century, the market for such 'livings' has been disguised: 'instead of direct purchase of office, one invests in educational credentials which in turn . . . are used to purchase a job protected from various aspects of labour market competition.'[25] This process *is* subject, however, to *certain* market forces, namely those of supply and demand. At the present time, according to Collins, we are witnessing a 'credential crisis'. More and more people are becoming increasingly well qualified, but the supply of sinecures is not expanding at the same rate. The acquisition of academic and professional certificates no longer has the same 'pay off' for individuals as in an earlier period. The result is widespread disillusionment, which may possibly involve the breakdown of the whole system.

Margaret Archer

Margaret Archer has been writing within the Weberian tradition for some years. Here we shall concentrate on her major work *Social Origins of Educational Systems*.[26]

At the beginning of the book Archer states that the questions she deals with are: 'how do state educational systems develop and how do they change?'[27] The basic answers to these questions, she says, are very simple, namely that:

education has the characteristics it does because of the goals pursued by those who control it . . . change occurs because new goals are pursued by those who have the power to modify education's previous structural form, definition of instruction and relationship to society . . . education is fundamentally about what people have wanted of it and have been able to do to it.[28]

Archer thinks it is important to stress the point that education is about the purposeful action of human beings, because so much of the literature in the sociology of education involves a belief in hidden hands, evolutionary mechanisms, structural determinants — such as we have already examined, for example, in our accounts of Durkheim and deterministic brands of Marxism.

At the same time she thinks it is important to avoid the opposite mistake of failing to take account of the 'social context of action'. 'Interactionists', for example, rightfully stress the independent contribution made by social interaction to the development of the educational system. However, they neglect to analyse the way that the social structure influences and conditions (but does not determine) the goals people pursue and the actions they take — even though that social structure is the product of past action. In Archer's view, therefore, 'an adequate sociology of education must incorporate statements about the structural conditioning of educational interaction and about the influence of independent action on educational change'.[29] In other words, it must focus on both 'macro' and 'micro' social processes. Such an approach, says Archer, is essentially Weberian in nature.

Archer goes on to say that the first thing to do, therefore, when examining education (or any other social institution) is to seek an understanding of the social structure in which social interaction takes place. This structure conditions the interaction, which in turn will lead to a change in, or modification of, the structure (structural elaboration). The whole process will then begin again in a neverending cycle. In Archer's terms, the process has three parts:

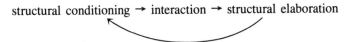

structural conditioning → interaction → structural elaboration

Archer then proceeds to analyse the educational systems of England and France in these terms, elaborating on several points as she goes along. She divides her book into two parts. Part One is devoted to an examination of the emergence of state educational systems in the two countries. Part Two is concerned with the influence of the newly developed systems upon subsequent interaction and change. The book is organised in this way because Archer believes that the emergence of state systems of education represents a crucial break in the history of education. This is for two reasons. With the development of a national system, education, for the first time, became closely connected to the state or political system; second, it also changed the relationship between education and other social institutions.

THE DEVELOPMENT OF STATE EDUCATIONAL SYSTEMS

Prior to the establishment of state systems — where 'overall control and supervision is at least partly governmental'[30] — education was a matter of 'private enterprise'. It was controlled by the various churches throughout Europe, who 'owned' it in the sense that they provided its facilities and supplied its teaching personnel. As a consequence, the churches moulded education to serve their own purposes, namely religious socialisation and the supply of ecclesiastical recruits. The educational system therefore possessed no autonomy, but was in a position of dependence. The churches held the purse strings and exercised close control over the services provided. It was they who defined the curriculum and determined teaching methods. In such circumstances, educational change could not be initiated from within — unlike today, when any explanation of change would be incomplete if it neglected the independent contribution of professional groups of teachers and organized groups of students.

With regard to the relationship between education and other social institutions in such a system of private ownership, Archer says that institutions other than the churches were not directly served by education. Of course, some may have benefited adventitiously. Others, however, were obstructed by the results of education. For example, Archer points out that in the first half of the nineteenth century there was no 'correspondence' or 'fit' between the needs of the economic system and the products of the educational system. Those leaving school had neither the values nor the skills required by the emerging capitalist system. As Archer says: 'the classical nature of secondary instruction was irrelevant to capitalist development while the catechistic nature of popular elementary instruction was an inadequate form of economic socialization for workers which did not teach sufficient respect for private property.'[31]

This, then, was the *structure* (structural conditioning) in which educational *interaction* took place. Such interaction, says Archer, essentially involved a struggle for control between the dominant group (the churches) and the 'assertive' group.[32] However, this struggle or conflict took different forms in France and England, and had different results.

In France there was a clear-cut transfer of control to the assertive group. The church could rouse little support for its position: 'Catholic domination sponsored a tradition of scholastic classicism which served its own purposes but increasingly meant that "a gap widened between it and society".'[33] Only the nobility joined forces with the church as they were 'united by social ties and similar vested interests in the retention of privilege'.[34] Furthermore, the struggle over education was superimposed on other types of social and political conflict. In the post-revolutionary period — in the first decades of the nineteenth century — control of education therefore passed to those who held the reins of political power. The political elite replaced the existing form of education with a state system which was in keeping with their purposes (the phase of structural elaboration). This national educational system, says Archer, 'gave priority to developing those forms of instruction from which political elites would gain most, while making shifting concessions to such sections of society whose support was needed'.[35] The system became a highly 'centralized' one, with control from the top down. In such a tightly integrated structure the individual parts of the system possessed very little autonomy.

In England the situation was different. Here a rival educational system grew up alongside that which was provided by the Anglican church. The reasons for this were twofold. Firstly, the dominant educational group (the Anglicans) had a close ally in the existing political elite. Amidst increasing working-class unrest in the early nineteenth century, this elite understood 'the contribution of religious instruction to social quietism'.[36] Tories and Whigs alike, says Archer, 'acknowledged the services of the church to social control and to legitimating elitist government'.[37] Secondly, the assertive group of middle-class entrepreneurs, dissenters and the working class was internally divided. Unlike France, 'political alignments in England fragmented educational alliances rather than cementing them'.[38] In addition, the assertive group did not possess the resources to overcome the resistance of the dominant group. This situation, therefore, 'led to the development of separate and alternative educational networks, outside the control of the dominant group',[39] such as the proprietary schools and the mechanics' institutes.

The result of this process of conflict between the dominant and assertive group was a situation of stalemate. Neither side was victorious. However, out of this situation there developed a state educational system (structural elaboration). For each side looked to the state to break the deadlock. In particular, the two sides formed alliances with the two major political parties. The outcome was the settlement of 1870 which, says Archer, 'reflected the balance of power between the two coalitions'.

> It established [she continues] the 'dual system': rate-aided school boards could be elected where the Education Department was satisfied that a shortage existed (a major advance for assertion); voluntary denominational schools were to continue receiving government grants but not to gain rate-aid (a continuing recognition of the Anglican Church which remained the largest proprietor).[40]

Thus, through a political process involving concessions and compromise the separate educational networks became incorporated into a national educational system. Nevertheless, unlike France it was very much a 'decentralised' system in which there was considerable local autonomy and little central control.

EDUCATIONAL SYSTEMS IN ACTION

In Part Two of the book, Archer examines the consequences of the emergence of state educational systems for subsequent interaction and further educational change. Again, she employs the notion of a cycle of structural conditioning, interaction and structural elaboration. The newly developed national educational systems are thus the structure which conditions the interaction that, in due course, modifies the structure.

Archer stresses that the development of state educational systems in England and France in the nineteenth century had a profound effect on what people did (their interaction was heavily structurally conditioned). As a consequence, she says, 'the relative simplicity of the domination and assertion approach must be left behind where it belongs, with the period antecedent to the emergence of educational systems'.[41] This is not to say that conflict between groups disappears; rather, that such conflict no longer involves straightforward competition and struggle, but 'negotiation' instead. Negotiation, states Archer, 'is now the most important process of educational change'[42] and is far more complex in nature than competitive conflict.

Negotiation and Change

There are three principal types of negotiation, and thus three sources of educational change. First, there is 'internal initiation' which means that educational change can now be initiated from within the educational system by teachers and administrators. According to Archer, 'this source of change is the school, the college and the university. It can be brought about on a small scale by independent initiative in a particular establishment, and on a much larger scale by collective professional action.'[43] As an example of this process she quotes: 'The transformation of English primary education along progressive lines [which] was accomplished without legislative intervention and was solely due to an exceptionally high degree of pedagogical consensus among teachers at this level, encouraged and spread by the NUT.'[44]

Secondly, there is 'external transaction', that is the way in which interest groups outside education negotiate with those inside it in order to develop forms of education which meet their specific needs. Basically, such groups offer money for services.

> For example, a particular local firm may offer equipment and facilities for a college to lay on a specialized form of training, the armed services may provide scholarships in return for the enrolment of their cadets, the police, farmers and various professional groups may sponsor or support specialized establishments, and industry may negotiate applied research in return for grants, professorships, laboratories, etc.[45]

The success of such groups in getting what they want depends, of course, on the co-operation of teachers and administrators, who will only agree to such arrangements if they feel they are in keeping with their own interests and/or professional standards.

Thirdly, there is 'political manipulation', which, in Archer's view, 'is the principal resort of those who have no other means of gaining satisfaction of their educational demands — despite the fact that they may be the least successful at manipulating the political machine'.[46] This method is therefore used by the majority of the population — the 'lower classes, immigrant groups and ethnic minorities'[47] — and involves working through local and national political parties. However, considerable success can be obtained by this means. As Archer puts it:

> By continually dragging class, ethnic and minority claims to the centre of the political arena, other groups are irresistibly drawn to debate in these terms when defending their own interests. For this reason, most of the central legislation passed will be found to concentrate on such issues.[48]

According to Archer, whilst these three types of negotiation are of roughly equal importance in decentralised systems such as in England, in centralised systems, such as in France, political manipulation is crucial. This is because of the tight control exercised by the political centre over all parts of the educational system. Individual institutions or sets of institutions possess very little autonomy and thus are unable to proceed with internal initiation or external transactions. All demands have to be channelled through the political system. Teachers and academics, for example, 'must go outside the system in order to influence it, by joining a national political organization or external pressure group'.[49]

In decentralised systems, on the other hand, the profession negotiates directly with the polity on an organised basis and, in so doing, affects policy formation. The relationship with government, therefore, 'becomes a two-way one with education no longer passively receiving directives, but with teachers collectively helping to frame legislation and mould practice'.[50] Similarly, external transactions often flourish within the more independent parts of the system.

> These transactions [says Archer] account for the development of preschool education, of preparatory establishments, of experimental or specialized secondary schools devoted to music, the arts, sectarianism or minority cultures, and commercial and industrial training; of technical, theological and trade colleges; of business schools and even of an independent university.[51]

Having considered the different types of negotiation, Archer makes some final additions to her theoretical framework by drawing upon the Exchange Theory of Peter Blau.[52] Her basic point is that, in addition to examining such types of negotiation in state educational systems, we need also to take into account the negotiating strength of the parties concerned. In decentralised systems such strength will depend upon the possession of wealth, power and expertise, whereas in centralised systems it is the distribution of power alone which is crucial.

Change in England

Archer then turns to an analysis of the nature of the changes in education in England and France since the emergence of state systems. The constraints of space, however, permit us only to scratch the surface of her account, and we shall therefore confine ourselves to illustrating the nature of her approach by considering her discussion of 'internal initiation' in England.

Archer points out that the role of internal initiation in educational change has increased enormously since the beginning of the present century. In the period up to the end of the First World War, the teaching profession was in a very weak bargaining position and, as a consequence, had little impact on the course of educational change. During the interwar years, however, this bargaining position was strengthened as a result of: an improvement in the level of qualifications among teachers; advances in control of entry to the profession; greater involvement by the teachers in shaping educational policy; the development of a new set of values (progressivism) which helped to reinforce and legitimate the above activities. By the time we reach the period 1945–64 the teachers possessed sufficient autonomy and power to be able to determine the nature of the curriculum. In addition, says Archer, they became able to participate in audacious structural reforms . . . For the partnership which emerged between the profession and the local authorities was tantamount to an alliance *against* the centre . . . This alliance was vital since the LEAs made all the running in structural innovation at this time, pioneering comprehensive reorganisation in opposition to central policy, which would have been impossible without strong professional support.[53]

The years between 1964 and 1975 were, however, 'the best yet for the school-teachers'. With the abandonment of the 11+, teachers' assessments of pupils came to be of paramount importance. Furthermore, the Plowden Report of 1965 gave official recognition to the progressive pedagogy. All of this was crowned by the teachers winning control of the new Schools' Council. In Archer's words, this meant that 'the chief agency concerned with the definition of instruction was now commanded by the teachers, thus officially reversing the respective roles of profession and polity as inherited from the nineteenth century'.[54]

Archer's account does not go beyond 1975. Clearly, the changes in the economic and political climate during the last decade must have affected the bargaining position of the teaching profession and the role of internal initiation in educational change. However, Archer points out that, once educational interest groups, such as teachers, have won significant negotiating strength, they tend to retain it. They remain important parties in the process of educational change despite fluctuations in their bargaining position.

Results of Negotiation

Finally, Archer turns to a discussion of the results of these processes of negotiation (structural elaboration). Firstly, she points out that a different pattern of change occurs in centralised and decentralised systems. In centralised systems there is a 'stop-go', jerky pattern of change in education. In decentralised systems, on the other hand, change is neverending, incremental and characterised by the absence of sharp breaks. Confining ourselves here to a discussion of decentralised systems, Archer maintains that there are two reasons for the incremental pattern. Firstly, the importance of internal initiation and external transactions mean that small, local changes frequently accumulate to produce a significant scale of change. Secondly, the considerable autonomy of educational institutions in such a system imposes constraints on political intervention and limits its scale. New legislation must take existing practices into account; indeed 'the ongoing practices and provisions have as much effect on polity-directed changes as legislative intervention on current educational activities'.[55] In addition, new central directives are often modified by action at a local and institutional level. Local authorities can be slow in their implementation of government policy. For example, 'schemes for comprehensive reorganisation were not forthcoming from 50 per cent of authorities when they fell due in 1966'.[56] Alternatively, local authorities can push legal provisions as far as they will go: 'in 1958 Leicestershire initiated full comprehensivization without official bye or leave'.[57] In addition, government legislation can be rejected by parts of the system. 'Examples include the recalcitrance of certain English LEAs vis-à-vis comprehensive reorganisation and the refusal of the majority of public and direct grant schools to associate themselves with it.'[58] In effect, then, centrally directed change in a decentralised system is limited by what exists at a local and institutional level, and by how well it is defended. There is a constant state of tension between the forces for standardisation and for diversification. As a consequence, says Archer

> central authorities cannot proceed like a general, deploying and disposing at will in order to achieve a grand planned strategy, because the parts fight back to defend their autonomy. Instead, the centre often has to work like a sheepdog patrolling the periphery, giving a nip here and a nip there, herding developments on the right trail.[59]

CONCLUSION

In this chapter we have examined three examples of a Weberian approach to education. In conclusion we would like to draw the threads together and briefly summarise the main features of this perspective.

The Weberian perspective is that form of interpretive sociology which is concerned with both micro and macro social processes. It seeks to 'interpret' the behaviour of individual human beings, to understand the subjective meaning of their actions. But it also attempts to locate individual conduct in its social context. All action takes place within a social and economic structure which, to some extent, limits what the individual can do. This structure is, of course, the result of past action. It has been constructed by innumerable men and women throughout history. Nevertheless, for each individual it forms an 'objective reality' that has to be reckoned with. Furthermore, the social system of which we are a part shapes our ideas, beliefs and values as well as controlling our actions. Our conception of the world and of ourselves is influenced by it. In turn, we may, as an individual, come to modify society's institutions; certainly, large numbers of individuals acting together in co-operation, competition and conflict will have such an effect.

A Weberian perspective, then, attends to the individual's action: to his intentions, purposes, goals and 'definition of the situation'. It also considers the 'interaction' of individuals. But, in addition, it examines the way that action and interaction are influenced by, and influence, the existing social and economic system. In doing this it pays attention to the following features of social life: power, authority and domination; the conflict over economic resources and rewards, the competition for status and prestige, the struggle for political control; and the role of bargaining, negotiation and compromise. It does not, however, prejudge the nature and outcome of conflict and struggle (as does Marxism). Rather, it is an 'open' approach which, like pluralism, recognises that class domination may be crucial at certain points in history, but not in others. It therefore provides a framework for analysis, and one which combines the strengths of both micro and macro sociology.

NOTES

1. R. King, 'Organisational Change in Secondary Schools: An Action Approach', *British Journal of Sociology of Education*, vol. 3, no. 1 (1982), p. 15.

2. R. King, 'Weberian Perspectives and the Study of Education', *British Journal of Sociology of Education*, vol. 1, no. 1 (1980), p. 20.

3. Ibid., p. 7.

4. Reported in R. King, *School Organisation and Pupil Involvement* (Routledge and Kegan Paul, London, 1973).

5. King, 'Organisational Change', p. 7.

6. Ibid., p. 10.

7. Ibid., p. 11.

8. In the language of phenomenology, it is 'taken-for-granted' as part of 'everyday life'.

9. King, 'Organisational Change', p. 6.

10. Ibid., p. 16.

11. R. Collins, 'Some Comparative Principles of Educational Stratification', *Harvard Educational Review*, vol. 47, no. 1 (1977), p. 1.

12. Ibid., p. 14.

13. Ibid., p. 15.

14. Ibid., p. 19.

15. Ibid., p. 20.

16. Ibid., p. 21.

17. Ibid., p. 23.

18. R. Collins, *The Credential Society* (Academic Press, New York, 1979), p. vii.

19. F. Parkin, *Marxism and Class Theory: A Bourgeois Critique* (Tavistock, London, 1979), Ch. 4.

20. Collins, *The Credential Society*, p. 93.

21. Ibid., p. 93.

22. Ibid., p. 189.

23. Ibid., p. 55.

24. Ibid., p. 57.

25. Ibid., p. 57.

26. M. Archer, *Social Origins of Educational Systems* (Sage, London, 1984). All references are to this abridged edition. The original book was first published in 1979 and was some 800 pages in length. The new edition has been reduced to a quarter of that length.

27. Ibid., p. 1.

28. Ibid., p. 1.

29. Ibid., p. 4.

30. Ibid., p. 19.

31. Ibid., p. 28.

32. Archer points out that the dominant group in education is not necessarily the same as the dominant group in society generally.

33. Ibid., p. 44.

34. Ibid., p. 46.

35. Ibid., p. 64.

36. Ibid., p. 45.

37. Ibid., p. 46.

38. Ibid., p. 50.

39. Ibid., p. 57.

40. Ibid., p. 70.

41. Ibid., p. 104.

42. Ibid., p. 98.

43. Ibid., p. 101.

44. Ibid., p. 182.

45. Ibid., p. 101.

46. Ibid., pp. 102–3.

47. Ibid., p. 109.

48. Ibid., p. 109.

49. Ibid., p. 114.

50. Ibid., p. 107.

51. Ibid., p. 108.

52. P.M. Blau, *Exchange and Power in Social Life* (Wiley, New York, 1964).

53. Archer, *Social Origins*, p. 150.

54. Ibid., p. 155.

55. Ibid., p. 184.

56. Ibid., p. 185.

57. Ibid., p. 186.

58. Ibid., p. 186.

59. Ibid., p. 195.

BIBLIOGRAPHY

Acton, H.B. *The Illusion of the Epoch* (Cohen and West, London, 1962)
Althusser, L. *For Marx* (Penguin, Harmondsworth, 1969)
—— 'Ideology and Ideological State Apparatuses' in B.R. Cosin *Education: Structure and Society* (Penguin, Harmondsworth, 1972)
Apple, M. (ed.), *Education and Power* (Routledge and Kegan Paul, London, 1982)
—— *Cultural and Economic Reproduction in Education* (Routledge and Kegan Paul, London, 1982)
Archer, M. *Social Origins of Educational Systems* (Sage, London, 1984)
Arnold, M. *Culture and Anarchy* (Cambridge University Press, London, 1971)
Aron, R. 'Social Structure and the Ruling Class', *British Journal of Sociology*, vol. 1, no. 1 (1950)
Auld, R. *Willian Tyndale Junior and Infants Schools Public Inquiry* (ILEA, London, 1976)
Bauman, Z. *Towards a Critical Sociology* (Routledge and Kegan Paul, London, 1976)
Becker, H. *Outsiders* (Free Press, New York, 1963)
Benyon, J. ' "Sussing Out" Teachers: Pupils as Data Gatherers' in M. Hammersley and P. Woods (eds.), *Life in Schools: The Sociology of Pupil Culture* (Open University Press, Milton Keynes, 1984)
Berg, L. *Risinghill, The Death of a Comprehensive School* (Penguin, Harmondsworth, 1968)
Berger, P. 'Some Observations Concerning the Problem of Work' in P. Berger (ed.), *The Human Shape of Work* (Macmillan, London, 1964)
—— *Invitation to Sociology: A Humanistic Perspective* (Penguin, Harmondsworth, 1966)
—— and Luckmann, T. *The Social Construction of Reality* (Allen Lane, London, 1967)
Berlin, I. *Karl Marx* (Oxford University Press, London, 1963)
—— 'Two Concepts of Liberty' in I. Berlin *Four Essays on Liberty* (Oxford University Press, London, 1969)
Bernstein, R. *Class, Codes and Control*, 2nd edn, 3 vols. (Routledge and Kegan Paul, London, 1977), vol. 3.
Blau, P.M. *Exchange and Power in Social Life* (Wiley, New York, 1964)
Blum, A. 'The Corpus of Knowledge' in M.F.D. Young (ed.), *Knowledge and Control* (Collier-Macmillan, London, 1971)
Bottomore, T. *Karl Marx: Early Writings* (Watts, London, 1963)
—— *Marxist Sociology* (Macmillan, London, 1975)
—— and Rubel, M. *Karl Marx: Selected Writings in Sociology and Social Philosophy* (Penguin, Harmondsworth, 1963)
Bourdieu, P. 'Cultural Reproduction and Social Reproduction' in R. Brown (ed.), *Knowledge, Education, and Cultural Change* (Tavistock, London, 1973)
—— 'Systems of Education and Systems of Thought' in R. Dale, G. Esland and M. MacDonald (eds.), *Schooling and Capitalism* (Routledge and Kegan Paul, London, 1976)
—— and Passeron, J.-P. *Reproduction in Education and Society* (Sage, London, 1977)
—— and Saint-Martin, M. de, 'Scholastic Excellence and the Values of the Educational System' in J. Eggleston (ed.), *Contemporary Research in the Sociology of Education* (Methuen, London, 1974)
Bowles, S. and Gintis, H. *Schooling in Capitalist America* (Routledge and Kegan Paul, London, 1976)
—— 'Contradiction and Reproduction in Educational Theory' in R. Dale *et al.* (eds.), *Education and the State*, vol. 1, *Schooling and the National Interest* (Falmer Press, Lewes, 1981)

Burke, E. *Reflections on the Revolution in France* (Penguin, Harmondsworth, 1968)

Burns, V. 'Review of *Learning to Labour*', *Harvard Educational Review*, vol. 50, no. 4 (1980)

Centre for Contemporary Cultural Studies (CCCS), University of Birmingham *Unpopular Education: Schooling and Social Democracy in England since 1944* (Hutchinson, London, 1981)

Cicourel, A. *Method and Measurement in Sociology* (Free Press, New York, 1964)

—— and Kitsuse, J. *The Educational Decision Makers* (Bobbs-Merrill, Indianapolis, 1963)

Cohen, P. *Modern Social Theory* (Heinemann, London, 1968)

Cohen, S. 'Symbols of Trouble', Introduction to the new edition *Folk Devils and Moral Panics* (Martin Robertson, Oxford, 1980)

Collins, R. 'Some Comparative Principles of Educational Stratification', *Harvard Educational Review*, vol. 47, no. 1 (1977)

—— *The Credential Society* (Academic Press, New York, 1979)

Comte, A. 'The Positive Philosophy' in K. Thompson and J. Tunstall (eds.), *Sociological Perspectives* (Penguin, Harmondsworth, 1971)

Cooper, D. *Illusions of Equality* (Routledge and Kegan Paul, London, 1980)

Corrigan, P. *Schooling the Smash Street Kids* (Macmillan, London, 1979)

Coulson, M.A. and Riddell, C. *Approaching Sociology* (Routledge and Kegan Paul, London, 1970)

Coxhead, P. 'Some Comments on Bowles and Gintis', Appendix to Unit 13 of E202 *Schooling and Society* (Open University Press, Milton Keynes, 1977)

Crosland, C.A.R. *The Future of Socialism* (Cape, London, 1964)

—— *Socialism Now and Other Essays* (Cape, London, 1975)

Dahl, R. *Who Governs* (Yale University Press, New Haven, 1961)

Dale, R. and Esland, G. 'Mass Schooling', Units 2–3 of E202 *Schooling and Society* (Open University Press, Milton Keynes, 1977)

Dawe, A. 'The Two Sociologies', *British Journal of Sociology*, vol. 21, no. 2 (1970)

Davie, R. and Butler, Neville R. *From Birth to Seven*, Second Report of the National Child Development Study (Longman, London, 1972)

Davies, I. 'The Management of Knowledge: A Critique of the Use of Typologies in Educational Sociology' in E. Hopper (ed.), *Readings in the Theory of Educational Systems* (Hutchinson, London, 1971)

Davis, K. and Moore, W.E. 'Some Principles of Stratification', *American Sociological Review*, vol. 10, no. 2 (1945)

Delamont, S. *Interaction in the Classroom* (Methuen, London, 1976)

Duncan, G. *Marx and Mill: Two Views of Social Conflict and Social Harmony* (Cambridge University Press, Cambridge, 1973)

Durbin, E.F.M. *The Politics of Democratic Socialism* (Routledge, London, 1940)

Durkheim, É. *Suicide: A Study in Sociology* (Routledge and Kegan Paul, London, 1952)

—— *Education and Sociology* (Free Press, New York, 1956)

—— *Moral Education* (Free Press, New York, 1961)

—— *The Division of Labour in Society* (Free Press, New York, 1964)

—— *The Rules of Sociological Method* (Free Press, New York, 1964)

—— 'Evolution of Educational Thought' in J. Karabel and A.H. Halsey (eds.), *Power and Ideology in Education* (Oxford University Press, New York, 1977)

Education and Science, Department of *A Framework for the School Curriculum* (HMSO, London, 1980)

Edwards, A.D. *Language in Culture and Class* (Heinemann, London, 1976)

Engels, F. 'On Authority' in K. Marx and F. Engels *Marx and Engels: Selected Works* (2 vols., Progress Publishers, Moscow, 1955), vol. 1

Erben, M. and Gleeson, D. 'Education as Reproduction' in M. Young and G. Whitty (eds.) *Society, State and Schooling* (Falmer Press, Lewes, 1977)

Esland, G. 'Teaching and Learning as the Organisation of Knowledge' in M.F.D. Young (ed.) *Knowledge and Control* (Collier-Macmillan, London, 1971)

Everhart, R. *Reading, Writing and Resistance* (Routledge and Kegan Paul, London, 1983)

Field, G.C. *Political Theory* (Methuen, London, 1963)

Frankena, W. *Ethics* (Prentice-Hall, Englewood Cliffs, 1973)

Furlong, V. 'Anancy Goes to School: A Case Study of Pupils' Knowledge of Their Teachers' in P. Woods and M. Hammersley (eds.) *School Experience: Explorations in the Sociology of Education* (Croom Helm, London, 1977)

—— 'Interaction Sets in the Classroom: Towards a Study of Pupil Knowledge' in M. Hammersley and P. Woods (eds.) *The Process of Schooling* (Routledge and Kegan Paul, London, 1976)

Finn, D., Grant, N. and Johnson, R. 'Social Democracy, Education and the Crisis' in The Centre for Contemporary Cultural Studies, the University of Birmingham *On Ideology* (Hutchinson, London, 1978)

Further Education Curriculum Review and Development Unit (FEU) *Beyond Coping: Some Approaches to Social Education* (FEU, London, 1980)

Galbraith, J.K. *The Anatomy of Power* (Hamish Hamilton, London, 1984)

Giroux, H. *Ideology, Culture and the Process of Schooling* (Falmer Press, Lewes, 1981)

—— 'Theories of Reproduction and Resistance in the New Sociology of Education: A Critical Analysis', *Harvard Educational Review*, vol. 53, no. 3 (1983)

Goffman, E. *The Presentation of Self in Everyday Life* (Allen Lane, London, 1969)

Goldthorpe, J.H. *Social Mobility and Class Structure in Modern Britain* (Clarendon Press, Oxford, 1980)

Gouldner, A. 'The Sociologist as Partisan' in A. Gouldner *For Sociology* (Allen Lane, London, 1973)

—— *The Two Marxisms* (Macmillan, London, 1980)

Greaves, H.R.G. *The Foundations of Political Theory* (Bell, London, 1966)

Haas, E. *Beyond the Nation State* (Stanford University Press, Stanford, 1964)

Hall, S. 'A Review of the Course', Unit 32 of E202 *Schooling and Society* (Open University Press, Milton Keynes, 1977)

Halsey, A.H. 'Theoretical Advance and Empirical Challenge' in E. Hopper (ed.) *Readings in the Theory of Educational Systems* (Hutchinson, London, 1971)

—— Heath, A.F. and Ridge, J.M. *Origins and Destinations* (Clarendon Press, Oxford, 1980)

Hammersley, M. 'Teacher Perspectives', Unit 9 of E202 *Schooling and Society* (Open University Press, Milton Keynes, 1977)

—— 'Some Reflections on the Macro–Micro Problems in the Sociology of Education', *Sociological Review*, vol. 32, no. 2 (1984)

—— and Turner, G. 'Conformist Pupils?' in M. Hammersley and P. Woods (eds.) *Life in Schools: The Sociology of Pupil Culture* (Open University Press, Milton Keynes, 1984)

Haralambos, M. with Heald, R. *Sociology: Themes and Perspectives* (University Tutorial Press, Slough, 1980)

Hargreaves, A. 'The Significance of Classroom Coping Strategies' in L. Barton and R. Meighan (eds.) *Sociological Interpretations of Schooling and Classrooms: A Reappraisal* (Nafferton Books, Driffield, 1978)

—— 'The Ideology of the Middle School' in A. Hargreaves and L. Tickle (eds.) *Middle Schools: Origins, Ideology and Practice* (Harper and Row, London, 1980)

—— 'Resistance and Relative Autonomy Theories: Problems of Distortion and Incoherence in Recent Marxist Analyses of Education', *British Journal of Sociology of Education*, vol. 3, no. 2 (1982)

Hargreaves, D. *Social Relations in a Secondary School* (Routledge and Kegan Paul, London, 1967)

—— *Interpersonal Relations and Education*, Student edition (Routledge and Kegan Paul, London, 1975)

—— 'Whatever Happened to Symbolic Interactionism?' in L. Barton and R. Meighan (eds.) *Sociological Interpretations of Schooling and Classrooms: A Reappraisal* (Nafferton

Books, Driffield, 1978)

—— 'A Sociological Critique of Individualism in Education', *British Journal of Educational Studies*, vol. 28, no. 3 (1980)

—— *The Challenge for the Comprehensive School: Culture, Curriculum and Community* (Routledge and Kegan Paul, London, 1982)

—— Hester, S.K. and Mellor, F.J. *Deviance in Classrooms* (Routledge and Kegan Paul, London, 1975)

Hickox, M.S.H. 'The Marxist Sociology of Education: A Critique', *British Journal of Sociology*, vol. 33, no. 4 (1982)

Hirst, P.H. and Peters, R.S. *The Logic of Education* (Routledge and Kegan Paul, London, 1970)

Hoare, Q. and Smith, G. Nowell (eds.) *Selections from the Prison Notebooks of Antonio Gramsci* (Lawrence and Wishart, London, 1971)

Hoggart, R. *The Uses of Literacy* (Penguin, Harmondsworth, 1958)

Hook, S. *Revolution, Reform and Social Justice* (Blackwell, Oxford, 1976)

Hopper, E. 'A Typology for the Classification of Educational Systems' in E. Hopper (ed.) *Readings in the Theory of Educational Systems* (Hutchinson, London, 1971)

HM Government, *Social Trends* (HMSO, London, 1978)

Jackson, B. and Marsden, D. *Education and the Working Class* (Penguin, Harmondsworth, 1966)

Jackson, L.A. 'The Myth of the Elaborated and Restricted Code' in B.R. Cosin *et al.* (eds.) *School and Society*, 2nd edn (Routledge and Kegan Paul, London, 1977)

Johnson, R. 'Notes on the Schooling of the English Working Class, 1780–1850' in R. Dale, G. Esland and M. MacDonald (eds.) *Schooling and Capitalism* (Routledge and Kegan Paul, London, 1976)

Joll, J. *Gramsci* (Fontana, London, 1977)

Kamenka, E. (ed.) *Community as a Social Ideal* (E. Arnold, London, 1982)

Karabel, J. and Halsey, A.H. (eds.) *Power and Ideology in Education* (Oxford University Press, New York, 1977)

Keddie, N. 'Classroom Knowledge' in M.F.D. Young *Knowledge and Control* (Collier-Macmillan, London, 1971)

King, R. *School Organisation and Pupil Involvement* (Routledge and Kegan Paul, London, 1973)

—— 'Bernstein's Sociology of the School', *British Journal of Sociology*, vol. 27, no. 4 (1976)

—— 'Weberian Perspectives and the Study of Education', *British Journal of Sociology of Education*, vol. 1, no. 1 (1980)

—— 'Organisational Change in Secondary Schools: An Action Approach', *British Journal of Sociology of Education*, vol. 3, no. 1 (1982)

Kolakowski, L. 'Althusser's Marx' in R. Miliband and J. Saville (eds.) *Socialist Register 1971* (Merlin Press, London, 1971)

—— *Main Currents of Marxism* (3 vols., Clarendon Press, Oxford, 1978)

Lacey, C. *Hightown Grammar* (Manchester University Press, Manchester, 1970)

Lukács, G. *History and Class Consciousness* (Merlin Press, London, 1971)

Lukes, S. 'Alienation and Anomie' in P. Laslett and W.G. Runciman (eds.) *Philosophy, Politics and Society*, Third series (Blackwell, Oxford, 1969). Reprinted in S. Lukes *Essays in Social Theory* (Macmillan, London, 1977)

—— 'Durkheim's "Individualism and the Intellectuals" ', *Political Studies*, vol. 17, no. 1 (1969)

—— *Émile Durkheim: His Life and Work* (Allen Lane, London, 1973)

—— *Individualism* (Blackwell, Oxford, 1973)

—— 'On the Social Determination of Truth' in S. Lukes *Essays in Social Theory* (Macmillan, London, 1977)

McLellan, D. (ed.) *Karl Marx: Early Texts* (Blackwell, Oxford, 1971)

—— (ed.) *Marx's Grundrisse* (Macmillan, London, 1971)

McRobbie, A. 'Working Class Girls and the Culture of Femininity' in The Centre for Contemporary Cultural Studies (CCCS), University of Birmingham *Women Take Issue* (Hutchinson, London, 1978)

MacDonald, Madeleine, 'The Curriculum and Cultural Reproduction', Unit 18 of E202 *Schooling and Society* (Open University Press, Milton Keynes, 1977)

Macdonald, M. 'Natural Rights' in P. Laslett (ed.) *Philosophy, Politics and Society* (Blackwell, Oxford, 1970)

Magee, B. *Popper* (Fontana, London, 1973)

—— *Men of Ideas* (BBC, London, 1978)

Mannheim, K. *Ideology and Utopia* (Routledge and Kegan Paul, London, 1960)

Marx, K. *Pre-Capitalist Economic Formations* (Lawrence and Wishart, London, 1969)

—— *Capital* (3 vols., Lawrence and Wishart, London, 1974), vol. 1

—— and Engels, F. *The German Ideology* (Lawrence and Wishart, London, 1965)

—— *Marx and Engels: Selected Works* in one vol. (Lawrence and Wishart, London, 1968)

Merton, R.K. 'The Self-Fulfilling Prophecy' in R.K. Merton *Social Theory and Social Structure* (Free Press, New York, 1957)

Miliband, R. *The State in Capitalist Society* (Weidenfeld and Nicolson, London, 1972)

—— *Marxism and Politics* (Oxford University Press, London, 1977)

Mill, J.S. *Considerations on Representative Government* (Dent, London, 1910)

—— *Utilitarianism* (Fontana, London, 1962)

—— *On Liberty* (Dent, London, 1910)

Mills, C. Wright, *The Sociological Imagination* (Oxford University Press, New York, 1959)

Moore, Jr. B. *Social Origins of Dictatorship and Democracy* (Penguin, Harmondsworth, 1969)

Musgrave, P.W. *The Sociology of Education* (Methuen, London, 1965)

Musgrove, F. *School and the Social Order* (Wiley, Chichester, 1979)

Nash, R. *Teacher Expectations and Pupil Learning* (Routledge and Kegan Paul, London, 1976)

Parekh, B. *Marx's Theory of Ideology* (Croom Helm, London, 1982)

Parkin, F. *Marxism and Class Theory: A Bourgeois Critique* (Tavistock, London, 1979)

Parsons, T. 'The School Class as a Social System' in A.H. Halsey, J. Floud and C.A. Anderson (eds.) *Education, Economy and Society* (Free Press, New York, 1961)

—— *Societies: Evolutionary and Comparative Perspectives* (Prentice-Hall, Englewood Cliffs, 1966)

—— 'An Outline of the Social System' in T. Parsons *et al.* (eds.) *Theories of Society* (Prentice-Hall, Englewood Cliffs, 1971)

—— *The System of Modern Societies* (Prentice-Hall, Englewood Cliffs, 1971)

—— and Shils, E. (eds.) *Toward a General Theory of Action* (Harper and Row, New York, 1962)

Partridge, P.H. *Consent and Consensus* (Pall Mall, London, 1971)

Payne, G. 'Making a Lesson Happen' in M. Hammersley and P. Woods (eds.) *The Process of Schooling* (Routledge and Kegan Paul, London, 1976)

Peters, R.S. *Ethics and Education* (Allen and Unwin, London, 1970)

Phillipson, M. 'Theory, Methodology and Conceptualization' in P. Filmer *et al. New Directions in Sociological Theory* (Collier-Macmillan, London, 1972)

Plamenatz, J.P. *German Marxism and Russian Communism* (Longman, London, 1954)

—— 'Electoral Studies and Democratic Theory', *Political Studies* (1958)

—— *Man and Society* (2 vols., Longman, London, 1963) vol. 2

—— *Karl Marx's Philosophy of Man* (Clarendon Press, Oxford, 1975)

Plant, R. *Community and Ideology* (Routledge and Kegan Paul, London, 1974)

Pollard, A. 'Goodies, Jokers and Gangs' in M. Hammersley and P. Woods (eds.) *Life in Schools: The Sociology of Pupil Cultures* (Open University Press, Milton Keynes, 1984)

Popper, K. *The Open Society and Its Enemies* (2 vols., Routledge and Kegan Paul, London, 1962) vol. 2

Poulantzas, N. 'The Problem of the Capitalist State' in R. Blackburn (ed.) *Ideology in Social Science* (Fontana, London, 1972)

Reisman, D. *Individualism Reconsidered* (Free Press, New York, 1954)

Rex, J. 'Thirty Theses on Epistemology and Method' in J. Rex (ed.) *Discovering Sociology* (Routledge and Kegan Paul, London, 1973)

Reynolds, D. 'Relative Autonomy Reconstructed' in L. Barton and S. Walker (eds.) *Social Crisis and Education* (Croom Helm, London, 1984)

—— and Sullivan, M. 'Towards a New Socialist Sociology of Education' in L. Barton *et al. Schooling, Ideology and the Curriculum* (Falmer Press, Lewes, 1980)

Rist, R. 'On Understanding the Process of Schooling: The Contributions of Labelling Theory' in J. Karabel and A.H. Halsey (eds.) *Power and Ideology in Education* (Oxford University Press, New York, 1977)

Roberts, R. *The Classic Slum* (Penguin, Harmondsworth, 1973)

Rousseau, J.-J. 'Discourse on the Origins of Inequality' (Dent, London, 1913)

Ryle, G. 'Can Virtue Be Taught?' in R.F. Dearden, P.H. Hirst and R.S. Peters (eds.) *Education and Reason* (Routledge and Kegan Paul, London, 1975)

Sarup, M. *Marxism and Education* (Routledge and Kegan Paul, London, 1978)

—— *Education, State and Crisis* (Routledge and Kegan Paul, London, 1982)

Sharp, R. *Knowledge, Ideology and the Politics of Schooling* (Routledge and Kegan Paul, London, 1980)

—— and Green, A. *Education and Social Control: A Study of Progressive Primary Education* (Routledge and Kegan Paul, London, 1975)

Smith, D. 'Selection and Knowledge Management in Educational Systems' in E. Hopper (ed.) *Readings in the Theory of Educational Systems* (Hutchinson, London, 1971)

Tawney, R.H. *Secondary Schools for All* (Allen and Unwin, London, 1922)

—— 'An Experiment in Democratic Education' in R. Tawney *The Radical Tradition* (Allen and Unwin, London, 1964)

—— 'The Workers Educational Association and Adult Education' in R. Tawney *The Radical Tradition* (Allen and Unwin, London, 1964)

Turner, R. 'Sponsored and Contest Mobility and the School System' in E. Hopper (ed.) *Readings in the Theory of Educational Systems* (Hutchinson, London, 1971)

Waller, W. *The Sociology of Teaching* (Wiley, New York, 1932)

Weber, M. *The Theory of Economic and Social Organization* (Free Press, New York, 1964)

Wellmer, A. *Critical Theory of Society* (The Seabury Press, New York, 1974)

Westergaard, J. and Resler, H. *Class in Capitalist Society* (Penguin, Harmondsworth, 1975)

Whitty, G. 'Sociology and the Problem of Radical Educational Change' in M. Young and G. Whitty (eds.) *Society, State and Schooling* (Falmer Press, Lewes, 1977)

Williamson, B. *Class, Culture and Community* (Routledge and Kegan Paul, London, 1982)

Willis, P. 'The Class Significance of School Counter-Culture' in M. Hammersley and P. Woods (eds.) *The Process of Schooling* (Routledge and Kegan Paul, London, 1976)

—— *Learning to Labour* (Saxon House, Farnborough, 1977)

—— 'Cultural Production and Theories of Reproduction' in L. Barton and S. Walker (eds.) *Race, Class and Education* (Croom Helm, London, 1983)

Woods, P. *The Divided School* (Routledge and Kegan Paul, London, 1979)

—— *Sociology and the School: An Interactionist Viewpoint* (Routledge and Kegan Paul, London, 1983)

Wrong, D. 'The Oversocialized Conception of Man in Modern Sociology' in L. Coser and B. Rosenberg (eds.) *Sociological Theory* (Collier-Macmillan, London, 1966)

Young, J. 'New Directions in Sub-Cultural Theory' in J. Rex (ed.) *Approaches to Sociology* (Routledge and Kegan Paul, London, 1974)

Young, M.F.D. 'An Approach to the Study of Curricula as Socially Organized Knowledge' in M.F.D. Young (ed.) *Knowledge and Control* (Collier-Macmillan, London, 1971)

—— *Knowledge and Control* (Collier-Macmillan, London, 1971)

INDEX

ability 41–4, 67, 260–2; knowledge and educational failure 290–3, 310
access to education 188–9
achievement 68–9, 73–5
action: context of 265, 328; subjectively meaningful 319
adaptation, modes of 266–70
Adorno, T.W. 121
affective-emotional abilities 41–4
affirmation of life 127
alienation 37, 124–6, 130, 137, 317
allocation function of education 73
Althusser, L. 114, 119, 122, 134, 151, 157–63, 186; on education as state apparatus 159–61
ambition, regulation of 82–5
anomie 14, 17, 23, 30, 36, 37, 56
anti-school *see* counter-school
Anyon, J. 217–18
Apple, M. 179–80, 187
approval-seeking 104–6; *see also* pleasing
arbitraries, cultural 164–6
Archer, M. on state educational system 327–35; in action 331–5; change in England 333–4; development of 327, 328, 329–31; negotiation and change 331–3, results of 334–5
Arnold, M. 189, 309, 311–12
Aron, R. 225
aspirations, infinite 14
assertive groups 329–30
authoritarian/totalitarian society 35–6, 98, 135, 147
authority 214–15, 271; *see also* control; resistance
autonomy *see* independence; relative autonomy

base *see* superstructure
Becker, H. 221, 304
Benyon, J. 275
Berger, P. 2, 22, 108, 209; on management of knowledge 89–92, 95; on work 298–9
Berlin, I. 39, 131, 199–200, 295–7, 310
Bernstein, B. 1, 21, 27, 44–6, 108, 166, 168; on changes in education 46–7; on educational knowledge 49–52; on pedagogy, types of 50, 53–5
Binstock, J. 146
Black Paper 194
Blau, P. 333
Bottomore, T. 122
Bourdieu, P. 21, 54, 93, 312; on reproduction 163–75, culture/cultural capital 164–70, educational system 170–1
Bowles, S. and Gintis, H. 134–48, 158–9, 205, 318; on capitalist system 135–42; on socialism as alternative 142–4, 147
Britain 152; comparison with France 93, 328–34
Burris, V. 208
busyness 261

Callaghan, J. 194
capital *see* culture/cultural
capitalism/capitalist: class 13, 136–7, 140, 145, 222–3; control 135–40; ideology and values 136–8, 204; and labour 16–17, 54, 135–6, 139–40; need for reproduction 135–42, correspondence principle 139–41, economic structure and education 141–2, education's contribution 137–8, socialisation 138–9; technocratic-meritocratic 136, 138, 317, 320
categories, changes in 47, 58–9
causal explanations of education 10, 11–13
CCCS *see* Centre for Contemporary etc.
centralised systems 332, 334
Centre for Contemporary Cultural Studies, on social democracy 186–95, 223; criticisms of 191–5; ideology of 187–9; policies of 190–1
change: in categories 47, 58–9; in

344

educational system 46–7, 331–4; and negotiation 331–5; social 11–12, 101–3, 120

China in T'ang dynasty 323–4

Cicourel, A. 2

class, social: and authority 214–15; and capitalism 13, 136–7, 140, 145, 222–3; confirmation and maintenance 155, 161, 164; conflict 123–4, 140; and conformity 214–16; consciousness 123; and control 149–51, 155; and credentialism 326; and cultural capital 167–73; and dignity 28; dominant/ruling 151–4, 167–70; and educational knowledge 311–14; and failure 192–3, 292; group 323; and inequality 192–3; and legitimation 205; of pupils 262, *see also* working class; and resistance 180–5, 208–20; and school systems 74–5; and socialisation 206–7; and social mobility 77–8, 84, 86; values and thought systems 24–5, 38, 45, 155, 211–13, 291–3, 311–12, 317–18; *see also* middle class; working class

classification 50–2, 53, 56–9

classroom *see* micro interpretive

codes 45, 50–2, 55, 57, 59, 166

cognitive achievement 73–4

cognitive-intellectual abilities 41–4

Cohen, P. 102–3

Cohen, S. 220, 227

collection code 50–2, 57

collective conscience 16

collective experiences 31–2; *see also* group

Collins, R. 322–7; on credentialism 325–7; on group conflict 323–5

colonisation mode of conformity 218–20, 267–8

commitment 10

common culture 68

communication 238; *see also* language

communications, control of 54

communism 126–30

community: -centred curriculum 41–4; and individualism 40–1; and modern social ills 37–41; sense of *see* group; *see also* social; society

compliance mode of conformity 218–19, 246, 266–8

Comte, A. 68–9

conceptualisation *see* self-conception

'concord' classroom 246

conflict: class 123–4, 140; group 323–5; interests 131; lack of 128; roles 241; in schools 147–8, 266, 269, 271, 280, 321–2, *see also* resistance; values 99–101, 131

conformity 268, 269, 271; modes of 218–19; working class 214–16

conscience, collective 16

consciousness: class 123; shaping 138; true and false 303

consensus 89, 98–9; on values 66–73 *passim*, 98–101

conservatism, theoretical 300–1

Conservative Party and social democracy 194

consistency, lack in classroom 272

conspiracy theory 141

constraints 91; social 8–9, 22, 49, 285; *see also* control

construction of relationships 91

content of education *see* 'new' sociology

contest norms 78–80, 81, 85, 88

context of action 265

'Contradiction, Unresolved' 122–3; *see also* conflict

contradictory goals 191

control/power: capitalist 135–40; differences in 104; and group conflict 323–4; lack of 139; in schools 144, 149, 165, 321, 333; social 49, 55, 60: hierarchy of 72, structure of 85, 88, of working class 149–51, 155; *see also* authority; constraints; disciplines; framing; order; resistance

Cooper, D. 295

co-operation 271

coping and survival strategies 275–6, 285–6

correspondence principle 139–41

Corrigan, P. 182

Coulson, M.A. 93

counter-school culture 28, 31, 211–12, 266, 272, 317; Willis on 182, 183–5; *see also* delinquency; deviance; resistance

Cox, H. 40

Coxhead, P. 145

creativity: of coping strategies 285; in schools 140, 145–6

credentialism, rise of 325–7

critical theory of Frankfurt School 121

Crosland, C.A.R. 191, 222–3, 227

culture/cultural: capital 164–70, 172–3,

265–6, arbitraries 164–6, dominant classes 167–70, socialisation 166–7; common 68; ideology and 252; national styles 93–4; system of society 71–3; *see also* counter-school
curriculum 41–4, 48–51, 59; hidden 139, 179–80; *see also* knowledge, educational

Dahl, R. 225–6, 228
Dahrendorf, R. 40
Dale, R. 148–50
Davies, I. 2, 316; on management of knowledge 92–4; on selection 76, 85–6, 88–90, 95
Davis, K. 138
Dawe, A. 2, 290
Debeauvais, M. 190
decentralised systems 332, 334
decision-making 90
definition of pupils, by teachers 301–5
definitions, failure to state origins of 282–4
Delamont, S. 266
delinquency 210–11, 220, 246; *see also* deviance
democracy 142–3; social 191–5, 221–6
democratic-pluralist theory 151
description *see* definition; labelling
determinism 103–4, 317; economic 114–15, 119–20, 122–3, evaluation of 198–200; social *see* Durkheim; Durkheimians
developmental individualism 33
deviance 267, 269, 271; labelling 304–5; as norm 302; typing 258; *see also* counter-school; delinquency; resistance
diffuse skills 82
dignity 28–9, 39
direct reproduction *see under* Marx and Marxism
discipline 18–21; *see also* control
'discord' classroom 246
division of labour 16–17, 54, 139–40
dominant groups 329–30; *see also* class, dominant
domination strategy 276
Duane, M. 165
Duncan, G. 99–100
Durbin, e. 200–2, 207
Durkheim, E. 1–2, 4, 7–26, 108, 301; on modern society 15–25, 30, 45, 48, 54, 155, 162–3; on sociology 7–10
Durkheimians, modern 27–63; *see also* Bernstein; Hargreaves, D.

economic/economy: activity *see* historical materialism; basic unit in society 157; democracy 142–3; determinism 114–15, 119–20, 122–3, evaluated 198–200; and education 203–4, 323; inequality 136; institutions 64; structure 151–6, 158, and capitalism 141–2; totalitarianism 135, 147
education *see* sociological interpretations
educational knowledge *see under* knowledge
egoism 30, 32, 36
elaborated code 45, 55
elite status *see* class, dominant; social, mobility
Ellis, T. 165
empirical forms of knowledge 295–6
employment *see* work
enabling interests 264–5
Engels, F. 114–17, 124, 149; on authority 215–16; as determinist 115–19
England *see* Britain
equality 190–1; before beginning school 73; as harmony 192; of opportunity 67–9, 190–1, 317; *see also* inequality
equilibrium, strain towards 102
Erben, M. 162
Esland, G. 148–50, 290–1, 300, 304
ethnomethodology 237, 277–9
Everhart, R. 182, 216
everyday activity 234; *see also* knowledge, everyday
Exchange Theory 333
exclusionary closure 325
expectations, role 66, 71–2
experiential knowledge 250, 262
expert knowledge 292
external: change 101–2; factors 322; social constraints 8–10, 49; transaction 331–2; *see also* internal

Fabians and social democracy 192
factory/shop-floor 182–6; *see also* work
failure, educational 172, 301–5; and class 292; and inequality 192–3; knowledge and ability 290–3, 310; false and true, distinction between

303

family: and achievement 68; as institution 64, 102; orientation, differences in 67; as site of social practice 147; and socialisation 45

fatalism *see* determinism

fear 105, 214

feedback, important to pupils 274

Field, G.C. 35

forces of production 115–17

formal forms of knowledge 295–6

Forster, E.M. 104

framing 50–2, 53, 59–61, 270; *see also* control

France 11, 324; comparison with Britain 93, 328–34; language in 169, 171, 173

Frankena, W. 33

Frankfurt School 121

fraternisation strategy 276

freedom 234

Freud, S. 37

Frith, S. 207

function of knowledge 297

functionalist approach to education 10, 13–15, 64–97; assessed 98–109, 162, 332; approval-seeking 104–6; change 101–3; consensus 98–101; determinism 103–4; social order, foundations of 64–6, socialisation, education as 67–85, *see also* Hopper; Parsons; Turner

fundamental values 155

Furlong, V. 105, 269, 281, 302; on pupils' knowledge of teachers 260, 272–5

Galbraith, J.K. 223–4, 227

Gintis, H. *see* Bowles and Gintis

Giroux, H. 181–2, 187, 219–20

Gleeson, D. 162

goals: achievement *see* strategies; contradictory 191; school 269

good–bad teacher dimension 273–4

Gouldner, A. 122, 221, 304–5

Gramsci, A. 119–22, 180, 307–8

'Great Debate' 194

Greaves, H.R.G. 35

Green, A. 59; *see also* Sharp and Green

group/s: conflict 323–5; dominant 329–30; interests and knowledge 297–9; organised *see* interest groups; social 18–20, 24–5, 30–1, 36

gynaecological analogy 119

Habermas, J. 121

habitual interaction 90–1

Hall, S. 119, 151, 157–9

Halsey, A.H. 53, 78, 88, 172–3

Hammersley, M. 233–4, 255–7; on pupils' self-conceptions 269–71

Haralambos, M. 276, 281, 282

Hargreaves, A. 227; on complexity of resistance 217–18; micro interpretive synthesis, attempted 284–7; on relative autonomy 198, 207

Hargreaves, D. 1, 4, 27–44, 59, 108, 182, 216, 270; on evaluation 210–12; on individualism 32–6; on modern social ills 36–44; on resistance 210–12; on social function of education 29–32; on symbolic interactionism 238–42, classroom applications 242–7; on teachers' knowledge of pupils 257–9, 272, 282–3

harmony 129–30, 192

Heath, A.F. 78, 129–30

Hegel, F. 130

Hickox, M.S.H. 205–7, 227

hierarchy of control 72

Hirst, P.H. 42, 290, 309–11

historical materialism 113–24; base/superstructure issue 113–15, 117, 119, 121; class conflict 123–4; evaluated 198–202; Marx and Engels as determinists 115–19; structuralist Marxists 119; 'Unresolved Contradictions' 122–3; voluntarist Marxists 119–22; *see also* Marx and Marxism

Hobbes, T. 37, 69

Hoggart, R. 212–13

honesty 213

Hook, S. 201–2

Hopper, E. 66, 76, 80–5; on ambition 82–5; criticised 85–9; on selection 80–2

humour, sense of 43

ideal pupil 261

ideals *see* values

ideas, role of 199–200, 307–8

identification of sociologist with underdog 221

Ideological State Apparatus 159–61

ideology; capitalist 136–8; concept of 175, 299–300; consensus on 89; as

culture 252; legitimation of 81–4; particular concept of 299–300; particularistic 82; of social democracy 187–9; universality of 82
independence/autonomy 40, 73; in school 140, 171, 204–5, of teachers 321, 333; *see also* relative autonomy
indifference 246
individual/individualism: and community 40–1; developmental 33; importance of 12, 14, 16, 18–19, 22; moral 33; motivation 67; non-egoistic 31, 32; and personal dignity 28–9; and self-development 33–4; and social aims 35–6; subjectively meaningful action 319; *see also* person; personal; personality
inequality: economic 136; and failure 192–3; legitimation of 137, 317; perpetuated by schools 276; *see also* class; equality
ingratiation mode of conformity 218–19, 266–7
institutions, social 64–5, 102–4, 329
integrated code 50–2, 57, 59
intellectual styles 93–4
intelligence 291; *see also* ability
interaction/interactionism 119, 277, 328–9; micro interpretive approaches 235; model 249–51; sets 273; symbolic 238–47, classroom applications 242–7; *see also* superstructure, and base interest groups 151, 224–5; *see also* groups
interests, conflict of 131
internal: change 101, 120; initiation 331, 333; social constraints 8, 10, 49; *see also* external
internalisation of values and norms 66
interpretive approach *see* micro interpretive: 'new' sociology; Weberian perspective
intervention threshold 258
intransigence mode of conformity 218–19, 267, 269
invisible pedagogy 53, 55

Jackson, B. 311–12
Japan 324
Johnson, R. 198, 206, 212
Joll, J. 121–2

Kamenka, E. 41

Karabel, J. 53
Keddie, N. 94, 304, 307; on ability, knowledge and educational failure 290, 292–3, 310; on teachers' knowledge of pupils 259, 260, 281
Kelly, G.A. 259
King, R. 58–9, 319–22; on organisational changes 320–2
knowledge: ability and educational failure 290–3, 310; conceptualisation of 256; educational and everyday 49–52, 294, 305–13, middle-class nature of 311–14, value of 306–11, *see also* curriculum; experiential 250, 262; expert and everyday 292; forms of 295–7; and group interests 297–9; management of 89–95; origin of 297; pupils', of teachers 250, 269; socially constructed 290–1, 295–9; *see also under* pupils; teachers; truth
Kolakowski, L. 113, 120, 123, 129–31, 201–2, 207

labelling 301–2, 304–5
labour: and capitalism 16–17, 54, 135–6, 139–40; and communism 127–30; *see also* alienation; division
Labour Party and social democracy 187–94
Lacey, C. 182, 291
language/speech 45, 55, 166–71, 173–4, 238; in France 169, 171, 173; in lessons 270, 277–9
Laski, H. 222
laws *see* rules
learning, concepts of 256, 274
legitimation: criticised 205–6; of ideologies 81–4; inequalities 137, 317; process 154
Lenin, V.I. 200, 307–8
liberalism 99, 309
life, affirmation of 127
limitations of other sociological approaches 316–18
Luckmann, T. 2, 22, 108, 290; on management of knowledge 89–92, 95
Lukács, G. 123
Lukes, S. 9, 10, 33–4, 54, 56, 126, 300
lumpenproletariat 149; *see also* working class

Macdonald, M. 297
macro approach 233–4; *see also* Durkheim; Durkheimians; functionalism; Marx
McRobbie, A. 182, 210
Magee, B. 202, 295
man, nature of 23
management of knowledge 89–95
manipulated consensus 98–9
Mannheim, K. 299–300
Manpower Services Commission 194
Marcuse, H. 121
Marsden, D. 311–12
Marx and Marxism 37, 301, 307–9, 317, 324; alienation 124–6, 130; communism 126–30; compared with Durkheimianism 37; and determinism 115–19; direct reproduction theories 134–78, 179, capitalism and socialism *see* Bowles and Gintis, evaluated 203–7, Open University course 148–50, structural 134, 150–6, *see also* Althusser, Bourdieu, Hall, Miliband, Poulantzas; and functionalism 108; historical materialism 113–24; ideas, role of 307–8; knowledge, educational 307–8; perspective, 113–33, alienation 124–6, 130, communism 126–30, historical materialism 113–24; perspective evaluated 198–230, direct reproduction 203–7, relative autonomy 207, resistance 208–21, society, state and social democracy, 221–6; procedural constraints 99–100; resistance, relative autonomy and voluntarism 179–97, 317–18, Apple on 179–80, 187, Centre for Contemporary Cultural Studies 186–95, evaluated 207–21, Giroux on 181–2, 187, 219–20, Willis on 182–6; voluntarist 119–22
Marxism-Leninism as contradiction 200
mass schooling 148–9
master patterns 166, 170
materialism *see* historical materialism
meaning 234–5, 239–40
mechanical solidarity 15–17, 45, 48
meritocracy 136, 138, 317, 320
Merton, R.K. 266, 303
micro and macro *see* Weberian
micro interpretive approaches 233–48; assumptions of 234–7; macro–micro approaches 233–4; variations within 237–47

micro interpretive approaches: studies of teachers and pupils 249–89; criticised 281–4, 287; definitions, failure to state origins 282–4; interaction model 249–51; narrow focus 281–2; observer's role 236, 289–1; pupils: interaction with teachers 275–9, knowledge of teachers 250, 260, 269, 272–5, 321, self-conceptions 250, 262–72; teachers: interaction with pupils 275–9, knowledge of pupils 244–5, 249–50, 255–62, 301–5, self-conceptions 242–5, 249–57
middle class: criticised by sociologists 221; cultural capital 168–70; nature of educational knowledge 311–14; new 53–5; pupils, thought system 293; values 155, 311–12; *see also* class
Miliband, R. 99, 114; on structural Marxism 134, 150–6
Mill, J.S. 37, 39, 99, 103–4, 297, 309
Mills, C. Wright 72, 291
mobility *see* social mobility
modern society *see under* social; society
Moore, B. 98–9
Moore, W.E. 138
moral/morality: achievement 73–4; characteristics of 17–19; education 17, 19–21; individualism 33; values 72–3
morale-boosting strategy 276
moralising effect of group life 36
motivation differences 67
Musgrave, P.W. 83, 93
Musgrove, F. 169, 312–13

Nash, R. 259, 262
national cultural styles 93–4
National Plan (1965) 193
nature, Marxist analogy 118–19, 120
negotiation 271; and change 331–3; classroom 237, 246–7; micro interpretive approaches 235–6; results of 334–5; strategies 275–7
'new' sociology of education 290–315; basic argument 290–1; knowledge, educational and everyday 294, 305–13; knowledge, socially constructed 290–1, 295–9; teachers, pupils and educational failure 301–5; truth and validity, socially

constructed 291–5, 299–301
non-egoistic individualism 31, 32
norms: consensus on 66; contest and
    sponsored 78–80, 81, 85, 88;
    deviance as 302; internalisation 66;
    of truth 291

objectification 127
objects, meaning of 239–40
observer role 236, 280–1
occupation *see* work
Open University course 148–50
opportunism 267
opportunity *see* equality
order, social 44, 52, 78, 88, 98; *see
    also* control
organic: analogy 65; solidarity 16–17,
    45, 48–9
organisational changes in secondary
    schools 320–2
origin of knowledge 297
'other', concept of 239–40

Parekh, B. 301
parents 239
Parkin, F. 325
Parsons, T. 1–2, 66–76, 137, 162, 317;
    on education as selection 75–6; on
    society and education 70–5, 100,
    162–3; on value consensus 67–70
particular concept of ideology 299–300
particularistic ideology 82
Partridge, P.H. 69
party group 323
Pascal, B. 300
path analysis 145
Payne, G. 278–9
Pearson, G. 149
pedagogy, types of 50, 53–5
peer approval 105–6
perceiving people 239–41
person, concept of 54, 56; *see also*
    individual
personal: approach 45; dignity 28–9;
    social abilities 41–2, 44; *see also*
    individual
personality system of society 71–3
perspectives for making sense of world
    265–6
Peters, R.S. 42, 309–11
phases of lessons 270
phenomenology 237
philosophical forms of knowledge 295,
    296–7
Plamenatz, J. 117, 130, 132, 200

Plant, R. 40–1
pleasing teachers 104–6, 245–6, 261
Plowden Report (1965) 334
pluralism 151, 224–6
plurality of factors 201
policy 85, 187–8, 190–1
political/politics: democracy 143;
    institutions 64, 103–4; liberal view
    of 99; manipulation 332
Pollard, A. 262–5, 271
Popper, K. 199, 202
positional approach to children 45
Poulantzas, N. 151, 156–7
power *see* authority; control
pre-industrial society 15–16
privacy 39
'problem pupils' *see* deviance
problematic situations in teaching
    252–3
problems, institutions to solve 103–4
procedural consensus 99–100
production, forces and relations of
    115–17, 137, 139
professionalisation 326
progressivism 334
proletariat 149; *see also* working class
pro-school group 266, 272
'pseudo-concord' 246
punishment 20–1
pupils: class of 262, *see also* working
    class; knowledge of teachers 250,
    260, 269, 272–5, 321; middle-class
    thought systems 293; self-
    conceptions 250, 262–72; and
    symbolic interactionism 245–6;
    teachers and 244–5, 249–50,
    255–62, 269 *passim*, 272–91,
    301–5, 321; *see also* failure

qualifications 325–7

reality 21–2, 90–2
rebellion mode of conformity 218–19,
    267
reification of society 316
Reisman, D. 34, 40–1
relations of production 115–17, 137, 139
relative autonomy theory 114, 198,
    200–2, 207, 317
religion 64, 69, 329
Renaissance 11–12
repertory grid technique 259
Repressive State Apparatus 159–60
reproduction, direct *see* capitalism;
    Marx and Marxism

resistance *see* counter-school; Marx and Marxism
Resler, H. 77
resource 277
respectability 213–15
restricted code 45
retreatism mode of conformity 218, 267–8
revolution, educational 67
Rex, J. 303
Reynolds, D. 203–5, 227, 307–8; on capitalist values 204; on economy 203–4; on school's independence 204–5
Ricardo, D. 297
Riddell, C. 93
Ridge, J.M. 78, 172–3
Rist, R. 74
ritualism mode of conformity 218–20, 267–8
Roberts, R. 213–15, 227
roles: conflict 241; educational 154–5; expectations 66, 71–2; ideas 99–200, 307–8; observers 236, 280–1; sex 73; social 71–2; state 223–5; symbolic interactionism 241–2; teachers 241–5, 255–6, changing 46–7, 58
Rousseau, J.-J. 28, 37, 69, 129
rules 8–9, 19, 23, 270
Russia 199, 324
Ryle, G. 43

Sarup, M. 182
school *see* micro interpretive
Schools Council 334
Schutz, A. 240, 272, 301
science and understanding 20–1
secondary deviance 258
selection: debate on 85–9, 90, 94; education as 75–6; Marxist view of 317; and social mobility 79, 83–4, 86–7, 89–90; types of 80–2
self: -conception: pupils 250, 262–72, teachers 242–5, 249–57; development and individualism 33–4; direction and dignity 39; -fulfilling prophecy 262, 301–4; -referential objections 300–1; and symbolic interactionism 238–9
Sex Discrimination Act (1975) 322
sex roles 73
Sharp, R. and Green, A. 22, 59, 251–5, 257; on headmasters' views 251–2; on teachers' knowledge of

pupils 260–1, 283–4; on teachers' views 252–5, of children 253, of school 253–5
shop-floor *see* factory
sites: of resistance 180; of social practice 147–8
skills, diffuse and technical 82
Smith, A. 297
Smith, D. 2, 76, 86–8, 89
social/society: aims and individualism 35–6; change 11–12, 120, and functionalism 101–3; class *see* class; constraints 8–9, 22, 49, 285; construction of knowledge 290–1, 295–9; construction of reality 90–2; construction of truth and validity 291–5, 299–301; context of action 328; control *see* control/power; democracy: criticism of 191–5, ideology 187–9, society and state 221–6; determinism *see* Durkheim; Durkheimians; function of education 29–32; groups 18–20, 24–5, 30–1, 36; ideology 187–9; ills, modern 36–44; institutions 64–5, 102–4, 329; meaning of 8; mobility 77–8, 83–4, 86–7, 89–90; modern, Durkheim on 15–25, 30, 45, 54, 155, 162–3; moral values 72–3; order *see* control; -personal abilities 41–2, 44; policies 190–1; power *see* control; practice, sites of 147–8; product, ability and intelligence as 291; relations 158; roles 71–2; solidarity 69; stability 98, 102–3; system 71–4
socialisation 8, 14, 56, 68, 70–3, 316; Bourdieu on 174; and capitalism 138–9; and class 206–7; criticised 206–7; and cultural capital 166–7; education as 67–85; family 45; and internalisation 66; Marxist view of 317; as strategy 275
socialism 223; as alternative 142–4, 147
society 21–2, 64–5, 316, 322; *see also* social
sociological interpretations of education *see* Durkheim; Durkheimians; functionalist; interpretive; Marx
sociology 7–10; methods 10–15; *see also* 'new' sociology
solidarity 15–17, 45, 48–9, 69
specialisation 51
speech *see* language
sponsored norms 78–80, 81, 85

stability, social 98, 102–3
state: apparatus, education as 159–61;
    educational system 331–5;
    inadequacy of 191–2; policy 85,
    187–8, 190–1; role 223–5; site of
    social practice 147–8; *see* social
    democracy
status: differentiation 88; elite, striving
    for *see* social mobility; group 323;
    Ideological Apparatus 159–61;
    rigidity 83
stereotypes 240–1, 243, 245, 250, 262
strain towards equilibrium 102
strategies 266, 275–7, 285–6
stratification 260–1; *see also* class
strict–soft dimension 273–4
structural Marxists 119
structuralism *see* Althusser
structure for interaction 329; *see also*
    economic structure
style 171, 174; intellectual 93–4
sub-cultures 221; *see also* delinquency
sub-roles, teacher 243, 245
sub-systems 65
subjectivist approach 236–7
suicide 14
Sullivan, M. 307–8
superstructure 199, 201; asnd base
    113–15, 117, 119, 121, 147, 202
survival *see* strategies
'sussing out' 275
symbolic interactionism 238–47;
    classroom application 242–7
synthesis, attempted 284–7
systems of society 71–4

Tawney, R.H. 39, 188–9, 306–7
teachers: ability concepts 293;
    autonomy 321, 333; definitions of
    pupils 301–5; ethnomethodological
    approach to discourse 277–9;
    knowledge concepts 249–50, 262,
    293; language 270, 277–9; power
    321, 333; and pupils 244–5,
    249–50, 255–62 *passim*, 269,
    272–91, 301–5, 321; roles, 241–5,
    255–6, changing 46–7, 58; self-
    conception 242–5, 249–57;
    strategies 275–6, 285–6; sub-roles
    243, 245; and symbolic
    interactionism 242–5
teaching perspectives 252
technical skills 82
technocratic-meritocratic capitalist 136,
    138, 317, 320

teleological explanation 103
theoretical conservatism 300–1
Thomas, W.I. 283
thought systems 291–4
threshold of intervention 258
time units in education 50
Tönnies, F. 40
topic 277
totalitarianism *see* authoritarian
trade unions 135–6
transactions 331–3
transmission of values 23–5, 45, 155
Trotsky, L. 200
trouble, pupils' definition of 273–4
true and false consciousness and
    definitions 303
truth 291, 297; and validity, socially
    constructed 291–5, 299–301, ability,
    knowledge and failure 291–3, self-
    referential objective 300–1, *see also*
    knowledge, educational etc.
Turner, G. 269–71
Turner, R. 2, 66, 76–80, 88–9; contest
    and sponsored norms 78–80, 81,
    85; social mobility 77–8, 81
typification of teachers by pupils 273
typing deviance 258

understanding 20–1, 42
United States: and Britain compared
    76–80, 88; and class 74–5;
    credentialism in 325–7; pluralism in
    225
unity and harmony 129–30
universality 82, 239
'Unresolved Contradiction' 122–3

Vaizey, J. 190
validity *see* truth
value/s: achievement 68–9, 73–5;
    capitalist 204; conflict 99–101, 131;
    consensus on 66–73 *passim*, 98–101;
    of educational knowledge 306–11;
    fundamental 155; internalisation of
    66; middle class 155, 311–12; moral
    72–3; and social groups 24–5,
    30–1, 36; transmission of 23–5, 45,
    155; working class 211–13, 317–18;
    see also thought systems
voluntarist Marxists 119–22

Wakeford, J. 266
Waller, W. 266
war analogy 280; *see also* conflict
Weber, M. and Weberian perspective 3,

89, 107, 271, 316–37; limitations of other approaches 316–18; sociology 318–35; Archer's 327–35, Collins's 322–7, King's 319–22
Weiner, M.J. 204
Wellmer, A. 121
Westergaard, J. 77
Whorf, B.L. 166
will, human 120
William Tyndale School 194
Williamson, B. 213, 220
Willis, P., on resistance 24, 182–6; on counter-school culture 182, 183–5; evaluated 208–10, 214–17, 221, 227; on preparation for factory 185–6
Wilson, H. 190
Woods, P. 105; on models of response 218–19; on pupils' self-conceptions 236, 262, 265–71, 275–6, 281–2,

forms of 266–9
work 138–41, 298–9, 326–7; *see also* factory
working class: and authority 214–15; communities, traditional 38–9; conformity 214–16; control of 149–51, 155; and cultural capital 168, 173; dignity 28; and educational failure 292; honesty 213; legitimation 205; resistance 180–5, 208–20; respectability 213–15; socialisation 206–7; thought systems and values 211–13, 291–3, 311–12, 317–18
Wright, E.O. 180
Wrong, D. 106

Young, M.F.D. 290–1, 294–5, 300, 305